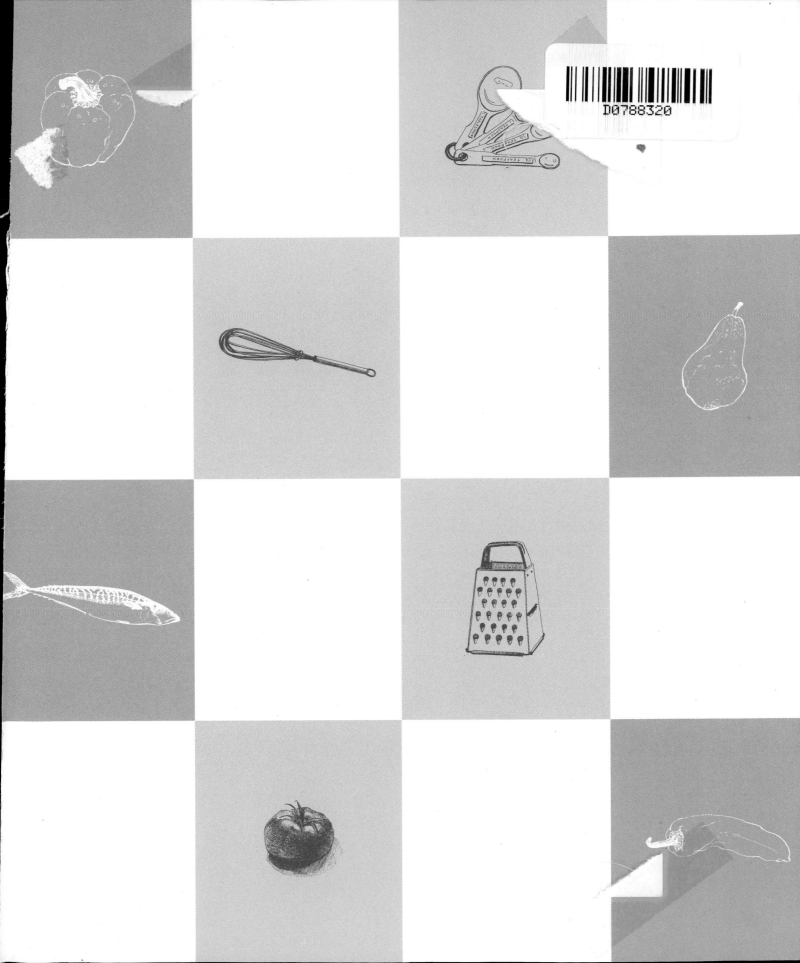

The New Canadian Basics Cookbook

The New *Canadian* Basics Cookbook

by Carol Ferguson with Murray McMillan

Enjoy!

Carol Ferguson

VIKING

A Denise Schon Book

A Denise Schon Book

VIKING
Published by the Penguin Group
Penguin Books Canada Ltd, 10 Alcorn Avenue,
Toronto, Ontario, Canada M4V 3B2

Penguin Books Ltd, 27 Wrights Lane,
London W8 5TZ, England

Penguin Putnam Inc., 375 Hudson Street,
New York, New York 10014, U.S.A.

Penguin Books Australia Ltd,
Ringwood, Victoria, Australia

Penguin Books (NZ) Ltd,
cnr Rosedale and Airborne Roads,
Albany, Auckland 1310, New Zealand

Penguin Books Ltd, Registered Offices:
Harmondsworth, Middlesex, England

First published 1999
10 9 8 7 6 5 4 3 2 1

Text copyright © Carol Ferguson, 1999
Illustrations © Andrew Leyerle, 1999

Produced by: Denise Schon Books Inc.
Design: Adams + Associates Design Consultants Inc.
Copy Editor: Shaun Oakey
Index: Barbara Schon
Printed and bound in Canada by Tri-graphic Printing Ltd.

Cataloguing in Publication Data

Ferguson, Carol
    The new Canadian basics cookbook
Includes index
ISBN 0-670-87909-6
1. Cookery.   I. McMillan, Murray.   II. Title.
TX715.6.F473 1999   641.5   C98-932302-1

Visit Penguin Canada's web site at www.penguin.ca

Table of Contents

Introduction

Cooking basics are different today. By design or circumstance, our priorities have changed. We're juggling busy schedules, concerned about nutrition, short of kitchen confidence. We want our food faster, easier, healthier than ever before.

But today we also demand great flavour. Our tastes have blossomed. We've learned to appreciate the heady fragrance of a perfect peach, the vibrancy of a sun-yellow pepper, the earthiness of a wild mushroom risotto, the sweetness of a just-steamed prawn. We delight in the spark of fresh ginger, the suave depth of balsamic, the layered complexity of a Thai curry. We're surrounded by intriguing international ingredients and want to explore new seasonings and techniques.

At the same time, we're rediscovering the pleasures of traditional comfort foods. We like the idea of a kitchen that smells delicious, that provides a gathering place, a haven for nurturing body and soul.

Can we still do it all? That's what this book is all about—sorting it out, simplifying life in the kitchen, balancing the practicalities and pleasures of cooking. We *can* cook faster, eat sensibly, explore the global pantry, keep traditions alive, gather friends around the table—and enjoy. Good cooking doesn't have to be complicated or expensive. Good food is *real* food. Some of the best food in the world is the simplest—a few fine ingredients tossed together with affection and imagination.

The New Canadian Basics Cookbook is designed for the way we cook today. It delivers the information you need and the recipes you want for everyday meals and special occasions. It includes all the must-haves, from the heritage recipes we still cherish to the latest flavours on our international food scene.

We hope this will be the book you reach for when you want supper on the table in twenty minutes or a make-ahead brunch for weekend guests; when you need cookies for the school bake sale or svelte snacks for a cocktail party; when you're wondering how to roast vegetables on the barbecue or how long to cook the Thanksgiving turkey; when you're mystified by an ingredient or looking for new ways to use a familiar one; when you want to try making that osso bucco or pad Thai you always order; when you're looking for the best-ever cinnamon buns or the ultimate bruschetta.

But this isn't a book about dictating style or taste or preaching how-tos (it's *your* dinner!). Every kitchen is different, every cook unique. We all have different levels of experience, from the can't-boil-water novice to the accomplished chocolate artist. Individual tastes and attitudes range wide: committed vegetarians and serious carnivores; busy parents of toddlers and teens; empty-nesters entertaining modestly but well; weight-worriers counting every gram of fat, starving students whose tastes have outgrown instant noodles; foodies who know every dish from abalone to zabaglione.

Many of today's younger generation of cooks have developed a broad range of tastes by eating out (or taking out), and often have two or three "specialties" that they enjoy preparing, but find themselves at a loss when it comes to everyday kitchen basics. They've told us they want simple, dependable recipes that produce great-tasting food. We hope this book fills the bill, while at the same time giving experienced cooks the information they want—updated traditional recipes and a roundup of the latest in ingredients and techniques.

Sorting it all out into one book has been challenging and satisfying for Murray and me. We are both food editors, and though we work thousands of miles apart, and in different media, our jobs have similar demands. We have to know what Canadians, in all their diversity, are eating; what our growers are bringing to market; and how cooks both at home and in fine restaurants are creating great things to eat. We travel to see what's cooking across the country and abroad. We keep in touch with culinary colleagues near and far (and are gratified that a number of them shared their thoughts and recipes for this book).

Covering food for our readers requires us to take a broad view, but any cookbook, including this one, is bound to be a little idiosyncratic and we confess to a few quirks. My family, for instance, has long regarded Jamaican rice and peas as a "basic," so it's here (with Murray's blessing as long as his teriyaki flank steak got equal room!). Living on the West Coast, he has an affinity for hunting down eye-popping sushi and haunting Fraser Valley produce stands; in my neighbourhood, I enjoy the proximity of little French bistros, Italian trattorias and local farmers' markets. His travels take him to Nothern California and spots around the Pacific; mine lean more to the Mediterranean and Caribbean.

But we also share common ground, much of it rooted in the Canadian Prairies. We happen to be cousins, so a mutual passion for saskatoon pie is forever linked to summer family picnics at a Saskatchewan lake. Canada's culinary wealth is what we know and love best: shopping for prawns at Vancouver's Granville Island Market, savouring the gelato of Toronto's Little Italy. What could top the flavour of a ripe melon in early fall in the Okanagan Valley? Or a cob of corn, just minutes off the stalk, in any corner of the country? A fresh peach shortcake in a Niagara orchard farm kitchen, a lobster feast in Prince Edward Island, a traditional Newfoundland scoff, a cozy bistro dinner in old Quebec City, an Alberta ranch-country barbecue?

Today in Canada we also enjoy an amazing global diversity of culinary tradition in home kitchens. Ever since the days of the first settlers from Europe, each wave of immigration has brought new layers of flavours from around the world for us to share. Today a neighborhood school might have children with 50 different first languages and just as many food traditions at home. Local food shops and restaurants reflect this diversity. In this book, we've included the international classics that have become or are becoming mainstream. Many of our "new basics" are simply the popular dishes of other countries added recently to our Canadian repertoire.

Experiences with the foods of different cultures, faraway places and other regions of our own country educate and enrich Canadian tastes. And when we apply them to our own local ingredients, cooking takes on a pleasurable new dimension. Canadians are blessed with a food supply of high quality, safety, variety and abundance that often amazes visitors from other countries. We can create a great variety of simple, great-tasting dishes with little effort and certainly don't need to depend on packaged or take-out "convenience" foods.

We hope that this book will help you sort out the basics, try some new flavours and techniques, and go on to wherever your tastes and interests take you. Meanwhile, even sticking with the basics definitely doesn't mean dull. (See pages 261-268 for a whole menu of menus from the recipes in this book). Enjoy!

Carol Ferguson, January 1999

About this book

Symbols:

✤ Heritage recipe (*Canadian regional or ethnic tradition or all-time favourite*)

🕐 Fast & easy

〰 Microwave

♥ Lower in fat

🥕 Vegetarian

🔥 Grill/barbecue

😊 Kid-pleaser

Unless specified otherwise, recipe ingredients are as follows:

Eggs are size large.

Milk is 2%.

Butter is salted.

Yogurt, sour cream, cream cheese and
    mayonnaise are low-fat (not no-fat) versions.

Light cream is 10% to 18%.

Vegetable oil is any good-quality
    neutral-flavoured oil such as canola.

Olive oil is extra-virgin.

Wine is dry.

Whole vegetables and fruit are medium-sized.

Lemon and lime juice are fresh, not bottled.

Cocoa is dry unsweetened.

Vanilla and other flavourings are pure, not artificial, extracts.

Coconut milk is unsweetened.

Rice vinegar is unseasoned.

Soy sauce: Light-coloured is preferred unless dark is specified.

Pepper is freshly ground black pepper.

Salt is the common fine-granulated kind, unless coarse salt (such as kosher, pickling or sea salt) is specified. Coarse salt is about half as salty as the same volume of fine salt; if substituting one for the other, adjust the amount to taste.

Stock (chicken, beef, vegetable, fish): see page 237.

Chicken breasts: see page 96.

For unfamiliar ingredients: see Global Pantry, page 244.

For unfamiliar terms and techniques: see page 242-43.

Microwaving: Cooking times are given for 750 watt oven, but are generally the same in a 650 watt oven of compact size. For larger or smaller ovens, adjust times. Recipes assume your oven has a turntable; if not, turn dish a few times during cooking. Be sure to use only microwavable dishes. For basic microwaving techniques and cooking charts, see your owner's manual; you will also find a large selection of microwave cookbooks in bookstores and libraries.

Serving sizes: Recipe yields give average adult-size portions (a little smaller than in most old cookbooks, a little larger than in most low-fat cookbooks). Calculate smaller portions for children, larger for very active teens and adults. (Remember to offer small portions of high-fat and high-calorie foods, larger portions of low-fat nutrient-rich foods.) The number of servings will also vary depending on how many other foods are being served with the dish, or if you want to allow for second servings.

How to use this book if you are a novice cook:

- Can't boil water? So you're not Julia Child. (Who is?)
How much or how little kitchen skill you start out with doesn't matter much, as long as you're interested in trying new things and in feeding yourself and others well. Learning to cook is a gradual process and even the most honoured chefs tell stories of their own kitchen disasters. Everyone has them. (A sense of humour is a great kitchen aid.) But you greatly improve your odds by looking for recipes that make you say, "I can do that!" This book has plenty of them. And look for those that carry the "Fast & Easy" symbol, too. Here are some suggestions composed with the beginner in mind, but cooks of all experience levels can benefit from a quick review of basic principles.

- Start with the easiest recipes (try Taco Dip, Greek Salad, Baked Potatoes with Toppings). Move on to some simple meat and vegetable dishes (Easy Oven Stew, All-Purpose Stir-Fry). Try your hand at some baking (Banana Bread, Quick Cinnamon Rolls). Make a simple supper for yourself and a friend (Pasta Primavera or Barbecued Spareribs with a salad). Soon you'll be putting together three-course menus (see suggestions page 261). Throw a party, invite your friends, impress your mother! You might even get asked for the recipes.

- You learn to cook by *really cooking*. As you work through the recipes, you'll learn basic techniques, how to measure, how to handle ingredients—and how real food is supposed to taste.

- When trying a new recipe: Read the recipe through to make sure you have all the ingredients and equipment and that you understand each step in the method (for unfamiliar terms and techniques, see page 242-43). If the listed ingredients are partially prepared (e.g. chopped, sliced), do this before you start the steps in the method. Assemble the ingredients so you can reach them easily as you work. Follow the recipe steps in order.

- Using the proper equipment makes cooking much easier but you don't need a lot of fancy gear.

- Don't be afraid to adjust recipes to your taste or available ingredients. Follow recipes carefully at first to learn basic techniques and to get a general guide to seasonings. Then, as you become more experienced, taste and adjust as you go along—decide what *you* like. Make up your own variations and note them on recipes.

- The only time you shouldn't adjust recipes is when baking. A cake or quickbread is a carefully balanced formula; you'll get the same results every time if you measure accurately.

- Expand your own tastes and food experiences. Canadian cooking includes lots of interesting regional specialties as well as a whole world of international flavours. Explore farmers' markets, city markets in ethnic neighbourhoods, specialty food shops. Talk to the butcher, the baker, the greengrocer. Or just check out the selection at any really good supermarket (there are probably hundreds of items you didn't know were there). Try something new. Check out web sites on the Internet and TV food shows. Browse in kitchen shops and cookbook stores. Accept any and all invitations to eat out in interesting restaurants, and especially at friends' homes with traditional cooking different from yours. Good food nourishes your body and soul and keeps you healthy and happy. And cooking can be half the fun.

Acknowledgements

No project of this size and scope can blossom through the work of just two writers. Many special people contributed in many ways, large and small. We thank them all.

Words of encouragement, candid advice and great recipes came from culinary colleagues and consultants coast-to-coast. They include, from west to east: chef Karen Barnaby, Asian food expert Stephen Wong, restaurateur Umberto Menghi, Barbara-jo McIntosh of Books to Cooks in Vancouver, Okanagan winery proprietor Sandra Hainle, *Edmonton Journal* food and travel writer Judy Schultz, *Calgary Herald* food editor Cinda Chavich, food writers/authors Rose Murray, Johanna Burkhard, Cynthia David and Pam Collacott in Ontario, Margaret Fraser (co-author, with Carol, of *A Century of Canadian Home Cooking),* *Toronto Star* food editor Marion Kane, cooking school owner/author Bonnie Stern, nutrition expert/author Anne Lindsay, Allison Fryer of the Cookbook Store in Toronto, Montreal *Gazette* food editor Julian Armstrong, and food writer/author Marie Nightingale in Halifax. Key people in food marketing groups and government departments were generous with their time and knowledge. Wine writer Frank Baldock brought his expertise to our Wine and Food Match-Maker section.

Yvonne Tremblay, associate food editor at *Homemaker's* magazine, did much of the recipe testing for this book, with her usual accuracy and good taste. Her expertise with preserves and herbs proved especially valuable, and she contributed several of her best recipes (including the jams and jellies that made her a grand champion prize-winner at the Royal Agricultural Winter Fair).

Lise Ferguson consistently created order out of chaos in both office and kitchen, managing mountains of paper, updating computer files, co-ordinating schedules and assisting with recipe testing and editing.

Writer/editor Don Douloff contributed many hours as researcher, candid comments as recipe-taster ("needs work") and good humour throughout.

Family members and friends helped smooth the way for us and lent some fine recipes to the cause. They include John Ferguson, Sarah Bromley, Jonathan Davies, Garry King, Donna McMillan, Denis Morin and Tom Parkinson. Brenda Thompson and Ruth Phelan, Murray's colleagues at the *Vancouver Sun* test kitchen, also gave consistent support.

Special appreciation goes to *Homemaker's* editor-in-chief Sally Armstrong and publisher Barry Wykes for their encouragement and ongoing support for this project.

Sincere thanks to Shaun Oakey for his meticulous copy editing, to France Simard for her hard work and heartfelt gratitude to Eva Quan and all at Denise Schon and Associates, especially Denise herself for her personal support and patient, professional guidance. Thanks also to everyone at Penguin Books Canada, who supported this project so enthusiastically from Day 1.

And finally, from our far-apart desks in Toronto and Vancouver, a big thank-you to Bell Canada, whose long-distance savings plan came along just when we needed it most!

Global Grazing...

Appetizers
Snacks
Starters

Need fast and fancy nibbles for a crowd? Easy
munchies for a kids' party? A dazzling first course
for dinner guests? No problem!

Antipasto Platter

"Antipasto" simply means before the meal, but if you've travelled in Italy (or have a good trattoria in your own neighbourhood), you'll know how tantalizing the selection of appetizers can be: colourful roasted peppers, grilled and marinated vegetables, seafood salads, artichokes, olives, mushrooms, cheeses, sliced salamis and prosciutto, melon, fresh figs. Though meant for leisurely sampling before dinner, antipasti can be just as enjoyable as the main event. Similar arrays of tasty little dishes, called tapas in Spain and meze in Greece, traditionally set the stage for all sorts of informal social gatherings. So whether your guests are seated comfortably around the dinner table, gathered elegantly on the terrace for pre-theatre drinks or just grazing during Stanley Cup playoffs, an antipasto platter fills the bill. Try some of these:

Marinated Roasted Peppers (page 236)
Marinated Vegetable Salad (page 57)
Grilled Vegetable Salad (page 57)
Antipasto Mixed Salad (page 55)
Mixed Bean Salad (page 55)
Tomatoes and Bocconcini with Basil (page 25)
Seafood Salad (Insalata di Mare) (page 54)
Steamed Mussels (page 69)
Oysters on the half shell (page 62)

Marinated Roasted Peppers (page 236)
Marinated Vegetable Salad (page 57)
Grilled Vegetable Salad (page 57)
Antipasto Mixed Salad (page 55)
Mixed Bean Salad (page 55)
Tomatoes and Bocconcini with Basil (page 25)
Seafood Salad (Insalata di Mare) (page 54)
Steamed Mussels (page 69)
Oysters on the half shell (page 62)

Tapas

As an alternative to Italian antipasti, switch the theme to Spanish tapas, using many of the same dishes (roasted red peppers, grilled vegetables, seafood salads, olives) plus sliced cured chorizo sausage, tiny sardines, small dishes of almonds, Garlic Shrimp, Fava Beans with Ham and Catalan Tomato Bread. Chilled dry sherry is the traditional accompaniment.

Garlic Shrimp: In large skillet over medium-high heat, heat 2 tbsp (30 mL) olive oil. Add 1 lb (500 g) large raw shrimp (peeled, deveined, tails left on), 3 minced garlic cloves and 1/4 tsp (1 mL) hot pepper flakes; sprinkle with salt. Cook, stirring, until shrimp turn pink, about 3 minutes. Sprinkle with the juice of half a lemon. **Makes about 6 servings.**

Fava Beans with Ham: This is typically Spanish and delicious made with best-quality beans. Canned fava and broad beans are now available in most supermarkets, but the quality varies; some are sweet and delicious, others quite bitter, so be sure to taste and note the brands you like. Large lima beans can be substituted in this recipe. In large skillet, heat 1/3 cup (75 mL) extra-virgin olive oil; add 1 can (19 oz /540 mL) fava or broad beans, drained; cook

Buy or Make?

For a small group, a simple platter needs only two or three items; for larger gatherings, offer a half-dozen or more choices. Arrange them all strikingly on one large platter or separately in small bowls. All you need as an accompaniment is crusty bread. Which antipasti to buy and which to make from scratch is your choice. Scan the selection at a good Italian deli and see what appeals. Pick up some prosciutto, salami and other sliced meats, two or three kinds of olives, marinated artichoke hearts, pickled peppers, good-quality solid-pack tuna in olive oil. Add small wedges of melon or fresh figs to wrap with the prosciutto. Other items can either be purchased or prepared at home.

over medium heat for 2 to 3 minutes, stirring gently. Add 3 thinly sliced garlic cloves and 4 oz (125 g) Spanish cured ham or prosciutto, cut in small pieces; cook, stirring, for 3 minutes. Add 1 tbsp (15 mL) dry sherry (or sherry vinegar for sharper taste) and cook for 1 minute, shaking the pan. Add a little chopped parsley and serve warm. **Makes about 6 servings**.

Bruschetta

The traditional rustic bruschetta of Italy is deliciously simple: crusty bread toasted on the grill, rubbed with garlic and drizzled with good olive oil. Today's dressed-up bruschetta ("broo-sketta" please, not "broo-shetta") comes with all sorts of toppings, hot and cold—everything from sun-dried tomato pesto, caramelized onions or spicy black bean salsa to herbed goat cheese with sautéed wild mushrooms. One of our family favourites is my son John's specialty: lightly grilled Italian bread topped with roasted red peppers (trimmed to fit), fresh basil and sliced friulano cheese, then broiled (or heated in covered barbecue) until the cheese melts.

Most popular of all is fresh-tomato-topped bruschetta, now standard appetizer fare in many restaurants and at barbecue parties. This is our ultimate homemade version, flavoured with fresh basil, garlic and the best extra-virgin olive oil.

Catalan Tomato Bread: This Spanish version of bruschetta is popular in tapas bars in Canada as well as Spain. Grill thick slices of crusty bread until toasted and rub on both sides with cut garlic. Then rub well with halved ripe tomatoes until the toast absorbs the tomato pulp and is well coloured. Drizzle with extra-virgin olive oil and sprinkle with salt.

1-1/2 lb	ripe plum tomatoes (about 9 medium)	750 g
2 tbsp	finely chopped onion	30 mL
2	large cloves garlic, minced	2
1/4 cup	chopped fresh basil	50 mL
2 tsp	balsamic or red wine vinegar	10 mL
6 tbsp	extra-virgin olive oil	90 mL
	Salt and pepper	
4	thick slices crusty Italian bread (about 5 inches/12 cm across)	4

➔ Cut tomatoes in half and squeeze out seeds and juice. Dice tomatoes and place in bowl. Add onion, garlic, basil, vinegar, half of the olive oil, and salt and pepper to taste. Let stand at room temperature for about 1 hour. Drain tomatoes. On grill or under broiler, toast bread on both sides until golden brown. Quickly brush one side of each slice with remaining olive oil. Spoon tomato mixture on top. Cut slices in half. Serve immediately. **Makes 4 servings** (2 pieces each).

Crostini

Crostini are Italian canapés— small, thin slices of bread grilled or toasted and topped with almost anything. Use any of the spreads on page 15, pestos, salsas, roasted garlic, caramelized onions, sautéed mushrooms, leftover ratatouille, purchased tapenade or caponata.

Olive and Sun-dried Tomato Spread: This is really addictive. In food processor (a mini food processor is ideal), combine 1 cup (250 mL) pitted black olives (preferably kalamata), 1/2 cup (125 mL) chopped sun-dried tomatoes (oil-packed, drained), 1 garlic clove and 1/4 cup (50 mL) extra-virgin olive oil.

Blend until almost smooth, adding about 1 tbsp (15 mL) water to give soft spreadable consistency. **Makes about 1 cup** (250 mL). Can be kept in covered container in refrigerator for up to 1 week.

Tip: Crush olives lightly with flat side of large knife and the pits will come out easily

Caponata

Vancouver chef Karen Barnaby's delectable version of Italy's traditional mixture is a perfect blend of sweet, sour and salty, with a creamy texture. Serve it with crusty bread or cheese as an appetizer; it's also great on pasta and with meat or fish.

1 lb	eggplant	500 g
1/4 cup	olive oil	50 mL
1	stalk celery, julienned	1
1	onion, cut into 1/2-inch (1 cm) lengthwise strips	1
1-1/2 cups	drained canned plum tomatoes, puréed and sieved	375 mL
8	each: black and green olives, pitted	8
1 tbsp	small capers	15 mL
1-1/2 tsp	golden raisins	7 mL
	Salt and pepper to taste	
1 tsp	balsamic vinegar	5 mL
1-1/2 tsp	coarsely chopped Italian parsley	7 mL
1/2 cup	coarsely chopped fresh basil	125 mL

➜ Prick eggplant several times with fork and place on baking sheet. Bake in 350F (180C) oven for 30 to 45 minutes or until eggplant is completely soft and collapsing. Slit eggplant open on one side. Place in colander, slit side down, to drain and cool completely. While eggplant is cooling, heat olive oil in large saucepan over medium heat. Add celery and onion; cook, stirring, until translucent. Add tomato purée, olives, capers and raisins. Cook, stirring occasionally, for 10 minutes or until slightly thickened and oil starts to separate from tomato mixture. When eggplant has cooled, peel off skin. Chop eggplant into 2-inch (5 cm) pieces. Add to tomato mixture and simmer for 10 minutes. Season with salt and pepper. Add vinegar, parsley and basil; remove from heat and let cool. Keeps for 1 week in the refrigerator. **Makes about 2 cups** (500 mL).

Gougères (Cheese Puffs)

Prepare Cream Puff dough (page 194). After beating in eggs, stir in 1 cup (250 mL) shredded gruyère or cheddar and 1/2 tsp (2 mL) dry mustard. Pipe dough or drop by small spoonfuls onto greased baking sheet. Bake at 425F (220C) for 10 minutes; reduce heat to 350F (180C) and bake 10 to 15 minutes longer or until firm to touch. Serve warm as hors d'oeuvre with drinks. Can be made a day ahead; reheat for about 5 minutes in 350F (180C) oven; do not microwave.

Dips and Spreads

Dips are all grown up these days. Blandly herbed, harshly spiced and store-bought types have been upstaged by easy-to-make combinations sparkling with fresh herbs or resonating with deep flavours. Based on low-fat dairy products, roasted vegetables and smooth beany mixtures, they complement whatever is used to scoop them up—crisp raw vegetables, jumbo shrimp, various crackers and chips, bagel and tortilla crisps, mini-pitas, soft breadsticks and little rounds of toast. Savoury spreads in all sorts of flavours are great to have on hand for bagels and snacks as well as party food. They're a lot better tasting and less expensive than store-bought. So are the crispy bases that go with them (see page 21).

Creamy Dips ☻ ♥

Just look in the fridge and you will probably find the makings of a quick dip for an impromptu party. Various combinations of dairy products provide the creamy base; low-fat versions of each work well.

For about 1-1/2 cups (375 mL) dip, start with:

1-1/2 cups (375 mL) drained yogurt (page 239) OR
1 cup (250 mL) plain yogurt plus 4 oz (125 g) softened cream cheese OR
1 cup (250 mL) sour cream or yogurt plus 1/2 cup (125 mL) light mayonnaise OR
1 cup (250 mL) smooth ricotta or creamed cottage cheese plus 1/2 cup (125 mL) sour cream or yogurt

➤ Blend together until smooth. Add ingredients for one of the Flavour Variations below. Add salt and pepper to taste. Cover and refrigerate for at least 1 hour to blend flavours.

Herbed: 1/4 cup (50 mL) chopped fresh chives and 2 tbsp (30 mL) each chopped fresh parsley and dill or basil.

Green Onion with Garlic: 1/4 cup (50 mL) finely chopped green onions and 1 or 2 minced garlic cloves.

Salsa: 1/2 cup (125 mL) (or to taste) bottled thick salsa (if thin, drain excess liquid).

Roasted Red Pepper: 1/2 cup (125 mL) well-drained and finely chopped bottled roasted red peppers, 1 minced garlic clove and a little lemon juice to taste. (For a smooth dip, purée in food processor.)

Caramelized Onion: 1/2 cup (125 mL) chopped caramelized onions (page 236), drained of any excess liquid and chilled.

Asian Peanut: 1/4 cup (50 mL) smooth peanut butter, 1 tbsp (15 mL) lime juice, 1 tbsp (15 mL) soy sauce, 1 tsp (5 mL) minced fresh ginger, 1 minced garlic clove, 1/4 tsp (1 mL) (or to taste) chile paste or hot pepper sauce.

Curried Shrimp: 1/2 cup (125 mL) minced cooked shrimp, 2 tbsp (30 mL) each minced green onions and celery, with curry powder or curry paste to taste.

Tzatziki: see page 109.

Hummus

This is the classic Middle Eastern bean dip, creamy textured and full flavoured. Serve with warmed pita wedges and raw vegetables.

2	large cloves garlic	2
1	can (19 oz/540 mL) chick peas, drained	1
1/2 cup	tahini (sesame paste)	125 mL
3 tbsp	lemon juice	45 mL
2 tbsp	extra-virgin olive oil	30 mL
1 tsp	ground cumin	5 mL
Dash	cayenne or hot pepper sauce	Dash
	Salt and pepper to taste	

➜ In food processor, chop garlic. Add chick peas and chop. Add remaining ingredients and purée until smooth. Blend in about 1/4 cup (50 mL) water to give dipping consistency. **Makes about 2 cups** (500 mL).

♥ **Low-Fat Hummus:** Use half as much tahini and olive oil; add a little more water or some yogurt to give dipping consistency. You can also omit the tahini and olive oil entirely and add 1 tbsp (15 mL) sesame oil for flavour.

Black Bean Dip OR White Bean Dip: These are both delicious with or without the tahini. They can be left chunky or puréed until smooth. Instead of chick peas, use canned black beans or cannellini (white kidney beans). Or use half chick peas and half black or white beans. Add 2 tsp (10 mL) chili powder and 2 tbsp (30 mL) chopped fresh coriander, plus a minced jalapeño pepper if you want extra heat.

Baba Ghanouj

Grilled eggplant gives a rich smoky flavour to this classic Middle Eastern dip for pita and vegetables.

2	medium eggplants (about 1-1/2 lb/750 g total)	2
2 tbsp	each: tahini, olive oil, lemon juice	30 mL
3	cloves garlic, minced	3
1/2 tsp	salt	2 mL
2 tbsp	finely chopped parsley	30 mL
1	green onion, finely chopped	1

➜ Prick eggplants all over with fork. Grill over medium-high heat (preferably on closed barbecue) or under broiler, about 6 inches (15 cm) from heat, turning occasionally, until soft and charred, about 40 minutes. Let cool. Cut in half lengthwise and scoop flesh into food processor. Add tahini, olive oil, lemon juice, garlic and salt; process until smooth. Stir in parsley and green onion. Add salt to taste if needed. **Makes about 2 cups** (500 mL).

Crudités (raw vegetables for dipping): Set out an interesting variety of colours, shapes and flavours, adding some less-common choices (fennel, celeriac, daikon, skinny green and yellow beans, asparagus spears, belgian endive, crisp inside leaves of romaine and radicchio, wedges of seeded plum tomato) along with the carrots, celery, peppers, broccoli, cauliflower, cucumbers, zucchini, snow peas, green onions, radishes, cherry tomatoes and small mushrooms. (For brighter colour and slightly softer texture, blanch broccoli, asparagus and snow peas very briefly in boiling water and refresh in ice water.) Arrange the vegetables on a large platter or in a large, shallow basket lined with plastic wrap; long skinny pieces look great in flower pots or shallow jugs, with the dips in smaller pots, seashells or hollowed-out sweet peppers.

Guacamole

Buttery-smooth ripe avocado, mashed and mixed with a little tropical heat, becomes a multipurpose sauce to scoop up with corn chips, spoon atop nachos or fajitas or serve with grilled meats.

2	small fully ripe avocados	2
1	plum tomato, seeded and chopped (optional)	1
2 tbsp	chopped fresh coriander (optional)	30 mL
2 tbsp	lime juice	30 mL
2	cloves garlic, minced	2
1 or 2	minced fresh or bottled jalapeño peppers or hot pepper sauce to taste	1 or 2
	Salt and pepper to taste	

➜ Pit and peel avocados; mash with fork until smooth or chunky as desired. Stir in remaining ingredients. Cover with plastic wrap directly on the surface to prevent discoloration. **Makes about 1-1/2 cups** (375 mL).

Tip: To pit avocado, cut in half lengthwise down to the pit; twist the two halves back and forth until they separate. Stick knife blade into pit and wiggle pit until it loosens.

Layered Taco Dip ⊕

This one never seems to lose its appeal and it's very easy to make. Vary the ingredients as you wish; the bean and avocado layers can be omitted if time is short or if your kids prefer it that way.

8 oz	low-fat cream cheese, softened	250 g
1/2 cup	low-fat sour cream	125 mL
1 cup	hot or mild salsa	250 mL
1/2 cup	chopped green onions	125 mL
1/2 cup	shredded iceberg lettuce	125 mL
4	plum tomatoes, chopped	4
1-1/2 cups	shredded cheddar cheese	375 mL
1/2 cup	sliced black olives	125 mL
	Tortilla chips	

➜ Beat cream cheese and sour cream together until smooth. Spread evenly in bottom of 9-inch (23 cm) ceramic quiche dish or glass pie plate. Spread salsa over cream cheese layer. Sprinkle evenly with onions, then lettuce, tomatoes, cheese and olives. Serve with tortilla chips. **Serves 6 to 8.**

Optional layers (spread in dish before adding cream cheese layer):

- Refried beans (14-oz/398 mL can mixed with a little sour cream, ground cumin and hot sauce)

- Guacamole (half of recipe above)

Crudités with Aioli: Aioli (page 47), a garlic mayonnaise, can be used as a dip, although in France it is traditionally served with tiny cooked vegetables. Choose an eye-appealing assortment: tiny new potatoes, green beans, baby carrots, baby beets, zucchini sticks, sliced fennel bulb, tiny globe artichokes. To prepare them, bring a saucepan of lightly salted water to boil. Cook vegetables, one kind at a time, just until crisp-tender. Remove with slotted spoon, refresh in cold water and dry on paper towels. Arrange vegetables in groups on a large platter and serve at room temperature. OR add some raw vegetables such as sliced plum tomatoes, seedless cucumber and small radishes (preferably a fresh bunch with leaves); cover platter with plastic wrap and chill for about an hour. Serve with bowl of aioli.

Hot Seafood Dip ※ ⊕

Warm savoury dips get scooped up immediately. And this one couldn't be easier—a few minutes to mix, three minutes in the microwave. Canned crab or shrimp is fine in this, but if you have some leftover cooked shrimp, crab or even lobster, all the better (chop it fine or chunky as you wish).

4 oz	cream cheese, softened	125 g
1/4 cup	mayonnaise	50 mL
1/4 cup	chopped green onions	50 mL
1	clove garlic, minced	1
2 tbsp	lemon juice	30 mL
2 tbsp	tomato paste	30 mL
Dash	hot pepper sauce (optional)	Dash
1	can (about 4 oz/113 g) crabmeat or tiny shrimp or 1 cup (250 mL) chopped cooked seafood	1
	Pepper and salt	

➜ In microwavable bowl, blend together cream cheese and mayonnaise. Stir in onions, garlic, lemon juice, tomato paste and hot pepper sauce. Blend in crabmeat or shrimp (if using canned shrimp, mash with fork). Add pepper to taste, and salt if needed. Microwave on High for 3 minutes or until very hot, stirring once halfway through. If too thick, blend in a little milk or water. (Dip may also be heated in small casserole in 350F/180C oven for about 20 minutes.) **Serves 6 to 8**.

Hot Artichoke Dip: Omit tomato paste, lemon juice and seafood. In food processor, chop 1 cup (250 mL) well-drained canned artichoke hearts (the plain kind, not marinated); stir into dip.

Hot Pizza Dip ⊕ ☻

This dip is great for kids' birthday parties (provide lots of paper napkins; also try to keep grownups at bay, or double the recipe). Serve with tortilla chips, pita crisps or soft breadsticks.

1	Italian sausage	1
1	small onion, chopped	1
2 cups	thick, chunky spaghetti sauce	500 mL
4 oz	cream cheese	125 g
1 cup	shredded mozzarella cheese	250 mL

➜ Remove casing from sausage and crumble meat into nonstick skillet over medium-high heat. Add onion and cook, stirring, until sausage is cooked through. Drain any excess fat. Stir in spaghetti sauce; simmer for 10 minutes or until thickened a little. Add cream cheese a bit at a time, stirring until melted. Add mozzarella and stir until melted. (Can be made ahead and reheated in microwave.) **Makes about 3 cups** (750 mL).

Hot Salsa Dip: You could get away with calling this Chili con Queso and serve it in a nice Mexican crockery pot. Instead of spaghetti sauce, use 1 cup (250 mL) bottled hot salsa (drained slightly if watery) and increase the cream cheese to 8 oz (250 g). For extra heat and flavour, stir in chopped jalapeños to taste.

Feta Spread or Dip

Ricotta smooths the texture and balances the salti-ness of the feta. Use a soft, mild feta if available.

4 oz	feta cheese, crumbled	250 g
4 oz	ricotta cheese (1/2 cup/125 mL)	250 g
1 tbsp	extra-virgin olive oil	15 mL
2 tsp	lemon juice	10 mL
2	cloves garlic, minced	2
1/2 tsp	dried oregano or mint	2 mL
2 to 4 tbsp	plain yogurt	30 to 60 mL

➜ In food processor, combine all ingredients except yogurt. Blend until smooth. Blend in enough yogurt to give spreading or dipping consistency as desired (mixture will thicken slightly when chilled). Taste; if too salty, add a little more ricotta. Transfer to bowl, cover and chill for at least 2 hours to blend flavours. **Makes about 1 cup** (250 mL).

To Serve: For appetizers with the flavour of Greek salad, spread feta mixture inside mini-pitas; fill with diced cucumber, tomato and black olives (or set out ingredients and let guests make their own). OR spread on small baguette slices and top with thinly sliced cucumber, tomato, olives and mint sprigs. OR spoon small dollops onto unpeeled cucumber slices or into scooped-out cherry tomatoes. OR serve as dip with pita chips, cucumber sticks, plum tomato wedges or other crudités.

Goat Cheese Spread or Dip: Use goat cheese (chèvre) instead of feta. (For mild flavour, use equal parts goat cheese and ricotta; for stronger flavour, increase the proportion of goat cheese.)

Chicken Liver Pâté

Having long abandoned (at least publicly) our beloved French country-style pâtés (the coarse-textured kind made with mixed meats, lots of pork fat and other sinful stuff), we turn to this slightly more virtuous alternative for occasional indulgence. It's easy to make, pleasantly smooth and a lot tastier than most store-bought versions.

1 lb	chicken livers	500 g
1 tbsp	butter	15 mL
3/4 cup	chopped onion	175 mL
2	cloves garlic, minced	2
2 tbsp	Madeira, port or brandy (optional)	30 mL
1/2 tsp	salt	2 mL
1/4 tsp	freshly ground pepper	1 mL
Pinch	each: dried thyme, allspice, ground cloves	Pinch
1/2 cup	chicken stock	125 mL
1/2 cup	butter, softened	125 mL
	Crushed black peppercorns	

➜ Cut livers in half and trim away any veins. In large nonstick skillet, melt 1 tbsp (15 mL) butter. Add livers and cook just until no pink colour remains. Add onion and garlic; cook, stirring, until softened. Stir in Madeira (if using), salt, pepper, thyme, allspice and cloves. Transfer to food processor; add stock and soft-ened butter. Process until very smooth. Taste and adjust seasoning. Spoon into 2-cup (500 mL) ramekin or other straight-sided dish. Cover tightly with plastic wrap and refrigerate for at least 4 hours or until firm spreading con-sistency. Sprinkle with crushed peppercorns. Serve with little toasts or thinly sliced baguette. **Makes about 2 cups** (500 mL).

Flavoured Cream Cheeses are easy to make in any flavour you fancy (and you can use low-fat cream cheese). Just soften the cheese and blend in minced ingredients to taste: fresh or dried herbs, green onions and garlic, roasted red peppers, sun-dried tomatoes, olives, capers, caraway seeds, smoked salmon, shrimp. Add a squeeze of lemon juice and salt and pepper to taste.

Veggie Cream Cheese: To 4 oz (125 g) softened cream cheese, add 2 tbsp (30 mL) each minced sweet red pepper, green onions and grated carrot, 4 minced green olives, 1 minced garlic clove (optional), pinch hot pepper flakes, squeeze of lemon juice, salt to taste.

Fruity Cream Cheese: To 4 oz (125 g) softened cream cheese, add 1/4 cup (50 mL) crushed strawberries, peaches or mango and a little lemon juice to taste.

Quick Fixes: A trayful of easy canapés in minutes

"Canapé" has a prissy sound, laden with images of silver trays. Cast the notion aside and imagine instead an array of good-looking, great-tasting, one- or two-bite morsels, all made with little effort. The key is interesting bases and intriguing toppings. Any of these bases will go with any of the toppings; mix and match is the name of the game.

Bases: small flatbread wedges or crisps (see page 21), baguette slices, tiny pumpernickel or rye bread rounds or squares, mini-bagels split horizontally, crackers, small toasts, grilled polenta slices, unpeeled cucumber or zucchini slices.

Toppings: flavoured cream cheeses, Feta or Goat Cheese Spread, Olive and Sun-dried Tomato Spread, Chicken Liver Pâté, Cheese Pâté (see pages 15-19). Top with a quick garnish of compatible flavour or something already in the spread (sprig or sprinkle of fresh herbs, sliced green onions, chopped peppers, sliced olives, sliced radishes, capers, tiny shrimp, thinly sliced smoked salmon, salmon or whitefish caviar).

Other holders and fillings:

- Leaves of belgian endive, romaine or scooped-out cherry tomatoes filled with any of the spreads on pages 15-19.

- Mini-pitas, tiny toast cups, wunton cups or phyllo cups (purchased or homemade, see page 21) filled with fresh salsas, hummus, baba ghanouj, guacamole, caramelized onions, tomato bruschetta topping, caponata (all can be purchased, or homemade; see index for recipes) or any of the Creamy Dips on page 15.

- Shiitake mushroom caps, grilled for about 1 minute on each side, then chilled; fill with chunky fresh salsa or pipe in a filling of flavoured cream cheese (page 19); top with matching garnish (tiny shrimps and sprigs of dill, chopped red peppers and basil, etc.).

Other Quick Fixes:

- Tortilla Roll-ups (see left Sidebar).

- Fruit cubes or small slices (melon, mango, papaya, plum, pear, apple, fig), wrapped with prosciutto if desired and secured with cocktail picks.

- Cheeses: Small log of goat cheese, rolled in finely chopped parsley or nuts, and sliced into rounds; small wedges of brie or camembert.

Serving Tips: Arrange canapés on large, good-looking trays; replenish occasionally to keep arrangement attractive (don't put out all your canapés at once!). On rectangular or square trays, canapés look best arranged in diagonal rows; on round trays, put them in wedge-shaped groupings. For garnish, use fresh herbs, edible flowers, miniature tomatoes, grape clusters.

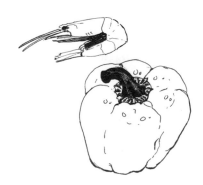

Tortilla Roll-ups: Spread 10-inch (25 cm) flour tortillas evenly with cream cheese, cover with a layer of thinly sliced smoked salmon and sprinkle with chopped capers or fresh dill (or use prosciutto and minced roasted red peppers OR smoked turkey and chopped green onions). Roll up tightly, wrap in plastic wrap and refrigerate until firm. Cut on slight diagonal into 1/2-inch (1 cm) slices.

Cheese Pâté: Serve this rather retro but always popular pâté in a small crock. Or shape it into a log or ball and coat the outside with toasted sesame seeds, finely chopped nuts or chopped parsley. In food processor, blend together until fairly smooth: 3 cups (750 mL) shredded old cheddar cheese, 8 oz (250 g) softened cream cheese, dash of Worcestershire sauce and 1/4 tsp (1 mL) (or to taste) hot pepper flakes. (For a variation, add about 4 oz/125 g crumbled gorgonzola, roquefort or other blue cheese.) Cover with plastic wrap and refrigerate; let stand at room temperature for about 30 minutes before serving. **Makes about 2 cups** (500 mL).

Base Hits

Tortilla crisps or pita crisps: Use small flour tortillas (plain or flavoured) or pita breads (split in half). Cut into wedges and place on baking sheet. Brush lightly on both sides with olive oil (or flavoured oil such as roasted garlic); if desired, sprinkle lightly with salt. For flavour variations, brush wedges with lightly beaten egg white and sprinkle with dried herbs such as oregano, chili powder or grated parmesan. Bake in 375F (190C) oven until crisp, about 5 minutes. Serve with dips or spreads or as canapé bases.

Bagel crisps: Cut stale bagels in half vertically (or into quarters if large), then cut horizontally into very thin slices. Arrange on baking sheet. Bake in 300F (150C) oven for 15 to 20 minutes or until dry and crisp. Serve with dips or spreads.

Grilled flatbread wedges: Brush focaccia or other flatbread lightly on both sides with olive oil. Grill on barbecue or stovetop ridged grill pan for a few minutes until lightly browned but still soft. Cut or tear into wedges and serve warm with spreads, soups or salads.

Grilled polenta slices: Use chilled homemade polenta (page 137) or purchased polenta roll. Cut into 1/2-inch (1 cm) slices; cut in half if large. Brush with olive oil and grill on barbecue or stovetop ridged grill pan until lightly browned on both sides. Use as canapé bases.

Toast cups: Trim crusts from thin slices of white bread. With rolling pin, roll out bread to flatten. For canapé-sized toast cups, cut slices into quarters and press into lightly oiled mini muffin cups; for larger cups, press whole slices into lightly oiled medium-sized muffin cups. Brush lightly with vegetable or olive oil. Bake in 350F (180C) oven for 5 to 7 minutes or until crisp and golden.

Phyllo cups: (For working with phyllo, see page 181.) Stack 4 layers of phyllo, each layer brushed lightly with melted butter; cut into squares and press into mini muffin cups (make squares large enough that points stick up over tops). Bake in 375F (190C) oven for 4 minutes or until golden.

Wunton cups: Separate wunton wrappers (available in Asian food shops and some supermarkets) and place one each in lightly oiled muffin cups. Bake in 375F (190C) oven for 6 to 7 minutes or until crisp and golden. Remove from tins and let cool on rack.

Quesadillas

These can be oven-baked, but we like them best cooked in a skillet for a more authentic taste and look, and they're not greasy when you use a lightly oiled nonstick pan. Quesadillas are made with flour tortillas or, less commonly, corn tortillas, and almost anything goes for the filling (cheese is the only must). Serve with salsa as appetizers or as accompaniments to salads or soups.

If using corn tortillas (about 6 inches/15 cm): Place 1 tortilla in lightly oiled nonstick skillet over medium-high heat. Sprinkle with about 2 tbsp (30 mL) shredded monterey jack cheese and top with a second tortilla. Cook for 2 minutes on each side or until tortillas are softened and lightly browned and cheese is melted. Cut into 4 wedges.

If using flour tortillas (about 8 inches/20 cm): Sprinkle half of each tortilla with about 1/3 cup (75 mL) shredded monterey jack cheese, keeping it away from the edges. Fold in half and press edges together. Heat nonstick skillet over medium-high heat. Brush with oil, add quesadilla and cook for 1 to 2 minutes on each side or until golden brown and cheese is melted. Cut into wedges. (Grilling works, too, and leaves nice grill marks; use a stovetop ridged grill pan if you're not barbecuing.)

Filling variation: Before adding cheese, spread tortilla with refried beans and sprinkle with minced jalapeños, green onions or chopped fresh coriander.

Nachos

For about 4 servings, arrange 30 to 40 round tortilla chips, just touching, in single layer in large shallow baking pan or ovenproof serving dish. Spoon 1/2 cup (125 mL) taco sauce or salsa evenly over chips. Sprinkle with 2 cups (500 mL) shredded cheddar or monterey jack cheese (or packaged shredded four-cheese mixture). Bake in 400F (200C) oven for 4 minutes (or broil) until cheese is melted. Serve with sour cream for dipping if desired.

Optional additions: Before adding cheese, top the chips with mashed or refried beans or leftover chili and/or sprinkle with chopped pickled jalapeños, sweet peppers, onions or tomatoes.

Chicken Fingers

These popular party snacks are also the first choice of most kids for supper. Cut boneless chicken breasts into strips, then coat with crumbs and bake (see Oven-Fried Chicken, page 100) OR simply marinate briefly (see Marinades, page 110) and grill or broil until cooked through, about 5 minutes. Serve with Dipping Sauces (see below).

Dipping Sauces

Plum Sauce: Mix together 1/2 cup (125 mL) yellow plum jam (if unavailable, apricot or peach will do; mash if lumpy), 1 minced small garlic clove and 1 tbsp (15 mL) each white vinegar, ketchup and mild honey mustard. You can also find good bottled plum sauces in Asian specialty stores and some supermarkets.

Honey-Garlic Dipping Sauce: Mix together 1/4 cup (50 mL) each liquid honey and light-coloured soy sauce, 2 tbsp (30 mL) ketchup, 1 minced garlic clove and 1/4 tsp (1 mL) ground ginger.

Hot and Spicy Dipping Sauce: Mix together 1/2 cup (125 mL) ketchup, 1/4 cup (50 mL) honey, 1 tbsp (15 mL) lemon juice and 1/4 tsp (1 mL) hot pepper flakes or hot pepper sauce to taste. Microwave on High for 1 minute or until hot.

Blue Cheese Dipping Sauce: Blend together 1/2 cup (125 mL) sour cream, 1/4 cup (50 mL) mayonnaise and 2 oz (50 g) (or to taste) crumbled blue cheese.

Spiced Nuts

A crisp spicy-sweet coating makes these popular as party nibbles or with after-dinner coffee. Double the recipe and wrap some up as great little gifts from your kitchen.

1	egg white	1
1 tbsp	water	15 mL
3 cups	pecan halves, blanched almonds, peanuts or mixture	750 mL
1/2 cup	granulated sugar	125 mL
2 tsp	cinnamon	10 mL
1/2 tsp	each: ground coriander, ginger, allspice	2 mL
1/4 tsp	each: nutmeg, pepper	1 mL
1 tsp	salt	5 mL

➜ In bowl, beat egg white with water until frothy. Stir in nuts and mix well. Pour nuts into sieve and let drain for a few minutes. In plastic bag, combine sugar, spices and salt. Add nuts and shake until well coated. Spread nuts in single layer on nonstick or lightly oiled baking sheets. Bake in 275F (140C) oven for about 45 minutes, stirring occasionally, until nuts are dried and crispy. Let cool. **Makes 3 cups** (750 mL).

Crispy Wings with Dips

Wings still claim top spot as pub and party food. For crispy wings, baking is a lot easier and healthier than deep-frying. For 4 to 6 servings, use about 3 lb (1.5 kg) wings. Cut off wing tips at joint (freeze them for use in stock). Cut remaining wings into two pieces at joint.

Arrange in single layer on nonstick or greased rimmed baking sheet. Sprinkle wings lightly on both sides with seasoned salt and pepper. Bake in 425F (220C) oven for 30 minutes or until crispy, turning them over halfway through. Serve with Dipping Sauces (see left Sidebar).

Glazed Chicken Wings

Coated with a spicy-sweet glaze, these wings make deliciously sticky finger food, or they can be served as a main course with rice.

2-1/2 lb	chicken wings (about 20)	1.25 kg
	Salt and pepper	
1/2 cup	each: soy sauce, liquid honey	125 mL
2 tbsp	ketchup	30 mL
2	cloves garlic, minced	2
1 tsp	grated fresh ginger (or 1/2 tsp/2 mL ground ginger)	5 mL

➜ Cut off wing tips at joint (freeze to use for stock). Cut remaining wings into two pieces at joint. Arrange wings in single layer in lightly greased or nonstick shallow baking pan. Sprinkle wings lightly on both sides with salt and pepper. Bake in 425F (220C) oven for 15 minutes; drain off fat in pan. Mix together soy sauce, honey, ketchup, garlic and ginger; pour over wings. Bake for 20 minutes longer, turning and basting often with sauce, until well glazed. **Makes 4 to 6 servings.**

Spring Rolls with Dipping Sauce

Southeast Asian cuisines include many versions of uncooked spring rolls, simply wrapped in rice paper—a fresh-tasting, low-fat alternative to the fried kind. Vary the filling as you wish.

2 oz	rice vermicelli noodles	50 g
1 cup	chopped cooked shrimp or chicken	250 mL
1/3 cup	(approx) each: bean sprouts, slivered cucumber, chopped water chestnuts, shredded carrot	75 mL
2 tbsp	chopped fresh coriander, parsley or mint	30 mL
About 20	6-inch (15 cm) round rice paper wrappers	About 20
	Leaf lettuce (optional)	

→ In bowl, cover noodles with boiling water; let stand for 3 minutes or until softened. Drain well and place in large bowl. Add shrimp, vegetables and coriander; mix gently. For each spring roll, submerge rice paper wrapper in bowl of warm water until flexible, about 1 minute; drain and pat dry on tea towel. If desired, place a lettuce leaf (trimmed to fit) on each rice paper wrapper. Spoon about 2 tbsp (30 mL) filling in centre of each. Roll up tightly, tucking in the sides (including lettuce along with wrapper) as you go. Rolls may be covered with plastic wrap and refrigerated for a few hours. To serve, cut rolls in half crosswise if desired. Serve with Dipping Sauce. (See Sidebar). **Makes about 40 pieces**.

Dipping Sauce for Spring Rolls: Combine 1/4 cup (50 mL) light-coloured for Spring Rolls soy sauce, 1/4 cup (50 mL) rice vinegar, 1 tbsp (15 mL) granulated sugar, 2 tbsp (30 mL) each minced green onion and shredded carrot, 1 minced garlic clove, dash of Chinese chile oil or paste (to taste).

Satays with Peanut Sauce

Grilled satays make great appetizers for a barbecue party. They can be marinated and threaded well ahead of time, and the grilling is fast and easy.

1 lb	boneless chicken breast, pork loin or beef sirloin	500 g
2 tbsp	peanut or vegetable oil	30 mL
2	cloves garlic, minced	2
2 tbsp	each: brown sugar, lime juice, soy sauce	30 mL

→ Cut meat into thin strips about 1 inch (2.5 cm) wide. In shallow dish, whisk together oil, garlic, brown sugar, lime juice and soy sauce. Add chicken, turning strips to coat; marinate, covered, in refrigerator for 2 to 8 hours. Soak about 16 small bamboo skewers in water for 30 minutes. Thread meat onto skewers; refrigerate if not cooking immediately. Grill, turning occasionally, just until cooked through, about 5 minutes. Serve with Peanut Sauce for dipping. **Makes 4 to 6 servings**.

Peanut Sauce: This has a popular spicy-sweet flavour but you can adjust ingredients to your taste (cooks across Southeast Asia make many different peanut sauces). The sauce is also good on rice or as a dressing for Asian noodle salads.

1/3 cup	smooth peanut butter	75 mL
3 tbsp	each: granulated sugar, soy sauce, rice vinegar or lime juice	45 mL
1 tbsp	each: minced garlic, minced fresh ginger, dark sesame oil	15 mL
1/2 tsp	(or to taste) chile paste or hot pepper sauce or flakes	2 mL
1/4 cup	(approx) warm water or coconut milk	50 mL

→ In food processor, blend ingredients together until smooth, adding a little more water if needed. Sauce may be refrigerated for up to 3 days; bring to room temperature before serving.

Herb-Marinated Goat Cheese

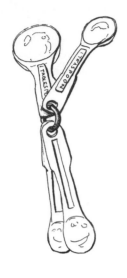

Creamy chèvre meets robust fresh herbs in this easy-to-prepare appetizer. The recipe is a favourite of Sandra Hainle of Hainle Vineyards Estate Winery in the Okanagan Valley and was created by David Forestell, chef at the winery's busy bistro. For a first course, the cheese can be served on its own, with some good bread, or on a bed of greens (such as mesclun) as a salad. (Dress the salad greens with some of the flavoured oil drained from the cheese, mixed with a little grapefruit or lemon juice to taste and seasoned with salt and pepper. At the bistro, the salad is garnished with edible flowers such as nasturtiums.)

2 tbsp	each: finely chopped fresh basil, oregano, marjoram, thyme, rosemary (mix together)	30 mL
1 tbsp	cracked black pepper	15 mL
1-1/2 tsp	fennel seeds	7 mL
1/2 tsp	juniper berries (optional)	2 mL
3	cloves garlic, flattened with broad side of knife	3
1-1/4 cups	good-quality olive oil	300 mL
8 oz	fresh chèvre (goat cheese)	250 g

➜ In stainless steel or other nonreactive saucepan, combine half of the herbs with pepper, fennel seeds, juniper berries (if using), garlic and oil. Heat just until mixture starts to bubble. Remove from heat; let cool. Strain through fine sieve or coffee filter; discard solids. Divide cheese into 8 portions and form into small discs (if using logs of cheese, cut into slices). Coat each disc with remaining chopped herbs, pressing them lightly into cheese to adhere. Place cheese in nonreactive container and completely cover with flavoured oil; add a bit more oil if needed. Seal tightly; marinate in refrigerator for at least 24 hours before serving. (Any leftover cheese will keep, covered with oil, for up to 1 week in the refrigerator.) **Makes 8 servings**.

Smoked Salmon Torta

In Canada we have some of the best smoked salmon in the world, and this layered pâté is one of Murray's favourite ways to show it off. Served with freshly sliced baguette or good crackers, it makes a luxurious appetizer for a special occasion and also transports well to a picnic (make it the day ahead).

1 lb	cream cheese, softened	500 g
1/2 cup	butter, softened	125 mL
	Salt	
	Sprigs fresh dill	
1/4 cup	chopped fresh dill	50 mL
1/2 lb	sliced smoked salmon	250 g

➜ Beat together cream cheese and butter; add salt to taste. Line an 8- x 4-inch (20 x 10 cm) loaf pan with piece of plastic wrap large enough to extend over edges of pan. Arrange a few dill sprigs on bottom. Carefully spread one-third of the cheese mixture in the pan to make an even layer. Sprinkle half of the chopped dill over cheese; top with half of the smoked salmon. Repeat layers, ending with cheese mixture. Press down lightly to compact layers. Cover and chill overnight. To serve, pull up edges of plastic wrap to loosen torta; invert onto plate and carefully remove wrap. Garnish as desired.

Beautiful Beginnings:
First courses for your sit-down dinners

How about chilled mango soup garnished with hibiscus blossoms? A salad of sizzling garlic shrimp atop colourful mesclun? Or some decidedly decadent shiitake-sauced creamy linguine? First impressions are important—experienced hosts often say that a dazzling starter and dessert, more than what's in between, are the secret to successful dinner parties.

For first-course inspiration, you'll find lots of recipes throughout this book; browse through Soups, Salads, Pasta, Eggs and Cheese, Fish and Seafood. Some recipes indicate appetizer-size portions; otherwise, allow about half a main-course serving for a starter portion.

Tomatoes and Bocconcini with Basil: This is a wonderful first course on its own or with a variety of other antipasti. It also makes a beautiful salad platter for a hot summer day when garden tomatoes and fresh basil are at their peak. Be sure to use top-quality cheese and olive oil. For 4 servings, you will need 4 ripe red tomatoes, sliced, and 1/2 lb (250 g) sliced bocconcini (balls of fresh mozzarella) or other mozzarella. On large platter or individual salad plates, alternate sliced tomatoes and cheese, overlapping slightly. Sprinkle lightly with salt and a few grindings of pepper. If desired, scatter with a few chopped green onions or rings of sweet onion. Sprinkle with about 1/2 cup (125 mL) slivered fresh basil. Drizzle with 2 tbsp (30 mL) balsamic or red wine vinegar and 6 tbsp (90 mL) extra-virgin olive oil. Let stand at room temperature for 30 minutes. Serve with crusty Italian bread.

Tip: To sliver basil, stack large leaves, then roll up tightly like a cigar; with sharp knife, slice thinly crosswise to make long shreds.

Prosciutto-Asparagus Bundles: This is one of Murray's springtime standbys. Wrap sliced prosciutto around 3 or 4 skinny crisp-cooked asparagus spears, allowing 2 wrapped bundles per serving. Arrange bundles, crisscrossed, on individual salad plates lined with mesclun. Drizzle with Balsamic Dressing (page 46) and top with shaved parmesan.

Baked Brie or Camembert Wedges: For 4 servings cut 1/2 lb (250 g) brie or camembert cheese into 8 wedges (use round cheeses, 1/4 lb/125 g each, if available). Brush wedges with olive oil, then roll in finely chopped almonds, pine nuts, sesame seeds or fresh breadcrumbs (mixed with chopped herbs if desired) to coat lightly and evenly on all sides. Place wedges on lightly oiled baking sheet. Cover and refrigerate for at least 1 hour. Bake uncovered in 325F (160C) oven for 10 to 15 minutes or until wedges are heated through but still holding their shape. Divide wedges among 4 salad plates (in autumn, the cheese looks nice sitting on bright-coloured maple leaves) accompanied by triangles of toast and a large spoonful of fresh fruit salsa or chutney. Garnish with thin slices of unpeeled apple or pear and sprigs of Italian parsley. Serve immediately. The cheese can also be served on salad greens or mesclun drizzled with a little olive oil and balsamic vinegar.

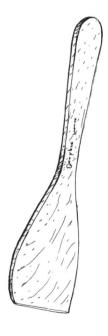

Mushrooms à la Grècque: One of my daughter-in-law Sarah's best concoctions, these are fast, easy and delicious. In large skillet over medium heat, combine 1/4 cup (50 mL) each olive oil and water, 2 tbsp (30 mL) white wine, 1 tbsp (15 mL) minced onion, 1 tbsp (15 mL) lemon juice, 1 minced garlic clove, 1 tsp (5 mL) tomato paste, 1 small bay leaf and a pinch each oregano, salt and pepper. Simmer for 5 minutes. Add 1/2 lb (250 g) white button mushrooms; simmer for 6 to 8 minutes or until just tender, stirring often. With slotted spoon, remove mushrooms to bowl. Boil liquid for about 2 minutes to reduce and thicken. Pour over mushrooms. Serve warm, spooned over grilled crusty bread and sprinkled with chopped Italian parsley; garnish with lemon wedges. **Makes 4 servings.** (Also good served room-temperature as antipasto.)

Avocado and Shrimp: There's something especially appealing about this international duo; the shapes, colours and flavours work so well together that almost any arrangement is a sure hit. For a refreshingly cool-looking, summery starter, arrange overlapping slices of avocado and honeydew melon on salad plates, scatter with a few perfect shrimp (chunks of poached salmon also work well); drizzle with a creamy citrus dressing and garnish with lime wedges and green grapes. OR, for a tropical twist, try a chunky salad of cubed avocado, mango, papaya and pineapple, dressed with a ginger-lime vinaigrette (looks great spooned into large stemmed glasses and topped with tails-on shrimp); OR make it Mexican with a salsa-flavoured dressing and leafy garnish of coriander; OR Thai-inspired, replacing the ripe fruit with slivers of unpeeled green mango and using a chile-laced vinaigrette. (For dressings, see pages 46-47).

And then there's **Avocado with Secret Sauce:** My brother Garry is a great cook who happily whips together four-course repasts for everyone who happens by. His repertoire of first courses (or "entrées" as he calls them, having spent his formative years in France) is legendary, but asked which one gets raves every single time, he somewhat reluctantly reveals this: Cut small ripe avocados in half and remove pits but don't peel; cut small slice from bottom so they sit flat on plate. Score surface of avocado with tines of fork. Drizzle liberally with Secret Sauce (3 parts extra-virgin olive oil and 1 part Worcestershire sauce whisked together). Provide small pointed spoons (or grapefruit spoons) and serve with thinly sliced baguette. *C'est tout.* (This looks and tastes great with a few nice pink shrimp atop the avocado, but I am among the purists who like it as is—and remind Garry that Worcestershire happens to be a very complex, though underappreciated, condiment!).

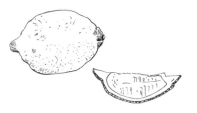

Sandwiches Wraps, Pizzas

Pack a panino, stuff a pita, wrap a roti,
grill a focaccia, trim a pizza.
Invent a new favourite—anything goes

Hot New Sandwiches

From Thai chicken salad in a warm pita to Caribbean curry in a roti wrap to grilled peppers and mushrooms in a fluffy focaccia wedge, sandwiches have entered a whole new world of flavour adventures. There are no rules for these between-the-covers meals, so unleash your imagination.

Grilled Focaccia Sandwiches

Filled-and-grilled focaccia is all the rage in sandwich shops and easy to make at home. Just slide any filling you fancy into split focaccia and grill in a skillet. The focaccia can be any shape or flavour, but should be fairly thin to heat through quickly. Slice focaccia in half horizontally; brush cut sides with olive oil. On bottom half arrange sliced prosciutto, salami or other Italian deli meats and sliced provolone or fontina cheese. Add a generous scattering of peppery arugula leaves and any extras you like—roasted red peppers, pickled hot peppers, sliced tomatoes. Add top half of bread and press down. Leave whole or cut into wedges or squares. Brush large nonstick skillet with olive oil and place over medium heat. Place filled focaccia in pan and press down firmly with spatula. Cook for about 5 minutes, turning once and pressing down again, until bread is browned and crispy and cheese is melted. For filling variations, try grilled chicken, veal, eggplant or portobello mushrooms.

Pick Your Panini

Take-out shops specializing in panini (oval, crusty Italian rolls with all kinds of hot and cold fillings) have expanded far beyond Italian neighbourhoods and offer not only a great choice for workday lunches but inspiration for do-it-yourself at home. Panini can be filled with anything from cold cuts and sliced cheese to sautéed veal with peppers and mushrooms. Some popular fillings from our favourite panini shop include grilled chicken with sun-dried tomatoes, pesto and bocconcini, and sliced Italian sausage with grilled vegetables, rapini and mushrooms (not to mention "mama's meatball sandwich"!).

For a lightened-up version of the traditional Italian veal parmigiana sandwich (fried breaded veal with tomato sauce), try a tasty **Turkey Parmigiana Panini:** Marinate turkey scaloppine briefly in a little lemon juice, olive oil and rosemary. Broil until just cooked through; drizzle with pizza sauce, sprinkle with parmesan and shredded mozzarella and broil just until cheese is melted. Serve in an Italian roll, crusty baguette or focaccia.

Wrap It Up

Pitas and tortillas have become popular wrappers for everything from cool chicken caesar salads to hot-and-spicy stir-fries. A pita pocket makes a handy holder, while the pocketless Greek pita wraps up stuffings in a snug blanket. Stuffed tortillas can be folded like an envelope or rolled up like a tube.

For cold fillings, try any of the chicken, bean, grain or rice salads on pages 52 to 57.

For hot fillings, try a spicy curry (page

116), chili (pages 80, 140), quick stir-fry (page 118) or grilled satays (removed from skewers) with peanut sauce (page 23).

Or try any of these combos:

- Store-bought or home-barbecued chicken cut in strips, red pepper strips, chopped avocado
- Grilled vegetables, fresh basil, crumbled feta or garlic mayonnaise

- Chunky chicken salad with fruit, or tuna salad niçoise
- Club sandwich wrap of grilled chicken or turkey breast, crisp bacon or pancetta, tangy coleslaw and thinly sliced tomatoes
- Leftover grilled honey-garlic or jerk chicken, grilled teriyaki salmon or flank steak with basmati rice and snow peas

Six Easy Melts ☺

Top toasted or grilled halved buns, baguette, focaccia or thickly sliced bread with whatever takes your fancy, sprinkle with cheese and slide under the broiler until melting-hot.

- Salmon or Tuna Melt: Combine drained canned salmon or tuna with a little chopped green onion and celery, a few chopped olives if desired, and enough mayonnaise just to moisten. Spread on toasted bun or bread and top with shredded cheddar.
- Scrambled Egg Melt: Spoon softly scrambled eggs on toasted bun or bread; top with chopped cooked bacon or ham if desired, sprinkle with shredded swiss or cheddar.
- Mushroom-Onion Melt: In skillet, cook sliced onion until soft; add an equal quantity of sliced mushrooms, a little minced garlic,

some dried basil or oregano, and salt and pepper to taste; cook until tender. Spread on toasted bun or bread; top with shredded cheddar or mozzarella.

- Turkey-Salsa Melt: Top toasted bread with thinly sliced monterey jack or mozzarella, sliced cooked turkey or chicken; spread with salsa and top with more sliced cheese.
- Italian Sandwich Melt: Top toasted focaccia or black olive bread with prosciutto, sliced cooked Italian sausage or pancetta, roasted peppers or tomatoes, and shaved asiago cheese.
- Grilled Vegetable Melt: Top toasted crusty Italian bread with leftover grilled vegetables (eggplant, peppers, fennel, zucchini), shredded mozzarella and grated parmesan.

In a Bun

In addition to panini with hot Italian-flavoured fillings, all kinds of other hot foods can be tucked into toasted buns for a quick, satisfying meal-in-hand. Here are some suggestions:

- A crispy-hot fish fillet (fresh from your grill, stovetop grill pan or oven; pages 64-65), topped with a grilled tomato slice and coleslaw (page 51) or tartar sauce.
- Thinly sliced grilled flank steak topped with grilled or sautéed mushrooms and

caramelized onions (page 236) or Mango Salsa (page 233).

- Barbecued chicken (purchased, freshly home-cooked or leftovers reheated in microwave; see grilled, baked or skillet chicken, pages 106-107) topped with thin slices of Vidalia or other sweet onions and some chopped crunchy greens.

French Toasted Sandwiches
This is a variation of the traditional croque monsieur of France (or a dressed-up grilled cheese sandwich, if you prefer). For 2 sandwiches: Spread 4 slices of white bread very lightly with Dijon mustard; make 2 sandwiches with 1 slice swiss cheese and 1 slice cooked ham in each. In shallow dish, beat together 2 eggs and 2 tbsp (30 mL) milk. Dip sandwiches in egg mixture, turning to coat both sides. In nonstick skillet over medium heat, melt 2 tsp (10 mL) butter. Add sandwiches and cook until golden brown underneath. Add another 1 tsp (5 mL) butter to skillet; turn sandwiches and brown the other side.

Fajitas (Beef, Chicken or Turkey) ☺ ♥

Grilled Beef Fajitas: Prepare lime juice mixture from recipe at right. Leave the steak in one piece; marinate in lime juice mixture for about 1 hour. Grill over high heat for about 3 minutes each side (it should be slightly charred), then slice into strips. If you want to be really authentic, use a less-tender cut of beef such as flank or round (about 1-1/2 lb/750 g), double the amount of marinade, and marinate in refrigerator for at least 8 hours. The onions and peppers can also be grilled; cut into large pieces, grill, then cut smaller before rolling.

Great in flavour, low in fat, fast and easy, these speedy fajitas are made with tender cuts of beef or poultry and a streamlined stir-fry method instead of the long marinating and grilling involved in traditional fajitas.

3/4 lb	sirloin steak or boneless chicken or turkey breast	375 g
2 tbsp	olive oil	30 mL
1 tbsp	lime juice	15 mL
1	clove garlic, finely minced	1
1/2 tsp	each: chili powder, ground cumin	2 mL
1/4 tsp	each: hot pepper flakes, pepper, salt	1 mL
8	flour tortillas (8-inch/20 cm)	8
1	large onion	1
2	sweet peppers (green, red, orange or yellow)	2

Toppings: salsa (mild or hot), sour cream or thick yogurt, shredded cheese, chopped tomatoes, chopped avocado or guacamole

➜ Slice meat into thin strips. In bowl, mix together 1 tbsp (15 mL) of the olive oil, lime juice, garlic, chili powder, cumin, hot pepper flakes, pepper and salt. Add meat strips and stir to coat; set aside. Wrap tortillas in foil and place in 350F (180C) oven for 5 to 10 minutes or until heated through. Cut onion in half lengthwise and slice into strips. Cut peppers into strips. In large nonstick skillet over medium-high heat, heat remaining 1 tbsp (15 mL) oil. Add onions and peppers; cook, stirring, for 3 or 4 minutes or until softened; remove to bowl and set aside. Add meat strips to skillet. Cook, stirring, for 3 to 4 minutes or until beef loses its red colour, or chicken or turkey is cooked through. Return onions and peppers to skillet; stir until hot, about 1 minute. To serve, spoon one-eighth of meat mixture down centre of each tortilla. Top with salsa and add other toppings as desired. Fold bottom of tortilla up over filling, then fold in sides, overlapping. **Makes 8 fajitas** (4 servings).

Basic Salad Sandwich Fillings

These are so easy it makes you wonder why so many are so unsatisfying. Here's a simple standby recipe—with good flavour, moistness and just a little crunch—that can be varied any way you wish (add chopped almonds, dried fruit, olives, peppers). You can use it for sandwiches OR chop the ingredients finely and use as a spread with crackers OR chop in larger pieces for chunky salads.

For Egg, Tuna, Salmon, Shrimp, Turkey or Chicken Salad Sandwiches: Use 3 coarsely chopped hard-cooked eggs OR 1 can tuna, salmon or shrimp (drained) OR 1 cup (250 mL) chopped cooked turkey or chicken. Add 2 chopped green onions, 1 chopped celery stalk, just enough mayonnaise to moisten, and salt and pepper to taste. **Makes enough for 3 sandwiches**.

For Open-Face Sandwiches: Top firm-textured bread with lettuce and/or alfalfa sprouts; mound filling on top.

Vegetarian Stacked Sandwich 🌿 ❤

Cooking school owner Bonnie Stern travels and cooks all over the world. In the '80s she introduced us to traditional New Orleans muffuletta: a big sandwich filled with cold cuts, cheese and an olive-based salad. This is her update on the theme—also stacked with great things and equally delicious, but much lower in fat.

2	eggplants, about 1 lb (500 g) each, cut into 1/4-inch (5 mm) slices	2
1	can (19 oz/540 mL) chick peas, rinsed and drained	1
2 tbsp	lemon juice	30 mL
1 tbsp	sesame oil	15 mL
1 tsp	ground cumin	5 mL
1	clove garlic, minced	1
1/2 tsp	each: salt, pepper, hot chile paste	2 mL
1	10-inch (25 cm) round loaf Italian bread	1
1	each: sweet red and yellow pepper, roasted, peeled and cut into chunks	1
1	bunch arugula or watercress, trimmed	1
1/3 cup	pesto	75 mL

➜ Grill eggplant on both sides until browned; reserve. In food processor, purée chick peas, lemon juice, oil, cumin, garlic, salt, pepper and chile paste. Taste and adjust seasonings and/or thin with water if necessary. Cut bread in half horizontally and remove some of the insides. Spread bottom half of loaf with chick pea purée and layer on eggplant slices, roasted peppers and arugula. Spread top half of bread with pesto and place firmly on top. Press down firmly; wrap tightly with plastic wrap. Refrigerate for about 1 hour; cut into 8 wedges and serve. **Makes 8 servings.**

Cool Combos

A dash of inspiration can turn favourite ingredients into classy satisfactions:

- On a crusty Italian roll, arrange in order: red leaf lettuce, prosciutto (in loose folds), sliced avocado, sliced onion, drizzle of balsamic vinegar and a scattering of fresh basil.

- A traditional Maritime Lobster Sandwich: chopped lobster meat, diced celery, chopped green onions, a little creamy dressing or mayo to moisten; spoon into large soft or toasted rolls.

- Good sourdough bread sandwiched around thinly sliced rare roast beef, creamy horseradish, sliced swiss cheese, dab of Dijon.

- Chilled poached fresh salmon fillet (page 67) with pickled zucchini or carrot slices and fresh alfalfa sprouts or arugula, on calabrese (Italian bread with cornmeal-sprinkled crust).

- Sliced chicken breast (such as chilled grilled chicken with Thai marinade, page 117) topped with chopped blanched bok choy and spicy tropical fruit salsa (page 233), on thick-sliced crisp-crusted country bread.

- Chilled grilled tuna on egg bread, with pickled ginger and watercress.

- Double-decker turkey or shrimp club sandwich on sliced brown bread or lightly toasted brioche: Fill bottom layer with sliced turkey or cooked shrimp (leftovers from the grill are great), a dab of mayo, sprinkle of capers and slice of mozzarella; fill top layer with sliced tomato, dab of mayo, crumbled cooked bacon and Boston lettuce.

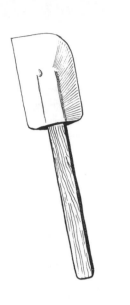

Pizza

Making your own pizza is easy, great fun for kids and nutritious, too, if you choose the toppings well.

Crust:

Store-bought pizza dough (usually refrigerated; if frozen, thaw in refrigerator) OR homemade pizza/focaccia dough (page 175) OR store-bought pizza crust (fully or partially baked) OR Italian-style thin flatbreads

Preparation:

If using purchased pizza crust, follow package directions. If using pizza dough, roll out on floured surface; place on ungreased baking sheet sprinkled lightly with cornmeal. Pinch edge of dough to form rim. Arrange your favourite toppings on crust (or choose from list at right).

To bake in oven:

Consult package directions when available. Otherwise, preheat oven to 450F (230C) for unbaked crust, 425F (220C) for partially baked, 400F (200C) for fully baked. Bake pizza until crust is crisp, toppings are hot and cheese is melted (usually 10 to 15 minutes; sometimes a few minutes less or more, depending on toppings).

To bake in covered barbecue:

If using unbaked or partially baked crust, preheat barbecue to medium-high. Place pizza crust on greased baking sheet; add toppings. Place pan on grill rack.

If using fully baked crust, turn on one side of barbecue to high heat; place pizza directly on grill rack on unheated side. Close lid and cook for 10 to 15 minutes or until bottom is crisp, toppings are hot and cheese is melted.

Toppings:

Spread crust with a thin layer of pizza sauce or lightly seasoned tomato sauce, then add your favourite embellishments; finish with a drizzle of olive oil.

- Italian Garden: fresh or grilled sliced tomatoes, sweet peppers, zucchini, eggplant and onion; sprinkle of minced garlic, oregano, parmesan or asiago.

- Assorted peppers and crumbled feta.

- Sliced mushrooms, sun-dried tomatoes, sweet onions, basil, mozzarella.

- Sliced canned (not marinated) artichoke hearts, prosciutto (or sliced pepperoni or salami), olives, feta.

- Sun-dried tomatoes, goat cheese, arugula.

- Four cheeses (mozzarella, fontina, goat cheese, parmesan) and sprinkle of basil or oregano.

- Shrimp, feta and mushrooms.

- Italian sausage (sliced or crumbled, lightly cooked), tomato sauce, sweet peppers, mozzarella.

- Tex-Mex: ground beef (crumbled, lightly cooked), minced jalapeño, spicy salsa, monterey jack cheese.

- Pesto (instead of pizza sauce), sliced tomatoes and bocconcini or goat cheese.

Simmered Satisfactions...

Soups &
Chowders

From homespun-and-hearty to the ultimate cool,
beautiful soups take top billing on today's menus

For **stocks (chicken, beef, fish, vegetable),** see page 237.

Minestrone Variations

Lentil Soup: Omit kidney beans, macaroni and cabbage. Add 1 cup (250 mL) dried lentils along with the tomatoes and stock; simmer for about 45 minutes or until lentils are tender.

Lentil Soup or Minestrone with Sausage: Lightly brown 1/2 lb (250 g) sliced or crumbled Italian sausage in saucepan before adding vegetables.

Minestrone

Honest, forthright, unadorned—that's the bravura of Italy's great soups, be they simple minestras, long-simmered vegetable minestrones, the twice-cooked ribollitas of Tuscany or simply zuppa, a catch-all term that echoes so close to "supper." This robust minestrone is hearty enough to be a meal on its own and can be varied (as it is in every Italian kitchen) by adding different spices or herbs, dried beans or any vegetables you wish.

2 tbsp	olive oil	30 mL
1 cup	finely chopped onions	250 mL
1/2 cup	each: finely chopped celery, carrot, sweet pepper	125 mL
2	cloves garlic, minced	2
1	can (28 oz/796 mL) tomatoes	1
2 cups	chicken stock	500 mL
1/2 tsp	each: dried oregano and basil	2 mL
2 cups	shredded cabbage	500 mL
1 cup	cooked or canned red kidney beans	250 mL
1/2 cup	uncooked macaroni	125 mL
	Salt and pepper	

➜ In large saucepan over medium heat, heat oil. Add onions, celery, carrot, sweet pepper and garlic. Cover and cook, stirring often, until softened but not browned, about 5 minutes. Add tomatoes (crush as you add them), chicken stock, oregano and basil; bring to boil, reduce heat and simmer for about 10 minutes. Add cabbage, beans and macaroni. Cover and simmer, stirring occasionally, for about 30 minutes. Add a little more stock or water if too thick. Add salt and pepper to taste. **Makes about 8 servings**.

Chunky Chicken or Turkey Soup ☻

Rich-flavoured soup with lots of tender noodles and chunky vegetables is the classic cure for winter chills. And as a bonus, it's fast and easy to make. Cooking cubed chicken or turkey in the broth gives a lot more flavour than adding already-cooked meat (although you could if you have leftover roast chicken or turkey).

2 tbsp	vegetable oil	30 mL
1	large onion, coarsely chopped	1
1	large leek (white and light green part), sliced	1
2	carrots, sliced	2
1	stalk celery, sliced	1
1	clove garlic, minced	1
6 cups	homemade chicken stock (or canned chicken broth diluted with water)	1.5 L
1	small bay leaf	1
1/4 tsp	each: dried thyme and rosemary	1 mL
2 cups	egg noodles (broad or medium)	500 mL
3/4 lb	boneless, skinless chicken or turkey breast or thigh meat, cut in small chunks	375 g
1/4 cup	chopped parsley	50 mL
	Salt and pepper	

➜ In large heavy saucepan, heat oil over medium-high heat. Add onion, leek, carrots, celery and garlic; cook, stirring, for 2 to 3 minutes or until slightly softened but not browned. Add chicken stock, bay leaf, thyme and rosemary. Bring to boil. Stir in noodles and chicken or turkey chunks. Reduce heat, cover and simmer for 10 minutes or until noodles are tender and meat is cooked through. Remove bay leaf. Stir in parsley. Add salt and pepper to taste. **Makes 6 servings.**

Harvest Soup and Other Vegetable Smoothies

From a flavourful base of leeks, onions and pota-toes, you can make almost any smooth vegetable soup you want (see Variations below for some suggestions). This harvest vegetable version, with its gorgeous golden colour and mellow flavour, is wonderful for supper on a crisp autumn evening or as a starter for Thanksgiving dinner. The tex-ture is beautifully smooth and creamy without any thickeners (the small amount of cream can even be omitted). A splash of white wine is also optional but really rounds out the flavour.

2 tbsp	butter	30 mL
2	large leeks (white and light green part), chopped	2
1	large onion, chopped	1
1	large potato, peeled and diced	1
2 cups	diced peeled squash (preferably butternut or buttercup)	500 mL
1 cup	diced carrots	250 mL
4 cups	chicken stock	1 L
1/2 cup	light cream or milk	125 mL
1/4 cup	white wine (optional)	50 mL
	Salt and pepper	
	Garnish: chopped green onions or chives	

➜ In large heavy saucepan over medium heat, melt butter. Add leeks and onion; cook, stirring often, until softened but not browned, about 10 minutes. Add potato, squash, carrots and stock. Bring to boil, reduce heat, cover and simmer, stirring occasionally, until vegetables are soft, about 20 minutes. In blender or food processor, purée mixture until very smooth (blender gives smoothest consistency). Return soup to saucepan. Stir in cream and wine (if using). Season to taste with salt and pepper. Heat until piping hot but do not boil. Garnish each serving with a sprinkle of green onions or chives. **Makes 6 servings.**

Harvest Vegetable Variations: Use pumpkin instead of squash, sweet potato instead of white, some parsnips along with the carrots, or add a tart apple, peeled and chopped. For flavour variations, add a touch of curry powder, nutmeg, ginger or savoury herbs.

Cream of Broccoli, Cauliflower OR Asparagus: Instead of the squash and carrots, add about 1-1/2 lb (750 g) coarsely chopped broccoli, cauliflower or asparagus.

Leek and Potato Soup: Serve this hot in winter, or as a classic chilled vichyssoise in summer. The hot soup can also be left chunky rather than smooth, if desired.

Follow recipe for Harvest Soup, omitting squash and carrots. Increase the leeks to 3 cups (750 mL) chopped (white part only for vichys-soise; light green part can be included for the hot version) and reduce onion to 1 small. Increase cream to 1 cup (250 mL). For vichys-soise, let cool, then chill until ice cold.

Roasted Vegetable Soup: For extra mellow and rich flavour, roast the vegetables before adding to pot. (See page 154)

Wild Mushroom Soup

Mellow and richly flavoured with a mixture of exotic mushrooms, this makes a satisfying lunch with some crusty bread, or a sophisticated starter for a dinner party. (To make the soup truly decadent, add a few drops of truffle oil to each serving.) For the mushrooms, use any combination of brown cremini, portobello, shiitake and oyster; include some white button mushrooms if you like. The dried mushrooms are optional but add additional depth to the flavour.

2 tbsp	butter	30 mL
2	onions, chopped	2
1	stalk celery, chopped	1
3	cloves garlic, chopped	3
1 lb	assorted mushrooms, coarsely chopped (about 8 cups/2 L)	500 g
2	potatoes, peeled and chopped	2
1/3 cup	dry sherry	75 mL
6 cups	vegetable or chicken stock	1.5 L
1	bay leaf	1
1/4 tsp	each: dried thyme and sage	1 mL
1/2 oz	dried mushrooms (porcini or mixed) (optional)	15 g
1/2 cup	milk or cream	125 mL
	Salt and pepper	
	Chopped fresh chives	

➜ In large heavy saucepan over medium heat, melt butter; add onions, celery and garlic; cook until softened, about 10 minutes (do not brown). Add fresh mushrooms; cook, stirring occasionally, for 10 minutes. Add potatoes, sherry, stock, bay leaf, thyme, sage and dried mushrooms (if using); bring to boil, reduce heat and simmer for 20 minutes or until potatoes are very soft. Remove bay leaf. Let soup cool slightly, then purée until smooth in blender or food processor; return to pot over low heat. Add milk (plus water if needed) to desired consistency, and salt and pepper to taste. Reheat gently; do not boil. Ladle into bowls and sprinkle with chives. **Makes 6 to 8 servings**.

Black Bean Soup

On a cold winter's day, take comfort in a smooth, spicy soup that conjures up sunny Mexican or Cuban cafés. Black bean soup comes in as many variations as there are cooks; this one is rich and hearty, with a touch of heat from the chiles. It is partially puréed for satisfying smoothness, with some beans left whole for pleasant texture and appearance. Canned black beans conveniently shorten the cooking time; you could substitute about 4 cups (1 L) cooked dried beans. Dried black bean flakes, available in some supermarkets and bulk food stores, produce a smooth-textured soup almost instantly (follow package directions).

2 tbsp	olive oil	30 mL
1	onion, chopped	1
2	cloves garlic, minced	2
1	carrot, chopped	1
1	stalk celery, chopped	1
1/2 tsp	each: dried oregano, ground cumin	2 mL
1/4 tsp	(or to taste) hot pepper flakes or sauce	1 mL
2	cans (19 oz/540 mL each) black beans, drained and rinsed	2
6 cups	chicken or vegetable stock	1.5 L
4	sprigs fresh coriander (optional)	4
1 to 2 tbsp	red wine vinegar or lime juice	15 to 30 mL
	Salt and freshly ground pepper	
	Sour cream or crème fraîche	

→ In large heavy saucepan over medium heat, heat oil. Add onion, garlic, carrot and celery; cook until softened, about 5 minutes. Stir in oregano, cumin and hot pepper flakes. Add beans and stock; bring to boil, reduce heat, cover and simmer for 30 minutes. Transfer half of soup to food processor or blender; add coriander (if using). Purée until smooth; return to saucepan and heat through. Add vinegar and salt and pepper to taste. Ladle into soup bowls and top each serving with a dollop of sour cream or crème fraîche. **Makes 8 servings**.

Easy Borscht ❦

Ever since eastern European immigrants put their first pot of borscht on a prairie homestead hearth, this soup has been made with whatever ingredients were available. Through thick and thin, literally, recipes evolved from sparse broths (made with a solitary beet) to hearty borschts made with meat and lots of homegrown vegetables (including beets, laboriously boiled, peeled and chopped). Today, we can unabashedly open a few cans and in half an hour have a gorgeous-coloured, low-fat, vitamin-loaded, full-flavoured borscht.

→ In large heavy saucepan over medium heat, heat butter and oil. Add onions and cook until softened. Add garlic and cabbage; cook, stirring, until cabbage is wilted. Add beets and their liquid, tomatoes, stock, vinegar, sugar and dillweed (if using dried). Cover and simmer for 30 minutes or until cabbage is very tender. Add fresh dill (if using fresh) and salt and pepper to taste. Garnish each serving with a dollop of sour cream. **Makes about 8 servings**.

1 tbsp	each: butter, vegetable oil	15 mL
1-1/2 cups	chopped onions	375 mL
2	cloves garlic, minced	2
2 cups	shredded red cabbage (shred with knife)	500 mL
1	can (19 oz/540 mL) diced beets,* undrained	1
1	can (28 oz/796 mL) tomatoes	1
4 cups	beef stock	1 L
1/4 cup	red wine vinegar	50 mL
1 tsp	granulated sugar	5 mL
2 tsp	dried dillweed (or 2 tbsp/30 mL chopped fresh dill)	10 mL
	Salt and pepper	
	Garnish: low-fat sour cream	

* If diced beets are unavailable, use whole or sliced canned beets; drain and reserve liquid; chop beets coarsely with knife or food processor.

Simple Starters ⊕

Light and easy but full of flavour, these make appealing first courses for a big dinner.

Scallop Soup: This simple, elegant soup is a favourite of Julian Armstrong, food editor of the Montreal *Gazette*. Be sure to use the freshest top-quality sea scallops and cook them very briefly. In large saucepan, combine 2 cups (500 mL) each white wine and fish stock (page 237). Add 1/2 cup (125 mL) each julienned carrots, turnips and leeks. Bring to boil, reduce heat and simmer for 5 minutes or until vegetables are just tender-crisp. Add salt and white pepper to taste. Add 20 sea scallops; simmer gently for 1 to 2 minutes or just until opaque. Serve immediately. **Makes 4 servings.**

Cranberry Consommé: This rosy-coloured soup is an excellent starter for Thanksgiving or Christmas dinner. In large saucepan, combine 5 cups (1.25 L) cranberry cocktail, 2-1/2 cups (625 mL) chicken stock, 2 chopped green onions, 2 orange slices, 1 lemon slice, 4 whole cloves and 1 small cinnamon stick. Simmer for 10 minutes; strain. Reheat, adding salt to taste if needed. Serve in soup cups or small bowls; garnish with sprinkle of sliced green onions and/or chopped dried cranberries. **Makes 6 servings.**

Avgolemono: Try this classic Greek egg-lemon soup as a first course for a festive Greek-themed dinner, such as roast lamb at Easter. As in Italian stracciatella or Chinese egg drop soup, beaten egg is added at the end, but here the eggs are blended in to create a creamy texture rather than floating as strands through the broth. In medium saucepan, bring 4 cups (1 L) chicken stock to boil. Add 1/2 cup (125 mL) rice or orzo (rice-shaped pasta); reduce heat, cover and simmer for 15 to 20 minutes or until tender. In small bowl, whisk 2 eggs well; whisk in 1/2 cup (125 mL) of the hot soup. Stirring constantly, gradually pour egg mixture into hot (not boiling) soup. Add 2 tbsp (30 mL) lemon juice and salt and pepper to taste. Serve garnished with thin lemon slices and snipped fresh dill if desired. **Makes 4 servings.**

Splendid Seafood Chowder ✦

Take your pick: a luxurious chowder of mixed seafood, a classic creamy clam chowder or a deliciously simple fish chowder—all easy variations of the same basic recipe. This satisfyingly thick, creamy chowder is made with less cream than most. If you want it extra-rich, use all cream instead of half milk; for a lighter version, replace cream with milk or low-fat evaporated milk.

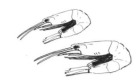

2 tbsp	butter	30 mL
1 cup	chopped onions	250 mL
1/4 cup	chopped celery	50 mL
2 tbsp	all-purpose flour	30 mL
	Salt and pepper	
2 cups	diced potatoes	500 mL
1-1/2 cups	water	375 mL
3 cups	mixed seafood (bite-size pieces of haddock or cod, scallops, lobster meat, small peeled shrimp)	750 mL
1 cup	each: milk, light cream	250 mL

➔ In large heavy saucepan over medium heat, melt butter. Add onions and celery; cook until softened (do not brown). Stir in flour; sprinkle lightly with salt and pepper. Add potatoes and water. Bring to boil; reduce heat and simmer until potatoes are tender, about 10 minutes. Add seafood, milk and cream; heat gently until simmering (do not allow to boil); simmer just until fish is cooked, about 5 minutes. Add salt and pepper to taste. **Makes 4 to 6 servings**.

Clam Chowder: Instead of mixed seafood, use canned clams (about 10 oz/284 mL). Replace part of the water with liquid drained from clams.

Traditional Fish Chowder: Instead of mixed seafood, use 1 lb (500 g) haddock or cod fillets cut in bite-size pieces.

Salmon Chowder: Instead of mixed seafood, use 1 lb (500 g) salmon fillets cut in bite-size pieces.

French Onion Soup ✦

Your friends will think they're in a French bistro when you serve them this gorgeous soup, and it's surprisingly easy to make. The secret to full flavour: cook the onions slowly, to a rich brown colour (the addition of a little sugar helps this happen).

3 tbsp	butter	45 mL
5 cups	thinly sliced onions	1.25 L
2	cloves garlic, minced	2
1/2 tsp	each: salt, granulated sugar	2 mL
3 tbsp	all-purpose flour	45 mL
6 cups	beef stock	1.5 L
1/2 cup	white wine	125 mL
	Salt and pepper	
6	thick slices slightly dry French bread (about 3 inches/8 cm across)	6
1-1/2 cups	shredded gruyère cheese	375 mL
1/4 cup	grated parmesan cheese	50 mL

➔ In large heavy saucepan over medium heat, melt butter. Add onions, garlic, salt and sugar. Cook, stirring often, for 30 minutes or until onions are dark golden brown. Stir in flour. Add beef stock and wine. Reduce heat and simmer for about 30 minutes. Add salt and pepper to taste. Toast bread under broiler until crisp and golden brown. Pour hot soup into ovenproof onion soup bowls (about 4 inches/10 cm wide). Float bread on top. Top with shredded cheese and sprinkle with parmesan. Broil until bubbly and lightly browned. **Makes 6 servings**.

Country Kitchen Pea Soup ✦

Thick, savoury pea soup is enjoying a comeback as one of the most nutritious, easy, inexpensive and satisfying of all homemade soups. This one has the flavour of old-fashioned French-Canadian pea soup made with whole yellow peas but is faster because it uses split peas (which don't have to soak overnight before cooking). Make it when you'll be home for a while to enjoy the aromas wafting from the soup pot. With a loaf of crusty country-style bread and a salad, it makes a complete supper. It's also very good reheated; add a little water if too thick.

2 cups	dried split peas	500 mL
6 cups	water	1.5 L
1	piece salt pork (2 oz/60 g)	1
1	large onion, chopped	1
1/2 cup	each: diced celery and carrots	125 mL
1	bay leaf	1
1/2 tsp	each: salt, dried savory	2 mL
1/4 tsp	freshly ground pepper	1 mL

➜ In large saucepan, combine all ingredients. Bring to boil; reduce heat, cover and simmer for 1-1/2 hours or until peas are very soft. Remove bay leaf and salt pork; reserve salt pork. Remove about 2 cups (500 mL) of soup from pot and purée in blender or food processor; stir puréed mixture back into pot (this makes the texture creamier). Finely chop salt pork and return it to the soup. Add more salt and pepper to taste if needed. **Makes about 6 servings**.

Hot-and-Sour Soup

A popular choice on Chinese restaurant menus, this invigorating soup has a delicious balance of hot and sour flavours. Chile oil is very hot, so add to taste; for those who like extra heat, pass chile oil at the table.

8	Chinese dried mushrooms	8
6 cups	chicken stock	1.5 L
1/2 lb	lean pork, slivered	250 g
8 oz	firm tofu, julienned or diced	250 g
1 cup	bamboo shoots, julienned	250 mL
3 tbsp	each: rice vinegar, light-coloured soy sauce	45 mL
2 tsp	minced fresh ginger	10 mL
	Salt and pepper	
2 tbsp	cornstarch	30 mL
1/4 cup	cold water	50 mL
1	egg, lightly beaten (optional)	1
2 tsp	sesame oil	10 mL
1 tsp	(or to taste) chile oil	5 mL
2	green onions, chopped	2

➜ In small bowl, cover dried mushrooms with warm water and let soak for 30 minutes; drain. Trim off any tough stems; slice mushrooms into julienne strips. In large pot, bring chicken stock to boil. Add mushrooms and pork; simmer, covered, for 5 minutes. Add tofu, bamboo shoots, rice vinegar, soy sauce, ginger, and salt and pepper to taste. Simmer, covered, for 5 minutes. Dissolve cornstarch in cold water; stir into soup; bring to boil, reduce heat and simmer for 2 minutes. If adding egg, drizzle into soup in a wide circle; stir gently to form streamers. Stir in sesame oil and chile oil. Stir in green onions. **Makes 6 servings**.

Tortilla Soup

A staple of Mexican cuisine, sopa de tortilla consists of a flavourful broth ladled over fried tortilla strips and topped with assorted garnishes. It's a meal in itself and great for a casual gathering at the table. Our family enjoys this fairly traditional version from my daughter-in-law Sarah, who grew up (with Australian parents and international tastes) in Mexico City. To round out the menu, we start with quesadillas and finish with an Aussie-Mexican flan (caramel custard flavoured with orange).

12	corn tortillas (6 inch/15 cm)	12
	Vegetable oil	
1	onion, chopped	1
2	cloves garlic, minced	2
4	tomatoes, skinned, seeded and chopped	4
8 cups	chicken stock	2 L
2	large sprigs fresh coriander*	2
	Salt to taste	
	Juice of 1 to 2 limes	

Garnishes: 6 ancho or pasilla chiles,**
   fried and chopped
   Crumbled queso fresco
   (Mexican fresh white cheese)
   or grated monterey jack cheese
   or crumbled mild feta
   Diced avocado
   Diced sweet onions
   Chopped fresh coriander
   Sour cream or crème fraîche

* If you are shopping in a Latin American market, fresh coriander will be called cilantro.
** Anchos and pasillas are medium-hot dried chiles. Fry them very lightly in an oiled skillet (they will puff up and soften slightly), then chop. They are added to taste to each serving of soup; for a little extra heat, you can also add one or two chiles to the soup while it simmers.

➜ With scissors, cut tortillas into thin strips; place on flat surface and let dry for about 1 hour. In large skillet, heat 1/4 cup (50 mL) oil; fry tortilla strips in batches for 2 minutes or until crisp and golden; drain on paper towels. In large heavy saucepan, heat 2 tbsp (30 mL) oil; add onion and garlic; cook until softened. Add tomatoes and cook, stirring constantly, until mixture forms a thick paste. Add stock and coriander; cover and simmer for 20 minutes. Strain and return to saucepan. Add salt and lime juice to taste; reheat if necessary. Place garnishes in separate bowls.

To serve: Place tortilla strips in large soup bowls; ladle soup on top. Let each person add chiles and cheese, plus additional garnishes, to taste. **Makes about 6 servings.**

Cool Cucumber Soup

1	seedless cucumber, unpeeled	1
2	green onions, coarsely chopped	2
2 tbsp	chopped fresh mint or dill	30 mL
2 cups	low-fat plain yogurt or buttermilk	500 mL
	Salt and pepper	
Garnish:	fresh mint	

➡ Cut a few very thin slices from one end of cucumber; reserve for garnish. Coarsely chop remainder of cucumber. In food processor (or in batches in blender), combine cucumber, green onions and mint or dill. Process until almost smooth. Add yogurt; process until smooth. Add salt and pepper to taste. Transfer to bowl, cover and chill thoroughly, about 2 hours. Serve garnished with cucumber slices and a sprig of mint or dill. **Makes 4 servings**.

Mango-Melon Soup

Use very sweet ripe fruit and fresh-squeezed juices; if desired, mango can be replaced with peach.

1	medium cantaloupe, peeled, seeded, cut in chunks	1
1	mango, peeled and coarsely chopped	1
3/4 cup	orange juice	175 mL
2 tbsp	each: lime and lemon juice	30 mL
	Honey or granulated sugar to taste (optional)	
Garnish:	fresh mint	

➡ In food processor or blender, process ingredients together until very smooth, adding a little honey or sugar to taste if needed. Transfer to bowl, cover and chill thoroughly, about 2 hours. Serve garnished with mint. **Makes 4 servings**.

Gazpacho

1	seedless cucumber, unpeeled	1
1	each: sweet red and green pepper	1
2	ripe tomatoes, peeled and seeded	2
1	small onion, coarsely chopped	1
2	cloves garlic	2
2 tbsp	red wine vinegar	30 mL
1 tbsp	extra-virgin olive oil	15 mL
1/4 tsp	hot pepper sauce	1 mL
3 cups	tomato juice	750 mL
	Salt and pepper	
	Chopped fresh coriander, croutons	

➡ Cut cucumber and peppers in half; dice one-half of each and set aside. Cut remainder into chunks and place in food processor. Add tomatoes, onion, garlic, vinegar, oil and hot pepper sauce. Process until smooth. (Can also be done in batches in blender.) Pour into large bowl. Stir in tomato juice, reserved diced cucumbers and peppers, and salt and pepper to taste. Cover and chill thoroughly, at least 3 hours or up to 12. Serve sprinkled with coriander and croutons. **Makes 6 servings**.

Dressing for Dinner...

Salads

Pleasure on your plate—
simple tosses, classic compositions
and scene-stealing new stars

Salad Basics

Oils

Olive oils: Available in wide range of qualities and prices. **Extra-virgin olive oil** has the least acidity and the most flavour and aroma and commands a premium price. It is produced with only one cold pressing (the term "first pressed" was used when less-powerful presses made it necessary to have more than one pressing). The colour (yellow to green) and wide range of flavour depend on a number of variables such as the variety of olive, growing conditions and production methods. Always use extra-virgin olive oil when flavour is foremost, such as in salads, brushing on grilled foods, drizzling on bread or into soup. **Regular pure olive oil** is further processed, lighter in colour and less flavourful, but fine for most frying and baking. **"Light" olive oils** are lighter in colour and flavour only, not lighter in fat or calories. All olive oils are high in monounsaturated fats (which reduce heart attack risk) and are much touted for health benefits.

Vegetable oils: Use when a light or neutral flavour is desired. All are high in polyunsaturated fats; canola is also high in monounsaturates. Canola, which was developed in Canada, is the country's most widely used vegetable oil. Combinations of canola and olive oil are available. Other popular oils include safflower, sunflower, corn and peanut, which has a mild peanuty taste.

Nut oils: (such as hazelnut or walnut) Rich nutty flavour combines well with mild vinegars. Purchase in small quantities because they go rancid quickly.

Sesame oil: Used in small amounts as flavouring in many Asian dishes. Dark sesame oil is made from toasted seeds and is much more flavourful than light-coloured sesame oils.

Flavoured oils: Olive or vegetable oils infused with a variety of flavours (garlic, herbs, chiles) conveniently add extra taste to dressings and other foods. (See Safety Tips, page 257)

Vinegars

Balsamic vinegar: Mellow, slightly sweet; wide range of qualities and prices. True balsamic is made from the juice of Trebbiano grapes and aged in wooden barrels. The finest balsamics have luxurious, complex flavour and high price tags. Most are rich brown in colour; there are a few white varieties. Cheaper balsamics usually are doctored wine vinegar and vary widely in quality, but some are pleasant for everyday use.

Cider vinegar: Golden colour; fruity flavour excellent for pickles and chutneys; too sharp for most salads.

Fruit and herb vinegars (e.g., raspberry, tarragon): Add interesting flavour variations to vinaigrettes.

Malt vinegar: Brown, fairly mild vinegar made from malted barley; traditional on fish and chips.

Rice vinegar: Chinese and Japanese varieties; mild flavour. Available unseasoned for most dishes or seasoned (usually with sugar and salt).

Sherry vinegar: Smooth, mellow flavour; light brown.

White vinegar: Distilled, with very sharp flavour; too harsh for salads but used widely in pickling and in small amounts in cooking.

Wine vinegars: Made from many varieties of red and white wines. Pleasantly pungent; red has fairly sharp flavour; white is milder.

Mesclun

This popular salad mixture (sometimes called "spring mix") is now a fixture in most produce stores and supermarkets. "Mesclun" comes from the Provençal word for mixture, referring to the young field greens gathered for salads. Today's mesclun mixtures, sold loose or in bags, are typically a combination of mild and bitter-flavoured tender young leaves of many colours. Mixtures can include red leaf and oak leaf lettuces, radicchio, frisée, dandelion greens, mâche, mizuna, tatsoi, arugula, baby spinach or beet greens, red mustard or others. To store mesclun, remove wilted or discoloured leaves; keep in plastic bag in refrigerator. Use as soon as possible. Although mesclun is often touted as pre-washed, some food safety authorities advise that it be washed and dried thoroughly just before using. Mesclun can be mixed with other lettuces such as Boston or leaf. Fresh herbs such as chervil, basil, summer savory, parsley or tarragon may be added. To dress a mesclun salad, use a lightly flavoured vinaigrette that doesn't overpower the greens.

Greens

To prepare greens: Wash them as soon as you get them home (swish in sink of cold water or rinse under cold running water). Dry in salad spinner or pat with paper towels or tea towel. Store in large plastic bag (along with extra paper towel or tea towel to absorb moisture) in refrigerator. Most will keep well for 3 or 4 days.

Arugula: Also called rocket; distinctive peppery flavour; smooth, notched dark green leaves.

Baby beet greens: Small dark green and burgundy leaves with a faint flavour of beets.

Baby spinach: Young tender leaves of spinach; mild flavour.

Belgian endive: Small head of elongated pale leaves with yellow to green edges; crunchy and pleasantly bitter.

Boston, Bibb or butter lettuce: Loosely packed heads; soft leaves, mild flavour.

Dandelion leaves: Green with jagged, pointy edges; slightly bitter; use young leaves for salads.

Endives: Curly endive is a bushy head of coarse, lacy-edged leaves (outer ones pale green; centres pale yellow to white). Frisée is a finer, lacier variety. Escarole has broad flat leaves. All have slightly bitter flavour.

Iceberg lettuce: Dependably crisp; very little flavour.

Leaf lettuce: Ruffled green leaves, sometimes red- or bronze-tipped; very mild and very tender.

Mâche (lamb's lettuce): Smooth, tongue-shaped small green leaves; delicate flavour.

Mint: Sprightly flavour adds a fresh dimension to mixed greens or tomato salads.

Mizuna: Small dark green, oak-leaf shaped with pointed tips; most delicately flavoured of the mustard family; mildly peppery taste.

Mustard greens: Dark green, slightly hot taste; use only small young leaves for salads.

Oak leaf lettuce: Oak leaf shape; green or red; mild flavour.

Parsley: Flat-leaf or curly; peppery flavour; a handful of whole leaves perks up bland salad mixtures.

Purslane: Small, round, light green leaves on ruby stems; mild and slightly lemony tasting.

Radicchio: Small compact heads, round or elongated shapes, of magenta leaves with ivory streaks; pleasantly bitter and slightly peppery.

Red mustard: Small scalloped-edged leaves; variegated red and green; faint but sharp mustard flavour.

Red leaf lettuce (lollo rosso): Large, frilly-edged, tender leaves tinged with deep red; mild, sweet flavour.

Romaine: Elongated sturdy, dark green leaves; inside leaves crisp and tender; mild flavour.

Tatsoi: Dark green, thick rounded leaves; assertive mustard taste.

Watercress: Tiny dark green leaves; peppery taste.

Edible Flowers

Flowers in salads, drinks and butters, and as garnishes for soups and desserts, are a delight for the eye, nose and palate. Flowers can be delicious, ranging in flavour from peppery to sweet. Taste and experiment with different combinations to give a pleasing balance of colours and flavours. In salads, nasturtiums and marigolds add spiciness; pansies and daisies are mild. Separate the petals of larger flowers such as roses and calendulas; use small flowers whole. For dressing flower salads, use mild vinaigrettes.

Colourful assortments of small edible blossoms, usually packaged in small, clear plastic boxes, are available from produce markets, gourmet shops, some supermarkets and organic flower growers. Floral "confetti," a mixture of petals, is sometimes available. Edible flowers must be free of pesticides and herbicides—never use florist flowers.

Varieties of edible flowers (Caution: Some flowers are not safe to eat; check a reliable source if flower is not on this list.) Apple blossom, begonia, calendula, carnation, chrysanthemum, daisy, daylily, elderberry, geranium, gladiola, hibiscus, hollyhock, honeysuckle, impatiens, jasmine, johnny-jump-up, lilac, marigold, nasturtium, pansy, petunia, primula, rose, snapdragon, tulip, violet, herb blossoms.

Salad Dressings

Italian Dressing: First of all, there is no such thing in Italy. The bottled dressings we see here, containing all kinds of herbs and spices and garlic, are a North American invention. Italian salads are traditionally dressed lightly and simply, right in the bowl, first with a generous drizzle of fine olive oil, then a small drizzle of good red wine vinegar and a sprinkle of salt.

The traditional proportions for a classic vinaigrette are 3 or 4 parts oil to 1 part vinegar, but vary according to the flavour and strength of both oil and vinegar used. Extra-virgin olive oil is very flavourful, so less is required to balance the acidity of the vinegar. Vegetable oil is quite neutral in taste and can be used for very mild dressings. A mixture of olive and vegetable oil can also be used. Vinaigrettes are best made fresh, but can be stored a day or two in the refrigerator. Most vinaigrettes, especially when made with dried herbs, are best if prepared an hour or two before using, to allow flavours to blend.

Basic Vinaigrette

This makes 1/2 cup (125 mL) of dressing, enough for 6 to 8 servings. Halve or double the recipe as required. The mustard is optional but helps to emulsify the dressing. Flavoured oils, nut oils, fruit vinegars (such as raspberry) and herbed vinegars can all be used; adjust proportions to taste.

2 tbsp	red or white wine vinegar	30 mL
1/2 tsp	Dijon mustard (optional)	2 mL
1/2 tsp	salt	2 mL
	Freshly ground pepper to taste	
6 tbsp	extra-virgin olive oil	90 mL

➜ In small bowl, whisk together vinegar, mustard (if using), salt and pepper; gradually whisk in oil. Taste dressing on a lettuce leaf; if flavour is too sharp, whisk in more oil.

If making dressing ahead, whisk again just before using.

Garlic: Add 1 garlic clove, minced or put through garlic press.

Shallot: Add 1 small shallot, minced.

Herbed: To basic or garlic vinaigrette, add 1 tsp (5 mL) dried herbs (or 1 tbsp/15 mL chopped fresh) such as basil, tarragon, oregano, thyme, dill, chives. Use one herb or a combination, or dried mixtures such as herbes de Provence or Italian herbs.

Mustardy: Increase Dijon to 2 tsp (10 mL) (or to taste); can also use grainy mustard.

Citrusy: Use lemon, lime or orange juice instead of vinegar.

Creamy: In blender, whirl together all ingredients (including mustard); dressing will become creamy.

Roasted Garlic: In blender, whirl together all ingredients, adding the squeezed pulp from 1 small head roasted garlic (page 154).

Thai: Use lime juice instead of vinegar, and vegetable oil instead of olive oil. Omit mustard. Add 2 tbsp (30 mL) fish sauce, 1 tbsp (15 mL) granulated sugar (or to taste) and a pinch of cayenne or dash of hot pepper sauce.

Balsamic Dressing: A very high quality balsamic vinegar can be used on salads without adding any oil. If using a more ordinary balsamic vinegar, make basic vinaigrette using equal parts vinegar and oil, or to taste.

Mayonnaise Variations

Store-bought mayonnaise is generally preferred these days, avoiding any risk associated with the raw egg used in homemade mayonnaise. Choose low-fat versions; some brands are very good. (Most no-fat versions, on the other hand, are awful.) Drained yogurt (page 239) can be substituted for mayonnaise (or mix half and half).

Easy Creamy Dressing: (for pasta or potato salads or coleslaw) Combine 1/2 cup (125 mL) each low-fat mayonnaise and sour cream, yogurt or buttermilk. Add garlic, onion, mustard or herbs to taste.

Thousand Island Dressing: Combine 1/2 cup (125 mL) mayonnaise, 2 tbsp (30 mL) ketchup or chili sauce, 2 tbsp (30 mL) minced sweet pickles or relish, 1 tbsp (15 mL) minced green onion; thin with a little milk if desired.

Ranch Dressing: Combine 1/2 cup (125 mL) buttermilk, 3 tbsp (45 mL) mayonnaise, 1 tbsp (15 mL) minced parsley, 1 minced garlic clove, 1 tsp (5 mL) cider vinegar and freshly ground pepper to taste.

Aioli (Garlic Mayonnaise): Stir 3 minced garlic cloves and 1 tsp (5 mL) lemon juice into 1 cup (250 mL) mayonnaise. See Crudités with Aioli (page 17).

Roasted Garlic Mayonnaise: Squeeze pulp from 1 head of roasted garlic (page 154) into 1 cup (250 mL) mayonnaise; mix well.

♥ **Reduced-Fat Dressings:** You can make a great variety of low-fat dressings in the same way as a basic vinaigrette by replacing most of the oil with low-fat yogurt, buttermilk, tomato juice or puréed tomatoes, fruit juice or chicken stock. (Keeping just a little oil smooths the mixture and adds minimal fat and calories.) Be generous with seasonings, adding a little extra garlic, mustard or herbs. And remember that a light drizzle of dressing is enough for most salads.

Easy Caesar Dressing

This avoids the raw egg used in classic Caesar dressings and is much lower in fat.

1 tbsp	each: red wine vinegar, lemon juice	15 mL
2	cloves garlic	2
2	anchovy fillets (or 1 tsp/5 mL anchovy paste)	2
1/2 tsp	each: Dijon mustard, Worcestershire sauce	2 mL
1/4 cup	grated parmesan cheese	50 mL
1/4 cup	olive oil	50 mL
1/2 cup	ricotta, cottage cheese or drained yogurt (page 239)	125 mL
1/4 cup	milk	50 mL
	Salt and pepper to taste	

➜ In blender, combine all ingredients and blend until smooth. Refrigerate for at least 1 hour to blend flavours. If too thick, thin with more milk. **Makes about 1 cup** (250 mL).

Easy Caesar Salad: Allow 1 head of romaine per 3 to 4 servings. Tear romaine into bite-size pieces; place in salad bowl. Toss with just enough Easy Caesar Dressing to coat leaves lightly. Add freshly grated parmesan cheese to taste; toss again. Top with croutons (page 237).

Winning Combinations ❖

A few top-quality ingredients (with complementary flavours, textures and colours), a compatible dressing, a quick toss—and you're all set for a satisfying solo supper or last-minute guests. To get you on your way to creating your own favourites, try some of these tasty combos for main-dish, side-dish and first-course salads:

Quick Tosses

Three factors join forces to create memorable salads that taste as if they were simply wished together. Textures—soft, crisp, crunchy—should play off one another. Flavours—mild, sharp, peppery—must be in balance so none overpowers the others. And colours, whether a range from palest to darkest green, or contrasting brights tossed together, should delight the eye. Simple is almost always better. Let just a few top-quality ingredients speak for themselves. Here are some samples (for the suggested dressings, see page 46):

Parsley is more than a decorative sprig. Try it as a salad (using either curly or flat-leaf variety or half of each). Toss with a garlicky vinaigrette and lots of freshly grated parmesan.

Watercress works well solo, creating a salad that looks delicate but has an assertive spiciness. Try it on its own with a mustardy vinaigrette OR add a small amount of crumbled blue cheese, slivers of pear and a balsamic dressing for an after-the-main-course dinner-party salad.

Cherry Tomato Salad: Fast, simple and delicious. Just toss together halved cherry tomatoes, very thinly sliced red onions and chopped fresh basil with a drizzle of balsamic vinegar and extra-virgin olive oil.

Broccoli and Roasted Red Pepper Salad: Combine broccoli florets (cooked tender-crisp, refreshed in cold water and drained well) with strips of roasted sweet red pepper (see page 154 or use bottled), thinly sliced red onion and a few black olives. Toss with Garlic Vinaigrette made with red wine vinegar (page 46); sprinkle with crumbled feta cheese.

Beet and Onion Salad: Cut into thin slices cooled roasted beets (page 154) (or, in a pinch, boiled or canned beets). Arrange them, overlapping, on a platter. Strew with thinly sliced onions and drizzle with vinaigrette (page 46) made with orange juice instead of vinegar. Thin crosswise slices of fresh orange can be alternated with the beets, or shreds of orange zest sprinkled on top.

Italian-Style Next-Day Salad: A great way to enjoy yesterday's best leftovers. Use cooked meat and vegetables at room temperature or chilled. Combine in shallow salad bowl: thinly sliced meat (grilled steak or lamb, roast turkey or chicken), new potatoes (small or cubed) and green beans or peas. Sprinkle with red onion (cut lengthwise into shreds), capers and chopped Italian parsley. Drizzle with dressing (1/2 cup/125 mL olive oil, 3 tbsp/45 mL red wine vinegar, 1 tsp/5 mL mustard, 2 chopped anchovies).

Cannellini and Tuna Salad: Combine drained canned solid white tuna (broken into chunks) with an equal quantity of cannellini (white kidney beans); some halved cherry tomatoes; chopped red onion, celery and sweet peppers; and slivered fennel bulb. Toss gently with enough dressing (such as Herbed Garlic Vinaigrette, page 46) to moisten. Sprinkle with chopped Italian parsley.

Minted Carrot Salad: Cook carrots (thinly sliced on the diagonal) until tender-crisp; refresh in cold water and drain thoroughly. Toss with vinaigrette made with 1 part orange juice, 1 part balsamic vinegar and 2 parts oil. Add chopped fresh mint and salt and pepper to taste. Scatter with toasted sesame or sunflower seeds or chopped pistachios. This is also good with a combination of carrots and broccoli, and chopped fresh coriander instead of mint. It can be kept in refrigerator for a day or two.

Warm Mushroom Spinach Salad: For 4 servings, divide washed spinach leaves (10 oz/284 g bag) among 4 individual salad plates. In 1 tbsp (15 mL) olive oil in large skillet, sauté 1/2 lb (250 g) sliced mushrooms (any combination) until tender. Add 2 tbsp (30 mL) more olive oil, 1/4 cup (50 mL) balsamic vinegar, and salt and pepper to taste. Spoon mushroom mixture over spinach. Sprinkle with toasted pine nuts or almonds.

Lentil Salad: Combine drained canned lentils (or even better, still-warm just-cooked lentils) with a dressing of 2 parts olive oil to 1 part lemon juice. Add a little minced garlic and season with a large pinch of cumin, salt and pepper. Add some chopped tomatoes and green onions, and chopped fresh mint and parsley to taste.

Orzo, Couscous or Rice Salad: Cold cooked rice or couscous can be used instead of orzo in these salad suggestions, so use whichever you have on hand. Orzo is a rice-shaped pasta that teams well with Italian flavours in a salad; toss with diced sweet peppers, tomatoes (fresh or sun-dried), chopped fresh basil and a garlicky vinaigrette. Or give orzo an Asian twist by tossing with shredded carrot, slivered green onions and chopped fresh coriander; use the same dressing as for Chinese Chicken Noodle Salad (page 52). Orzo cooks very quickly if you don't have any left over in the fridge; boil just until tender but still firm, rinse in cold water and drain well.

Fennel-Orange Salad: On serving platter, arrange alternating slices of fennel bulb (thinly sliced lengthwise) and orange (peeled and thinly sliced). Strew with red onion rings. Drizzle with herbed vinaigrette made with parsley, arugula or mint. Garnish with pitted black olives.

Quick Tosses

Mesclun salad almost makes itself. Its contrasting colours and textures need little more than a light vinaigrette, softly flavoured with fresh herbs and mellow balsamic or fruity vinegar.

Spinach does yeoman service for the salad bowl all year round, yet its flavour can be pallid, so add some spark with citrus segments or sliced specialty mushrooms and thin rings of sweet onion; dress lightly with a citrusy vinaigrette.

Radicchio, the deep-red Italian lettuce, adds eye appeal but is bitter on its own. Mix with neutral greens such as spinach or romaine, then toss with a herbed garlic vinaigrette.

Arugula has a peppery bite that contrasts well with a mixture of milder greens or with the cooling tang of orange or grapefruit sections. Slices of ripe olives add a Mediterranean note. Drizzle with a simple wine vinegar vinaigrette.

Asparagus Vinaigrette

The season's best salads often begin with the market's star attraction—such as asparagus at its springtime prime—cooked briefly, embellished with a light sauce and little more. Green or yellow beans (even better, some of each) are also splendid treated the same way; add some fresh herbs such as basil or tarragon if you like.

1-1/2 lb	asparagus, trimmed	750 g
3 tbsp	lemon juice	45 mL
2 tbsp	olive oil	30 mL
1	clove garlic, minced	1
1 tsp	salt	5 mL
2	green onions, chopped	2

➜ Peel asparagus stalks unless very thin. Microwave asparagus or cook in skillet of boiling water just until tender-crisp. Drain and refresh in cold water. Whisk together lemon juice, olive oil, garlic and salt; stir in green onions. Arrange asparagus on 6 salad plates and drizzle dressing over. **Makes 6 servings**.

Variation: Add 1/2 lb (250 g) cooked shrimp and/or 2 coarsely chopped hard-cooked eggs before drizzling with dressing.

Salade Niçoise

Prepare this classic version, close your eyes and dream of the south of France. Or try a fresh-flavoured springtime variation, substituting asparagus for the beans, fresh salmon and shrimp for the tuna and anchovies, and using white wine vinegar instead of red. Serve with French bread and unsalted butter.

Dressing:

1/4 cup	each: red wine vinegar, extra-virgin olive oil	50 mL
2	cloves garlic, minced	2
1 tsp	Dijon mustard	5 mL
1/2 tsp	each: salt, dried basil, dried oregano	2 mL
	Freshly ground pepper to taste	

Salad:

1 lb	small new potatoes (or 4 medium), cooked and cubed	500 g
2 cups	crisp-cooked green beans (skinny or French-cut; see page 155)	500 mL
1	red onion, thinly sliced	1
1	sweet green or red pepper, cut into thin strips	1
12	cherry tomatoes, halved	12
2	cans (about 7 oz/200 g each) solid light tuna, drained	2
12	anchovy fillets	12
3	hard-cooked eggs, quartered	3
12	black olives	12
	Lettuce leaves to line platter	

Dressing: Whisk together all ingredients; set aside.

Salad: In large bowl, combine potatoes, beans, onion, peppers, tomatoes and tuna (broken into chunks). Add enough dressing to moisten, tossing gently. Mound on lettuce-lined platter or in shallow salad bowl. Garnish with anchovies, eggs and olives. Drizzle with a little more dressing. **Makes about 6 servings**.

Make-Ahead Coleslaw

This is a tangy slaw that everyone likes and it keeps conveniently in the fridge for 3 or 4 days.

8 cups	shredded cabbage	2 L
1	large carrot, grated	1
1	small onion, chopped	1
1/2 cup	white vinegar	125 mL
1/4 cup	granulated sugar	50 mL
1/4 cup	vegetable oil	50 mL
1 tsp	salt	5 mL
1/2 tsp	celery seed	2 mL
Pinch	pepper	Pinch

➔ Finely shred cabbage with large sharp knife; place in large bowl. Add carrot and onion. In glass measuring cup, combine remaining ingredients; microwave on High for 1 minute or until boiling; stir to dissolve sugar. Pour hot dressing over cabbage mixture; stir to mix well. Add more salt and pepper to taste. Cover and chill. **Makes about 8 servings.**

Creamy Coleslaw: In large bowl, toss finely shredded or coarsely grated cabbage (plus some grated carrot or chopped green onions if desired) with enough Easy Creamy Dressing (page 47) to moisten lightly. Add salt and pepper to taste; for sharper flavour, stir in a little vinegar to taste. Chill before serving.

Chinese Cabbage Slaw: Use recipe for Chinese Chicken Noodle Salad (page 52), omitting noodles, chicken, cucumber, bean sprouts and peanuts. Increase shredded cabbage to 4 cups (1 L). Add some snow peas (thinly sliced on the diagonal) if desired. Toss with the same dressing. Chill before serving. **Makes 4 to 6 servings.**

Mixed Slaw with Apples and Lentils: In large bowl, combine 4 cups (1 L) shredded cabbage (mixture of green and red), 1 cup (250 mL) cooked or canned lentils, 1/2 cup (125 mL) each grated carrot and chopped celery, 2 chopped green onions, 1 diced unpeeled red apple and 2 tbsp (30 mL) raisins. For dressing, whisk together 3 tbsp (45 mL) cider vinegar, 1 tbsp (15 mL) each lemon juice, vegetable oil and granulated sugar, and 1/2 tsp (2 mL) salt. Pour over salad and mix well. Chill for at least 2 hours. **Makes 4 to 6 servings.**

Chef's Salad: The never-know-what-you'll-get salad that used to be on every small restaurant's menu has its place on our own dining tables today, but it's better thought out. We still use an array of ingredients, traditionally presented on top of greens, but now choose two or three meats and cheeses where the chef tossed in five or six; the chicken or turkey is grilled or roasted rather than processed, and rubbery cheeses are replaced with creamy chèvre or chunky feta. For a firm foundation of greens, forget the traditional iceberg (your salad will meet the same fate as the Titanic) and use romaine or other crunchy-firm lettuces. Then select vegetables with contrasting colours and textures—grilled peppers or eggplant, sliced fresh tomatoes or radishes, grated young carrots or slivered fennel. Arrange all the ingredients in rows or groupings atop the greens on a large platter, or layer all in a clear glass bowl. A mild herby dressing (made a little creamy in the blender) joins the elements together; drizzle it in a zigzag over top, or pass separately for diners to add as they wish.

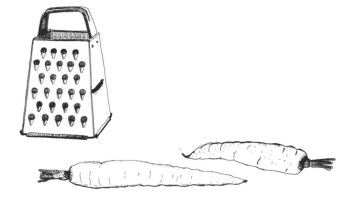

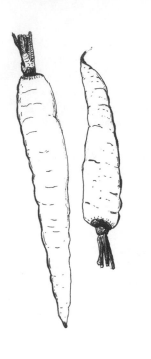

Chinese Chicken Noodle Salad

A great way to introduce some interesting Asian flavours and ingredients into your salads, this is good with either vermicelli-type noodles or flat noodles.

Salad:

4 oz	rice vermicelli or other thin noodles such as capellini or spaghettini or flat Chinese noodles or similar pasta such as linguine	125 g
2 cups	cooked chicken breast cut in thin strips	500 mL
1 cup	seedless cucumber cut in thin strips	250 mL
1 cup	fresh bean sprouts	250 mL
1 cup	shredded napa (Chinese) cabbage (shred with knife)	250 mL
1/2 cup	shredded carrot	125 mL
2	green onions, chopped	2
2 tbsp	chopped fresh coriander or parsley	30 mL
2 tbsp	coarsely chopped peanuts	30 mL

Dressing:

2 tbsp	rice vinegar	30 mL
1 tbsp	each: soy sauce, lemon juice, sesame oil	15 mL
1	clove garlic, minced	1
1 tsp	minced fresh ginger	5 mL
1 tsp	granulated sugar	5 mL
Dash	Chinese chili sauce or other hot pepper sauce (optional)	Dash

Salad: In pot of boiling water, cook rice vermicelli for 3 minutes; if using other noodles, cook until tender but firm. Drain in colander and rinse under cold running water; drain well. In large bowl, combine noodles, chicken, cucumber, bean sprouts, cabbage, carrots, green onions and coriander.

Dressing: Whisk ingredients together. Pour over salad and toss thoroughly. Cover and chill for about 2 hours to blend flavours. Sprinkle with peanuts. **Makes 4 to 6 servings**.

Autumn Salad with Honey-Broiled Apples

Julian Armstrong, food editor of the Montreal Gazette, recommends this delicious salad as an attractive way to show off our fine autumn apples.

Cider Dressing:

1 tbsp	each: cider vinegar, dry apple cider	15 mL
1 tsp	minced shallots	5 mL
1/4 cup	olive oil	50 mL
	Salt and pepper to taste	

Salad:

4	firm tart apples	4
1/4 cup	liquid honey	50 mL
4	large belgian endives	4
1	head Boston lettuce	1
	A few leaves red-tipped lettuce or radicchio	

Dressing: Whisk ingredients together; set aside.

Salad: Peel apples; core and slice each into 4 equal rings. Drizzle with honey. Grill briefly under hot broiler, turning once, until lightly browned. On each of 4 individual serving plates, arrange 4 endive leaves around the edge, pointing outward. Toss lettuces with dressing; arrange in centre of plates. Top with broiled apple slices. **Makes 4 servings**.

Chunky Chicken Salad

Diced fruit, crunchy celery and nuts make this one of the most popular versions of chicken salad. For a little more tropical flavour, stir a little curry powder or spicy mango chutney into the dressing. For another variation, replace the diced fruit with sweet peppers, cucumber, tomatoes and black olives. For the chicken, you can use leftover roasted, grilled, poached or even take-out chicken. OR cook 4 boneless, skinless chicken breast halves (about 1-1/2 lb/750 g) on grill or poach in simmering water for 15 minutes or until just cooked through).

3 cups	cooked chicken cut in bite-size chunks	750 mL
2	stalks celery, sliced	2
1	green onion, chopped	1

1/2 cup	each: diced pineapple, unpeeled apple, mango (or melon or peach), seedless grapes	125 mL
1/2 cup	light mayonnaise	125 mL
1/4 cup	plain yogurt	50 mL
2 tsp	lemon or lime juice	10 mL
	Salt and pepper	
	Leaf lettuce; radicchio (optional)	
1/4 cup	toasted almond or pecan pieces	50 mL

➜ In large bowl, combine chicken, celery, green onion and fruit. Whisk together mayonnaise, yogurt, lemon juice, and salt and pepper to taste. Pour over salad and stir gently to mix. On platter or individual salad plates, arrange leaf lettuce (with radicchio if using). Mound salad on top. Sprinkle with nuts. **Makes 4 servings.**

Spicy Salsa Salad with Rice, Barley and Beans ♥

Hot salsa spices up the easy dressing, and corn and peppers add a Mexican touch in this high-fibre, low-fat, nutrient-packed salad. Spoon some into pitas for lunch, or eat it with corn muffins or sourdough bread.

1/4 cup	pearl barley	50 mL
1 cup	water	250 mL
Pinch	salt	Pinch
2 cups	cooked rice (long-grain white, brown or mixture)	500 mL
1/2 cup	each: black beans, red kidney beans (cooked or canned)	125 mL
1/2 cup	each: corn kernels, chopped celery, chopped sweet red pepper	125 mL
1/4 cup	chopped onion	50 mL
2 tbsp	chopped mild chiles (canned or fresh)	30 mL

2 tbsp	chopped fresh coriander or parsley	30 mL

Dressing:		
3 tbsp	bottled hot salsa	45 mL
1 tbsp	olive or vegetable oil	15 mL
2 tsp	white vinegar	10 mL
1 tsp	chili powder	5 mL
	Salt and pepper to taste	

➜ In saucepan, combine barley, water and salt. Bring to boil; reduce heat, cover and boil gently until tender but still slightly chewy, about 40 minutes; drain any water that hasn't been absorbed. In bowl, combine barley, rice, beans, corn, celery, peppers, onion, chiles and parsley.

Dressing: Whisk ingredients together. Pour over salad and toss to mix. (Can be refrigerated, covered, for up to 2 days.) **Makes 4 servings.**

Grilled Seafood Salad ♨

Grilled Chicken, Steak or Mushroom Salad: For 4 servings, grill 4 boneless, skinless chicken breasts (page 106) OR 1 marinated flank steak (page 76) OR 4 large or 8 medium portobello mushroom caps. Toss about 8 cups (2 L) mixed salad greens (include some fairly sturdy varieties such as romaine and radicchio) with dressing (such as Herbed Garlic Vinaigrette or Balsamic Dressing, page 46) and arrange on individual serving plates. Slice hot grilled steak or chicken diagonally across the grain, or slice mushrooms into thick strips; arrange on top of greens. Scatter thinly sliced rings of sweet onion on top as garnish. Drizzle with a little more dressing.

For **Sesame-Crusted Salmon on Greens,** see page 65.

Warm salads make sensational starters for dinner parties, or light summer suppers on their own. A modest amount of seafood can serve 6 this way; use more if budget allows, or add some cubes of firm-fleshed fish, which is delicious grilled. The seafood can also be cooked in a stovetop ridged grill pan or broiled. For the greens, use a mix of fairly sturdy leaves such as romaine, radicchio and watercress.

3/4 lb	fresh shrimp (about 18 medium-large)	375 g
1/2 lb	fresh scallops	250 g
1/4 cup	lime juice	50 mL
1/4 cup	white wine vinegar or tarragon vinegar	50 mL
1/4 cup	minced shallots or mild onion	50 mL
2	cloves garlic, minced	2
1 tsp	Dijon mustard	5 mL
1 tsp	salt	5 mL
	Freshly ground pepper	
1 cup	olive oil	250 mL
1/4 cup	finely chopped parsley	50 mL
12 cups	mixed salad greens	3 L

➔ Peel and devein shrimp, leaving tails on. Combine with scallops in bowl. Whisk together lime juice, vinegar, shallots, garlic, mustard, salt and pepper; gradually whisk in oil. Pour about half of marinade over seafood; marinate in refrigerator for 15 to 30 minutes. Add parsley to remaining marinade; set aside to use for dressing. Thread shrimp and scallops separately onto presoaked bamboo skewers. (To hold shrimp securely, curve each into a C-shape and skewer through both ends.) Grill over medium heat, turning occasionally, just until cooked through, about 4 minutes for shrimp, 6 to 8 minutes for scallops. Meanwhile, toss salad greens with enough of the reserved dressing to coat lightly; arrange on 6 salad plates. Remove seafood from skewers and arrange on top of greens. Drizzle with a little more dressing. **Makes 6 servings.**

Insalata di Mare (Fresh Seafood Salad)

A popular choice for an antipasto buffet or as a first course on its own, this can be made with different combinations of fresh fish and seafood. Here's a classic version:

Steam 2 lbs (1 kg) fresh clams and/or mussels (see Moules Marinière, page 69 ; clams can be steamed the same way); remove from shells and set aside in large bowl. In large saucepan, combine 4 cups (1 L) water and 1 cup (250 mL) white wine; bring to simmer. In this liquid, cook the following fish and shellfish, one kind at time; remove with slotted spoon and add to the bowl of clams and/or mussels: 1/2 lb (250 g) fresh scallops (cook for 2 minutes or until opaque); 1/2 lb (250 g) shrimp (cook for 1 to 2 minutes or until pink); 1 lb (500 g) firm-fleshed white fish, cut into small chunks (cook for 2 to 3 minutes or until opaque); 1/2 lb (250 g) squid*, cut into rings (cook for 30 seconds). For dressing, whisk together 1/3 cup (75 mL) each lemon juice and extra-virgin olive oil, 2 minced garlic cloves, 3 tbsp (45 mL) chopped parsley, pinch of hot pepper flakes, and salt and pepper to taste. Add to seafood, mix well, cover and chill. **Makes about 6 servings.**

* Squid (calamari) is available cleaned, fresh or frozen, at most fish markets; it must be cooked very briefly or will become tough.

Greek Salad

Greek salads vary as much in modern Greece as they do in Canada. But a traditional homestyle Greek salad (called horiatiki) is a simple, sunny-flavoured combo of ripe red tomatoes, crisp cucumbers, feta cheese, black olives, fresh oregano and no lettuce. Make this in midsummer with garden-fresh cucumbers and tomatoes (regular, plum or beefsteak) or at other times of year with top-quality Canadian greenhouse vegetables.

Dressing:

1 tbsp	red wine vinegar	15 mL
2 tsp	lemon juice	10 mL
1	clove garlic, minced	1
1/4 tsp	salt	1 mL
	Freshly ground pepper	
1/3 cup	extra-virgin olive oil	75 mL
2 tbsp	chopped fresh oregano (or 2 tsp/10 mL dried)	30 mL

Salad:

4	medium-sized ripe tomatoes	4
1	seedless cucumber	1
1	small red onion, coarsely chopped	1
4 oz	feta cheese, broken into small chunks	125 g
1/2 cup	kalamata olives	125 mL

Dressing: Whisk together vinegar, lemon juice, garlic, salt and a generous grinding of pepper; gradually whisk in oil. If using dried oregano, add to dressing. Let stand for about 1 hour to blend flavours.

Salad: Cut tomatoes in half; if very juicy, gently squeeze out some of the juice so it doesn't dilute the dressing. Cut tomatoes and cucumber into bite-size chunks. Place in salad bowl and add onion. Add fresh oregano, if using. Toss with enough dressing to coat vegetables, adding more pepper and salt to taste if needed (the feta will add saltiness). Scatter feta and olives on top; toss gently before serving. **Makes 6 servings.**

Mixed Bean Salad

A sweet-and-sour dressing enhances this updated version of an ever-popular salad. Canned mixed beans are now available in most stores; otherwise, use any combination you like.

2 cups	each: crisp-cooked green and yellow beans	500 mL
2	cans (19 oz/540 mL each) mixed beans or any mixture (about 4 cups/1 L) of chick peas, red kidney beans, pinto or romano beans	2
1 cup	chopped celery	250 mL
1/2 cup	each: chopped onion, chopped sweet peppers (any colour)	125 mL
1/2 cup	each: white vinegar, vegetable oil	125 mL
1/4 cup	granulated sugar	50 mL
1 tsp	salt	5 mL
1/2 tsp	freshly ground pepper	2 mL

➜ In large bowl, combine fresh and canned beans, celery, onion and peppers. Whisk together vinegar, oil, sugar, salt and pepper. Pour over beans and mix well. Cover and chill for at least 3 hours, stirring occasionally. (Salad will keep for up to 3 days in refrigerator.) Drain before serving. **Makes about 8 servings.**

Antipasto Mixed Salad: In large bowl, combine 1 cup (250 mL) each: drained canned chick peas and red kidney beans, crisp-cooked broccoli florets, halved cherry tomatoes, canned artichoke hearts (halved or quartered), cubed mozzarella cheese. Add 1 sweet pepper (any colour) cut into strips, half a seedless cucumber cut into chunks, and 1/4 cup (50 mL) kalamata olives. For dressing, whisk together 3 tbsp (45 mL) red wine vinegar, 2 minced garlic cloves, 1/2 tsp (2 mL) each dried basil and oregano, 4 tbsp (60 mL) extra-virgin olive oil, and salt and pepper to taste. Pour over vegetable mixture and toss gently. Cover and refrigerate for at least 1 hour or up to 8 hours, stirring occasionally. Serve sprinkled lightly with crumbled feta cheese. **Makes about 8 servings.**

Panzanella

Half a baguette left over from yesterday's dinner? Plump red tomatoes perfectly ripe and ready for something? Time for panzanella, Tuscany's great rustic bread salad—it sings of summer. This version is a favourite of Murray's, who says, "This was once a way to use up day-old bread; now it's worth buying extra bread for." Fresh field-ripened tomatoes—preferably meaty beefsteaks—make this dish, but when they're not available, hothouse-raised do just fine. Each ingredient sits all but unadorned, so use the best quality possible.

2 cups	cubed or torn day-old French or Italian crusty bread	500 mL
3/4 lb	ripe tomatoes, chopped coarse or cubed	375 g
1/2	sweet onion (preferably red), thinly sliced	1/2
1	stalk celery, diced	1
1/4 cup	lightly packed fresh basil leaves, slivered	50 mL
1 or 2	cloves garlic, minced	1 or 2
1/2 cup	pitted green olives, halved or sliced	125 mL
1 tbsp	(or to taste) balsamic or red wine vinegar Salt to taste	15 mL
2 tbsp	(or to taste) extra-virgin olive oil	30 mL
	Freshly ground pepper	

➜ Put torn bread in salad bowl. Add tomatoes, onion, celery, basil, garlic and olives. Toss gently. Sprinkle with vinegar and salt; drizzle with olive oil; toss gently again. Grind pepper over it; toss a final time. Cover and let stand for 30 to 60 minutes at room temperature. **Makes 3 to 4 servings**.

Tabbouleh Salad

This version of the famous Middle Eastern bulgur-and-parsley salad uses a little less parsley than usual and has a minty-cool, fresh taste that is excellent with grilled lamb or chicken.

1 cup	bulgur	250 mL
2 cups	boiling water	500 mL
1 cup	diced unpeeled seedless cucumber	250 mL
14	cherry tomatoes, quartered	14
1 cup	finely chopped parsley	250 mL
1/4 cup	snipped fresh chives	50 mL
2 tbsp	finely chopped fresh mint	30 mL
1	small clove garlic, minced	1
4 tbsp	olive oil	60 mL
2 tbsp	lemon juice	30 mL
	Salt and pepper to taste	

➜ Place bulgur in large bowl; stir in boiling water; cover and let stand for 30 minutes. Drain well, pressing out excess water; let cool to room temperature. Stir in cucumber, tomatoes, parsley, chives and mint. In small bowl, combine garlic, oil and lemon juice; pour over salad and mix well. Season with salt and pepper. Refrigerate for 1 hour or up to 6 hours. Remove from refrigerator 15 minutes before serving. **Makes 6 servings**.

Marinated Vegetable Salad

This is a very attractive, healthful vegetable dish and salad all in one.

1 cup	each: sliced carrots, cut green beans, broccoli florets, cauliflower florets	250 mL
1/2 cup	each: sweet pepper strips (any colour), sliced celery	125 mL

Marinade:

1/2 cup	olive oil	125 mL
1/4 cup	white wine vinegar	50 mL
2 tbsp	lemon juice	30 mL
1	clove garlic, minced	1
1/2 tsp	salt	2 mL
1/4 tsp	pepper	1 mL
2 tbsp	chopped parsley	30 mL

→ In saucepan of boiling lightly salted water, separately cook carrots, beans, broccoli and cauliflower until slightly tender but still crisp (about 4 minutes for carrots, 2 minutes for the others). Or separately microwave on High for 1 to 2 minutes each. Drain vegetables and refresh in cold water (this keeps their colour bright). Drain in colander, then place in large bowl. Add peppers and celery. Combine marinade ingredients; pour over vegetables and stir well. Taste and add salt if needed. Cover and refrigerate for about 2 hours, stirring occasionally. **Makes about 4 servings.**

Mediterranean Pasta Salad

With sunny flavours reminiscent of Italy and southern France, this salad is perfect for summer meals outdoors. For a main-course salad, add about 1 cup (250 mL) diced cooked chicken, chunk tuna or cooked shrimp.

2 cups	pasta (fusilli, rotini or penne)	500 mL
1	small sweet pepper (any colour), chopped	1
1	stalk celery, chopped	1
3	green onions, chopped	3
1 cup	canned artichoke hearts (not marinated), drained	250 mL
10	cherry tomatoes, halved	10
	Easy Caesar Dressing (page 47) or Herbed Garlic Vinaigrette (page 46)	
Garnish:	Italian parsley	

→ In large pot of boiling salted water, cook pasta until tender but firm, about 10 minutes. Drain in colander and rinse under cold running water; drain well. In large bowl, combine pasta, pepper, celery, green onions, artichokes and tomatoes. Add just enough dressing to coat lightly; mix gently. Spoon into serving bowl. Garnish with parsley. **Makes 4 to 6 servings.**

Grilled Vegetable Salad: Serve this as antipasto or as an accompaniment to grilled meats. Choose a colourful assortment of vegetables and grill until tender but still firm (see Grilled Vegetables, page 154). For 6 servings, a good combination would be: 3 sweet peppers of assorted colours (cut lengthwise into eighths), 2 zucchini (sliced diagonally), 1 fennel bulb (sliced lengthwise) and 1 eggplant (sliced crosswise; cut slices in half if large). Place grilled vegetables in large shallow serving bowl. Drizzle with 3 tbsp (45 mL) each balsamic vinegar and extra-virgin olive oil. If desired, sprinkle with 1/4 cup (50 mL) chopped Italian parsley or fresh basil, or 2 tbsp (30 mL) chopped fresh thyme or oregano. Mix gently, adding salt and freshly ground pepper to taste. Serve warm or at room temperature.

Traditional Potato Salad

A good potato salad is a satisfying dish for simple summer meals. In this easy, flavourful version, the potatoes are drizzled while warm with oil and vinegar, then dressed lightly with mayonnaise. Use new potatoes for best texture.

6	medium potatoes, peeled and halved	6
2 tbsp	each: vegetable oil, white vinegar	30 mL
1	small onion, chopped	1
4	green onions, chopped	4
1/2 cup	chopped celery	125 mL
4	hard-cooked eggs	4
3/4 cup	(approx) low-fat mayonnaise	175 mL
1 to 2 tbsp	Dijon mustard (regular or grainy)	15 to 30 mL
	Salt and pepper	
Garnish:	sliced radishes, parsley sprigs	

→ Boil potatoes in lightly salted water until tender but still quite firm, about 20 minutes. Drain and let stand until cool enough to handle. Cut into small cubes and place in large bowl. Drizzle with oil and vinegar; toss. Add onions, celery and two of the eggs (cut up). Add enough mayonnaise to coat potatoes. Add mustard to taste. Season with salt and pepper to taste, mixing thoroughly; cover and refrigerate for about 2 hours. Spoon into serving bowl. Slice remaining eggs. Garnish top of salad with egg, radish slices and parsley. **Makes 4 to 6 servings**.

Bistro Potato Salad: Cook 2 lb (1 kg) new potatoes (unpeeled) in lightly salted boiling water just until tender when pierced with small knife; drain. As soon as cool enough to handle, peel if desired, cut into slices and place in large bowl. Whisk together 2 tbsp (30 mL) each white wine and white wine vinegar, 1 tsp (5 mL) Dijon mustard, 1/4 tsp (1 mL) salt and 6 tbsp (90 mL) olive oil. Add 2 tbsp (30 mL) each chopped green onions and parsley. Pour over warm potatoes; mix gently, adding salt and pepper to taste. Serve at room temperature. **Makes 4 to 6 servings**.

From Sea to Sea...

Fish & Seafood

A netful of ways to make the most of
our maritime bounty

At the Fish Market

The fish counter presents oceans of opportunities. Schooling yourself even modestly in how each of the better-known fish tastes and which cooking methods give best results will make your shopping easier and your dining more pleasurable.

Some experts suggest you go to the fish counter with no set idea of what you want to prepare. If you're flexible, and know which fish can substitute easily for another in both flavour and cooking method, you're on your way to fine dining—and perhaps a new taste experience.

In the market, whole fish should look fresh—bright-eyed, scales glistening, no bruises. It should smell fresh and sea-like, and feel firm to the touch. Ocean-caught fish may be at sea several days before coming to market as a "fresh" product (much of the catch is frozen at sea). Properly handled, most fish still looks fresh and stays firm. To make your shopping easier, find a knowledgeable, reliable fish retailer.

Fish to Cook Every Which Way

Most of the following can be baked, grilled or poached whole or in large pieces (depending on the size of the fish). Steaks and fillets can be grilled, broiled, baked or sautéed.

From salt water

Salmon begin and end their lives in fresh water but spend most of their life in the ocean, where they are commercially fished. They're prized on both east and west coasts, though the wild species in each place are distinctly different. What's called "Atlantic salmon" is caught in open Atlantic waters and also farmed on both coasts, so fish labelled "Atlantic salmon" may in fact come from Pacific Coast farms. Five species dominate the wild Pacific catch: deep-red-fleshed chinook; orange-red sockeye; pinks and chum, both having pale pink flesh; and pink-to-red coho. Price is a rough guide to quality, but is influenced by the appeal of each species' depth of colour. Some paler ones aren't as eye-catching but can be extremely flavourful.

Arctic char, a northern Canadian specialty now farm-raised in fresh water, has become famous internationally. From the same family as salmon, char has a milder flavour and deli cate yet firm texture; it can be prepared in the same ways as salmon.

Cod encompasses a large group of groundfish found on both Atlantic and Pacific coasts. Most are lean, white-fleshed and prized for delicate flavour and texture. Pacific cod has grey-to-brown flesh.

Haddock, hake and **pollock** are related, although the pollocks—Atlantic (also called **Boston bluefish**) and Alaskan (also called walleye pollock)—are two different things.

Blackcod, also called sablefish and (aptly) butterfish, is of a different family and is caught in the northern Pacific. Rich and fatty, it has large white flakes when cooked. Cod is sold numerous ways: fresh and frozen fillets and steaks, and as dried salt cod, which must be rehydrated before using.

Halibut, a huge deepwater flatfish that's part of the flounder family, appears on both coasts in closely related species. (The Pacific halibut is slightly smaller.) They can weigh several hundred pounds, though most are considerably smaller. Markets carry steaks and roasts, which are highly versatile. The lean, firm flesh makes halibut popular.

Ocean perch is the trade name in Canada and the U.S. for redfish, rosefish and some others in the rockfish family. Ocean perch are small (up to 3 lb/1.5 kg) inhabitants of deep Atlantic waters. The flesh is mild, with a fine, flaky texture.

Snapper encompasses more than 100 species, and some fish sold as snapper in Canada don't even belong to that group. True red snapper can be deep red to pink, and comes from temperate-to-warm Atlantic and Caribbean waters. Snappers weigh up to 30 lb (15 kg) and can be roasted or grilled whole; fillets can be baked or poached. A reddish-pink member of the Pacific rockfish family is often sold as red snapper. It is similar in texture to real snapper.

Smelts are tiny—as small as 5 oz (140 g)—with sweet flesh. They live in both ocean and inland waters. Many species fall into this group; common ones are the rainbow smelt of the Great Lakes and southeastern Canada, and the eulachon of the Pacific Coast.

Sea bass has splashed onto menus everywhere. Often called Chilean sea bass, it is more correctly called white sea bass, a member of the croaker family, and shouldn't be confused with true sea bass, which is part of the huge **grouper** clan. Family relations aside, all these basses are excellent, with firm, sweet flesh. The groupers number close to 400 species, mostly from temperate and tropical Atlantic waters.

From fresh water

Many freshwater fish are called **bass**, often with a modifier attached. White bass from eastern lakes and rivers are usually just a few pounds, and quite versatile. Freshwater white bass are part of a large family of sport fish.

Pike (also **Northern pike** or **jackfish**), valued for sport, is also taken commercially from central lakes and rivers. Its lean, firm flesh suits many cooking techniques.

Pickerel (also known as **walleye pike**, though not related to true pike) is an adaptable freshwater fish.

Trout, part of the salmon family, are widely found in fresh water across North America. Several species, the **rainbow** foremost, are also farmed. Trout are small—8 to 12 oz (250 to 375 g) is common—making them ideal for individual servings. **Salmon trout** is a pink-fleshed trout, not a salmon. Another cousin of the salmon, **whitefish**, is found in cold northern lakes. It is versatile, with delicate, sweet-tasting flesh.

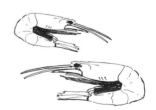

Fish to Cook Gently

The delicate texture of some fish requires careful handling. The following are usually sold as fillets, and are best poached, baked or gently sautéed. Grilling isn't advised.

"Sole" and **"flounder"** cover many flatfish (so named because of their compressed, oval shape) caught on both **Atlantic and Pacific coasts. They include Atlantic flounder, fluke, sole, plaice and turbot;** and **Pacific sole, flounder and dab.** There are also **English sole** (not to be confused with true **Dover sole**), **West Coast dover sole** (ditto), **butter sole** and **petrale sole.** (**Halibut** is also part of this mixed family, but its size allows it to be treated much differently.)

Skate, sometimes called **ray**, appears in a number of species off both coasts. Sometimes whole triangular wings appear in markets, but more often it's the filleted flesh, cut from between the long cartilage "bones" of the wing. Sautéed with brown butter and capers, skate makes a memorable dish

Shellfish

If you relish the sweetness of ocean-fresh lobster or the briny delicacy of a just-shucked oyster, find a reputable fish retailer and befriend the staff; they're your surest guide to shellfish excellence. Use your own senses, too. If possible, have a sniff, hoping for the clean, clear scent of the sea. Avoid those with cracked or broken shells. Clams, mussels and oysters should be alive; if the two shells are gaping, rap one of them; if it clams shut, it's alive. These shellfish are commonly sold fresh in Canadian markets. Some are wild-caught; increasingly, many are farmed. Sometimes that affects taste; consult your retailer. (All are sold frozen or canned, too, but fresh seafood promises optimum taste and texture.)

Clams range from the Pacific's thumb-wide Manilas and small Atlantic quahogs, through larger cherrystones and ocean quahogs (up to 4 inches/10 cm wide) to the long, narrow razor clams on both coasts. The geoduck (pronounced "gooey-duck") is a Pacific behemoth that can reach 10 lb (4.5 kg) and carries an equally weighty price because of its value in Asian markets.

Crab is best purchased live, cooked quickly, then devoured (messy, but the rich sweet flavour is worth it). Specialty markets in major cities, especially ones catering to an Asian clientele, often have live crab in tanks. The long-legged snow crab (also called spider, queen or tanner crab) and the less-bright rock crab are prominent in Atlantic markets. The West Coast favourite is dungeness, which can reach 4 lb (2 kg) and offers excellent meat.

Lobster, the famed "king of seafood" from the Atlantic coast, can be bought live from tanks in major centres across Canada. Usual size is 1 to 5 lb (0.5 to 2.5 kg). Lobster is also sold cooked (whole or meat only, fresh or frozen; frozen canned lobster is excellent for use in recipes calling for cooked lobster meat). Clawless spiny lobsters (sometimes called langouste) are caught in the warmer waters of the Americas. Miniature lobsters known as Dublin Bay prawns (langoustine in France, scampi in Italy) are harvested in northern Atlantic and Mediterranean waters.

Boiled Lobster: Freshly boiled lobster, served with melted butter for dipping, is a delicious feast. Lobster can be grilled or steamed, but the easiest and most common way is boiling in salted water. Use a large deep pot with a lid, and fill with enough water to cover lobster. Add 1 tbsp (15 mL) salt per 4 cups (1 L) water. Bring to full rolling boil. Grasp lobster by the back with your hand or tongs, and plunge it headfirst into water. Cover pot and return to boil; reduce heat to simmer. Cook lobster based on 12 minutes for the first pound (500 g) plus 4 minutes for each additional pound.

Serving Oysters: To serve on the half shell, shuck oysters using oyster knife, retaining liquid in bottom shell; discard top shell. (If you're not expert with an oyster knife, an easy way to open oysters is to place them on a barbecue grill for a few minutes until they open enough to pry open easily.) Slide knife under oyster to sever it from shell. Serve on a bed of ice. Accompany with lemon wedges and hot pepper sauce.

Oysters are also delectable in traditional oyster stew and chowders, wrapped in bacon and grilled, or lightly breaded and quickly sautéed.

Mussels abound naturally on both coasts, but the Atlantic excels in production. The common blue mussel is farmed extensively in Prince Edward Island. Larger green-lipped mussels, with distinctive orange and white flesh, are imported from New Zealand.

Oysters appear all around North America's coasts—famed Malpeques from Prince Edward Island and Caraquets from New Brunswick have many close relatives, often with local place names. The common Pacific oyster, first imported from Japan, has been joined by numerous cultivated types, such as the Golden Mantle.

Scallops appear in our markets in two general types: tiny bay scallops, and the much larger (and more flavourful) sea scallops, which thrive in deep waters off both coasts (Atlantic production predominates). Very sweet scallops weighing several ounces each are taken from northern Pacific waters off Alaska, but most go to restaurants. Scallops are sold by the pound, out of the shell, in most markets. In coastal cities, scallops are sometimes available in the shell, occasionally with the delicious orange roe intact.

Shrimp and **prawns** cause confusion because the terms can be carelessly used. In commerce, shrimp means the smaller species; prawn is the larger. Canada's Pacific coast is home to 85 varieties, with large, deep-water spot prawns especially prized. (They're also highly perishable, but sometimes available in specialty markets.) Shrimp and prawns are sold fresh and frozen, cooked and raw, peeled and unpeeled. Sizes range from tiny to jumbo.

Squid, the familiar kalamari/calamari of Greek and Italian menus, is harvested in the waters of Atlantic Canada. Much of what comes to market has been processed and frozen, often at sea.

Exotics

Aquaculture and efficient international transportation bring us intriguing and exotic species. Mild, versatile **orange roughy** is caught off New Zealand and Australia; North Americans almost always see it as fillets. **Tilapia** describes a group of species farmed in fresh water around the globe; much of what comes to Canadian markets (sold mainly as fillets) is farmed in the U.S. **Catfish** is usually from the American South, and often appears already marinated.

Some of the more exotic imports have the appeal of a prime steak; they are dense, meaty fish. Among the better known are **mahi-mahi** (its Hawaiian name), or **dolphinfish** (not to be confused with dolphins, which are mammals), which appears mainly in tropical waters; **monkfish**, an ugly creature if ever there was one, but whose dense, chunky fillets are sweet and almost lobster-like; and **swordfish**, a large inhabitant of warm Atlantic and Pacific waters that shows up in our markets as steaks or cubes for brochettes. Swordfish is very lean; cook carefully to avoid drying out.

Tuna has been part of every Canadian's life, but only recently have we come to know the real fish—fresh, rather than the pale, often bland, canned product. "Tuna" describes a large segment of the mackerel family; many species roam the warm and temperate waters of both Atlantic and Pacific. Deep-red tuna steaks appear in many markets, and the cuts can be cooked like the other dense, steak-like fish.

Fast Fish ♥

Quick Cooking Method

🔥 Grilled Fish

Fish steaks and fillets are quick, easy and delicious on the grill—whether outdoor barbecue, indoor grill or stovetop ridged grill pan. Oven-broiling is basically the same, although the grill marks and smoky flavour will be missing. Choose fish that is firm-fleshed and fairly thick so it is easy to turn during cooking. Rub a little oil over both sides and sprinkle with salt and pepper or other seasonings. Cook on greased grill over medium-high heat, turning once halfway through cooking, just until fish looks opaque in centre. When tested with a fork, the flakes of flesh should lift apart but not too easily (if you wait until fish flakes very easily, it is likely overcooked). Total cooking time will be about 10 minutes per inch (2.5 cm) of thickness. For extra flavour, fish can be marinated before grilling or brushed with flavoured mixtures during grilling. See Marinades, page 110; they can also be used as brush-on mixtures. Marinating time should be no more than 30 minutes or the fish will begin to "cook" in the acidic marinade.

For quick, easy, healthful and tasty midweek suppers, just pop some fish fillets into the microwave or oven. Add a kaleidoscope of flavours with just a few ingredients; choose from the toppings suggested here, or make up your own. These quantities make about 3 servings. Serve with rice or pasta.

1 lb	fish fillets	500 g
2 tbsp	lemon juice or white wine Salt and pepper	30 mL

Lemon-Almond Topping:

1/2	lemon, thinly sliced	1/2
2 tbsp	chopped parsley	30 mL
1/4 cup	toasted almonds (add after cooking)	50 mL

Mushroom-Herb Topping:

1 cup	sliced mushrooms	250 mL
1/4 cup	chopped green onions	50 mL
1 tbsp	chopped fresh basil or tarragon (or 1 tsp/5 mL dried)	15 mL

Tomato-Parmesan Topping:

1/2 cup	chopped drained canned tomatoes	125 mL
2 tbsp	each: finely chopped onion and sweet green pepper	30 mL
1/2 tsp	dried oregano	2 mL
1/4 cup	grated parmesan cheese	50 mL

➔ **To Microwave:** In microwavable baking dish, arrange fillets in single layer or slightly overlapping, with thicker parts at edges of dish. Tuck thinner parts under to give even thickness. Sprinkle with lemon juice and a little salt and pepper. Scatter desired topping ingredients over fish. Cover with parchment or waxed paper. Microwave on High for 5 to 7 minutes or until fish is opaque.

To Oven-Bake: In baking dish, arrange fish fillets in single layer, tucking thin parts under to give even thickness. Sprinkle with lemon juice and a little salt and pepper. Scatter desired topping ingredients over fish. Cover with lid or foil. Bake in 425F (220C) oven for 15 minutes or until fish is opaque. Remove fish with slotted lifter; discard any liquid in dish.

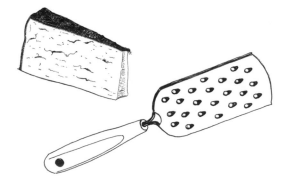

Sesame-Crusted Salmon on Greens

For 25 years at her Toronto cooking school, Bonnie Stern has taught classes on cooking fish correctly and creatively. This is one of her favourite recipes and can be used with sea bass, halibut or any thick, firm-textured fillets. Crispy fish atop a colourful salad mixture makes a gorgeous presentation; Bonnie likes to serve it with basmati rice, quinoa or couscous. The recipe is a great example of the skillet-to-oven technique, commonly used by chefs and being picked up by home cooks: quickly sear to give the fish a nice colour, then transfer to oven to cook through without drying out. You can use the same method for any thick fillet of fish, without the sesame coating.

6	4-oz (125 g) fillets fresh salmon, skin removed	6
1 tbsp	each: honey, light-coloured soy sauce	15 mL
1 tsp	sweet hot mustard	5 mL
1 tbsp	sesame seeds	15 mL

Salad:

8 to 12 cups	mixed greens	2 to 3 L
1 lb	cooked asparagus, cut into 2-inch (5 cm) pieces (or green beans or broccoli)	500 g
1	sweet red pepper, cut into strips	1
1	orange, peeled and sectioned	1
2 tbsp	chopped fresh coriander or parsley	30 mL
2 tbsp	chopped chives or green onions	30 mL

Orange-Ginger Dressing:

1	clove garlic, minced	1
1 tsp	minced fresh ginger	5 mL
3 tbsp	orange juice	45 mL
2 tbsp	light-coloured soy sauce	30 mL
2 tbsp	rice vinegar or balsamic vinegar	30 mL
2 tsp	each: sesame oil, honey	10 mL
1/4 tsp	Chinese chile paste or hot pepper sauce	1 mL

➜ Pat salmon dry. In small bowl, combine honey, soy sauce and mustard; rub over both sides of salmon. Sprinkle both sides with sesame seeds. In oiled ovenproof skillet over high heat, brown salmon lightly, about 1 minute on each side. Transfer to 425F (220C) oven and bake for 7 to 8 minutes or until just cooked through. In large bowl, combine salad ingredients; whisk together dressing ingredients and toss with salad. Serve salad topped with salmon. **Makes 6 servings**.

Quick Cooking Method

Pan-fried Fish Fillets

Pan-frying is also referred to as sautéing (which sounds fancier), and this method is used everywhere—fresh-caught whitefish in cast iron skillets over campfires; sole in copper sauté pans in French restaurants. Dry the fillets on paper towels, then dredge in flour seasoned with salt and pepper; shake off excess flour. In large skillet over medium-high heat, melt a generous amount (about 4 tbsp/60 mL) of butter or a mixture of butter and oil. (You can use a nonstick skillet and much less butter if you wish.) Cook fillets, turning once, until lightly browned on both sides, about 5 minutes total for thin fillets, 10 minutes for thicker. Check to see that fish is opaque in the centre; don't overcook. Serve very hot, with lemon wedges alongside. OR splash a little white wine or vermouth into the pan, cook for about 15 seconds, pour over fish and sprinkle with parsley.

Oven-Fried Fish and Chips 😊

Crave the old-time satisfaction of fish and chips but not the bad old fat content? Then bake them both in the oven. Cornflake crumbs give the fish a crisp, light, golden coating (much better than breadcrumbs); if you don't have packaged crumbs, crush cornflakes in plastic bag with rolling pin, then measure. Little kids love to help with the crushing and with dipping the fish. For the chips, see Oven-Baked French Fries (page 157).

1/2 cup	all-purpose flour seasoned with 1 tsp (5 mL) salt	125 mL
Pinch	pepper	Pinch
1	egg, lightly beaten	1
1 cup	cornflake crumbs	250 mL

1 lb	fish fillets (fresh, or thawed in refrigerator)	500 g
	Lemon wedges	
	Tartar Sauce	

➜ Place seasoned flour, egg and crumbs in 3 separate shallow bowls. Dredge fish lightly in flour, dip into egg, letting excess run off, then into crumbs, pressing crumbs to stick. Place on baking sheet (nonstick, oiled or lined with parchment). Bake in 450F (230C) oven for 7 to 9 minutes or until fish is just cooked through. Serve with lemon wedges and/or tartar sauce. **Makes about 4 servings**.

Baked Fish Steaks Mediterranean-Style

Sunny colour and flavour make this a great dish for a cold winter day, or for midsummer when you can make it with fresh ripe red tomatoes. Similar dishes are common all around the Mediterranean and Aegean, from Spain to the Middle East.

Be sure to use extra-virgin oil and don't skimp on the amount (it's important for authentic flavour, and olive oil is good for you!). It's also an easy dish to vary; sliced black olives, red pepper strips, capers and shreds of lemon zest are all good additions.

3 tbsp	extra-virgin olive oil	45 mL
1	large onion, chopped	1
4	cloves garlic, minced	4
2 cups	chopped canned or fresh tomatoes (peeled, seeded)	500 mL
2 tsp	chopped fresh herbs (basil, rosemary, oregano or thyme) (or 1/2 tsp/2 mL dried)	10 mL

1/4 cup	white wine	50 mL
	Salt and pepper	
1-1/2 lb	fish steaks or fillets such as cod or halibut	750 g

➜ In large skillet over medium heat, heat 2 tbsp (30 mL) of the oil. Cook onion and garlic until softened. Add tomatoes, herbs and wine; cook, stirring occasionally, for about 5 minutes (the sauce should be thick because more moisture will come from the fish during baking). Add salt and pepper to taste. Arrange fish in single layer in oiled baking dish. Pour sauce over. Drizzle with remaining olive oil. Bake in 425F (220C) oven for 15 minutes or just until fish is cooked through. **Makes 4 servings**.

Fish en Papillote: Serving fish "en papillote" (wrapped in parchment packages) makes a nifty presentation, and the puffed-up packages also waft a lovely fragrance when they're opened at the dinner table. This technique may sound complex, but it's basically the same as oven-baking in a tightly covered dish.

For each serving: Use a 6-oz (175 g) fillet of fish and about 1 cup (250 mL) julienned strips of carrot, celery and leek. Cut parchment paper in large round or heart shape. (Foil can also be used but doesn't look as nice and may discolour fish.) Butter one half of the paper and place half of the julienned vegetables on it; drizzle with a little melted butter and sprinkle with salt and pepper. If fish fillet is thick, cut it in slices. Place fish on top of vegetables; place rest of vegetables on top of fish. Drizzle with a little more melted butter; sprinkle with salt and pepper. Fold paper over to enclose fish; fold edges over twice and crimp together well to seal all around. Place packets on rimmed baking sheet. Bake in 400F (200C) oven for 20 minutes. Serve fish packets on dinner plates, letting guests cut open their own.

Roasted Fish Caribbean-Style

Any whole fish (3 to 4 lb/1.5 to 2 kg) can be roasted this way. We've enjoyed snapper, grouper and sea bass all done in a similar fashion in the Bahamas and West Indies. For a simpler version (which also works well with salmon and other northern fish), omit the tomato mixture, brush the fish with oil and roast as is—a delicious treat, especially when the fish is so fresh it still tastes of the sea.

Here's the basic method: cut 2 diagonal slashes almost to the bone in thickest part of fish on both sides. Squeeze juice from 2 small limes all over fish, inside and out. Place fish in large oiled baking pan. Sprinkle inside of fish with salt and pepper, 2 sliced garlic cloves and a few sprigs of fresh thyme. In oiled skillet, cook together over medium heat until softened: 2 chopped ripe tomatoes, 1 chopped small onion, 1 chopped small sweet green pepper, 1 chopped celery stalk and 1 chopped small chile pepper; add salt and pepper to taste. Spread mixture over fish. Cover very loosely with foil. Bake in 400F (200C) oven for 30 minutes; remove foil and bake for about 10 minutes longer or until thickest part of fish is opaque when flaked with tip of a knife. **Makes 6 servings**.

Herbed Rainbow Trout

Fresh herbs, garlic and lemon enhance the delicate flavour of trout in this low-fat treatment. Wrapped in foil, the fish can be cooked on the barbecue or in the oven. Using 1 rainbow trout (about 12 oz/375 g) per serving, cut 2 diagonal slashes almost to the bone on both sides of fish. Insert a sliver of garlic, a thin slice of lemon and a sprig of fresh tarragon or a basil leaf in each slash. Place each fish on a large piece of foil. Sprinkle inside of each fish lightly with salt, lemon juice and olive oil; add a few sprigs of fresh tarragon or basil. Enclose fish completely in foil. Bake in 450F (230C) oven (or in covered barbecue) for 20 to 25 minutes or until fish is opaque when flaked with tip of a knife. The trout can also be steamed (without the foil wrapping) over simmering water in a covered wok fitted with steaming rack (or on a rack in a large covered saucepan).

Steamed Sea Bass with Black Bean Sauce

Steaming fish fillets retains their flavour and texture while avoiding extra calories. Catherine Liang, of Ocean Park, B.C., entered this recipe in a Vancouver Sun *contest seeking fast, delicious dinner ideas. She won first prize.*

1-1/4 to 1-1/2 lb	sea bass fillets (1-1/2 inches/4 cm thick)	625 to 750 g
3 tbsp	black bean garlic sauce	45 mL
1	slice (1/2-inch/1cm) fresh ginger, julienned	1
1	green onion, cut into 2-inch (5 cm) pieces	1
1/2 tsp	peanut oil	2 mL

Fresh coriander leaves for garnish

➜ Place steam rack in wok or large frypan. Fill wok with water to about 1 inch (2.5 cm) below rack. Cover and bring to boil. Meanwhile, rinse fish fillets and pat dry. Place in single layer in 10-inch (25 cm) glass pie plate. Spread black bean garlic sauce over tops and sides of fillets. Top with ginger and green onion. Drizzle with oil. Place pie plate on rack in wok; cover and steam for 12 minutes or until fish flakes easily when tested with a fork. Remove from steamer and garnish with coriander. **Makes 4 servings**.

Skillet-Poached Salmon: This simple technique produces moist, tender salmon to serve hot or cold with a simple sauce, or to use for salads or sandwiches. Other fish fillets can be poached the same way. In large deep skillet, combine 1 cup (250 mL) each white wine and water, 1 sliced small onion, 1 tsp (5 mL) salt, a few peppercorns and parsley sprigs, and 1 bay leaf. Bring to simmer. Add 4 salmon fillets (about 6 oz/ 175 g each); return to simmer. Cover and simmer gently until fish is barely cooked (almost opaque at centre), about 4 minutes. Remove pan from heat and let fish sit in liquid for 2 minutes. Remove and serve hot, cold or at room temperature. Serve with lemon wedges, Quick Herbed Sauce (see Sidebar) or Cucumber Raita (page 102).

Quick Herbed Sauce: Mix together equal parts light mayonnaise and plain yogurt (or drained yogurt, page 239). Add two or three chopped fresh herbs—chives, dill, tarragon, parsley, basil, etc.—to taste. (My cousin Donna McMillan calls this "grass-clippings sauce," using a variety of herbs from her West Vancouver garden.) Add a squeeze of lemon juice and salt and pepper to taste (you can also add a little crushed garlic if desired). Serve with hot or cold poached salmon (also delicious with hot grilled fish).

Whole Salmon Baked in Foil

For years I've used this method because it ensures succulent fish and is so easy, including a neat technique for transferring a large fish to a serving platter. Sprinkle inside of fish with salt, pepper, fresh dill or other herbs and juice of half a lemon. Brush outside of fish with oil and place on large rectangle of heavy foil. Drizzle with white wine. Fold long sides of foil over fish; seal edges together in a double fold. Fold ends of foil over top. Place on large baking sheet. Bake in 450F (230C) oven until thickest part of fish is opaque when flaked with tip of a knife (about 45 minutes for a 5-lb/2.2 kg salmon; or 10 minutes per inch/2.5 cm of thickness measured at thickest part).

To transfer to serving platter: With fish still on baking sheet, fold back foil and use small sharp knife to peel off skin on exposed side of fish. Drain any liquid from inside foil. Invert large platter on top of fish; holding both platter and baking sheet firmly, flip whole thing over. Lift off baking sheet and remove foil. Peel off skin from second side of fish.

Garnish if desired with lemon slices and fresh dill or parsley.

To serve: Using fish knife and fork, lift fish away from backbone in serving-size portions. Remove tail and pull backbone and head off in one piece; serve bottom layer of fish in portions. Serve with Quick Herbed Sauce (page 67) or Cucumber Raita (page 102).

Cedar Planked Salmon ✦

"Planking" is an ancient tradition of Native Canadian cooking, using large fish, especially salmon, split and skewered on willow branches to cook beside an open fire. In pioneer days, fish were commonly cooked on hardwood planks in front of the open hearth. And early in this century, fish was also "planked" by being baked or broiled on a board, then garnished with piped potato rosettes. In recent years, planked fish has become fashionable again; cooking fish on a cedar plank in a hot oven or closed barbecue adds a wonderfully woodsy flavour; some fish shops sell the boards. My daughter Lise, who enjoys culinary research as part of her work in archaeology, developed this recipe for a contemporary version. This recipe is also very good made with fresh whitefish.

4	salmon fillets (6 oz/175 g each), skin on, about 1 inch (2.5 cm) thick	4
1 tbsp	butter, melted	15 mL
1/2 tsp	each: salt, coarsely crushed dried savory	2 mL
	Freshly ground pepper	
	Garnish: lemon slices, parsley	

➡ Use a cedar plank large enough to hold the fillets, at least 12 x 12 inches (30 x 30 cm) and 1/2 to 3/4 inch (1 to 2 cm) thick. Be sure the wood is clean and not chemically treated. Soak the plank in water overnight, using weights to keep it submerged. Place fish fillets, skin side down, in single layer on the soaked plank. Brush fish with melted butter; sprinkle with salt, savory and a few generous grindings of pepper. Bake in 450F (230C) oven or in a closed barbecue for 10 minutes or until the fish flakes easily with a fork. (For thinner or thicker fillets, allow 10 minutes cooking time per inch/2.5 cm of thickness measured at thickest part of fillets.) Serve fish on the plank, garnished with lemon and parsley. **Makes 4 servings**.

Moules à la Marinière ⊕

The simplest and most popular way of cooking mussels is the classic French method given here along with some variations, one typically Italian, one exotically Asian. Serve in large shallow bowls, with small forks for the mussels, lots of crusty baguette for mopping up the broth, and a side dish for empty shells.

4 lb	fresh mussels	2 kg
1 cup	white wine	250 mL
1/2 cup	minced shallots or onion	125 mL
2	cloves garlic, minced	2
2 tbsp	finely chopped parsley	30 mL

➔ Scrub mussels well; remove beards. Discard any mussels that are not tightly closed. Put wine, shallots and garlic in large pot. Bring to boil. Add mussels, cover and steam, shaking pot occasionally, until shells open, 4 to 5 minutes. Discard any that don't open. Remove mussels with slotted spoon and put them in bowls. (Some recipes recommend straining the stock through a paper-lined sieve in case there is any grit, but this is not usually necessary with cultured mussels.) Add parsley to broth and pour over mussels. **Makes 4 servings**.

Moules à la Crème: After removing mussels, strain broth if desired. Add 1/4 cup (50 mL) whipping cream to broth; bring to simmer, add parsley and pour over mussels.

Mussels with Tomatoes and Basil: To wine mixture in pot, add 1 cup (250 mL) chopped canned or fresh tomatoes; simmer for 5 minutes before adding mussels. After removing cooked mussels, add 2 tbsp (30 mL) chopped fresh basil along with parsley. For a further variation (my favourite, after tasting it at an Italian restaurant in my neighbourhood), stir in a little tomato purée and whipping cream at the end for a slightly richer, smoother sauce; add more basil to taste if desired.

Mussels Thai-Style: Follow recipe for Thai Green Curry (page 117), using mussels instead of shrimp and omitting snow peas.

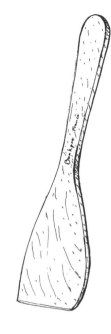

Canadian Cioppino

An all-Canadian fish stew can be just as distinctive and delicious as the famous fisherman's stews of San Francisco (cioppino) or Marseilles (bouillabaisse). This one borrows a bit from both, with superb flavour and fragrance. You can use any combination of fish and shellfish; the only rule is to use the freshest catch of the day. See what's best at the fish market and stew up a dish that's easy, fast and fabulous.

2 tbsp	olive oil	30 mL
1 cup	chopped onions	250 mL
3	cloves garlic, minced	3
1	carrot, chopped	1
2	stalks celery, chopped	2
1	small fennel bulb, chopped	1
1	can (28 oz/796 mL) tomatoes	1
2 cups	fish or chicken stock	500 mL
1 cup	white wine	250 mL
1/2 tsp	saffron (optional)	2 mL
1/4 tsp	each: dried tarragon, thyme, oregano	1 mL
1	bay leaf	1
	Salt and pepper	
2 lb	mussels and/or clams, scrubbed	1 kg
1 lb	fish fillets, cut in chunks (a mix of 2 or 3 kinds such as cod, halibut, snapper, salmon)	500 g
1/2 lb	peeled large raw shrimp or prawns (optional)	250 g

➜ In large heavy pot over medium-high heat, heat oil. Add onions, garlic, carrot, celery and fennel. Cook until softened but not browned. Add tomatoes (crush as you add them), stock, wine, saffron (if using), herbs and bay leaf. Simmer for about 30 minutes. Add salt and pepper to taste. Add mussels and clams; cover and cook for 3 minutes. Add fish chunks and simmer for 5 minutes. Add shrimp (if using). Simmer for 3 to 5 minutes or until shrimp are pink and fish is opaque. Discard any mussels or clams that haven't opened. Remove bay leaf. Add salt and pepper to taste if needed. **Makes 6 servings**.

Crab Cakes

The best crab cakes are made with crab and not much else; for best texture use good-quality crabmeat, which gives a chunky texture to the cakes.

1/3 cup	mayonnaise	75 mL
1/2 cup	fine fresh breadcrumbs or crushed soda crackers	125 mL
1	egg	1
1/4 cup	finely chopped green onions	50 mL
1 tbsp	minced parsley	15 mL
1 tsp	Worcestershire sauce	5 mL
1/2 tsp	dry mustard (or 2 tsp/10 mL Dijon)	2 mL
1/4 tsp	(or to taste) hot pepper sauce or cayenne	1 mL
1 lb	cooked crabmeat	500 g
2 tbsp	vegetable oil	30 mL

➜ In bowl, combine all ingredients except crabmeat and oil; mix thoroughly. Stir in crabmeat (mix well but leave some chunky bits). Taste and adjust seasoning. Shape mixture into 8 cakes. (If desired, dust lightly with additional fine breadcrumbs.) In large skillet over medium-high heat, heat oil. Cook crab cakes until golden brown, about 3 minutes on each side. Serve with mayonnaise (garlic-, mustard-, lemon- or basil-flavoured if desired; see page 47). **Makes 4 servings**.

Prime Time...

Meats

Beef, lamb, pork and veal take centre-stage—
with the spotlight on versatility and flavour

Beef

Shopping for beef got a whole lot easier when a new labelling system was introduced in 1998 by Canada's beef industry. Research showed the majority of shoppers didn't understand the various cuts or how to match them with proper cooking methods. The new system, in place at many retail meat counters, displays beef cuts according to cooking method, with signs indicating Grilling Steaks, Pot Roasts and so on. Those categories are repeated on the package labels, along with the name of the cut (for example, Rib-Eye Grilling Steak, Short Rib Pot Roast). Many retailers have also added labels with new basic cooking instructions developed by Canada's Beef Information Centre. Here are the industry's new categories and methods:

Matching Cuts to Cooking Methods

Premium Oven Roasts

Cuts: prime rib (standing or rolled), tenderloin, sirloin.

Basic Method: Place roast, fat side up, on rack in roasting pan. Season to taste. Insert meat thermometer into centre of roast, avoiding fat or bone. Roast uncovered at 325F (160C) to desired doneness.

Doneness	Internal Temp.	Roasting Time
Rare	140F (60C)	20 min. per lb (500 g)
Medium	160F (70C)	25 min. per lb (500 g)
Well	170F (75C)	30 min. per lb (500 g)

Oven Roasts

Cuts: rump, eye of round, inside round, outside round, sirloin tip (2 to 5 lb/1 to 2.4 kg).

Basic Method: Add water to roasting pan to depth of 1/2 inch (1 cm). Place roast, fat side up, on rack over water in pan. Do not add extra fat. Season roast to taste. Insert meat thermometer into centre of roast, avoiding fat or bone. Place in preheated 500F (260C) oven for 30 minutes. Don't open oven door; reduce temperature to 275F (140C). Cook an additional 1-1/4 to 1-3/4 hours for medium doneness (internal temperature 160F/70C).

Pot Roasts

Cuts: cross rib, short rib, blade, shoulder, brisket. (Outside round and rump roasts can also be pot roasted.)

Basic Method: Season roast and brown on all sides in a small amount of oil in Dutch oven or deep heavy pot or pan. Add 1 to 2 cups (250 to 500 mL) liquid such as stock or wine. Cover and simmer on stovetop or in 325F (160C) oven until tender, at least 3 hours. Add vegetables for final 1/2 hour if desired.

Grilling Steaks

Cuts: rib, rib-eye, strip loin, tenderloin, T-bone, wing, sirloin.

Basic Method: Season with pepper or seasoning rubs but do not salt. Grill or broil using medium-high heat, turning only once or twice with tongs.

Thickness	*Minutes Per Side*		
	Rare	Medium	Well
1/2 to 3/4 inch (1 to 2 cm)	3 to 5	5 to 7	7 to 9
1 inch (2.5 cm)	5 to 7	7 to 9	9 to 11

Marinating Steaks

Cuts: flank, sirloin tip, inside round, outside round, eye of round

Basic Method: Pierce steak numerous times with fork. Marinate in acidic liquid (wine, citrus juice, etc.) plus seasonings for 12 to 24 hours in refrigerator. (For Marinades, see page 110.) Grill or broil, turning only once or twice with tongs. Do not cook past medium.

Thickness	*Minutes Per Side*	
	Rare	Medium
1/2 to 3/4 inch (1 to 2 cm)	3 to 5	5 to 7
1 inch (2.5 cm)	5 to 7	7 to 9

Simmering Steaks

Cuts: cross rib and blade. (Simmering means braising; cuts labelled Marinating Steaks can also be braised.)

Basic Method: Braising is essentially the same as pot roasting (long, slow cooking in a small amount of liquid in a covered pan). Season meat and brown on all sides in lightly oiled pan. Add sliced onion, garlic, etc., if desired. Add 1/2 to 1 cup (125 to 250 mL) liquid such as stock, juice, wine or canned tomatoes. Cover and simmer on stovetop or in 325F (160C) oven until tender, at least 1-1/4 hours.

Stewing Beef

Cuts: stewing cubes, short ribs, shank.

Basic Method: Lightly coat cubes or short ribs with mixture of flour, salt and pepper. Brown in small amount of hot oil; add onions and other seasonings as desired. Add liquid (such as stock, tomato juice, wine) to cover beef. Cover and simmer on stovetop or in 325F (160C) oven for 2 hours or until tender. Add cut-up vegetables for final 1/2 hour if desired.

Gather-the-Clan Roast Beef Dinner

If Sunday roast beef dinner is but a distant memory at your house, you're not unusual. Families are either off in all directions on weekends, or no one knows how to cook a roast anymore (or both). Relax—rounding up the gang may be tough, but the roast beef is easy.

With today's very lean beef, you won't find a lot of drippings in the roasting pan; you'd have to add a lot more fat to do all the traditional trimmings (roast potatoes around the meat, lots of gravy and Yorkshire pudding as well). Instead, here's how to do an oven roast with lots of flavour instead of fat. The meat is seasoned first, roasted at high temperature to sear it, then at low temperature to keep it moist and tender. Don't be concerned about turning the oven way up to 500F (260C); although some advice about high-temperature roasting includes cautions about fat splattering in the oven and suggests turning off your smoke alarm (don't!), the Beef Information Centre's method of adding water to the roasting pan eliminates any hazards.

4- to 5-lb	oven roast (rump, sirloin tip or inside round)	2 to 2.2 kg
Seasoning Rub:		
1 tbsp	each: olive oil, Worcestershire sauce, Dijon mustard	15 mL
2	cloves garlic, minced	2
1 tsp	each: dried thyme and savory	5 mL
1/2 tsp	freshly ground pepper	2 mL

→ Combine ingredients for Seasoning Rub. Rub all over roast. Add water to roasting pan to depth of 1/2 inch (1 cm). Place roast, fat side up, on rack over water in pan. Place in preheated 500F (260C) oven for 30 minutes. Don't open oven door; reduce heat to 275F (140C). Roast for about 1-3/4 hours longer for medium doneness (160F/70C on meat thermometer). Transfer roast to cutting board; tent with foil and let stand for 15 minutes before carving. Meanwhile, make gravy (see Sidebar). Serve with mashed potatoes or Popovers (page 168) if desired. **Makes 8 to 10 servings**.

Good Gravy (for meat or poultry): We're not making old-fashioned gravy very often anymore; adding a little stock or wine to pan juices and reducing over high heat is preferred to thickening with flour. But for traditional feasts where gravy is back by popular demand, this easy method can be used with any oven-roasted meats or poultry. The flavour and colour of the gravy will be best when sufficient browned residue and fatty drippings are left in the roasting pan. For 2 cups (500 mL) gravy, you'll need about 1/4 cup (50 mL) fat, to which you will add 1/4 cup (50 mL) flour and 2 cups (500 mL) water or stock (beef, chicken or turkey); use the same proportions for larger or smaller quantities of gravy. Measure the fat in the pan (or just go by eye). Drain off any excess (such as from a large turkey); or if you don't have enough (such as from a small or very lean roast), add butter to make up the difference. Place roasting pan over medium-high heat. Stir flour into fat in pan; cook, stirring, for 1 minute. Stir in stock or water. Bring to boil, stirring to scrape up brown bits from bottom of pan. Reduce heat and simmer, stirring often, for 3 minutes or until thickened and smooth. (If too thin, simmer longer until reduced; if too thick, stir in more liquid.) Season with salt and pepper to taste.

Traditional Pot Roast ✤

Nothing beats the aroma of a savoury pot roast simmering away on a wintry afternoon.

This one has wonderful flavour and lots of sauce to spoon over mashed potatoes. For a simpler traditional version, omit the chopped vegetables and tomatoes; add quartered potatoes, carrots and onions to the pot for the last half-hour of cooking.

4-lb	boneless short rib, cross rib, blade or rump roast	2 kg
	All-purpose flour, salt, pepper	
2 tbsp	vegetable oil	30 mL
2	large onions, chopped	2
1 cup	each: chopped celery and carrots	250 mL
2	cloves garlic, minced	2
1 cup	chopped canned tomatoes (or 1 tbsp/15 mL tomato paste)	250 mL
2 cups	beef stock	500 mL
1	bay leaf	1
1/2 tsp	dried thyme	2 mL
4 to 6	potatoes, peeled and quartered (optional)	4 to 6
2	large carrots, cut in thick slices (optional)	2

➜ Dredge meat lightly in flour and sprinkle with salt and pepper. In Dutch oven or large heavy-bottomed pot, heat oil over medium-high heat. Brown meat well on all sides; remove and set aside. To pot, add chopped onions, celery, carrots and garlic; cook, stirring, until softened. Add tomatoes, stock, bay leaf and thyme. Bring to simmer and return meat to pot. Cover and cook over low heat (or transfer pot to 325F/160C oven) for 2-1/2 to 3 hours or until very tender. If desired, add potatoes and carrots for the last 30 minutes of cooking. Remove meat (and potatoes and carrots, if using); cover with foil and keep warm. Remove bay leaf and skim fat from liquid in pot. Pour contents of pot into blender or food processor; purée until smooth. Return sauce to pot and reheat, adding salt and pepper to taste if needed. If sauce is too thick, add a little water; if not thick enough, whisk in about 2 tsp (10 mL) cornstarch dissolved in a little cold water and bring to boil, stirring until thickened. Slice meat and arrange with vegetables on serving platter. Pass sauce separately. **Makes 6 to 8 servings**.

Italian Pot Roast: A classic dish of northern Italy, where it is known simply as "rump of beef braised in red wine." You can make it exactly like the traditional pot roast recipe above, using canned tomatoes and substituting red wine for the beef stock. It is usually prepared ahead, allowed to cool, then sliced, arranged on an ovenproof platter and reheated with sauce poured over. It tastes wonderful served with soft polenta (page 137).

Spicy Salsa Pot Roast: This shortcut sauce produces a very easy, satisfying dish. Instead of the chopped vegetables, stock and herbs in the traditional pot roast recipe, use a mixture of 1 cup (250 mL) bottled salsa, 1/2 cup (125 mL) each ketchup and water, 2 tbsp (30 mL) brown sugar and 1 tbsp (15 mL) red wine vinegar.

Good Gravy Variations: For extra flavour, cook some chopped onions in the fat before adding flour; strain gravy, if desired, before serving. For wine flavour, stir in about 2 tbsp (30 mL) red or white wine or dry sherry along with each cup (250 mL) stock or water. For flavourful turkey gravy, use Giblet Stock (page 92).

Teriyaki Flank Steak

This marinade is a long-time favourite of Murray's. He also recommends it for pork tenderloin and chicken pieces. It makes about 1/2 cup (125 mL), enough for a small flank steak; for larger quantities of meat, double the recipe.

1	flank steak (about 1 lb/500 g)	1

Teriyaki Marinade:

1/3 cup	soy sauce	75 mL
1/4 cup	olive oil	50 mL
2 tbsp	dry sherry	30 mL
1 tbsp	grated fresh ginger	15 mL
1	clove garlic, minced	1
1-1/2 tsp	grated orange rind	7 mL

➜ If flank steak is not already scored, use a sharp knife to score both sides in a diamond pattern. Mix together marinade ingredients; pour over steak in shallow glass dish or zip-top plastic bag; turn to coat both sides. Marinate in refrigerator for at least 12 hours or up to 2 days, turning steak occasionally. Grill over medium-high heat, or broil, for 5 to 7 minutes on each side for medium-rare. Let stand on cutting board for 5 minutes before carving. Carve into thin slices across the grain. **Makes 2 to 4 servings.**

Other Grilled Marinated Steaks

See "Marinating Steaks" (page 73) for cuts and basic method. For the marinade, use Teriyaki Flank Steak marinade (above) or Red Wine Marinade (page 110).

Sautéed Steak with Red Wine Shallot Sauce

You could save this recipe just for Valentine's Day, but why not give in more often?

This updated version of a French classic is still seductively flavourful but slimmed down, using today's lean beef and much less butter. Serve tiny potatoes, baby carrots and fresh green beans alongside the steak.

2 tsp	each: vegetable oil, butter	10 mL
2	rib-eye steaks, about 1 inch (2.5 cm) thick	2
	Salt and freshly ground pepper	
1/2 cup	chopped shallots	125 mL
1/2 cup	red wine	125 mL
1/4 cup	beef stock	50 mL
1 tbsp	chopped parsley	15 mL

➜ In nonstick skillet over medium-high heat, heat oil and butter. Add steaks and cook for about 3 minutes on each side for medium-rare. Sprinkle with salt and pepper. Transfer to plate; place in warm oven. To skillet, add shallots; cook, stirring, until softened, about 2 minutes. Add wine and stock; increase heat and boil rapidly until liquid reduces and thickens slightly. Pour in any juices accumulated on steak plate. Stir in parsley. Place steaks on dinner plates; spoon sauce over. **Makes 2 servings.**

Easy Oven Stew

With this recipe, you don't have to brown the meat first (so it's much easier and lower-fat, too) but it still makes a rich-tasting stew or thick, chunky soup. Serve in large shallow soup bowls with lots of crusty bread. Leftovers reheat and freeze well.

3 lb	stewing beef	1.5 kg
2	large onions, chopped	2
4	cloves garlic, minced	4
1/2 cup	all-purpose flour	125 mL
1 tsp	salt	5 mL
1/2 tsp	each: pepper, dried thyme	2 mL
3 cups	beef stock	750 mL
1 cup	red wine or water	250 mL
1	can (14 oz/398 mL) tomato sauce	1
1	bay leaf	1
4	medium carrots, sliced	4
4	medium potatoes, diced	4

→ Trim beef and cut into 1-inch (2.5 cm) chunks. Place in roasting pan or large casserole. Add onions, garlic, flour, salt, pepper and thyme; mix well. Stir in stock, wine and tomato sauce. Add bay leaf. Cover with lid or foil. Bake in 350F (180C) oven for 1 hour; stir in carrots, cover and bake for 1 more hour; stir in potatoes and bake for 30 minutes longer or until meat is very tender. If too thick, add a little water; if too thin, remove lid and let the liquid cook down. Remove bay leaf. Taste and add salt or pepper if needed. **Makes about 8 servings**.

Chunky Beef Vegetable Soup: Add extra vegetables such as diced rutabaga, sliced green beans or green peas. Add a little water to give desired thickness.

Oven Beef Bourguignon: Use 2 cups (500 mL) each red wine and beef stock. Instead of carrots, add 24 peeled pearl onions; instead of potatoes, add 24 small white mushrooms.

Beer-Braised Beef

Turn inexpensive braising steak into a full-flavoured saucy stew to serve over mashed potatoes for a deliciously comforting dinner. (For a chunkier stew, buy an extra-thick steak, and cut beef and vegetables into larger cubes.) Or for meat pies taken to new heights, transform the same stew into individual Deep-Dish Steak Pies with puff pastry toppings (recipe below)—perfect fare for a pub party at your house.

2 lb	boneless blade, cross rib or round steak	1 kg
1/2 cup	all-purpose flour	125 mL
2 tsp	salt	10 mL
1 tsp	pepper	5 mL
2 tbsp	vegetable oil	30 mL
1 cup	chopped onions	250 mL
2	cloves garlic, minced	2
2 cups	beef stock	500 mL
1	bottle or can beer (about 340 mL), preferably ale	1
1 cup	plain tomato sauce (or 7-1/2-oz/ 213 mL can)	250 mL
1 tbsp	Worcestershire sauce	15 mL
1	bay leaf	1
1/2 tsp	dried thyme	2 mL
2	carrots, diced	2
2	potatoes, peeled and diced	2
1/2 cup	diced celery	125 mL
1 cup	halved small mushrooms	250 mL

➡ Cut beef into small cubes. In plastic bag, combine flour, salt and pepper. Add beef and shake to coat; reserve remaining flour mixture. In large heavy saucepan over medium-high heat, heat oil; brown beef cubes well in batches, adding a little more oil if necessary. Add onions and garlic; cook until softened. Add stock, beer, tomato sauce, Worcestershire sauce, bay leaf and thyme. Bring to boil, stirring well to scrape brown bits from bottom. Reduce heat, cover and simmer for 1 hour or until meat is nearly tender. Add carrots, potatoes and celery; cover and simmer for 30 minutes; add mushrooms and simmer for 15 minutes longer or until meat and vegetables are tender. If mixture needs thickening, mix reserved flour mixture with a little cold water until smooth; stir into beef mixture and bring to boil, stirring; simmer for 5 minutes. Remove bay leaf. Taste and adjust seasoning. **Makes about 6 servings**.

Deep-Dish Steak Pies

Prepare Beer-Braised Beef (may be made ahead and refrigerated for up to 2 days).
You will need 8 individual casserole dishes of about 1-1/4-cup (300 mL) capacity.

Thaw 1 package (about 14 oz/400 g) frozen puff pastry. On lightly floured surface, roll out to 1/8-inch (3 mm) thickness; cut into 8 rounds about 1 inch (2.5 cm) larger in diameter than the casseroles (pastries will puff up during baking and shrink slightly in diameter). Place on baking sheet. Chill for about 15 minutes. Brush with lightly beaten egg. Bake in 400F (200C) oven for 15 minutes or until puffed and golden brown. (Pastries can be made up to a day ahead; cover with tea towel and store at room temperature.) Divide beef mixture among casseroles. Cover with foil. Bake in 400F (200C) oven for 15 minutes or until bubbling hot. Remove foil; top each with baked puff pastry and return to oven for 5 minutes. Serve hot. **Makes 8 pies**.

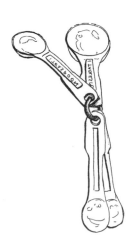

Shepherd's Pie with Garlic Potato Topping ✦

A golden topping of garlic mashed potatoes updates this comfort-food favourite. If you prefer a traditional version, just omit the garlic. A standby dish for many generations, shepherd's pie was originally made with lamb (for obvious reasons); the beef version was sometimes called cottage pie.

1-1/2 lb	ground beef	750 g
1 cup	chopped onions	250 mL
2	cloves garlic, minced	2
1/4 cup	all-purpose flour	50 mL
1/4 tsp	each: pepper, salt, dried thyme and savory	1 mL
2 cups	beef stock	500 mL
2 tsp	Worcestershire sauce	10 mL
1	bay leaf	1
1/2 cup	each: finely diced carrots, corn kernels	125 mL

Topping:

2 lb	potatoes (5 to 6 medium), peeled and cubed (preferably Yukon Gold)	1 kg
6	cloves garlic, peeled and lightly crushed	6
3/4 cup	buttermilk or 2% milk	175 mL
	Salt and pepper to taste	
1	egg, lightly beaten	1

→ In large nonstick skillet over medium heat, cook ground beef until no longer pink, breaking it up as it cooks; drain any excess fat. Add onions and garlic; cook until softened. Stir in flour, pepper, salt, thyme and savory. Add stock, Worcestershire sauce, bay leaf and carrots. Cover loosely and simmer, stirring occasionally, for 20 minutes or until quite thick and carrots are tender. Stir in corn. Add salt to taste. Remove bay leaf. Spread mixture in 11- x 7-inch (28 x 18 cm) baking dish. Let cool slightly.

Topping: In boiling salted water, cook potatoes with garlic until tender. Drain well and mash. Beat in buttermilk, salt and pepper. Reserve 1 tbsp (15 mL) of beaten egg; beat remainder into potatoes. Spread over meat mixture (easiest if you start from the edges); brush with reserved egg. Bake in 400F (200C) oven for 20 minutes or until filling is bubbling. **Makes 6 servings**.

Quick Chili

Countless recipes for chili con carne continue to make the rounds, with an equal number of debates on what's best—authentic Texas-style or '50s diner-style, with beans or without, ground beef or cubed, fiery-hot or darkly mysterious (with a little chocolate as the secret ingredient). Meanwhile, when the kids clamour for a bowlful, or you're having a snack attack that shouts "Chili!" this is a dependable standby.

1-1/2 lb	ground beef	750 g
1 cup	chopped onions	250 mL
2	cloves garlic, minced	2
1 tbsp	chili powder	15 mL
2 tsp	dried oregano	10 mL
1 tsp	ground cumin	5 mL
1/2 tsp	(or to taste) hot pepper flakes or minced jalapeño peppers	2 mL
1/4 tsp	black pepper	1 mL
1	can (28 oz/796 mL) tomatoes (or tomato sauce if you're in a hurry; omit beef stock)	1
1/2 cup	beef stock, beer or water	125 mL
1	can (19 oz/540 mL) red kidney beans, drained	1
	Salt and pepper to taste	

➜ In large nonstick or lightly greased skillet over medium heat, cook ground beef until no longer pink, breaking it up well. Drain off fat. Add onions and garlic; cook until softened, about 3 minutes. Add chili powder, oregano, cumin, hot pepper flakes and black pepper; cook for 1 minute. Add tomatoes (crushed) and their juice; add beef stock. Stir in beans. Cover and simmer for 15 minutes, stirring occasionally. Uncover and simmer for 30 minutes or until desired thickness. Add salt and pepper if needed (or a dash of hot pepper sauce for more heat). Serve in bowls with thick slices of crusty bread or toasted egg bread, OR cook chili until thicker and spoon into taco shells or pitas, OR wrap up in tortillas and serve as burritos. Chili can also be served over rice with toppings of salsa, chopped avocado, sour cream or shredded cheese. **Makes about 6 servings**.
For Marvellous Meatless Chili, see page 140.

Beef and Pork Chili with Ancho Sauce

This deliciously spicy black bean chili is a favourite among many recipes collected by Calgary Herald food editor Cinda Chavich in her research of "Wild West" cooking (old and new). Chilis of all kinds have been popular in Alberta since chuckwagon days.

2	dried ancho chiles	2
1/4 cup	olive oil	50 mL
1 lb	each: pork shoulder meat and beef chuck steak, cut into 1/2-inch (1 cm) cubes	500 g
1	large onion, chopped	1
5	cloves garlic, minced	5
1/4 lb	hot Italian sausage, casings removed	125 g
1 tbsp	ground cumin	15 mL
2 tsp	(or to taste) hot pepper flakes	10 mL
2	cans (19 oz/540 mL each) canned tomatoes, chopped	2
1/4 cup	rye whisky	50 mL
1 tbsp	dried oregano	15 mL
1-1/2 cups	cooked black beans (or 19-oz/540 mL can, drained and rinsed)	375 mL
1/4 cup	tomato paste	50 mL
	Salt and pepper	

➜ Soak anchos in hot water for 20 minutes or until softened; drain. Chop, discarding stems and seeds; set aside. In large Dutch oven over medium-high heat, heat oil. In several batches, brown pork and beef well; remove with slotted spoon and set aside. Reduce heat to medium-low. Add onion, garlic and sausage. Cook, stirring to break up sausage, until onion is soft and sausage is no longer pink, about 4 minutes. Stir in anchos, cumin and hot pepper flakes; cook for 5 minutes. Stir in browned pork and beef, tomatoes and their juice, whisky and oregano. Bring to boil, reduce heat, cover and simmer for 1-1/2 hours. Stir in beans and tomato paste; simmer for 15 minutes. Add salt and pepper to taste. **Makes 8 servings**

Tamale Pie

Tex-Mex fills the bill when you're in the mood for a comforting meal with a zap of hot-and-spicy. This one, from Toronto Star food editor Marion Kane, is a great meatless dish for starving students who will appreciate its low cost. For a meat version, instead of the beans, add 1 lb (500 g) ground beef to the onion mixture and cook for 5 minutes or until no longer pink.

1 tbsp	vegetable oil	15 mL
1	large onion, chopped	1
2	cloves garlic, minced	2
2	cans (19 oz/540 mL each) red kidney beans, drained and rinsed	2
2 tbsp	chili powder	30 mL
1/2 tsp	each: ground cumin, dried oregano, salt	2 mL
1	can (28 oz/796 mL) tomatoes, undrained, chopped	1
1-1/2 cups	corn kernels	375 mL

Cornmeal Topping:

1 cup	all-purpose flour	250 mL
3/4 cup	cornmeal	175 mL
2 tbsp	granulated sugar	30 mL
1 tbsp	baking powder	15 mL
1 cup	milk	250 mL
1	egg	1
2 tbsp	butter, melted	30 mL
1-1/2 cups	shredded cheddar cheese	375 mL

➜ In large skillet over medium-high heat, heat oil. Add onion and garlic; cook until softened, about 4 minutes. Empty one can of beans into bowl; crush with potato masher. Add to onion mixture, stirring to combine. Add remaining can of whole beans. Stir in chili powder, cumin, oregano and salt; cook for 1 minute. Add tomatoes and corn. Bring to boil, reduce heat and simmer for 10 minutes. Pour into 13- x 9-inch (33 x 23 cm) baking dish.

Topping: In bowl, mix together flour, cornmeal, sugar and baking powder. In another bowl, whisk together milk, egg and butter. Pour into flour mixture; stir just until moistened. Spoon topping evenly over bean mixture and sprinkle with cheese. Bake in 350F (180C) oven for 45 minutes or until topping springs back when lightly touched. **Makes 6 servings.**

Beef Noodle Skillet Dinner 👦

Youngsters love this busy-day standby—and it's good for them, too. You could always play a game with them: "Find the Four Food Groups." (Well, maybe not.) Any kind of pasta will do (try it with rotini spirals), and Italian-seasoned tomato sauce or stewed tomatoes can stand in for the spaghetti sauce.

2 cups	egg noodles	500 mL
1/2 lb	ground beef	250 g
1	small onion, chopped	1
1	small sweet green pepper, chopped	1
1/2 cup	coarsely chopped mushrooms	125 mL
2 cups	meatless spaghetti sauce (homemade or store-bought)	500 mL
	Salt and pepper to taste	
1/2 cup	diced cheddar or mozzarella cheese	125 mL

➜ Cook noodles in large pot of boiling salted water until tender but still firm, about 6 minutes. Drain and set aside. Meanwhile, in large nonstick skillet over medium heat, cook ground beef until no longer pink; stir often to break up meat as it cooks. Drain off fat. Add onion, green pepper and mushrooms. Cook, stirring often, until softened, about 2 minutes. Stir in sauce. Season with salt and pepper if needed. Stir in cheese. Add noodles to skillet. Stir to combine, then cover for 1 to 2 minutes or until heated through. **Makes about 4 kid-size servings**.

Beef Noodle Casserole: Prepare skillet dinner as above, omitting diced cheese. Pour into 6-cup (1.5 L) casserole dish. Sprinkle with 1/2 cup (125 mL) shredded cheese. Cover with lid or foil. Bake in 350F (180C) oven for about 20 minutes or until bubbling.

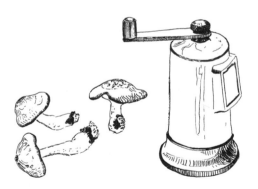

Pork

Today's pork is very lean and should be cooked to medium (160F/70C on meat thermometer) with a hint of pink in the centre. Cooking to a higher temperature dries out and toughens the meat. The exceptions are ground pork and sausage, which, like all ground meats, should be cooked through thoroughly (no pink colour remaining).

Broiling: (steaks, side or back ribs, chops, ground pork burgers, kabobs) Broil 3 to 5 inches (8 to 13 cm) from heat source.

Barbecuing/Grilling: (side, back or country-style ribs; loin roasts, leg roasts, rack, steaks, chops, sausage, burgers, kabobs) Cook over low to medium heat.

Stir-frying: (strips, cubes, ground) Use small amount of oil over medium-high heat.

Pan-frying: (chops, steaks, tenderloin, cutlets, scaloppine, sausage, burgers) In small amount of oil, brown on high heat, then cook at medium-high until done.

Roasting: (loin roasts, leg roasts, rack, crown roast, shoulder butt roast, tenderloin) Roast uncovered in 325F (160C) oven (375F/190C for tenderloin).

Braising: (shoulder butt or picnic roast, leg steaks and roasts, loin or rib steaks and chops, shoulder steaks and chops; side, back or country-style ribs; leg cutlets, pork strips or cubes) Use small amount of liquid in pan; simmer, covered, over low heat on stovetop or in 325F (160C) oven until tender.

Stewing: (cubes, strips; side, back or country-style ribs; shoulder steaks and chops) Brown meat in a little fat; cover with liquid; simmer, covered, over low heat or in 325F (160C) oven until tender.

Pork Roasting Guide

	Minutes per lb (500 g) (325F/160C oven)
Loin: centre cut or	
rib end, bone-in	20–25
single loin, boneless	20–25
double loin, boneless	30–35
crown roast	10–15
Leg: boneless	20–25
Shoulder: butt or picnic	
boneless	30–35
bone-in	25–30

Roast Loin of Pork with Cider

Apple is a traditional accompaniment to roast pork, and here a little apple cider adds moistness as well as a mellow flavour that's compatible with whichever of these seasoning rubs you choose. Roasted potatoes and root vegetables (page 154) or baked squash can cook in another pan alongside. If you buy a bone-in roast, have the butcher crack the chine bone, which runs the length of the roast, so it can be carved easily.

Herb Seasoning Rub:

3 tbsp	grainy mustard	45 mL
1 tbsp	olive oil	15 mL
2	cloves garlic, minced	2
1 tsp	each: dried sage, savory, rosemary, thyme	5 mL

Spicy Seasoning Rub:

2 tsp	each: chili powder, ground cumin, ground coriander, brown sugar	10 mL

1/2 tsp	each: cinnamon, salt, pepper	2 mL
2 tbsp	olive or vegetable oil	30 mL
3-lb	boneless pork loin roast (or 5 lb/2.2 kg bone-in)	1.5 kg
3/4 cup	apple cider or juice	175 mL

➜ Mix together ingredients for either Herb or Spicy Seasoning Rub. Rub all over roast. Place in shallow roasting pan just large enough to hold it. Roast, uncovered, in 425F (220C) oven for 20 minutes. Pour cider around meat. Reduce heat to 325F (160C) and roast, basting meat occasionally with pan juices, for 1 to 1-1/2 hours or until meat thermometer registers 160F (70C). Remove meat, tent with foil and let stand for 10 minutes before carving. If desired, place roasting pan over high heat and reduce pan juices to serve with the meat. **Makes 6 servings**

Stuffed Pork Tenderloin

Easy but impressive, this dish is perfect for entertaining. The mushroom-spinach stuffing is stylish, or try any of the poultry stuffings on page 95, reducing the recipes to give about 2 cups (500 mL) stuffing.

Mushroom-Spinach-Pine Nut Stuffing:

For 2 pork tenderloins (about 3/4 lb/375 g each). In skillet over medium-high heat, melt 1 tbsp (15 mL) butter. Sauté 1 chopped small onion, 1 minced garlic clove and 1 cup (250 mL) chopped mushrooms for 3 minutes or until softened. Stir in 4 cups (1 L) fresh spinach leaves; cover and cook for 2 minutes; uncover and cook for 2 minutes or until liquid evaporates. Transfer to bowl. Stir in 1 cup (250 mL) fresh breadcrumbs, 1/4 cup (50 mL) toasted pine nuts, a squeeze of lemon juice and salt and pepper to taste.

Tenderloin:

Butterfly each tenderloin by slicing almost in half lengthwise; open them out and pound to flatten slightly. Spread stuffing down centres, leaving a 1-inch (2.5 cm) border around edges. Bring long edges together and secure with string or skewers, tucking narrow end of meat inside. In oiled skillet over medium-high heat, brown tenderloins on all sides, about 5 minutes. Transfer to small roasting pan. Roast in 375F (190C) oven for 25 to 30 minutes or until juices run clear when meat is pierced with skewer. Remove string or skewers and cut meat into thick slices. **Makes 4 servings**.

Ribs: Spareribs (also called side ribs) and back ribs (which are meatier) can be interchanged in most recipes. Country-style ribs are cut from the rib end portion of a pork loin and include loin meat as well as ribs; this cut can be cooked like a roast or grilled over medium-low heat.

Other Ways to Cook Pork Tenderloin

Roasted or Grilled: Marinate if desired (see Marinades, page 110) OR rub with either of the seasoning rubs for Roast Loin of Pork, cover and refrigerate for about 1 hour. Roast in 400F (200C) oven OR grill over medium heat, turning occasionally, for 25 to 30 minutes or until cooked through (a hint of pink in centre is fine).

Saucy Medallions: Cut tenderloin into 1-inch (2.5 cm) slices; pound to flatten slightly. Sauté in skillet and add desired sauce, just as for pork chops in Speedy Skillet Chops (page 107). Sliced pork tenderloin can also be used in stir-fries.

Barbecued Spareribs (grilled or baked)

The secret to tender, juicy ribs with lots of flavour is to simmer them first, then marinate in sauce before grilling or oven-baking.

3 to 4 lb	pork spareribs or back ribs	1.5 to 2 kg
	Barbecue Sauce (page 238)	

➜ Cut ribs into portions of about 3 ribs each. In large saucepan, cover ribs with salted water. Bring to gentle boil; cook, covered, for 45 minutes or until tender. Drain and place ribs in large zip-top plastic bag or large dish. Add choice of Barbecue Sauce; turn ribs to coat well. Marinate in refrigerator for at least 2 hours or up to 24.

To Grill: Remove ribs from sauce (reserve sauce) and place on grill over medium heat. Grill for 15 to 20 minutes, turning occasionally and brushing with reserved sauce.

To Oven-Bake: Arrange ribs (with sauce) in single layer in shallow roasting pan. Bake in 400F (200C) oven for about 40 minutes, turning ribs occasionally and basting with sauce. **Makes about 4 servings**.

Barbecued Pork Chops or Chicken: Instead of ribs, use pork chops or chicken pieces. Eliminate precooking. Remove skin from chicken; trim visible fat from chicken or chops. Marinate in the sauce, then grill or bake same as for ribs.

Pork Chops

Today's pork chops (especially loin chops) are very lean and cook fast. To keep them moist and tender, the cardinal rule is Don't Overcook.

Loin or rib chops (bone-in or boneless, 3/4 inch/2 cm thick)

To pan-fry: Season chops with salt and pepper. In lightly oiled nonstick skillet over medium-high heat, cook for 3 minutes on each side or until just cooked through (a hint of pink is fine); don't overcook. A ridged grill pan on the stovetop is an excellent alternative to a skillet for cooking pork chops (they can be marinated or simply sprinkled with salt and pepper); it cooks them quickly without drying out and leaves attractive grill marks.

Breaded chops: A light, crisp crumb coating helps to keep very lean pork or veal chops moist and tender. Prepare chops in the same way as Speedy Schnitzel (page 115). Brown the chops lightly on both sides, then reduce heat and cook, turning once or twice, until dark golden brown and just cooked through (don't cover pan or crumbs will get soggy).

Grilled Chops: see page 106.

Skillet Chops with sauces: see page 107.

Barbecued Chops, baked or grilled: see page 85.

Shoulder chops or steaks are best braised: Brown first, then add a small amount of liquid, cover and simmer over low heat or in 325F (160C) oven until tender, about 30 minutes.

Smoked and Cured Cuts

Cottage roll: Boneless shoulder butt cured in brine ("sweet-pickled"). To cook: Remove plastic wrapper, leaving netting in place. Cover with water in large pot. Bring to boil, reduce heat, cover and simmer for 35 minutes per pound (500 g).

Smoked picnic shoulder: Smoked and cured; boneless or bone-in. To cook: Cover with water in large pot. Bring to boil, reduce heat, cover and simmer for 2 to 2-1/2 hours (160F/70C on meat thermometer).

Peameal bacon: Cut from loin; cured in brine. Generally coated in cornmeal. *To cook whole:* Place in baking pan with 1/2 cup (125 mL) water or apple juice. Cover and bake in 325F (160C) oven for 20 minutes per pound (500 g). *To cook sliced:* Cut into thick or thin slices; pan-fry or grill until lightly browned and liquid has evaporated.

Smoked back bacon: Sold as whole piece or sliced. It is fully cooked and needs only heating; pan-fry or broil.

Pancetta: An Italian bacon that is cured but unsmoked, usually sold rolled up; commonly used (usually chopped) in Italian cooking.

Prosciutto: Italian ham that is salt-cured and air-dried, not smoked. Ready to eat and best eaten as is, but can be added at end of cooking. True prosciutto di Parma is highest quality.

Tourtière ✦

This famous meat pie was once a symbol of French-Canadian cooking. Now it's made for special occasions and still tastes wonderful—especially made with today's much leaner ground pork. Serve the tourtière warm, with chunky chili sauce, chutney-type relish or pickled beets.

1-1/2 lb	ground pork	750 g
1 cup	water	250 mL
3/4 cup	finely chopped onion	175 mL
1/4 cup	finely chopped celery	50 mL
2	cloves garlic, minced	2
1 tsp	salt	5 mL
1/2 tsp	dried savory	2 mL
1/4 tsp	each: dried thyme, ground cloves, pepper	1 mL
1	bay leaf	1
1/2 cup	mashed potato	125 mL
	Pastry for double-crust 9-inch (23 cm) pie	

Glaze: 1 egg yolk beaten with 1 tbsp (15 mL) milk

➜ In large heavy saucepan, combine pork, water, onion, celery and garlic. Cook over medium high heat until bubbling, stirring to break up meat. Add salt, savory, thyme, cloves, pepper and bay leaf. Reduce heat, cover and simmer, stirring occasionally, for 30 minutes. Remove bay leaf. Stir in mashed potato, mixing well. Taste and add more salt and pepper if needed. Let cool, stirring occasionally (mixture will thicken as it cools). Line pie plate with pastry. Fill with meat mixture. Cover with remaining pastry; seal and crimp edges; cut a few steam vents. Brush top crust with glaze. If desired, decorate with pastry cutouts; brush with glaze. Bake in 425F (220C) oven for 15 minutes; reduce heat to 375F (190C) and bake for 20 to 25 minutes longer or until golden brown. **Makes about 6 servings**.

Glazed Baked Ham

For festive feasts, especially at Easter, a big shiny glazed ham traditionally gets the spotlight. Here are three glazes for a special-occasion bone-in ham; you can use the same glazes on small boneless hams (use half the quantity and just brush on during the last 15 to 30 minutes of heating). Serve glazed ham hot for dinner, or let cool completely and serve cold for a buffet; enjoy leftovers in sandwiches and salads.

To bake ham (4 to 5 lb/2 to 2.2 kg):
➜ Remove rind from ham. Score fat surface in diamond pattern; if desired, stud with whole cloves. Place ham in shallow roasting pan. Bake in 325F (160C) oven for 1 hour. Spread glaze over ham. Bake for 30 minutes longer, basting occasionally with melted glaze in pan. For darker colour, increase heat to 425F (220C) for the last few minutes. Let stand for 15 minutes before carving. **Makes 10 to 12 servings**.

Traditional Glaze: Mix together 1 cup (250 mL) brown sugar, 1 tbsp (15 mL) all-purpose flour, 1 tsp (5 mL) dry mustard, 2 tbsp (30 mL) cider vinegar.

Maple-Mustard Glaze: Mix together 1/4 cup (50 mL) each maple syrup, brown sugar and Dijon mustard.

Orange or Apricot Glaze: Mix together 1/2 cup (125 mL) apricot jam or orange marmalade, 2 tbsp (30 mL) Dijon mustard, 1 tsp (5 mL) ground ginger.

Hamming It Up

The choice is yours—today's hams come in all shapes and sizes. Nearly all are cured, smoked and sold fully cooked, often labelled "ready-to-serve." They can be eaten as is but benefit from heating through in the oven.

To heat: Place in shallow roasting pan and bake in 325F (160C) oven for 15 minutes per pound (500 g) or until meat thermometer registers 140F (60C). Let stand for 10 to 15 minutes before carving to allow juices to settle.

- Bone-in hams (skin-on) are available in whole, shank end, and butt end cuts.

- Boneless "whole-muscle" ham is pressed into a football shape and usually has a netting pattern on the surface. Often labelled "Black Forest Style," it is generally less watery than many hams and carries a higher price; it is sold whole, halved or quartered.

- Boneless "dinner hams" are made from chopped meat packed into a cylindrical shape and are lower priced.

- Ham steaks (usually vacuum packed) can be grilled, pan-fried or heated in oven to warm through.

Veal
Veal Scaloppine

A perennial classic on Italian menus and appropriate for both casual and elegant dining, thin slices of sautéed veal are very easy to make at home in any of the traditional variations. The quality of the dish depends, of course, on the quality of the veal, so the first step is finding a butcher shop selling the very best. You can also make this with chicken scaloppine (less expensive and quite satisfactory, though very different in taste). This recipe makes 2 servings, which is manageable in one skillet. If you increase the recipe, cook the scaloppine in batches (don't overcrowd the pan); allow about 4 oz (125 g) scaloppine per serving (slices vary in size).

1/2 lb	veal scaloppine	250 g
	Salt, pepper, all-purpose flour	
2 tsp	each: olive oil, butter	10 mL

➜ If necessary, pound scaloppine lightly to a little less than 1/4-inch (5 mm) thickness. Sprinkle each piece lightly with salt and pepper; dredge lightly in flour, shaking off excess. In large skillet over medium-high heat, heat oil and butter. Cook scaloppine for 1 to 2 minutes on each side or until golden brown. Remove from skillet and keep warm. Continue with variation of your choice, then arrange veal on serving plate and pour sauce over.

Veal Piccata: To skillet, add 3 tbsp (45 mL) each white wine and lemon juice; bring to boil, stirring; reduce heat and simmer until reduced a little. Whisk in 2 tbsp (30 mL) softened unsalted butter, 2 tsp (10 mL) finely chopped parsley and, if desired, 1 tbsp (15 mL) capers. Return veal to skillet and simmer for 2 minutes.

Veal Marsala: To skillet, add 1/4 cup (50 mL) dry Marsala, stirring to deglaze pan. Add 1/4 cup (50 mL) veal or chicken stock; cook over medium heat until reduced by one-third. Stir in 2 tbsp (30 mL) softened unsalted butter. Add salt and pepper to taste. Return veal to skillet and simmer for 2 minutes.

Veal with Mushrooms: Before browning veal in skillet, cook 1-1/2 cups (375 mL) sliced mushrooms until softened; remove and set aside. Add a little more butter and oil; brown and remove veal. Add 1/4 cup (50 mL) dry Marsala or white wine and 1/4 cup (50 mL) whipping cream; cook until reduced and thickened. Add salt and pepper to taste. Return veal and mushrooms to skillet and simmer for 2 minutes.

Sautéed Calf's Liver

This is one of those dishes that stays popular in restaurants, yet most people say they don't make it at home, or are unhappy with the results. The most important step to success is finding top-quality liver—young, tender, light in colour, thinly sliced, no gristle. Then, don't overcook.

➜ Sprinkle liver lightly with salt and pepper; dredge lightly in flour, shaking off excess. In nonstick skillet, heat a little oil (or half oil, half butter) over medium-high heat. Add liver and sauté, turning once, for about 2 minutes on each side, until nicely browned and just cooked through (or a little pink inside, if you prefer); don't overcook. If desired, stir in a splash of balsamic vinegar. Serve immediately.

For **Veal Chops:**
Speedy Skillet Chops (page 107)
Grilled Chops (page 106)
For **Osso Bucco** (page 89)

Other Meats

In among all the usual packages at the supermarket meat counter, you may have noticed a few newcomers, mysterious to many Canadians but familiar to others who've always enjoyed them in traditional dishes.

Rabbit is common in Britain and most European countries (try substituting it for chicken in braised dishes and stews).

Goat is a favourite in West Indian curries and in Greek and other Mediterranean traditions, especially at Easter.

Bison, venison, wild boar (farm-raised game) have become extremely popular in specialty butcher shops. Also watch for *ostrich* and *emu,* meaty-textured birds that have become trendy on the restaurant scene. All of these specialty meats are raised in Canada and becoming much more readily available. All of them also happen to be very lean, making them popular for their healthy attributes as well as novel flavours.

Lamb

Roast Leg of Lamb

Rosemary, garlic and lamb are made for each other and send lovely aromas wafting through your kitchen. This makes a fine centrepiece for a dinner with an Eastern Mediterranean theme (see Menus, pages 261-268).

4-lb	(approx) leg of lamb (bone-in, short shank)	2 kg
3	cloves garlic, slivered	3
2 tbsp	olive oil	30 mL
1 tbsp	lemon juice	15 mL
2 tbsp	chopped fresh rosemary (or 2 tsp/10 mL dried)	30 mL
1 tsp	salt	5 mL
1/4 tsp	freshly ground pepper	1 mL

➡ Using sharp knife, remove the fell (thin parchment-like covering) from lamb. With tip of knife, cut small slits all over lamb and insert slivers of garlic. Combine oil, lemon juice, rosemary, salt and pepper; rub all over lamb. (Alternatively, crush garlic, combine with rest of ingredients and rub over surface and into slits.) Place in shallow roasting pan; let stand for 30 minutes at room temperature. Roast lamb at 475F (240C) for 15 minutes. Reduce heat to 325F (160C) and roast for 1-1/2 to 2 hours longer or until meat thermometer registers 140F (60C) for rare or 160F (70C) for medium. Cover with foil and let stand for 10 minutes before carving. **Makes about 6 servings.**

Roast Rack of Lamb

This is the classic herb-crusted rack of lamb, just right for a special dinner. This recipe uses packaged frozen racks (packed 2 per box), which are quite small. Other racks usually weigh about 1 lb (500 g) each. If using larger racks, roast for 5 to 10 minutes longer (cover loosely with foil if coating starts to brown too much). The racks should be "frenched" (fat and meat cleaned off the top inch or two of the bones); you can do it yourself or ask the butcher to do it.

4	racks of lamb (two 1-1/4 lb/625 g frozen packages, thawed)	4
1/2 cup	fine dry breadcrumbs	125 mL
1/4 cup	finely chopped parsley	50 mL
2 tsp	each: finely chopped fresh oregano and rosemary (or 1/2 tsp/2 mL dried)	10 mL
2	cloves garlic, minced	2
	Salt and pepper to taste	
1 tbsp	olive oil	15 mL
2 tbsp	Dijon mustard	30 mL

➡ Mix together breadcrumbs, parsley, oregano, rosemary, garlic, salt, pepper and oil. Brush lamb racks with mustard; press crumb mixture evenly on top. Roast in 425F (220C) oven until meat thermometer inserted in thickest part of meat registers 130F (54C) for rare, 140F (60C) for medium-rare, about 20 to 25 minutes. Remove from oven, cover with foil and let stand for 5 minutes. To serve, slice between bones to separate chops. **Makes 4 to 6 servings.**

Lovely Lamb

Fresh lamb is a treat. It's available in season (locally raised or imported, mostly from New Zealand and sometimes Australia) and worth watching for at the meat counter. Good-quality frozen lamb is readily available year-round in a wide variety of cuts:

Leg roasts: Bone-in (short shank) and boned (with tunnel for stuffing) can both be oven-roasted. Boneless butterflied leg can be marinated and grilled or broiled, or stuffed, rolled and oven-roasted.

Shoulder roasts: Usually boned and rolled; can be roasted but best braised.

Lamb racks: Usually 6 or 7 ribs per rack weighing up to 1 lb (500 g); roast or grill.

Lamb chops: Loin, rib (grill or pan-fry); shoulder (braise, or marinate and grill or pan-fry).

Lamb loins: Grill or roast whole or cut into medallions.

Lamb tenderloins: Tiny and delicious; grill or sauté.

Glazed Grilled Rack of Lamb: Trim most of fat from racks; make tiny slits in surface and insert slivers of garlic. Grill over medium-high heat in covered barbecue for about 10 minutes on each side or until medium-rare. Brush during last 5 minutes with glaze (about 1/4 cup/50 mL for each rack). For Orange Glaze, mix equal parts honey and orange juice concentrate; for Apricot Glaze, mix apricot jam with a little soy sauce and Dijon mustard.

Braised Lamb Shanks

Hearty, flavourful and the very essence of comfort food, this dish takes the chill out of a wintry evening and makes family and guests smile. Lamb shanks are perfect weekend fare; once the preparation is done, put them in the oven and savour the aroma of dinner to come. Serve with garlic mashed potatoes, polenta, rice or couscous.

2 tbsp	olive oil	30 mL
4	lamb shanks (about 3 lb/1.5 kg)	4
1-1/2 cups	chopped onions	375 mL
4	cloves garlic, minced	4
1 cup	chopped carrots	250 mL
1/2 cup	chopped celery	125 mL
1	can (19 oz/540 mL) tomatoes with juice, crushed	1
3/4 cup	each: beef stock, red wine	175 mL
2	strips lemon rind	2
1/2 tsp	each: dried thyme, rosemary, salt, pepper	2 mL
1	bay leaf	1
1/4 cup	chopped parsley	50 mL

Gremolata:

1/4 cup	minced Italian parsley	50 mL
2	cloves garlic, minced	2
2 tbsp	coarsely grated lemon rind	30 mL

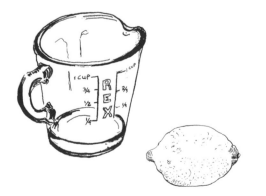

➜ In Dutch oven or large heavy pot over high heat, heat oil. Add lamb shanks. Brown well on all sides; remove. To pot, add onions, garlic, carrots and celery; reduce heat to medium. Cook, stirring occasionally, until softened, about 10 minutes. Add tomatoes, stock, wine, lemon rind, thyme, rosemary, salt, pepper and bay leaf; bring to boil. (If you're not using an ovenproof Dutch oven, transfer mixture to large casserole.) Return shanks to sauce. Cover and bake in 350F (180C) oven for 2 to 2-1/2 hours or until tender. Uncover and bake 30 minutes longer, or until sauce is thickened and meat is very, very tender. Add salt and pepper if needed. Remove bay leaf and lemon rind. Skim fat. Combine ingredients for gremolata (a traditional garnish) and sprinkle over each serving (or just sprinkle with parsley). **Makes 4 servings**.

Osso Bucco, or braised veal shanks, is an Italian classic that's been around forever, but its rustic satisfaction has been rediscovered, making it popular on restaurant menus and in home kitchens. Veal shanks are readily available at many butcher shops, and you can make a terrific Osso Bucco by following the Braised Lamb Shanks recipe. Instead of lamb, use 4 to 6 pieces meaty veal shanks, about 1-1/2 inches (4 cm) thick. Sprinkle them with salt and pepper and dredge in flour before browning. You can use chicken stock and white wine (as some traditional recipes do), but beef stock and red wine give a rich, dark colour and flavour that is wonderful with meat so tender it falls off the bones. A garnish of gremolata is a must.

Grilled Butterflied Leg of Lamb

Butterflied leg of lamb is quick cooking, easy to carve and an ideal cut for grilling or broiling. Butterflied means boned and opened up, and because it has thick and thinner sections, it provides a choice of rare and more well done meat.

3-lb	(approx) butterflied leg of lamb	1.5 kg
	Herbed Citrus or Red Wine Marinade (page 110)	

➡ Trim fat from lamb. Place in large shallow glass dish or zip-top plastic bag. Combine marinade ingredients; pour over lamb, turning to coat both sides. Cover and marinate in refrigerator for 4 to 8 hours. Remove from refrigerator 1 hour before grilling. Preheat grill to high. Sear lamb for about 3 minutes on each side. Reduce heat to medium (or move lamb to unheated side of grill). Close lid if using covered barbecue. Cook for 10 minutes, turn and cook for about 10 minutes longer (the thinnest parts will be medium to well done but the thickest part should be still quite rare in the centre because it will continue to cook as it stands). Transfer lamb to cutting board, cover with foil and let stand for 10 minutes. Carve across the grain into thin slices. **Makes about 6 servings**.

Broiled Butterflied Leg of Lamb: Broil about 6 inches (15 cm) below heat for 25 to 30 minutes, turning two or three times and brushing with any remaining marinade.

For **Lamb Chops:**

See *Speedy Skillet Chops* (page 107)

See *Grilled Chops* (page 106)

Quick Mixed Grill: A great standby for easy family meals, and special enough for a weekday dinner guest. Broil lamb chops and vegetables all on the same broiler pan (or use stovetop ridged grill pan if making only 2 servings). The chops can be marinated in the morning and refrigerated, or at the last minute just brushed with olive oil and sprinkled with salt, pepper, crushed garlic and a little rosemary or mixed herbs. Choose vegetables that will cook in about the same length of time as the chops (sliced eggplant, peppers, fennel, zucchini; plum tomato halves, mushrooms); brush with oil and sprinkle with seasonings (same as chops). Broil or grill for 8 minutes, turning once, or until chops are medium-rare and vegetables tender (if some vegetables are cooked before the others, remove and set aside). Serve with crusty bread.

Navarin of Lamb

Among the many classic lamb stews we know and love—Irish lamb stew, Lancashire hot pot, ragoût of lamb with flageolet beans—this French casserole is one of the most flavourful.

2 lb	lean boneless lamb	1 kg
1 tbsp	each: olive oil, butter	15 mL
1/4 cup	brandy	50 mL
1/2 cup	finely chopped onion	125 mL
4	cloves garlic, minced	4
2 tbsp	each: all-purpose flour, brown sugar, red wine vinegar, tomato paste	30 mL
2 cups	beef stock	500 mL
1/2 tsp	each: dried rosemary, thyme, salt, pepper	2 mL
1	bay leaf	1
	Strip of lemon rind (4 inches/10 cm)	
3	carrots, sliced	3
1 cup	cubed white turnip or rutabaga	250 mL
6	small new potatoes, halved	6
18	pearl onions, peeled	18
1 cup	halved snow peas or frozen green peas	250 mL
1/4 cup	chopped parsley	50 mL

➡ Cut lamb into 1-1/2-inch (4 cm) cubes. In large skillet over medium-high heat, heat oil and butter. Brown lamb in batches, removing it to a large casserole. Pour brandy into skillet, stirring to scrape up brown bits. There should be about 2 tbsp (30 mL) drippings left in skillet (add a little more oil if necessary). Add onion and garlic; cook until softened. Stir in flour, brown sugar, vinegar and tomato paste. Gradually stir in stock. Bring to boil, stirring. Add rosemary, thyme, salt, pepper, bay leaf and lemon rind. Pour contents of skillet over meat in casserole. Cover and bake in 350F (180C) oven for 1 to 1-1/2 hours or until meat is nearly tender. Add carrots, turnips, potatoes and onions. Cover and cook for 30 minutes longer or until meat and vegetables are tender. Add peas and cook for about 10 minutes longer. Remove bay leaf and lemon rind. Taste and adjust seasoning. Serve sprinkled with chopped parsley. **Makes about 6 servings**.

Let's Talk Turkey, and Chicken, and Duck...

Poultry

Large or small, a bird in the hand solves
mealtime puzzles—family-style, company-classy,
simply grilled or decadently sauced

Roast Turkey

A cooked-to-perfection bird—tender, juicy, well browned—is what every cook wants to achieve for a special holiday dinner. Here's how in six easy steps. (For self-basting turkeys, follow package directions.)

1. Rinse turkey inside and out with cold water; pat dry. Spoon stuffing into neck cavity; pull neck skin over stuffing and fasten with skewer. Spoon stuffing loosely into body cavity; cover stuffing with slice of bread or close opening with skewer. (For unstuffed turkey, sprinkle inside with salt and pepper; if desired, add a cut-up onion, squeeze of lemon or orange juice and sprinkle of herbs.)

2. Return legs to tucked-in position under band of skin; or tie together with string.

3. Place turkey, breast side up, on rack (a cake cooling rack will do) in shallow roasting pan. Brush turkey with melted butter (about 1/4 cup/50 mL for medium-sized bird); sprinkle lightly with salt.

4. Cover wings with foil or tuck wing tips behind back. Cover turkey loosely with foil, tucking it in at ends and leaving it open at sides.

5. Roast in 325F (160C) oven (see chart for times). Remove foil for the last hour to allow turkey to brown; baste or brush occasionally with pan drippings.

6. Remove from oven and tent with foil to keep warm; let stand for 20 minutes before carving.

Turkey Tips

Thawing frozen turkey: Leave turkey in original plastic wrapper. Thaw in refrigerator, allowing 5 hours per pound (10 hours per kg). (A 20-lb/9 kg bird will take about 4 days to thaw completely.) For faster thawing, place wrapped turkey in sink and cover completely with cold water. Allow 1 hour per pound (2 hours per kg); change water frequently to keep it cold. Refrigerate or cook turkey immediately after thawing. Never thaw turkey at room temperature; never refreeze uncooked turkey. (For other safety tips, see page 257.)

Good Gravy: See page 74. To make turkey gravy extra-flavourful, use Giblet Stock: In saucepan, cover turkey neck and giblets (except the liver) with salted water; add a halved small onion and a few celery leaves. Simmer for 1 hour; strain.

Roasting Times for Stuffed Turkeys: The turkey industry's recommended roasting times are shorter than they used to be; for moist, tender meat, it's important not to overcook. Follow the chart below for approximate roasting times, but allow some extra time because many variables affect cooking time (shape and initial temperature of bird, size of pan, accuracy of oven, etc.); times can vary by an hour or more. When turkey is done, the thickest part of the drumstick will feel soft when pressed, but the most accurate measure of doneness is the temperature of the meat. Use a meat thermometer inserted in the thickest part of inner thigh, not touching bone; turkey is done when thermometer reads 180F (82C) for stuffed turkey, 170F (77C) for unstuffed.

(For unstuffed turkeys, reduce times by 30 minutes.)

Weight	Approximate Roasting Time (325F/160C oven)
6 to 8 lb (3 to 3.5 kg)	3 to 3-1/4 hrs
8 to 10 lb (3.5 to 4.5 kg)	3-1/4 to 3-1/2 hrs
10 to 12 lb (4.5 to 5.5 kg)	3-1/2 to 3-3/4 hrs
12 to 16 lb (5.5 to 7 kg)	3-3/4 to 4 hrs
16 to 22 lb (7 to 10 kg)	4 to 4-1/2 hrs

High-temperature roasting: Although roasting at moderately low temperature (325F/160C) and covering loosely with foil ensures that the breast meat will be juicy and tender, today's shorter roasting times don't always produce as much browning or pan drippings as some people like. Removing the foil for the last hour allows the bird to brown lightly, but for darker browning of the skin (and also for browner, more flavourful drippings for making gravy), try a high-temperature start: Roast at 450F (230C) for the first 45 to 60 minutes. Then reduce heat to 325F (160C) and roast until done, removing foil for the last 30 to 60 minutes and brushing occasionally with pan drippings. Start testing for doneness about 30 minutes earlier than on the chart, but don't be surprised if the total time is about the same.

Roasting pan: Use a metal roasting pan about 2 inches (5 cm) deep; too deep a pan will steam rather than roast the bird. Avoid aluminum foil pans.

Turkey Stuffing

Savoury onion-and-herb stuffing is always popular and adapts easily to new variations. You could offer a choice of stuffings by using one kind in the body and one in the neck cavity (halve the quantity for stuffing neck only). This recipe makes enough stuffing for a 10- to 12-lb (4.5 to 5.5 kg) turkey; for a larger bird, use 1-1/2 times the recipe; for a smaller bird, halve the recipe. The stuffing can also be baked separately in a covered casserole in 350F (180C) oven for about 30 minutes.

1/3 cup	butter	75 mL
2 cups	chopped onions	500 mL
1 cup	chopped celery	250 mL
2 tsp	each: crushed dried sage and savory	10 mL
1/2 tsp	each: dried thyme, pepper	2 mL
1 tsp	salt	5 mL
1/4 cup	chopped parsley	50 mL
8 cups	slightly dry bread cut into small cubes or very coarsely crumbled	2 L

➜ In skillet over medium heat, melt butter. Add onions and celery; cook until softened. (Alternatively, microwave on High for 10 minutes or until softened, stirring once or twice during cooking.) Stir in sage, savory, thyme, pepper, salt and parsley. In very large bowl, combine bread and onion mixture; toss well until moistened. If you prefer a very moist stuffing, or if baking stuffing separately, stir in a little chicken broth.

Roasted Garlic and Apple Stuffing: To cooked onion mixture, add 2 chopped tart apples and the pulp squeezed from 2 heads roasted garlic (page 236).

Mushroom Stuffing: Cook 3 cups (750 mL) sliced mushrooms with onion mixture.

Sausage Stuffing: Cook 1/2 lb (250 g) sausage meat (or Italian sausage with casings removed) with onion mixture.

Cranberry-Apricot Stuffing: Add 1/2 cup (125 mL) each dried cranberries and chopped dried apricots to bread mixture.

Chestnut or Pecan Stuffing: Add 1-1/2 cups (375 mL) chopped roasted chestnuts (see page 236) or pecans to bread mixture.

Roast Turkey Breast

Low-fat, quick-cooking turkey breast gets top marks for versatility: it can be cut into strips or cubes for stir-fries, sliced into cutlets, or butterflied for grilling. Roast turkey breast is easy for family meals anytime and perfect for special occasions when a whole turkey would be too much.

To roast turkey breast: Brush with melted butter and sprinkle with salt and pepper. Cover loosely with foil. Roast in 325F (160C) oven until meat thermometer registers 160F (70C). A turkey breast weighing 2 lb (1 kg) will take about 1 hour, but time will vary according to shape and thickness.

To roast turkey breast with stuffing: Halve the stuffing recipe above; mound stuffing in baking pan, place turkey breast on top and cover with foil.

Glazed turkey breast: Remove foil for last 15 minutes of roasting; brush several times with mixture of 1/4 cup (50 mL) teriyaki sauce and 1 tbsp (15 mL) honey OR mixture of 1/4 cup (50 mL) orange marmalade and 1 tbsp (15 mL) Dijon mustard.

Stuffing

Use slightly dry bread for these stuffings. (If too fresh, spread on baking sheet and let dry for a few hours at room temperature, or place in 350F/180C oven for a few minutes until slightly dry.) To cut into cubes, stack bread slices and cut lengthwise, then crosswise, to make 1/2-inch (1 cm) cubes. To crumble bread, place in food processor and pulse a few times to make very coarse crumbs. Stuff turkey just before roasting. Don't pack stuffing; spoon in loosely for even cooking.

Turkey thighs: Can be roasted like turkey breast. Roast thighs to temperature of 170F (77C) on meat thermometer; 1 lb (500 g) boneless, skinless thighs will take about 1 hour. Braising is another good method for thighs: Brown in Dutch oven, add 1 to 2 cups (250 to 500 mL) liquid such as chicken stock or tomato sauce; cover and simmer until very tender. Thigh meat can also be cut into steak-size portions (pound to flatten) for grilling, or into chunks or strips for stir-frying, kabobs, fajitas or chili.

Turkey drumsticks and wings: (Remove wing tips; reserve for stock if desired.) Simmer in water for 30 minutes, drain and let cool for 10 minutes. Brush with barbecue sauce (see recipes, page 238). Grill over low heat for 30 to 45 minutes (depending on size), or bake in 325F (160C) oven for 1 to 1-1/2 hours or until tender.

Roast Chicken

Two kinds of roast chicken are my ultimate favourites: simple bistro-style poulet rôti (reminiscent of cozy little Left Bank cafés on cold, drizzly days) and traditional stuffed roast chicken like my mother made (and which always prompts my kids to say, "Uh-oh, Mom needs a hug," when they find me roasting chicken on a Sunday afternoon). Both kinds are old-fashioned comfort foods, no apology. But roast chicken is back on the fashionable food scene, too. Though Granny would never recognize it ("Where's the stuffing?"), it's aimed directly at stressed-out urbanites who need a hug (and respite from red peppers, coriander and balsamic on everything). Which is not to say that the new homestyle lacks flavour—in fact, flavour with less fat is what it's all about. But the seasonings are generally calming (mellow garlic scented with sage; lemon soothed with rosemary), rather than revved-up. So take your pick—traditional stuffed chicken or fast and flavourful unstuffed. Here's how to do both at home.

Roast Chicken with Lemon, Rosemary and Garlic

You can vary this with different herbs and citrus fruits, but otherwise the preparation is a popular new basic for a simple, satisfying roast chicken. The main variable you'll find in recipes is roasting temperature. Some call for a fast, high-temperature roasting (450F/230C or even higher), others a long, steady 325F (160C), others a combination of the two. Some even call for turning the bird several times or other unnecessary manoeuvres. Forget all that. A straightforward roasting at 400F (200C) produces crispy, nicely browned skin and moist meat—no fuss, lots of flavour. Serve with another updated comfort food: mashed potatoes with garlic, green onions or herbs (page 157).

➜ Rinse chicken inside and out; pat dry. Squeeze juice from lemon into cavity of chicken. Place the squeezed lemon, onion, rosemary and garlic in the cavity. Tie legs together; tuck wings under back of chicken. Brush outside of chicken with olive oil; sprinkle with salt and pepper. Place chicken, breast side up, on rack in shallow roasting pan. Roast in 400F (200C) oven, basting occasionally with pan juices, for 1-1/4 hours or until chicken is golden brown and juices run clear when thigh is pierced with the point of a sharp knife. **Makes 4 servings**.

1	chicken (about 3 lb/1.5 kg)	1
1/2	lemon	1/2
1	onion, quartered	1
2	large sprigs fresh rosemary (or 1 tsp/5 mL dried)	2
4	cloves garlic	4
	Olive oil, salt, pepper	

Basic Stuffed Roast Chicken

Many people don't think a small chicken can be stuffed and roasted, but this method works fine for any bird between about 2 1/2 and 5 lb (1.25 to 2.5 kg)—just reduce or increase the roasting time by about 30 minutes; use the same test for doneness as in recipe for Roast Chicken with Lemon, Rosemary and Garlic. Larger chickens can be roasted just like small turkeys (page 92). Nothing beats the aroma and flavour of a slow-roasted stuffed chicken, so this is the recipe to choose if you're a starving student away from home (or anyone else, even a mom, just wanting "mom food").

1	chicken (about 4 lb/2 kg)	1
2 tbsp	butter, melted	30 mL

Stuffing:

4	slices slightly dry bread	4
1/4 cup	butter	50 mL
1	small onion, chopped	1
1	stalk celery, chopped	1
2 tsp	dried herbs (mix of sage, savory, thyme)	10 mL
1/4 tsp	salt	1 mL
Pinch	pepper	Pinch

➜ Rinse inside of chicken with cold water; pat dry.

Stuffing: Stack bread slices; with bread knife, cut into small cubes (you should have about 4 cups/1 L); place in large bowl. In large glass measuring cup or bowl, combine butter, onion, celery, herbs, salt and pepper; microwave on High for 1-1/2 minutes or until butter is melted and onion and celery are softened, stirring halfway through. Add to bread and toss well. Taste and add more seasoning if needed. Fill cavity of chicken with stuffing. Cover opening with an end slice of bread or fasten shut with a metal skewer. Tie legs of chicken together tightly with string. Place chicken, breast side up, in shallow roasting pan (a large rectangular cake pan is fine). Brush chicken with the 2 tbsp (30 mL) melted butter. Cover chicken very loosely with foil, tucking it in at the ends but leaving sides open. Roast in 350F (180C) oven for 1-1/4 hours; remove foil and brush chicken with pan drippings. Roast uncovered for 30 minutes longer or until golden brown. (Don't overcook—check occasionally that the chicken is done; the thigh should feel soft when pressed, and the juices should be clear, not pink, when thigh is pierced with the point of a sharp knife.) **Makes 4 servings**. (For gravy, see page 74.)

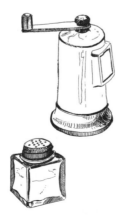

Roast Cornish Hens with Orange-Almond Rice Stuffing

Cornish hens make great dinner-party fare, especially with a flavourful stuffing like this one. The birds are easy to cut in half for serving. You can also roast Cornish hens unstuffed, exactly like chicken (see Roast Chicken with Lemon, Rosemary and Garlic, page 94); reduce roasting time to 45 to 60 minutes.

1 tbsp	butter	15 mL
1/4 cup	slivered blanched almonds	50 mL
1/3 cup	each: chopped onion and celery	75 mL
2 tbsp	shredded orange rind	30 mL
1-1/2 cups	cooked rice (preferably mixture of white and wild)	375 mL
	Salt and pepper	
2	Cornish hens (about 1-1/2 lb/750 g each)	2
	Melted butter	

➜ In large skillet over medium-high heat, melt 1 tbsp (15 mL) butter. Add almonds and cook, stirring, until lightly browned; remove and set aside. Add onion and celery to skillet; cook until softened. Stir in orange rind. Combine with cooked rice, tossing well to mix. Add salt and pepper to taste. Stuff into hen cavities; close openings with small skewers. Tie legs together and tuck wings under backs. Place hens, breast side up, in roasting pan. Brush lightly with melted butter. Roast in 375F (190C) oven, brushing occasionally with pan juices, for 1 hour or until golden brown and juices run clear when thighs are pierced. To serve, remove stuffing. With kitchen shears, cut hens along each side of the backbone; cut rib cage to divide hens in half. Spoon stuffing onto each dinner plate and place hen half on top. **Makes 4 servings**.

Herb-Roasted Chicken Breasts with Garlic, Potatoes and Carrots

Food writer Rose Murray is a pro at updating flavours and streamlining methods. I love the technique she uses here to produce nicely browned, crispy chicken atop savoury vegetables—all in one easy dish.

2 tbsp	each: lemon juice, olive oil	30 mL
1/2 tsp	each: salt, dried rosemary and thyme	2 mL
1/4 tsp	pepper	1 mL
12	cloves garlic, peeled	12
1-1/2 lb	small red potatoes, halved	750 g
4	carrots, cut in small chunks	4
1/2 lb	small mushrooms	250 g
4	chicken breasts	4
1 cup	chicken stock	250 mL

➜ Combine lemon juice, oil, salt, rosemary, thyme and pepper; set aside. In large shallow baking dish, toss together garlic, potatoes, carrots, mushrooms and half of the herb mixture; spread out in pan. Arrange chicken, skin side up, on top of vegetables. Sprinkle with remaining herb mixture. (Can be covered and refrigerated for up to 1 day; let stand at room temperature for 30 minutes before baking.) Bake, uncovered, in upper third of 450F (230C) oven for 20 minutes. Reduce heat to 375F (190C). Bake for 25 minutes longer or until chicken is cooked through and vegetables are tender. Transfer chicken and vegetables to heated platter. Add stock to pan and bring to boil, scraping up any brown bits from bottom of pan. Boil until syrupy, about 5 minutes. Pour over chicken and vegetables. **Makes 4 servings**.

Coq au Vin

A bistro classic that we will love forever, this can be cooked entirely in the skillet, but transferring it to the oven means less pot-watching. The dish holds well at low heat if dinner guests are tardy (just don't let it overcook or the chicken will fall off the bones). Red wine and beef stock are uncommon in chicken dishes but give coq au vin its traditional flavour and colour.

3 lb	chicken pieces	1.5 kg
1 tbsp	each: butter, vegetable oil	15 mL
1/4 cup	brandy	50 mL
16	small white mushrooms	16
1/2 cup	chopped onion	125 mL
2	cloves garlic, minced	2
24	pearl onions, peeled	24
2 tbsp	all-purpose flour	30 mL
1 cup	each: beef stock, red wine	250 mL
1/4 tsp	dried thyme	1 mL
1	bay leaf	1
	Salt and pepper	
	Chopped parsley	

➜ Trim any excess fat from chicken. In large nonstick skillet over medium-high heat, heat butter and oil. Brown chicken pieces well on all sides. Remove chicken and place in baking dish. To skillet, add brandy and mushrooms; cook until nearly tender; remove to a bowl. To skillet, add chopped onion, garlic and pearl onions; cook until golden, about 3 minutes. Stir in flour, then stock, wine, thyme and bay leaf. Bring to boil, stirring. Pour over chicken in baking dish. Cover and bake in 350F (180C) oven for 30 minutes or until tender. Add mushrooms; bake for 10 minutes longer. Add salt and pepper to taste. Remove bay leaf. Transfer to deep serving platter; sprinkle with parsley. **Makes 4 servings**.

Company Chicken

Chicken tops every cook's no-fuss-feed-'em-well-and-make-'em-smile list of company favourites. For dishes that can be made ahead and popped into the oven when guests are due, see: Maple-Hoisin Chicken and Lemon-Garlic Chicken (this page), Herb-Roasted Chicken Breasts with Garlic, Potatoes and Carrots (page 96), Tagine of Chicken (page 99), Tandoori-Style Chicken (page 102), Jerk Chicken (page 101), Coq au Vin (page 97), Chicken Cacciatore (page 101) and Baked Chicken Pieces with various marinades (page 106).

Maple-Hoisin Chicken

Ideal for no-fuss dinner parties, this flavourful chicken dish and the Lemon-Garlic version (below) take only a few minutes' preparation. Marinate in refrigerator, then bake when needed. For either recipe, you could use chicken thighs, quarters or mixed pieces instead of breasts. Serve with rice and a fresh vegetable such as green beans or sautéed broccoli (page 155).

1/3 cup	each: hoisin sauce, maple syrup	75 mL
2 tbsp	each: soy sauce, rice vinegar, ketchup	30 mL
1 tbsp	each: minced garlic and fresh ginger	15 mL
8	chicken breasts (bone-in, skin-on or skinless)	8

➜ In large shallow bowl, mix together all ingredients except chicken. Add chicken and turn to coat well on all sides. Cover and refrigerate for at least 2 hours or up to 8 hours; turn chicken occasionally. Place chicken pieces slightly apart in single layer in large shallow baking dish (use two if necessary; chicken will brown best if not crowded). Drizzle any extra marinade over chicken. Bake in 400F (200C) oven for 35 to 40 minutes, brushing chicken once or twice with pan juices during last 10 minutes, until browned and cooked through (juices run clear when chicken is pierced); don't overcook. **Makes 8 servings**.

Lemon-Garlic Chicken: A Middle Eastern blend of ingredients (lemon, garlic, spices and honey) gives great flavour to the chicken and helps it to brown nicely as it cooks. Follow recipe above, replacing Maple-Hoisin marinade with this one: Mix together 1/4 cup (50 mL) each lemon juice and liquid honey, 1 tbsp (15 mL) grated lemon rind, 4 minced garlic cloves, 2 tbsp (30 mL) olive oil and 1/2 tsp (2 mL) each ground cumin, cinnamon, paprika, salt and pepper.

How to bone a chicken breast: If desired, pull skin off breast. Place breast, bone side down, on cutting board. Starting at thickest end of breast, with point of sharp knife make shallow cut between meat and bone. Holding knife almost flat against rib bones, cut with short strokes between meat and bones, lifting meat away from bones.

How to cut up a chicken: Use a very sharp knife; poultry shears are also very helpful. Place chicken, breast side up, on cutting board. Bend one leg away from body until thigh joint pops loose; cut through skin and joint to separate leg from body. If desired, separate thigh and drumstick by cutting through joint. Repeat with other leg. With poultry shears or knife, cut along both sides of backbone and remove. Cut along breastbone to separate breast into 2 halves. If desired, cut off wings at joint OR cut breast halves into two portions (cut crosswise on a diagonal; this leaves 2 breast pieces with wings attached and 2 without); cut off wing tips if desired.

Tagine of Chicken

You don't have to travel to Morocco or even to a Canadian Moroccan restaurant to enjoy a sample of the cuisine. A tagine is a fragrantly spiced stew made with whatever the cook decides that day—meat, fish, poultry, often vegetables, sometimes fruit. Taking the same liberties, we can create a pleasantly exotic, if not totally authentic, dish with chicken and some typically Moroccan ingredients (spices, garlic, preserved lemon, prunes, olives). In place of the traditional conical-lidded earthenware cooking pot (also called a tagine), a Dutch oven does nicely. Serve with couscous.

2 tbsp	olive oil	30 mL
4 lb	chicken thighs	2 kg
	Salt and pepper	
2	onions, thinly sliced	2
4	cloves garlic, minced	4
1 tsp	each: ground cumin, coriander, ginger, paprika	5 mL
1/2 tsp	cinnamon	2 mL
1/4 tsp	hot pepper flakes	1 mL
1	can (28 oz/796 mL) tomatoes	1
1 cup	pitted prunes	250 mL
1 cup	pitted green olives	250 mL
2 tbsp	lemon juice	30 mL
1	preserved lemon, peel only, cut into strips or shredded zest of 1 lemon	1
1/4 cup	chopped fresh coriander	50 mL

➜ In Dutch oven or large heavy pot, heat oil over medium-high heat. Brown chicken in batches, sprinkling with salt and pepper. Remove chicken; set aside. Drain all but 2 tbsp (30 mL) fat from pan. Reduce heat to medium. Add onions, garlic and all the spices; cook, stirring often, for 3 minutes. Crush tomatoes well; stir into pan. Bring to boil. Return chicken to pan. Cover and simmer for 30 to 40 minutes or until chicken is tender. Add prunes, olives, lemon juice and preserved lemon peel. Simmer for a few more minutes until hot. Stir in coriander. Taste and adjust seasoning if necessary. **Makes 6 servings**.

To make ahead: After chicken has simmered until tender, it can be covered and refrigerated for up to 1 day. Reheat gently, adding remaining ingredients, OR instead of simmering chicken on stovetop, transfer to large baking dish and bake in 350F (180C) oven. Refrigerate for up to 1 day. Add remaining ingredients and reheat in oven for 30 minutes or until hot.

Preserved Lemons

A popular ingredient in Moroccan cooking, lemons preserved in salt are available in some specialty shops but can also be made at home. They are used as a condiment and as an ingredient in dishes such as tagines. Usually just the softened rind, not the pulp, is used. For a 4-cup (1 L) canning jar, you will need about 6 small lemons. Scrub them thoroughly and quarter each one lengthwise, but don't cut through stem end. Spread each lemon apart and sprinkle inside liberally with salt (about 1 tbsp/15 mL per lemon). Pack lemons tightly, stem ends down, in sterilized jar. Press them down firmly as you pack them so that no space is left and the juice rises to the top. Squeeze in as many as possible; the top layer should be covered with juice. Cover jar with tight lid and store in cool, dark place for 3 to 4 weeks before using; shake the jar gently every few days. Refrigerate after opening. Rinse lemons before using.

Chicken Breasts with Prosciutto and Fontina

For supper with Italian flair, try this suave version of a classic: breast of chicken rolled around a primo stuffing.

4	boneless, skinless chicken breasts (about 1-1/2 lb/750 g)	4
3 oz	thinly sliced prosciutto	90 g
1 cup	shredded fontina or provolone cheese (or 4 slices)	250 mL
1/4 cup	grated parmesan cheese	50 mL
1-1/2 tsp	chopped fresh sage (or 1/2 tsp/2 mL dried)	7 mL
	Salt and pepper	
1 tbsp	each: olive oil, butter	15 mL
1/2 cup	each: chicken stock and white wine or dry Marsala	125 mL

→ Pound chicken breasts between sheets of plastic wrap to 1/4-inch (5 mm) thickness. Place breasts, smooth side down, on work surface. Top each with one-quarter of the prosciutto, cutting it to fit; top with one-quarter of the fontina, parmesan and sage. Roll up, tucking in sides; secure with toothpicks. Sprinkle rolls lightly with salt and pepper. (Can be covered with plastic wrap and refrigerated for up to 1 day.) In large skillet over medium-high heat, heat oil and butter. Add chicken and cook, turning often, until browned on all sides. Drain excess oil. Add stock and wine, bring to boil, reduce heat, cover and simmer for 10 to 15 minutes or until chicken is cooked through. Remove chicken and cut into slices. Meanwhile, over high heat, reduce liquid in skillet until quite thick; drizzle over chicken. **Makes 4 servings**.

Oven-Fried Chicken ♥ 👨

Baking crispy chicken pieces in the oven is much healthier than frying, and so easy that kids can do it themselves. The chicken can be coated with seasoned breadcrumbs or various other mixtures, but for crispness and colour, we prefer good old cornflake crumbs.

→ For 8 pieces of chicken (bone-in, skin removed; use thighs, breasts or mixed pieces): In shallow dish, mix 1 cup (250 mL) cornflake crumbs with 1/4 tsp (1 mL) each salt and pepper. (Use packaged crumbs, or finely crush 4 cups/1 L cornflakes.) In another dish, combine 1/4 cup (50 mL) Dijon mustard with 1/4 cup (50 mL) yogurt, mayonnaise or creamy salad dressing.

Spread chicken pieces with mustard mixture, then roll in crumb mixture to coat. Place on baking sheet lined with parchment paper, or on lightly oiled or sprayed nonstick baking sheet. Bake in 375F (190C) oven for 40 to 45 minutes or until crisp and cooked through (juices run clear when chicken is pierced).

Chicken Fingers or Nuggets: Cut boneless, skinless chicken breasts into strips or chunks. Prepare same as for Oven-Fried Chicken. Bake for 15 minutes, turn and bake for 10 minutes longer or until crisp and cooked through. For Dipping Sauces, see page 22.

Chicken Cacciatore

A dish that absolutely everyone seems to love, especially if the sausage is included. Serve over pasta, polenta or mashed potatoes.

2 lb	chicken pieces	1 kg
	All-purpose flour, salt, pepper	
1 tbsp	olive oil	15 mL
3	Italian sausages (optional)	3
1	medium onion, chopped	1
2	cloves garlic, minced	2
1	small sweet green pepper, cut into strips	1
1-1/2 cups	sliced mushrooms	375 mL
1/2 cup	chopped celery	125 mL
1	can (28 oz/796 mL) tomatoes	1
1/2 tsp	each: dried basil and oregano	2 mL
	Salt and pepper	
2 tbsp	chopped Italian parsley	30 mL

➜ Dust chicken with flour and sprinkle lightly with salt and pepper. In large deep skillet over medium heat, heat oil. Brown chicken pieces lightly on all sides. Remove and set aside. If using sausages, brown in same pan, then cut into small pieces and set aside with chicken. To skillet, add onion, garlic, green pepper, mushrooms and celery. Cook, stirring occasionally, for 5 minutes or until softened. Add tomatoes (crush as you add them) and herbs. Cover and simmer for 30 to 40 minutes or until chicken is very tender. Season to taste with salt and pepper and garnish with parsley. **Makes 4 servings**.

Jerk Chicken

Spicy grilled chicken Jamaica-style is popular party food. Scotch bonnet peppers are fiery-hot, so add to taste and handle with care (see page 152).

3 lb	chicken pieces (whole legs, drumsticks, thighs or breasts)	1.5 kg
Marinade:		
1 tbsp	granulated sugar	15 mL
2 tsp	each: allspice, dried thyme	10 mL
1 tsp	each: salt and pepper	5 mL
1/2 to 1 tsp	hot pepper flakes or sauce	2 to 5 mL
1/2 tsp	each: cinnamon, nutmeg	2 mL
1/4 cup	each: lime juice, red wine vinegar, soy sauce, vegetable oil	50 mL
1	onion, finely chopped	1
3	cloves garlic, minced	3
1	(or to taste) Scotch bonnet pepper, seeded and minced	1

➜ In large bowl, combine all marinade ingredients, mixing thoroughly. Add chicken, turning to coat with marinade. Cover and refrigerate for 4 to 8 hours. Grill over medium heat, turning occasionally, for 30 to 40 minutes or until cooked through. (Alternatively, place chicken on rack in large roasting pan and bake in 400F (200C) oven for 50 to 60 minutes; turn chicken occasionally and brush with pan drippings until well browned and very tender.) **Makes 6 servings**.

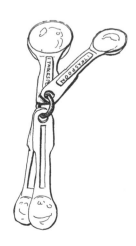

Caribbean Curry Chicken

Strange how family food traditions evolve. Our clan acquired this recipe years ago from our Jamaican friend Claire Ebanks, and it has been a special favourite ever since for family gatherings in the summer. With Caribbean food getting so popular in Canada, we can even get curry like Claire's at a local take-out. Traditionally made with bone-in chicken pieces or goat meat, it is also made with boneless meat and wrapped in a roti. West Indian curry powder gives authentic flavour, colour and aroma; you'll find it in West Indian food shops and some supermarkets. Regular curry powder can be used but the flavour will be a bit different.

2	chickens (about 2 1/2 lb/1.25 kg each), cut into about 10 pieces	2
	Salt and freshly ground pepper	
2	large sprigs fresh thyme (or 2 tsp/10 mL dried)	2
2	onions, chopped	2
4	cloves garlic, minced	4
3 tbsp	vegetable oil	45 mL
2 tbsp	(approx) West Indian curry powder	30 mL
1 cup	chicken stock	250 mL
	Hot pepper sauce to taste	

➡ In large bowl, sprinkle chicken pieces with salt and pepper. Add thyme, onions and garlic; mix well; let stand for about 30 minutes, stirring occasionally. In large deep skillet or heavy pot over medium-high heat, heat oil. Add chicken mixture and cook, stirring often, until lightly browned, about 10 minutes. Add curry powder, stock and hot pepper sauce. Reduce heat, cover and simmer, stirring occasionally, until tender, about 40 minutes. **Makes about 8 servings**.

Tandoori-Style Chicken

Traditional tandoori chicken, cooked in the searing heat of an Indian tandoor (charcoal-fired clay oven), emerges spicy, crisp and terra-cotta-coloured. A reasonable facsimile can be produced in a covered barbecue, but this oven-baked version is much easier. Dark meat is ideal because it doesn't dry out as fast, so you might prefer to use whole legs or thighs only.

3 to 4 lb	chicken pieces (whole legs, thighs, breasts)	1.5 to 2 kg
Marinade:		
1 cup	plain yogurt	250 mL
1/4 cup	lemon or lime juice	50 mL
2 tbsp	each: minced garlic and fresh ginger	30 mL
1 tbsp	paprika	15 mL
1-1/2 tsp	each: ground cumin, ground coriander, turmeric, curry powder, salt	7 mL
1/4 tsp	each: cinnamon, cayenne, pepper	1 mL

➡ Remove skin from chicken. With sharp knife, make 2 or 3 deep slashes almost to bone in each piece. Place in large bowl. Combine marinade ingredients and pour over chicken, turning each piece to coat well and rubbing marinade into slits. Cover and marinate in refrigerator for about 8 hours. Arrange in single layer in large shallow baking pan lined with foil. Bake in 475F (240C) oven for 15 minutes; reduce heat to 400F (200C) and bake for 20 to 30 minutes longer or until cooked through, then place under broiler for a few minutes until browned and crisp. Serve with Cucumber Raita. **Makes 4 servings**

Cucumber Raita: Raita is a cooling Indian condiment served with spicy meats. Combine 1 medium cucumber (peeled, seeded and finely chopped) with 1 cup (250 mL) plain yogurt and 1 tbsp (15 mL) finely chopped fresh mint.

Chicken or Turkey Pot Pie ✦

Pot pies do three things: they make great use of leftovers, they warm the soul on a chilly night, and they bring back great memories of times when every meal was comfort food.

2 tsp	each: butter, vegetable oil	10 mL
3/4 cup	chopped onion	175 mL
1/2 cup	chopped celery	125 mL
2	cloves garlic, minced	2
3/4 tsp	dried thyme	4 mL
1	bay leaf	1
3 cups	chicken or turkey stock	750 mL
1 cup	each: sliced or baby carrots, peeled pearl onions, small mushrooms	250 mL
3 tbsp	cornstarch	45 mL
1/4 cup	whipping cream	50 mL
3/4 cup	frozen green peas	175 mL
2 cups	cooked chicken or turkey in bite-size pieces*	500 mL
	Salt and pepper	
	Topping: see right	

* If you don't have leftover roast turkey or chicken, simmer about 1 lb (500 g) boneless, skinless chicken thighs and/or breasts in chicken stock until tender and cut into bite-size pieces.

➜ In heavy saucepan over medium-low heat, heat butter and oil. Add chopped onion, celery and garlic; cook until softened but not browned. Add thyme, bay leaf, 2-1/2 cups (625 mL) of the stock, carrots, pearl onions and mushrooms; cover and simmer for 10 minutes or until carrots are tender. Whisk together cornstarch and remaining stock until smooth; stir into saucepan. Bring to boil, stirring until thickened. Stir in cream, peas and chicken. Add salt and pepper to taste. Remove bay leaf. Pour into 8-cup (2 L) casserole or four 2-cup (500 mL) casseroles. Cover with desired topping. Bake in 400F (200C) oven for 20 minutes or until topping is golden and filling is bubbling. **Makes 4 servings.**

Toppings:

Biscuit topping: (plain, herbed or cheese) Use Tea Biscuits recipe (page 169). Roll out dough and cut to fit top of casserole(s). Place over filling. Brush with glaze (1 egg yolk beaten with 1 tbsp/15 mL milk).

Pastry topping: Use recipe for single-crust pie, page 216. Proceed same as for biscuit topping.

Puff pastry topping: Use 1/2 pkg frozen puff pastry, thawed. Proceed same as for regular pastry topping but use some of the glaze to brush rim of casserole; press pastry firmly to rim.

For **Grilled Chicken,** see page 106

For **Skillet Chicken,** see page 107

For **En Brochette,** see page 108

For **more chicken curries,** see pages 116-117

For **Chicken or Turkey Burgers,** see page 112

For **Terrific Turkey Loaf,** see page 115

For **Chicken or Turkey Schnitzel,** see page 115

For **Stir fries,** see page 118

For **Chicken or Turkey Fajitas,** see page 30

Other Birds

Duck: To roast a 5-lb (2.2 kg) duck: Prick skin all over (don't pierce meat). Sprinkle inside and out with salt and pepper. Tuck 2 garlic cloves and a strip of lemon or orange rind into the cavity. Place on rack in roasting pan. Roast in 450F (230C) oven for 30 minutes; drain fat from pan. Reduce heat to 325F (160C) and roast, basting occasionally, for 1-1/2 hours longer or until juices run clear when thigh is pierced. **Makes 3 to 4 servings**.

Duck breasts are not always easy to find, but when you do spot them at a butcher shop, try them for their rich flavour. Boneless breasts are sometimes called magrets. One of the best ways to cook them so they are not fatty or dry is to score the skin crisscross, then sear them in a hot skillet for about 3 minutes on each side, draining off fat as it accumulates. Transfer to 425F (220C) oven and roast to desired doneness (about 10 minutes for medium-rare). The pan can be deglazed with a little red wine or balsamic vinegar for a sauce; apple or pear slices (cooked and glazed with a little sugar in the pan) also make a complementary finish. To serve, slice duck meat at an angle.

Pheasant and guinea hen (pintade/pintelle): Farm-raised game birds weighing 2 to 3 lb (1 to 1.5 kg); very lean with delicate flavour and texture. Both can be cooked in same ways as chicken. To roast: Brush with butter; roast in 400F (200C) oven, basting occasionally, for 1 hour or until juices are slightly pink when thigh is pierced. **Makes 4 servings**.

Quail: Tiny and delicious (eat them with your fingers!). Quail can be grilled or roasted whole, or boned and broiled or sautéed. They are also good braised in tomato or wine sauce and serve over polenta. Allow about 3 per person. To roast quail: Marinate for 4 hours (see Marinades, page 110); drain and reserve marinade. Place quail in small roasting pan. Roast, brushing occasionally with marinade, in 400F (200C) oven for 30 minutes or until juices are slightly pink when thigh is pierced. Cover with foil and let stand for 5 minutes.

Goose: A rich-flavoured bird, but it has a lot of fat that needs to be drained off during cooking. To roast a 10-lb (4.5 kg) goose: Stuff if desired. Prick skin all over (don't pierce meat); place breast side down on rack in shallow roasting pan. Place in 425F (220C) oven and pour 2 cups (500 mL) boiling water over goose (this helps to release fat). Roast for 1 hour. Reduce heat to 325F (160C). Pour off liquid in pan, turn goose over and prick skin again. Roast, occasionally basting and pricking skin, for 2 hours or until meat thermometer inserted in thigh registers 185F (85C). **Makes 6 to 8 servings**.

Themes & Variations

Stir-fries... schnitzels... curries... kabobs... burgers... meatloaves... chicken & chops...

Main-Course Magic

Match your method to your mood—or what's in the fridge! That's what this section is all about: basic recipes that can star a variety of meats, poultry or seafood. Change a few ingredients—and taste transformations occur. With the basic techniques mastered, you'll soon be creating your own variations on the themes.

Grilled Chops or Chicken

Easy techniques for marinating and grilling ensure tender, juicy, flavourful chops and chicken every time.

Cuts for Grilling: Chops (pork, veal, lamb): Loin or rib chops are best for quick marinating and grilling. Shoulder chops can be used if marinated at least 8 hours to tenderize.

Chicken pieces: Whole legs, drumsticks, thighs or breasts (bone-in or boneless, skin-on or skinless) are all suitable for quick marinating and grilling. Chicken quarters or halves are best precooked in microwave or oven and finished on the grill, or cooked more slowly over indirect heat in a covered barbecue. To ensure even cooking of boneless chicken breasts and thighs, pound them lightly to an even thickness.

To Marinate: Remove most of the visible fat from chops or chicken and place in shallow dish or heavy plastic bag. Add your choice of marinade (see Marinade recipes, page 110), turning pieces to coat all sides. Cover dish or seal bag; marinate in refrigerator for at least 1 hour or up to 8 hours.

To Grill: Over medium heat on barbecue, indoor grill or stovetop ridged grill pan, or under preheated broiler. Approximate cooking times below.

Chicken: Breasts about 7 minutes per side; thighs, drumsticks or whole legs about 10 minutes per side. Be sure chicken is cooked through (no pink colour in centre; juices run clear when chicken is pierced) but don't overcook.

Chops: (1 inch/2.5 cm thick) Pork and veal, 4 to 6 minutes per side or until just cooked through (a hint of pink in centre is okay); lamb, about 4 minutes per side for medium rare, 5 to 6 minutes per side for medium; don't overcook.

Baked Chicken Pieces: Place marinated chicken pieces on rimmed baking sheet lined with parchment or foil. Bake in 375F (190C) oven until cooked through, 30 to 40 minutes for boneless pieces, 45 to 60 minutes for bone-in pieces. You can also bake the chicken until almost cooked through, then finish on the grill to brown the surface and add smoky flavour.

Speedy Skillet Chops or Chicken ⊕

Fire up the skillet—supper's in 20 minutes! What will it be? Chicken or chops? Pork, veal or lamb? Take your pick, because the basic technique is the same: a quick browning, an easy sauce and a few minutes of simmering. Serve with rice or noodles and a salad or crisp-cooked vegetables.

Basic How-To (for 4 servings) Use 4 pork or veal chops (3/4-inch/2 cm thick), 8 lamb loin chops or 4 boneless, skinless chicken thighs or breasts (bone-in chicken pieces can be used, but increase simmering time to about 15 minutes or until cooked through).

In large nonstick skillet over medium-high heat, heat 2 tsp (10 mL) vegetable oil. Add chops or chicken; brown on both sides, sprinkle with salt and pepper. Reduce heat to medium. Continue with variation of your choice:

Sweet and Sour: Top each browned chop or chicken piece with 1 or 2 thin slices of onion and unpeeled lemon. In small bowl, whisk together 1/4 cup (50 mL) brown sugar, 2 tsp (10 mL) cornstarch, 1/4 cup (50 mL) orange juice, 2 tbsp (30 mL) white vinegar and 1 tbsp (15 mL) soy sauce. Pour into skillet, reduce heat, cover and simmer, spooning sauce over meat occasionally (and adding a little water if sauce gets too thick), for about 8 minutes or until cooked through.

Creamy Mushroom: To skillet, add 1 chopped small onion and 2 cups (500 mL) sliced mushrooms; stir to distribute around the meat; cook for 2 minutes or until mushrooms are slightly softened. Stir in 1/4 cup (50 mL) white wine or chicken stock; reduce heat, cover and simmer for about 6 minutes or until meat is cooked through. Stir in 1/4 cup (50 mL) whipping cream or drained yogurt (page 239); cook uncovered for about 2 minutes or until sauce reduces and thickens a bit. Add salt and pepper to taste.

Spicy Tomato-Pepper: To skillet, add 1 chopped small onion and 1 minced garlic clove; cook, stirring, for 1 minute or until softened. Add 1 sliced small sweet red pepper, 1/2 cup (125 mL) tomato sauce and 1/4 tsp (1 mL) each chili powder, ground cumin and hot pepper flakes. Reduce heat, cover and simmer for about 8 minutes or until meat is cooked through. Add salt and pepper to taste.

Barbecue: Add 1/2 cup (125 mL) bottled or homemade barbecue sauce (see Barbecue Sauces in References). Reduce heat, cover and simmer for about 8 minutes or until meat is cooked through.

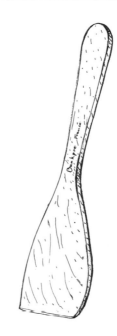

En Brochette

Whether you call them kabobs, kebabs, shishkebabs, brochettes or souvlaki, the array of skewered morsels sizzling on our grills these days gets top marks for eye appeal, tantalizing aroma and taste. All can be served as appetizers or main courses. See also Satays, page 23.

Skewers: Wooden skewers (usually bamboo) look nicer than metal, especially for appetizers; to prevent scorching, soak wooden skewers in water for 30 minutes before threading. Metal skewers should be flat-sided, rather than round, to hold foods securely. For appetizers, use short skewers; for main-course kabobs, use one long skewer or several short ones per serving.

Choose your favourites: Skewers can be threaded with almost any kind of meat, poultry, seafood, vegetables or fruit, alone or in combination (three kinds per skewer is plenty). For mixed skewers, choose foods that cook in the same length of time, or precook those that take longer. For foods with different cooking times, use separate skewers. When threading, leave a small space between each piece for even cooking.

Quantities: Plan on 2 to 4 oz (60 to 125 g) of boneless meat, poultry or seafood per serving for appetizers with dipping sauces, or 4 to 6 oz (125 to 175 g) for main course with other foods. Cut into small cubes for appetizers, larger cubes for main courses. For mixed kabobs, calculate quantities based on 6 to 8 pieces of food per large skewer, 3 or 4 on short skewers.

Marinating or Basting: For added flavour, skewered foods benefit from even a brief marinating, either before or after threading on skewers. Marinate meat or poultry in refrigerator for 1 to 4 hours (tender meats are best for kabobs; if tougher cuts are used, marinate for at least 8 hours to tenderize). Most fish and shellfish should be marinated for no longer than 30 minutes (acidic marinades will start to "cook" the fish and soften the texture; a strong marinade will also overwhelm the flavour of delicate fish). Firm, meaty fish such as swordfish can be marinated longer. Fish and shellfish can also be cooked without marinating at all; just brush or baste with marinade during grilling. Vegetables and fruits need just a quick toss in marinade before grilling and/or occasional basting during grilling. For Marinade recipes, see page 110. All can also be used as basting sauces.

Grilling: Grill kabobs over medium-high heat on barbecue (preferably with cover), indoor grill or stovetop ridged grill pan, or under pre-heated broiler, turning two or three times and brushing with marinade.

Approximate Cooking Times
(for 1-inch/2.5 cm cubes)

Meats and seafood:

- Beef, lamb: 8 to 10 minutes (medium-rare to medium)
- Pork, chicken, turkey: 10 to 15 minutes (just cooked through)
- Shrimp: about 5 minutes
- Scallops, fish: 8 to 10 minutes (just cooked through)

Vegetables and fruits:

- soft (e.g., cherry tomatoes, zucchini, mango): about 5 minutes
- medium-firm (e.g., peppers, onions, mushrooms, pineapple): about 10 minutes
- partially precooked (e.g., potatoes, carrots): about 10 minutes

Serving: Leave on skewers and arrange attractively on each plate, or remove from skewers and place on top of rice, pilaf, couscous or salad greens (or in toasted buns accompanied by fresh salsa; see page 233).

Mixed Kabobs (suggested combos that can be grilled on same skewer)

Marinate cubes of meat, poultry or seafood (see Marinade recipes, page 110), then thread alternately with other ingredients onto skewers:

Chicken (Herbed Citrus Marinade), button mushrooms, red onion wedges (zucchini and tomatoes on separate skewers)

Pork tenderloin (Hoisin Marinade), pre-cooked pearl onions, cubed squash, apple wedges

Lamb (Minted Balsamic Marinade), shiitake mushroom caps (cherry tomatoes on separate skewers)

Swordfish (Thai Marinade), firm mango cubes, sweet pepper squares

Shrimp or scallops (Teriyaki Marinade), onion and sweet pepper squares, pineapple cubes

Tip: To hold shrimp securely on skewers, curl shrimp and thread skewer through both ends.

Souvlaki: This popular Greek specialty is great as either an appetizer or a main course. For 6 servings, use 1-1/2 lb (750 g) boneless lamb leg or shoulder cut into 1-inch (2.5 cm) cubes. Marinate in Greek Marinade (page 110) for 2 to 4 hours in refrigerator. Thread onto skewers and sprinkle with salt. Grill for about 8 minutes, turning occasionally and brushing with marinade, until browned outside but still pink inside. Souvlaki can also feature chicken, beef or pork. Serve with Tzatziki (see right Sidebar). For a main course, serve with couscous, grilled vegetables and roasted peppers.

Tzatziki: Use as a sauce for souvlaki, grilled meats, chicken or fish, or as a dip with vegetables or pitas. Peel and grate half a seedless cucumber and place in strainer over bowl. Sprinkle with 1/4 tsp (1 mL) salt and let drain for 30 minutes; squeeze out excess moisture. Combine cucumber with 1 cup (250 mL) drained yogurt (page 239), 3 minced garlic cloves and 2 tbsp (30 mL) chopped fresh dill or mint. Add salt and pepper to taste. Makes about 1-1/2 cups (375 mL).

Marinades

Why Marinate?

The purpose of marinating is to add flavour or to tenderize or both. For tender cuts, a few minutes is often enough; 4 hours is about the limit. Less-tender cuts usually need at least 8 hours in a marinade that contains acidic ingredients (vinegar, tomato, citrus juice, wine). Add salt just before grilling, rather than to the marinade.

All kinds of ready-to-cook marinated and seasoned meats, poultry and fish are now available in supermarkets and butcher shops. Some are great, some are not. Try them when you're really short of time and note which ones you like. Marinating your own, on the other hand, usually pays off in flavour versus convenience. For recipes using the marinades below, see Main Dishes (Meats, Poultry, Fish and Seafood) or look under "Grilling" in index. For each marinade, combine the listed ingredients. You don't need a lot—just enough to coat the pieces. Each makes about 1/2 cup (125 mL), sufficient for 6 veal or pork chops, fish steaks, chicken pieces or turkey cutlets; 12 small lamb chops; 1 flank steak; 2 pork tenderloins; 1-1/2 lb (750 g) cubes for kabobs. For larger cuts such as butterflied leg of lamb, double the recipe.

Herbed Citrus Marinade: (for lamb, veal, pork, chicken, turkey, fish) 1/4 cup (50 mL) extra-virgin olive oil, 1/4 cup (50 mL) lemon or lime juice, 2 tsp (10 mL) grated lemon or lime rind, 2 tsp (10 mL) Dijon mustard, 2 minced garlic cloves, 2 tbsp (30 mL) chopped fresh rosemary (or 2 tsp/10 mL dried), 1-1/2 tsp (7 mL) chopped fresh thyme (or 1/2 tsp/ 2 mL dried).

White Wine Marinade: Use white wine instead of lemon juice. *Balsamic Marinade:* Use balsamic vinegar instead of lemon juice. *Minted Marinade:* (for lamb) Use either balsamic vinegar or lemon juice; replace herbs with 2 tbsp (30 mL) chopped fresh mint. *Greek Marinade:* Omit mustard; use oregano instead of thyme. *Provençal Marinade:* Omit mustard; replace herbs with 1 tbsp (15 mL) dried herbes de Provence. *Moroccan Marinade:* Omit mustard and rosemary; add 1/2 tsp (2 mL) each ground cumin and coriander and 1/4 tsp (1 mL) each cinnamon and pepper.

Red Wine Marinade: (for beef or lamb) 1/3 cup (75 mL) red wine, 2 tbsp (30 mL) extra-virgin olive oil, 2 minced garlic cloves, 2 tsp (10 mL) each chopped fresh rosemary and thyme (or 1/2 tsp/2 mL dried), a few grindings of pepper.

Hot and Spicy Marinade: (for chicken, turkey, beef, pork) 1/3 cup (75 mL) bottled hot salsa, 2 tbsp (30 mL) red wine vinegar, 2 tsp (10 mL) each Dijon mustard and Worcestershire sauce, 1/4 tsp (1 mL) (or to taste) each pepper and hot pepper sauce or flakes.

Hoisin Marinade: (for chicken or pork) 1/3 cup (75 mL) hoisin sauce and 2 tbsp (30 mL) each orange juice concentrate and rice vinegar.

Thai Marinade: (for chicken, pork, fish) 4 tbsp (60 mL) fish sauce, 3 tbsp (45 mL) lime juice, 2 tbsp (30 mL) vegetable oil, 2 tbsp (30 mL) brown sugar, 2 tsp (10 mL) each minced garlic and fresh ginger, 1/4 tsp (1 mL) (or to taste) Thai curry paste or minced hot chiles, 1/4 cup (50 mL) chopped fresh coriander (optional).

Teriyaki Marinade: (for fish, veal, chicken, turkey; for beef teriyaki marinade, see Teriyaki Flank Steak, page 76): 1/3 cup (75 mL) light-coloured soy sauce, 2 tbsp (30 mL) brown sugar, 2 tbsp (30 mL) rice vinegar or lemon juice, 1 tsp (5 mL) each minced fresh ginger and garlic.

Tandoori Marinade: see Tandoori-Style Chicken, page 102.

The Best Burgers on the Block

How our horizons have expanded! Not long ago, biting into a burger meant biting into beef, and that fine old basic is still hard to beat, especially with some nifty new toppings. But the carnivorous crowd now has a feast of choices including lamb, turkey and chicken. And the centre of attraction need not be meat at all; veggie burgers and grilled portobello mushrooms could well charm those meat-eaters into a whole new flavour realm.

Grilled Beef Burgers

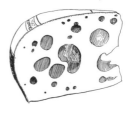

For the best burgers, use high-quality medium or lean ground beef. I prefer to use medium for better moistness and tenderness (the small amount of extra fat drains off during grilling), seasoned with salt and pepper, and with no egg or fillers. If you prefer, add 1 egg and 1/4 cup (50 mL) fresh breadcrumbs per 1-1/4 lb (625 g) ground beef.

Basic Burgers: 5-oz (125 g) patties make a good medium-sized burger. For 4 patties, mix 1-1/4 lb (625 g) ground beef with 1/2 tsp (2 mL) salt and 1/4 tsp (1 mL) freshly ground pepper. Shape into patties of even thickness (1/2 to 3/4 inch/1 to 2 cm). For best texture, handle gently. Patties hold together best if chilled before cooking. Grill over medium-high heat on barbecue, indoor grill or stovetop ridged grill pan just until no longer pink in centre, about 4 to 5 minutes on each side. To keep burgers juicy, turn only once, don't press down and don't overcook. Serve in lightly toasted fresh buns with traditional toppings (sliced tomatoes, sweet onions, salsa, pickles) or try caramelized onions, roasted peppers, grilled vegetables or mushrooms. **Makes 4 servings**.

Herbed Burgers: To basic burger mixture, add 1 minced garlic clove and 1/2 tsp (2 mL) each dried oregano and basil. Serve in crusty Italian or Portuguese buns or small focaccia.

Toppings: roasted peppers, sweet onions, asiago cheese.

Hot and Spicy Burgers: To basic burger mixture, add 1 minced small onion, 1 or 2 minced jalapeños and large pinch ground cumin and chili powder. Serve in cornmeal buns or tortilla wraps.

Toppings: hot salsa or barbecue sauce, sliced avocado or guacamole (page 17), lettuce, shredded cheese.

Teriyaki Burgers: To basic burger mixture, add 2 chopped green onions and 1 tsp (5 mL) each minced garlic and fresh ginger. Brush with teriyaki sauce during grilling. Serve in sesame buns.

Toppings: slivered sweet peppers, shredded lettuce, sprouts. (Go ahead—put on your hula skirt and grill pineapple slices if the urge strikes.)

Turkey or Chicken Burgers

Ground turkey and chicken make great low-fat burgers and adapt well to all kinds of seasonings. This tasty basic version and two variations will get you started on creating your own (try adding mushrooms, a little teriyaki sauce or barbecue sauce). For best texture and moistness, handle gently and don't overcook. Serve in toasted buns, grilled focaccia or warmed pitas.

1 lb	ground turkey or chicken	500 g
1/2 cup	fresh breadcrumbs	125 mL
1/4 cup	low-fat mayonnaise	50 mL
1/4 cup	finely chopped onion	50 mL
1	clove garlic, minced	1
1/2 tsp	salt	2 mL
1/4 tsp	pepper	1 mL

➡ In large bowl, combine all ingredients. Shape into 4 patties about 1/2 inch (1 cm) thick. Grill or broil (or cook in lightly oiled nonstick skillet) for 4 to 5 minutes on each side or until just cooked through. Top with salsa, sliced tomatoes, onions, grilled peppers or mushrooms. **Makes 4 servings**.

Honey-Dijon: To basic mixture, add 2 tbsp (30 mL) honey Dijon mustard (or mild honey mustard for little kids).

Black Olive and Sun-Dried Tomato: To basic mixture, add 2 tbsp (30 mL) each chopped kalamata olives, sun-dried tomatoes (oil-packed, drained) and sweet red peppers, and 1/2 tsp (2 mL) dried oregano.

Lamburgers

Try something new on the barbecue. Served in pitas, these Middle Eastern–flavoured burgers are deliciously different. Food consultant Yvonne Tremblay, who created the recipe, likes them mini-sized (so she can call them lamburgini). Ground lamb is available at some supermarkets and butcher shops, or the butcher will grind it for you.

1 lb	ground lamb	500 g
2	cloves garlic, minced (or 1 head roasted garlic, page 236)	2
1/3 cup	chopped green onions	75 mL
2 tbsp	chopped parsley	30 mL
1 tsp	ground cumin	5 mL
1/2 tsp	each: ground coriander, salt	2 mL
1/4 tsp	pepper	1 mL

➡ Mix together all ingredients. Shape into 4 patties (or 12 mini-patties) about 1/2 inch (1 cm) thick. Grill or broil for 5 minutes on each side or until just cooked through. Serve in warmed pitas and top with Tzatziki (page 109). If using mini-patties, tuck 2 or 3 into pocket pita halves; OR, for appetizers, tuck individually into mini-pitas. **Makes 4 servings**.

Veggie Burgers

For the vegetarians in the crowd, or just for a change, try these tasty patties. They are quick and easy in a skillet but can be cooked (on foil) on a grill. Be sure the patties are chilled thoroughly before cooking so they hold their shape.

4 tsp	vegetable oil	20 mL
1 cup	each: chopped onions, chopped mushrooms	250 mL
1/2 cup	coarsely grated carrot	125 mL
1/4 cup	each: finely chopped celery, finely chopped sweet red and/or green pepper	50 mL
2	large cloves garlic, minced	2
1 cup	each: canned or cooked lentils, white kidney beans (or 19-oz/540 mL can lentils, drained)	250 mL
2 tbsp	dry breadcrumbs	30 mL
1/4 tsp	(or to taste) each: salt and pepper	1 mL
	Dry breadcrumbs for coating	
4	wholewheat buns or pitas, warmed	4

Toppings:

salsa, tzatziki, roasted red peppers, sliced tomatoes and cucumbers, alfalfa sprouts

→ In large nonstick skillet over medium heat, heat half of the oil. Add onions, mushrooms, carrot, celery, peppers and garlic; cook until slightly softened. In food processor, or with potato masher, coarsely mash lentils and beans. Stir in vegetable mixture, breadcrumbs, salt and pepper; mix thoroughly. Shape into 4 patties 1/2 inch (1 cm) thick; coat lightly with breadcrumbs. Chill for at least 1 hour. In nonstick skillet over medium heat, heat remaining oil. Cook patties for about 4 minutes on each side or until golden brown. Serve in buns or pitas with choice of toppings. **Makes 4 servings.**

Portobello Burgers

Big, meaty-textured portobello mushroom caps are flavourful and juicy and really do look like meat patties. Cut off stems; marinate caps for 10 minutes in Herbed Citrus or Balsamic Marinade (page 110) OR just brush with olive oil and sprinkle with salt and pepper. Grill for 5 minutes on each side or until tender. Serve in lightly toasted buns, topped with grilled peppers and onions, a few leaves of fresh basil and a little garlic mayonnaise.

Not Your Average Meatloaf

Down-home favourites remain as popular as ever, with new meat mixtures and international spice combinations offering great alternatives to the traditional.

Basic Meatloaf ❖

This red-topped meatloaf is flavourful, moist and very satisfying when you're in a comfort-food mood. Using oats rather than breadcrumbs gives a pleasantly coarse texture. Instead of all beef, you can use half ground pork or veal or a mixture of all three. Any leftovers reheat well (thickly sliced) in the microwave, are also very good thinly sliced in toasted sandwiches, or can be frozen. Recipe can be halved for a small loaf.

2 lb	ground beef	1 kg
1 cup	finely chopped onions	250 mL
2	cloves garlic, minced	2
3/4 cup	quick-cooking oats (not instant)	175 mL
1/2 cup	milk	125 mL
2	eggs	2
1 tbsp	Worcestershire sauce	15 mL
1-1/2 tsp	salt	7 mL
1 tsp	freshly ground pepper	5 mL
1/4 tsp	hot pepper flakes or sauce (optional)	1 mL
2/3 cup	(divided) ketchup, chili sauce, salsa or barbecue sauce	150 mL

➜ In large bowl, combine all ingredients (save half of the ketchup for topping); mix thoroughly with spoon or hands. Pack into lightly greased 9- x 5-inch (23 x 13 cm) loaf pan. Spread reserved ketchup over top. Bake in 350F (180C) oven for 1 to 1-1/4 hours or until cooked through (meat thermometer inserted in centre should register 170F/75C). Drain off fat in pan. Remove loaf and cut into slices. **Makes 8 servings**.

Italian: Use 1-1/2 lb (750 g) ground beef and 1/2 lb (250 g) Italian sausage (sweet or hot, casings removed, crumbled); add 1/2 tsp (2 mL) each dried thyme and oregano.

Tex-Mex: To basic mixture, add 1/2 tsp (2 mL) each ground cumin and dried oregano, 1/2 cup (125 mL) chopped sweet red or green pepper and 1 or 2 minced small fresh chiles or canned chipotles or jalapeños. Use salsa instead of ketchup.

Cheddar Chunk: To basic mixture, add 6 oz (175 g) old cheddar cheese, cut into tiny cubes.

Oven-Roasted Meatballs: Cooking meatballs in the oven is much easier than in a skillet, and you can prepare lots at once; they can be used right away, refrigerated for a day or two or frozen for up to 2 months. They defrost quickly in the microwave or can be added directly to spaghetti sauce and simmered for about 15 minutes until heated through. Meatballs can also be used instead of browned chicken or chops in any of the sauces for Speedy Skillet Chops or Chicken on page 107.

To prepare meatballs: Use same mixture as Basic Meatloaf, omitting ketchup and using breadcrumbs instead of oats if you want a finer texture. Shape into small balls (makes about 75 1-inch/2.5 cm or 50 1-1/2-inch/4 cm balls). Place on rimmed baking sheet. Roast in 400F (200C) oven for 15 to 25 minutes, depending on size, until browned and cooked through.

To freeze: Let cool, freeze in single layer, then transfer to plastic freezer bags.

Terrific Turkey Loaf ♥

Lean and light but very flavourful, this has a pâté-like texture and taste. Serve hot or cold with a spicy chutney.

1/2 cup	finely chopped onion	125 mL
1	clove garlic, minced	1
1 cup	chopped fresh mushrooms	250 mL
1 tbsp	vegetable oil	15 mL
1-1/2 lb	ground turkey	750 g
1 cup	fresh breadcrumbs	250 mL
1/2 cup	chopped parsley	125 mL
1 tsp	salt	5 mL
1/4 tsp	each: dried thyme and savory	1 mL
	Pepper	

➜ Sauté or microwave onion, garlic and mushrooms in oil until softened. Mix with turkey, breadcrumbs, parsley, salt, thyme, savory and pepper to taste. Pack lightly into 8-1/2- x 4-1/2-inch (22 x 12 cm) greased loaf pan. Bake in 350F (180C) oven for 1 hour or until juices run clear. **Makes about 6 servings**

Speedy Schnitzel 🕑

Today's wide selection of thin-sliced very lean meats makes for great flash-in-the-pan suppers. Chicken, turkey and pork are popular alternatives to veal for classic dishes like schnitzel. A crumb coating keeps the meats moist and tender and, with a brief cooking, they are crisp, light and satisfying, whether served with traditional accompaniments like braised red cabbage or topped off with roasted red peppers or a zippy salsa.

1 lb	chicken, turkey, veal or pork scaloppine or cutlets	500 g
1	egg, lightly beaten	1
3/4 cup	fine dry breadcrumbs	175 mL
	Salt and pepper	
2 tbsp	vegetable oil	30 mL
	Lemon wedges	

➜ If cutlets are more than 1/4 inch (5 mm) thick, place between two pieces of parchment or waxed paper and pound with meat mallet or bottom of a pot. Dip slices in egg, then into breadcrumbs to coat evenly. Sprinkle lightly on both sides with salt and pepper. Let stand on wire rack for about 10 minutes to set coating. In large nonstick skillet over medium heat, heat oil. Add cutlets and cook, turning once, until golden brown and just cooked through, about 3 minutes on each side. Serve with lemon wedges. **Makes 4 servings**.

Skillet Parmigiana: Pour 1 cup (250 mL) tomato sauce around cooked schnitzel in skillet. Top each piece with sliced mozzarella cheese; sprinkle with 1/4 cup (50 mL) grated parmesan. Cover and simmer until cheese is melted, about 2 minutes.

Grilled Turkey Cutlets: (without crumb coating) Brush cutlets with olive oil and sprinkle with herbs or other seasonings, or marinate for a few minutes to add flavour (see Marinades, page 110). Grill on barbecue, indoor grill or stovetop ridged grill pan for about 3 minutes on each side, until just cooked through. Can also be cooked in a nonstick skillet.

Curries

Curry means a multitude of things to a multitude of peoples. The universal connotation is spicy heat. But a hearty chicken, lamb or vegetarian curry in an Indo-Canadian restaurant is a far different dish from a fragrantly-sauced seafood curry in a Thai establishment just down the street. The last few decades have brought us an international array of spicy dishes, and in most Canadian cities we can choose not only Indian or Thai curries, but also dishes from Malaysia, Indonesia, Vietnam, Sri Lanka and the West Indies that carry the curry name and heat, but with their own distinct interpretations. Still, two styles predominate: Indian curries are usually made with dry spice mixtures; Thai and other Southeast Asian versions generally use curry pastes. A wide variety of curry powders, pastes and sauces (some true to their origins, some not) are available in grocery stores; explore the choices, experiment and enjoy! For Caribbean Curry Chicken, see page 102.

An Indian Curry (Chicken, Lamb or Beef)

Here's a basic, flavourful sample of an Indian-style curry. There are countless famous versions in every region of India and no such thing as a definitive curry. You could substitute about 2 tbsp (30 mL) store-bought curry powder or Indian-style curry paste for the mixture of spices given here, but the flavour of the dish will vary with brands and qualities.

2 tbsp	vegetable oil	30 mL
2 cups	finely chopped onions	500 mL
4	cloves garlic, minced	4
1 tbsp	minced fresh ginger	15 mL
2 tsp	each: ground coriander, ground cumin	10 mL
1 tsp	turmeric	5 mL
1/2 tsp	cayenne or hot pepper flakes	2 mL
1/4 tsp	each: ground cardamom, cinnamon, ground cloves, black pepper and salt	1 mL
1 cup	chopped drained canned tomatoes	250 mL
1 cup	water or stock	250 mL
1 lb	boneless chicken thighs,	500 g
	lean lamb or beef, cut into large bite-size chunks	
2 to 4 tbsp	whipping cream or plain yogurt	30 to 60 mL
	Salt and pepper to taste	

➜ In large skillet over medium-high heat, heat oil. Add onions and cook, stirring, until softened but not browned, about 5 minutes. Add garlic, ginger and all the spices; cook, stirring, for 2 minutes. Stir in tomatoes and water. Add chicken or meat, cover and simmer until tender, about 20 minutes for chicken, 45 minutes for meat; add more water if needed. Stir in cream to taste. Add salt and pepper if needed. **Makes 4 servings**.

Shrimp Curry: After adding the water, let mixture simmer for 15 minutes. Instead of chicken or meat, add peeled raw shrimp; simmer for 5 minutes.

Vegetable Curry: Instead of meat, use a mixture of vegetables such as small new potatoes, cauliflower florets, cubed squash or sliced carrots. Simmer them just until tender.

Thai Red Curry with Beef or Chicken

If you're not familiar with Thai cooking, this easy recipe is a pleasant introduction to typical flavours. Adjust the curry paste to taste (Thai curry paste is very hot).

1 tbsp	vegetable oil	15 mL
1 tbsp	(or to taste) red curry paste	15 mL
1/2 cup	chopped onion	125 mL
3/4 lb	beef stir-fry strips or boneless, skinless chicken breasts, cut into thin strips	375 g
1	sweet red pepper, cut into thin strips	1
3/4 cup	coconut milk	175 mL
1 tbsp	fish sauce	15 mL
1 tbsp	lime or lemon juice	15 mL
3 cups	cooked jasmine rice	750 mL

➜ In large skillet over medium-high heat, heat oil. Add curry paste and cook, stirring, for 30 seconds. Add onion; cook, stirring, for 1 minute. Add beef or chicken strips; cook, stirring, for 2 minutes or until almost cooked through. Add red pepper; cook, stirring, for 1 minute. Stir in coconut milk, fish sauce and lime juice. Bring to simmer; cook, stirring often, for about 3 minutes. Add more fish sauce (for saltiness) if needed. Serve over jasmine rice. **Makes 2 to 3 servings**.

Thai Green Curry with Shrimp or Salmon

For an East-West fusion of ingredients, Canadian salmon makes a delectable alternative to shrimp in this popular Thai dish. You could also turn it into a mixed seafood curry by using both shrimp and salmon (or other fish such as grouper) and adding some mussels (add them to skillet and cook for about 5 minutes before adding the shrimp; discard any that don't open). This dish is often made without any vegetables, but the green snow peas look wonderful with the pink of the seafood. Green curry paste is fiery-hot, so add to taste. Seafood curries like this one generally have lots of sauce and are meant to be served over rice.

1	can (14 oz/398 mL) coconut milk	1
1/4 cup	minced shallots or onion	50 mL
1 tsp	each: minced fresh ginger and garlic	5 mL
1 tbsp	(or to taste) green curry paste	15 mL
2 tbsp	fish sauce	30 mL
1 tbsp	lime juice (or 2 kaffir lime leaves, torn in thirds)	15 mL
1 lb	large raw shrimp, peeled and deveined or fresh salmon fillet, cubed	500 g
1/4 lb	snow peas, cut in half on the diagonal (or 1/4 cup/50 mL frozen green peas)	125 g
2 tbsp	each: chopped fresh coriander and basil	30 mL
4 cups	cooked jasmine rice	1 L

➜ In large skillet, bring 1/2 cup (125 mL) of the coconut milk to gentle boil. Add shallots, ginger and garlic; cook, stirring, for 2 minutes. Add curry paste; cook, stirring, until it dissolves. Add remaining coconut milk, fish sauce and lime juice; boil gently for 3 minutes or until thickened a little. Add shrimp or salmon; simmer, stirring occasionally, until shrimp are pink (about 3 minutes) or salmon is cooked through (about 5 minutes). Add snow peas for the last minute of cooking. Stir in coriander and basil. Serve over rice. **Makes about 4 servings**.

Thai curry pastes (red and green) are available in Asian grocery stores and many supermarkets. They contain chiles, galangal, garlic, coriander, kaffir lime leaves, lemongrass and other ingredients that give authentic flavour. Thai curry pastes are very hot; although "red" suggests fiery and "green" seems cool, green curries can be scorching. If you're not sure of your heat tolerance, start with a small amount of curry paste and work up. The amount indicated in these recipes is about average; add more if you know you like it even hotter. Indian-style curry paste can be substituted in these recipes but will give a very different flavour.

Thai Green Curry with Chicken: Instead of shrimp or salmon, use boneless, skinless chicken breasts cut into small chunks. Simmer for about 10 minutes or until cooked through.

All-Purpose Super Stir-Fry ⊛

Master this basic recipe and you'll never wok alone—everyone will want to know what new meat and vegetable combos you've dreamed up. Convenient packages of stir-fry strips are available at most meat counters. This recipe makes 2 to 3 servings; it can be doubled (use an extra-large skillet).

2 tbsp	vegetable oil	30 mL
1/2 lb	boneless beef, pork, chicken or turkey cut in strips or small cubes, or large raw shrimp, peeled and deveined, or firm tofu, cut into strips or cubes	250 g
1	small onion, coarsely chopped	1
1	large clove garlic, minced	1
1 tsp	minced fresh ginger	5 mL
2 cups	raw vegetables*	500 mL
1/2 cup	chicken stock	125 mL
2 tbsp	soy sauce	30 mL
2 tsp	cornstarch	10 mL
	Salt and pepper to taste	

* Use a combination of 3 or 4 vegetables: strips of sweet peppers (any colour), broccoli or cauliflower florets, diagonally sliced celery or green onions, snow peas, sliced zucchini, carrots or fennel, sliced water chestnuts, bean sprouts or mushrooms. If using firm vegetables such as carrots, add them a minute or two before the others. A sprinkling of toasted cashews or peanuts can also be added at the end.

➜ In wok or large skillet over medium-high heat, heat half of the oil. Add meat, poultry or shrimp; stir-fry for 3 to 4 minutes or until just cooked through. Remove to a bowl. Add remaining oil to pan; add onion, garlic, ginger and vegetables; stir-fry for about 1 minute. Add stock; cover and let steam for 2 to 3 minutes or until vegetables are tender-crisp. Return meat to pan. Mix together soy sauce and cornstarch; stir into pan. Cook, stirring, until thickened, about 1 minute. Add salt and pepper if needed.

Hoisin Stir-Fry: Add 1 tbsp (15 mL) hoisin sauce to the soy-cornstarch mixture.

Orange-Chile Stir-Fry: Instead of all chicken stock, use 1/4 cup (50 mL) stock plus 2 tbsp (30 mL) each dry sherry (or rice wine) and orange juice concentrate. Stir in 1 to 2 tsp (5 to 10 mL) Chinese chile paste (to taste) and the shredded rind of a small orange.

Pasta, Grains & Beans

Superbly healthful, infinitely versatile—
a global gathering of uncomplicated pleasures

Pasta Basics

With dozens of pasta sizes and shapes available in supermarkets (and even more in Italian grocery stores), matching them up with appropriate sauces is easier when you keep a few basic guidelines in mind. (Also, be sure to choose good-quality dried pasta made from durum semolina, a granular hard wheat flour that gives the proper al dente texture to cooked pasta.) In general, pair delicate pastas with light sauces, sturdier pastas with more robust sauces. Long thin shapes such as fettuccine, tagliatelle, linguine and spaghetti are best with creamy or oil-based sauces that will cling to the smooth surfaces. The thinnest strands—capelli d'angelo (angel hair) and the slightly larger capellini and vermicelli—need light, delicate sauces. Short pasta with twists, grooves or hollows—such as fusilli and rotini (corkscrew spirals or springs), penne (quills), farfalle (bows or butterflies), conchiglie (shells)—match well with sauces that fill up the nooks and crannies, such as chunky sauces containing small pieces of meat, seafood or vegetables. Small pasta also comes in all kinds of kid-pleasing fanciful shapes, from orecchiette (little ears) to radiatore (radiators) to rotelle (wagon wheels), and these can go with almost any kind of sauce. Tubular shapes like macaroni, ziti and rigatoni take well to substantial sauces and stay firm in baked dishes; larger tubes (cannelloni, manicotti) are for stuffing. Soup pastas include tubetti, ditali, tiny shells and stars, and rice-shaped orzo. Lasagne noodles are available in regular and no-boil varieties. Coloured and flavoured pasta is made with spinach, tomato, carrot, peppers, herbs or even squid ink.

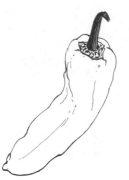

Fresh Pasta: Homemade pasta, made with eggs and shaped into fettuccine or other flat noodles, has an ethereal texture that is nothing like dried pasta. Fresh pasta is meant to be eaten the same day it's made or refrigerated for only a day or two. A lot of store-bought "fresh" pasta isn't very fresh, so unless you make your own or have a reliable source nearby, you're much better off with high-quality dried pasta. Some stores do have good-quality fresh or frozen ravioli and tortellini (small stuffed pastas) and also gnocchi (small pasta-like dumplings, often made with potato). Fresh lasagne sheets (often in packages of about 16) are also available; this pasta has usually been precooked and so requires no boiling; it's also very convenient for making cannelloni (wrap the pasta around the filling rather than stuffing the tubes).

How Much Pasta? For each main-course serving, allow 3 to 4 oz (100 to 125 g); for first-course servings, about 2 to 3 oz (50 to 100 g). A 3/4-to-1-lb (375 to 500 g) package is about 4 main-course servings. If measuring short pasta by volume, 3/4 lb (375 g) equals 3 to 4 cups (750 mL to 1 L). To measure long thin strands, grasp a handful tightly at one end; a diameter of 1-1/2 inches (4 cm) is about 3/4 lb (375 g).

Cooking Pasta: For dried pasta, use a large pot and lots of water, about 20 cups (5 L) per pound (500 g) of pasta. Adequate water and frequent stirring eliminate any problems with sticking. Never add oil to the water; it makes pasta slippery and the sauce won't cling. Bring the water to a full rolling boil (it will boil faster if pot is covered and if salt is not added until boil is reached). Add about 1 tbsp (15 mL) salt per 20 cups (5 L) water. Add pasta to rapidly boiling water, stirring to separate pieces. Boil uncovered, stirring occasionally, just until al dente (tender but still firm to the bite). Taste often so you don't overcook it. Cooking time varies by size and brand, but most dried pasta takes 8 to 10 minutes, larger shapes about 12, fine strands 3 to 5 minutes. Fresh pasta requires less water to cook and takes only 1 to 3 minutes. As soon as pasta is al dente, drain in large colander (some pasta pots come with a separate perforated liner basket for draining). Save some of the cooking water to add to sauced pastas that need to be a bit saucier. Toss hot, drained pasta thoroughly with the sauce; each strand or piece should be lightly coated. But pasta should never be served swimming in sauce; you want to taste pasta, not just sauce.

Noodles and Dumplings ❦

Packaged dried egg noodles (fine, medium, broad, extra-broad) are quick-cooking and convenient for adding to soups and casseroles, or for serving instead of rice or potatoes to accompany saucy foods.

Fresh egg noodles and pasta-like dumplings are used in many traditional European dishes, and recipes with old-country origins remain favourites with many Canadians. They include Austrian/German spaetzle (tiny noodles or dumplings served as a side dish or stirred into soup) and similar Mennonite, Hungarian and other Eastern European versions; Jewish kugel (baked noodle cakes) and kreplach (dumplings resembling ravioli); and the ever-popular Polish and Ukrainian perogy/varenyky (small stuffed dumplings, boiled, then sometimes fried). Frozen perogies are available in many supermarkets; follow package directions for reheating.

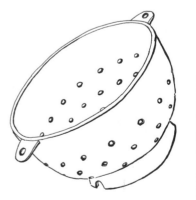

Basic Tomato Sauce

Countless recipes exist for tomato sauces—from simple, unseasoned purées to chunky, robust pasta sauces. I particularly like this lightly seasoned version because it can be adapted easily to tastes and needs (see variations below.) It's a simple, satisfying, homestyle sauce—the kind sold fresh or bottled in Italian food shops. It's medium-thick, fairly smooth in texture and flavoured lightly with onion, garlic and herbs. It can be used as is on pasta, doctored a bit with extra seasonings or used as the base for many other dishes.

1	can (28 oz/796 mL) plum tomatoes	1
1 tbsp	extra-virgin olive oil	15 mL
1	small onion, finely chopped	1
2	cloves garlic, minced	2
2 tbsp	tomato paste	30 mL
1/2 cup	water	125 mL
1 tsp	dried basil	5 mL
1/2 tsp	dried oregano	2 mL
1/4 tsp	each: salt and pepper	1 mL

➔ Crush tomatoes thoroughly (see Sidebar); set aside. In large heavy saucepan over medium heat, heat oil. Add onion and cook for about 2 minutes until softened. Add garlic and cook for about 30 seconds (do not brown). Stir in crushed tomatoes, tomato paste, water, basil, oregano, salt and pepper. Bring to boil, reduce heat and simmer, partially covered, for about 40 minutes or to desired thickness, stirring often. Add salt and pepper to taste if needed. **Makes about 3 cups** (750 mL).

Basic Tomato Sauce Variations

The sauce can be made meatless or with meat or varied in any of the following ways: If you want a very smooth sauce, purée the tomatoes in a food processor, or purée the finished sauce after cooking. If you want it seedless, put the tomatoes through a food mill. (You can also buy bottled strained tomatoes called passato in Italian food shops and some supermarkets.) You can make it chunkier by chopping instead of crushing the tomatoes. You can use only onion or garlic instead of both; or add a finely chopped celery stalk and carrot (adds sweetness if the tomatoes are too acidic). For extra basil flavour, stir in a few slivered fresh basil leaves at the end. The sauce can also be made with fresh, ripe plum tomatoes (about 3 lb/1.5 kg, peeled, seeded and chopped). The recipe can be doubled or tripled and frozen in small quantities for convenience.

Tomato Sauce with Meat: (use for Lasagne, page 123) Add 3/4 lb (375 g) ground beef to saucepan before the onions; cook until no longer pink, breaking up meat thoroughly. Increase onions to 1 cup (250 mL). Add 1/2 cup (125 mL) more water, beef stock or red wine along with the tomatoes. **Makes about 4 cups** (1 L). (Instead of all ground beef, you can use part ground pork, ground veal or crumbled Italian sausage.)

Tomato Sauce with Mushrooms and Vegetables: (use for Mushroom-Vegetable Lasagne, page 123) In skillet, along with the onions, add 1 finely chopped small carrot and celery stalk, 3 cups (750 mL) sliced mushrooms and 1 chopped sweet red or green pepper (or half of each); cook until softened, about 5 minutes. **Makes about 3-1/2 cups** (875 mL).

How to Crush or Chop Canned Tomatoes

Many recipes call for crushing or chopping canned tomatoes before adding. One of the best ways to do this is to drain and reserve the juice, put tomatoes in a bowl and crush them with your hands, removing any bits of skin and the hard cores from the stem ends; the tomatoes can be thoroughly crushed or left a little chunky as desired. Alternatively, you can crush the tomatoes with a potato masher or do as many traditional Italian cooks do—simply crush them with your fingers as you add them to the pot. Another good method is to drain and reserve the juice, then chop the tomatoes with a knife or kitchen scissors right in the can. You can also use canned tomatoes labelled "crushed" or "diced," but try a few brands to find one you trust; crushed and diced tomatoes vary greatly in quality and many have inferior flavour.

Fresh Tomato Sauce with Basil ☻

Light, fresh, quickly cooked tomato sauces are stylish as well as delicious and healthful. Adding sun-dried tomatoes makes this extra-flavourful. Enjoy it with pasta or as a bruschetta topping.

2 tbsp	extra-virgin olive oil	30 mL
2	cloves garlic, minced	2
Pinch	hot pepper flakes	Pinch
2	large ripe tomatoes, chopped	2
2 tbsp	coarsely chopped sun-dried tomatoes (oil-packed)	30 mL
2 tbsp	coarsely chopped black olives (optional)	30 mL
1/4 cup	slivered fresh basil	50 mL
	Salt and freshly ground pepper	
	Shaved parmesan or crumbled feta cheese (optional)	

➜ In skillet over medium heat, heat oil; cook garlic and hot pepper flakes for a few seconds (do not brown). Add fresh and sun-dried tomatoes; cook, stirring, for 2 minutes or until fresh tomatoes are softened a little. Add olives (if using), basil, a little salt if needed, and pepper to taste. Serve over hot, drained pasta (about 8 oz/250 g); sprinkle with cheese (if using). **Makes 2 servings**.

For bruschetta topping: Spread sauce on grilled crusty bread; top with grated parmesan and broil until golden.

Lasagne

A perennial favourite for potluck and casual entertaining, lasagne can have satisfyingly traditional flavour and be quick to prepare. In this recipe, the meat sauce can be made ahead (refrigerate up to 3 days or freeze up to 3 months) and an easy ricotta mixture fills in nicely for the classic besciamella (béchamel) sauce. (If you prefer you can use 1 1/2 cups Béchamel page 238).

9	lasagne noodles (about 8 oz/250 g)	9
1-1/2 cups	ricotta cheese	375 mL
1/2 cup	freshly grated parmesan cheese	125 mL
1	egg, beaten	1
1/4 tsp	each: pepper, nutmeg	1 mL
1 cup	chopped cooked spinach (optional)	250 mL
4 cups	Tomato Sauce with Meat (page 122)	1 L
3 cups	shredded mozzarella cheese (12 oz/375 g)	750 mL

➜ In large pot of boiling salted water, cook lasagne noodles until tender, about 15 minutes; drain and rinse in cold water. If ricotta is not smooth, blend briefly in food processor. Mix together ricotta, half of the parmesan, egg, pepper, nutmeg and spinach (if using). In lightly greased 13- x 9-inch (33 x 23 cm) baking dish, spread thin layer of Tomato Sauce with Meat. Cover with three of the noodles; spread with half of ricotta mixture, then one-third of remaining meat sauce and one-third of mozzarella. Repeat layers of noodles, ricotta, sauce and mozzarella. Top with remaining noodles, sauce and mozzarella. Sprinkle with remaining parmesan. Cover loosely with foil. Bake in 375F (190C) oven for 20 minutes; remove foil and bake for 20 minutes longer or until bubbly. Let stand for 10 minutes before serving. **Makes 8 servings**.

Tip: Packaged oven-ready or no-boil lasagne noodles can be used, but check package directions; most require the addition of more liquid.

Mushroom-Vegetable Lasagne: Instead of Tomato Sauce with Meat, use Tomato Sauce with Mushrooms and Vegetables (page 122). Include the spinach in the ricotta mixture.

Sauce-and-Toss Fast Pasta

It's 5:40 p.m. and everyone's chanting, "What's for supper?" With some staple ingredients in the pantry and a few fresh essentials in the fridge, you can walk in the door, put a large pot of water on to boil, and then take off your coat—knowing that dinner can be on the table in 20 minutes or even less. Here are some easy sauces to make while the pasta is cooking (see basic instructions for cooking pasta, page 121; if the pasta is done a little ahead of the sauce, just drain, return to pot and cover).

No-Sauce Toss is the simplest of all (best with quickly cooked, good-quality fresh linguine or fettuccine): Toss hot, drained pasta with extra-virgin olive oil to coat lightly, a generous sprinkling of chopped fresh herbs such as basil or Italian parsley, and lots of freshly ground pepper. To this, you could also add some chopped fresh or sun-dried tomatoes (oil-packed) or any grilled vegetables. If you'd like it a bit saucier, add a little of the pasta cooking water.

Pesto Pasta: Toss hot, drained pasta with Pesto (page 234) to coat lightly; if pesto is too thick, add a little of the pasta cooking water or olive oil. If desired, add some halved cherry tomatoes, chopped sun-dried tomatoes and toasted pine nuts. Season with freshly ground pepper and top with shaved or grated parmesan.

Spaghetti Carbonara: In skillet, heat 2 tsp (10 mL) each butter and olive oil; add 1 chopped small onion, 2 minced garlic cloves and 4 oz (125 g) chopped bacon or pancetta; cook until onion is soft and bacon almost crisp. In small bowl, beat 2 eggs; set aside. Meanwhile, cook 8 oz (250 g) spaghetti in boiling salted water; drain quickly and return to pot over medium heat. Immediately stir in eggs; toss for about 30 seconds until pasta is coated. Stir in 1/4 cup (50 mL) freshly grated parmesan and the bacon mixture. Serve immediately. **Makes 2 to 3 servings**.

Clam Sauce: Cook 6 oz (175 g) linguine or spaghetti. Meanwhile, in skillet, heat 2 tbsp (30 mL) butter; cook 1 chopped small onion and 2 minced garlic cloves until softened but not browned. Stir in 1/4 cup (50 mL) white wine and the liquid drained from a 5-oz (142 g) can clams; cook until reduced by half. Add drained clams, 1/4 cup (50 mL) chopped parsley and freshly ground pepper to taste; cook for 1 minute. Toss with hot, drained pasta and sprinkle with freshly grated parmesan. **Makes 2 servings**.

Puttanesca Sauce: Cook 12 oz (375 g) spaghetti or other pasta. Meanwhile, in saucepan, combine 2 cups (500 mL) Basic Tomato Sauce (page 122), 1/4 tsp (1 mL) hot pepper flakes, 1/2 cup (125 mL) sliced black olives and 2 tbsp (30 mL) capers; simmer for 5 minutes. Add chopped Italian parsley and freshly ground pepper to taste. Toss with hot, drained pasta and top with freshly grated parmesan. **Make 4 servings**.

Sausage, Red Pepper and Broccoli Sauce: Cook 12 oz (375 g) pasta such as fusilli. Meanwhile, in skillet, heat 1 tbsp (15 mL) olive oil; add 1 chopped onion and 3 minced garlic cloves; cook until softened. Remove casings from 1/2 lb (250 g) Italian sausage (hot or mild) and crumble into skillet; cook for 3 minutes. Add 1 slivered sweet red pepper, 3/4 cup (175 mL) tomato sauce and 1 tsp (5 mL) dried basil. Cover and simmer for 3 minutes. Add 2 cups (500 mL) cooked broccoli florets and salt and pepper to taste. Toss with hot, drained pasta and top with grated parmesan. **Makes 4 servings**.

Creamy Tomato Sauce: Cook 12 oz (375 g) tortellini, fettuccine or other pasta. Purée 1-1/2 cups (375 mL) tomato sauce (such as Basic Tomato Sauce, page 122) in blender or food processor until smooth. Pour into saucepan; stir in 1/2 cup (125 mL) whipping cream; simmer for about 5 minutes. Toss with hot, drained pasta. **Makes 4 servings**.

Pasta Primavera Two Ways 🌱

Fresh-tasting, fast and easy, this colourful toss of pasta and vegetables can be sauced with either cream or fresh tomatoes. "Primavera" means spring, but any seasonal vegetables (such as asparagus, snow peas, green beans, green peas, carrots, cauliflower or summer squash) can be added or substituted for those suggested here.

➜ In large pot of boiling salted water, cook 8 oz (250 g) fettuccine, spaghetti, penne or other pasta until tender but still firm to the bite. Meanwhile, in large skillet, heat 2 tbsp (30 mL) olive oil. Add 1 chopped small onion, 2 minced garlic cloves and about 1/2 cup (125 mL) each coarsely chopped sweet red pepper, sliced zucchini, small broccoli florets and sliced mushrooms. Cover and cook until nearly tender, about 2 minutes.

For a fresh tomato sauce, add 2 chopped ripe tomatoes OR for a creamy sauce, add 1/2 cup (125 mL) whipping cream. Cook, stirring, for 2 to 3 minutes, until tomatoes are softened or cream is bubbling. Stir in 1/4 cup (50 mL) freshly grated parmesan cheese and 2 tbsp (30 mL) chopped parsley or basil if desired. Season with salt and pepper to taste. Toss with hot, drained pasta. Top with more parmesan if desired. **Makes 2 to 3 servings**.

Fettuccine Alfredo

This is the real thing, rich and decadent. Share it with someone special, or serve smaller portions as a first course.

8 oz	fettuccine (fresh or dried)	250 g
2 tbsp	butter	30 mL
3/4 cup	whipping cream	175 mL
3/4 cup	freshly grated parmesan (preferably Parmigiano-Reggiano)	175 mL
	Freshly ground pepper	

➜ In large pot of boiling salted water, cook fettuccine until tender but firm, about 3 minutes for fresh or 6 minutes for dried; drain. Meanwhile, in large skillet over medium heat, melt butter. Add whipping cream and heat, stirring constantly, until bubbling. Stir in parmesan. Add fettuccine to skillet; toss until well coated with sauce. Serve immediately, sprinkled with freshly ground pepper and more parmesan if desired. **Makes 2 main-course** or **4 appetizer servings**.

Fettuccine with Smoked Salmon and Asparagus: To Fettuccine Alfredo, add 3 oz (90 g) smoked salmon cut in strips, 1/2 lb (250 g) cooked asparagus cut in small pieces, 1 tbsp (15 mL) chopped fresh tarragon or dill and 1 tsp (5 mL) grated lemon rind. Simmer for 1 minute to heat through.

Fettuccine with Shiitake Mushrooms: Make same as Fettuccine Alfredo, except before adding cream to skillet, add 2 minced shallots and 4 oz (125 g) shiitake mushrooms (stems removed, sliced thick); cook until tender.

♥ **Low-Fat Creamy Fettuccine:** You can use low-fat evaporated milk instead of whipping cream (or white sauce thickened with flour), as long as you call it Fettuccine Cousin Vinnie or anything other than Alfredo, who would be most offended.

Ravioli or Tortellini Casserole

In pot of boiling salted water, cook 8 oz (250 g) fresh or frozen ravioli or tortellini until tender but still firm, about 10 minutes. Drain well. In 6-cup (1.5 L) casserole, combine pasta with 2 cups (500 mL) Basic Tomato Sauce (page 122) or a favourite bottled brand. Sprinkle with 1 cup (250 mL) shredded mozzarella and 1/4 cup (50 mL) grated parmesan. Bake in 350F (180C) oven for 20 minutes or until bubbling hot. (Or microwave on High for about 3 minutes.) **Makes about 3 servings**.

Baked Cannelloni ❦

Pasta tubes stuffed with a creamy cheese mixture and baked in tomato sauce make a popular dish for casual entertaining as well as family dinners.

1-3/4 cups	ricotta cheese	425 mL
1 cup	shredded mozzarella cheese	250 mL
1/4 cup	grated parmesan cheese	50 mL
1	egg	1
1/2 cup	well-drained chopped cooked spinach	125 mL
1-1/2 tsp	dried basil	7 mL
1/4 tsp	nutmeg	1 mL
12	cannelloni tubes, cooked according to package directions	12
3 cups	Basic Tomato Sauce (page 122) or good-quality store-bought, puréed until smooth	750 mL
2 tbsp	grated parmesan cheese	30 mL

➜ In large bowl, combine ricotta, mozzarella, 1/4 cup (50 mL) parmesan, egg, spinach, basil, nutmeg, salt and pepper. Stuff into cooked cannelloni shells. Spoon half of sauce into 13- x 9-inch (33 x 23 cm) baking dish. Place filled cannelloni in single layer in dish. Spoon remaining sauce over top; sprinkle with 2 tbsp (30 mL) parmesan. Cover with foil. Bake in 375F (190C) oven for 30 minutes. Remove foil and bake for another 10 minutes or until bubbling. **Makes 4 servings**.

Tip: Cannelloni are easiest to stuff with a piping tube. Fresh pasta squares, available from some Italian food shops and supermarkets, are even easier; just spoon filling down the centres and roll up; place seam side down in baking dish. It's important to use a smooth tomato sauce with good Italian flavour in this recipe.

Pasta e Fagioli ❦

On a trip to Italy a few years ago with my archae-ology-oriented daughter Lise, I learned that her idea of heaven was spending an entire day in the Roman Forum and then discovering a tiny trat-toria serving up fragrant bowlfuls of pasta e fagioli. This flavourful rendition of the traditional Italian soup-stew—a hearty medley of pasta and beans—is one of her vegetarian specials; some ver-sions start with sautéeing some chopped pro-sciutto, pancetta or salt pork before the onions.

2 tbsp	extra-virgin olive oil	30 mL
1	onion, chopped	1
2	cloves garlic, minced	2
1	stalk celery, including leaves, chopped	1
4 cups	chicken or vegetable stock	1 L
1	can (28 oz/796 mL) tomatoes	1
1/4 tsp	hot pepper flakes	1 mL
1 tsp	dried basil (or 1 tbsp/15 mL chopped fresh)	5 mL
1	can (19 oz/540 mL) great northern beans or cannellini (white kidney beans), drained and rinsed	1
2 cups	tubetti, ditali or macaroni	500 mL
	Freshly grated parmesan or romano cheese	
	Chopped Italian parsley (optional)	

➜ In large heavy saucepan over medium heat, heat oil. Add onion, garlic and celery; cook for 3 to 5 minutes or until softened (do not brown). Add stock, tomatoes (crushed or chopped) and their juice, hot pepper flakes and dried basil (if using). Bring to boil; reduce heat and simmer, partially covered, for 10 minutes. Add beans and simmer for another 10 minutes. Remove 1/2 cup (125 mL) of the mixture and purée in food processor until smooth; return to pot. Add pasta and cook for 10 minutes or until tender but still firm to the bite. Add fresh basil (if using) and salt and pepper to taste. Serve sprinkled generously with cheese and parsley (if using). **Makes 4 to 6 servings**.

Easy Macaroni and Cheese

Make this easy but rich-tasting cheese sauce in the microwave while the macaroni is cooking, then simply combine the two for a speedy, satisfying supper when you're in a hurry. For a traditional baked macaroni and cheese with crispy crumb topping, bake in oven (see Variations below).

2 cups	elbow macaroni	500 mL

Microwave Cheese Sauce:

1/4 cup	butter	50 mL
1/4 cup	all-purpose flour	50 mL
2 cups	milk	500 mL
1 tsp	Dijon mustard (or pinch dry mustard)	5 mL
1/2 tsp	salt	2 mL
Pinch	pepper	Pinch
3 cups	shredded cheddar cheese	750 mL

Topping:

1 cup	shredded cheddar cheese	250 mL
1-1/2 cups	fresh breadcrumbs	375 mL
1/4 cup	butter, melted	50 mL

→ In pot of boiling salted water, cook macaroni until tender, about 12 minutes; drain well.

Microwave Cheese Sauce: In 4-cup (1 L) glass measuring cup or microwavable bowl, melt butter (about 20 seconds on High). Stir in flour, milk, mustard, salt and pepper. Microwave on High for 2 minutes; stir with whisk. Microwave on High for 2 minutes longer; stir with whisk. Stir in cheese until melted. Taste and add a little more salt and pepper if needed. (Alternatively, use stovetop method for cheese sauce; see Variations below.) Combine sauce with drained macaroni. Turn into microwavable baking dish.

Stovetop method for Cheese Sauce: In heavy saucepan over medium heat, melt butter. Stir in flour until smooth. Gradually add milk, stirring with a whisk. Stirring constantly, bring to boil and boil gently for about 2 minutes, until thickened and smooth. Add mustard, salt and pepper. Stir in cheese just until melted; remove from heat.

Topping: Sprinkle with shredded cheese (omit crumbs and butter). Microwave on High for 1 minute or until cheese is melted. **Makes about 4 servings**.

Oven-Baked Macaroni and Cheese: Turn macaroni and sauce into greased 8-cup (2 L) baking dish. Topping: Sprinkle with shredded cheese. Toss together breadcrumbs and melted butter; sprinkle over cheese. Bake in 375F (190C) oven for 25 to 30 minutes or until bubbly and lightly browned.

Asian Noodles

Sorting out which Asian noodles are which, and what they're made from, can be as tangled as the packaged nests of them that sit on market shelves. Unlike European pastas, which are mostly made from wheat, Asian noodles are made from rice, wheat, buckwheat, yam or bean flour. And they're sold in an equally wide range of shapes and thicknesses. But when approached with some simple divisions in mind, the distinctions become clearer. Most Asian noodles are sold dried, but packages are also available frozen or fresh. Shapes and thicknesses govern cooking times. Texture comes primarily from the flour from which the noodles are made (See Sidebar).

Pad Thai

You can make this popular stir-fried noodle dish with or without the shrimp, or replace either chicken or shrimp with small cubes of fried tofu (available in Asian food shops). The preferred noodles for Pad Thai are flat, linguine-shaped noodles, sometimes labelled rice sticks; some versions of this dish use the thinner vermicelli.

1/2 lb	dried rice noodles	250 g
1/4 cup	each: fish sauce, ketchup	50 mL
2 tbsp	lime juice	30 mL
2 tsp	granulated sugar	10 mL
2 tsp	(or to taste) Asian chile paste or sauce	10 mL
1/4 cup	vegetable oil	50 mL
2	large cloves garlic, minced	2
1/2 lb	boneless, skinless chicken breast, cut into thin strips	250 g
1/2 lb	shrimp, peeled and deveined	250 g
2	eggs, lightly beaten	2
2 cups	fresh bean sprouts	500 mL
4	green onions, chopped	4
1/2 cup	roasted unsalted peanuts, coarsely chopped	125 mL
	Fresh coriander leaves; lime wedges	

➡ In large bowl, cover noodles with warm water; let soak for 20 minutes; drain. Mix together fish sauce, ketchup, lime juice, sugar and chile paste; set aside. In wok or very large skillet over medium-high heat, heat oil. Add garlic, chicken and shrimp; stir-fry until chicken loses its pink colour, about 2 minutes. Push chicken and shrimp aside and pour in egg; let set slightly, then stir to scramble. Add noodles, bean sprouts, green onions and reserved sauce. Stir-fry until noodles are softened and everything is mixed together and hot, about 3 minutes. Serve immediately, sprinkled with peanuts and coriander leaves and garnished with lime wedges. **Makes 4 servings**.

Kinds of noodles

Wheat flour produces flat, pasta-like egg noodles, wunton (or wonton) noodles and wrappers, fat Shanghai noodles, thin chow mein, thick round Japanese noodles called udon, and curly Japanese ramen sold in fast-food noodle blocks and cups. **Rice** flour is used for flat noodles, curly bands, long sticks and curly sticks (all are often labelled "rice stick noodles" with little regard to shape), thin paper-like sheets, and delicate vermicelli that resembles angel-hair pasta. Rice noodles can be pure white, greyish-white or translucent. **Bean thread** noodles are made from bean starch and are often translucent or glassy and brittle. The most common buckwheat noodles are Japanese soba, which are thick, round and greyish; some are made from pure **buckwheat** flour, some include wheat or yam flour as well.

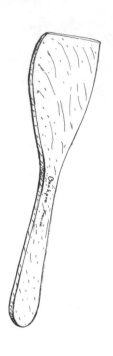

Rice Basics

Rice is the staple grain of many countries around the world, and Canadians are discovering the delights of the many kinds—Italian, basmati, jasmine and other Asian varieties, along with the familiar white and brown rices—widely available in supermarkets and specialty food shops. Most rices can be substituted for each other or used in combinations; experiment to find your preferences for pilafs, puddings and stuffings. Long-grain rice tends to separate into fluffy grains; short-grain tends to cling together. When desired for additional flavour, stock (chicken, beef or vegetable) can be used instead of water. Aromatic rices such as jasmine and basmati match perfectly with the spicy dishes of their Asian homelands but also make good alternatives to regular rice. Serve them as accompaniment to main dishes or experiment with incorporating them into favourite recipes; the results are often very flavourful and interesting (for example, rice pudding is wonderful made with aromatic rice, seasoned with cardamom and sprinkled with chopped pistachios).

How to Cook Rice

Do not rinse except when specified below. Follow package directions if available; quantities and times vary somewhat by brand. Some recommend stirring the rice into boiling water (as for parboiled rice, see below). However, the generally preferred method for most rices is to combine rice and water in a heavy saucepan, bring to boil, reduce heat, cover and simmer until water is absorbed. This method results in uniform cooking of the grains and is virtually foolproof—if you don't peek. The rice has to steam undisturbed; don't lift the lid or stir during cooking. At end of cooking time, remove from heat and let stand for a few minutes. Fluff with fork to separate grains.

Regular white rice (long-grain or short-grain) has been polished to remove the outer bran layer. *To cook:* In heavy saucepan, combine 1 cup (250 mL) rice and 2 cups (500 mL) water. Add 1/2 tsp (2 mL) salt if desired. Bring to boil, reduce heat to low, cover and simmer for 15 minutes. Remove from heat and let stand, covered, for 5 minutes. Fluff with fork. **Makes about 3 cups** (750 mL).

Brown rice is the whole grain with outer bran layer and germ intact. It is more nutritious than white rice and requires longer cooking. *To cook:* In heavy saucepan, combine 1 cup (250 mL) rice and 2-3/4 cups (675 mL) water. Add 1/2 tsp (2 mL) salt if desired. Bring to boil, reduce heat to low, cover and simmer for 45 minutes. Remove from heat and let stand, covered, for 10 minutes. **Makes about 3 cups** (750 mL). Brown rice can also be cooked in a large amount of gently boiling water until tender, then drained.

Parboiled rice (also called converted) has undergone processing so that it cooks into fluffy separate grains. The processing retains slightly more nutrients than in regular white rice. *To cook:* Cook according to package directions OR in heavy saucepan, stir 1 cup (250 mL) rice into 2-1/2 cups (625 mL) boiling water. Add 1/2 tsp (2 mL) salt if desired. Reduce heat to low; cover and simmer for 20 minutes or until water is absorbed. Fluff with fork. **Makes about 3-1/2 cups** (875 mL).

Arborio (superfino is the top grade) and other Italian-style rice (carnaroli, vialone nano) is short-grain rice with a starchy surface that produces a creamy product. Do not rinse the rice before cooking. Use for risotto (page 134) and creamy rice pudding (page 193).

Jasmine rice is a fragrant long-grain white rice; varieties grown in Thailand and the United States are available in many grocery stores. The cooked grains are soft and slightly clingy. Before cooking, rinse rice thoroughly (place in large bowl, cover with cold water and swish well; drain and repeat 2 or 3 times until water runs clear); drain rice in sieve. *To cook:* In heavy saucepan, combine 1 cup (250 mL) rinsed rice and 1 1/2 cups (375 mL) water. Bring to vigorous boil, cover, reduce heat to very low and cook for 15 minutes. Without lifting lid, remove from heat and let stand for 10 minutes. Turn rice gently to fluff. **Makes about 3 cups** (750 mL).

Basmati rice is an aromatic long-grain rice common in Indian cuisine. Rinse and cook same as jasmine rice. For brown basmati, double the amount of water and cooking time.

Japanese-style rice (grown in California) is available in Asian grocery stores and some supermarkets. It has short, rounded white grains and tends to clump together a little, making it easy to eat with chopsticks. It is cooked with less water than most rices, and without salt. *To cook:* Rinse 1-3/4 cups (425 mL) rice thoroughly in 2 or 3 changes of cold water (see jasmine rice, left). In saucepan, combine rice with 2 cups (500 mL) cold water; let soak for 30 minutes. Bring to vigorous boil, cover, reduce heat to very low and cook for 10 minutes. Without lifting lid, remove from heat and let stand for 15 minutes. Turn rice gently with rice paddle or wooden spoon. **Makes about 4 cups** (1 L).

Sushi rice is made with plain Japanese rice flavoured with seasoned rice vinegar. **Sticky rice** (also called glutinous rice) is a different kind of rice; it can be long- or short-grain and is used in China, Japan and all over Southeast Asia in savoury dishes and sweets. **Chinese rice** is usually a plain long-grain or medium-grain rice (not aromatic or parboiled).

Wild rice is not rice but an aquatic grass. It is harvested in northwestern Ontario, Manitoba and Saskatchewan. *To cook:* In heavy saucepan, combine 1 cup (250 mL) wild rice and 2-1/2 cups (625 mL) water. Bring to boil, reduce heat to low, cover and simmer for 40 to 50 minutes or until tender but still firm to the bite. **Makes about 3 cups** (750 mL). Wild rice can also be cooked in a large amount of gently boiling water until tender, then drained.

Basic Rice Pilaf

An easy way to dress up rice, savoury pilaf is great with most meat dishes, especially lamb or chicken.

2 tbsp	butter	30 mL
1/2 cup	finely chopped onion	125 mL
1/4 cup	finely chopped celery	50 mL
3/4 cup	long-grain rice	175 mL
1-1/4 cups	chicken stock	300 mL
1/2 tsp	salt (if stock is not salty)	2 mL
2 tbsp	chopped parsley	30 mL
	Salt and pepper to taste	

➜ In large heavy saucepan over medium-high heat, melt butter. Add onion and celery; cook until softened but not browned, about 2 minutes. Add rice and cook, stirring often, for 2 minutes. Stir in stock and salt; bring to boil. Reduce heat, cover and simmer for 20 minutes or until rice is tender and liquid is absorbed. Stir in parsley, salt and pepper. **Makes about 4 servings.**

Bulgur or Quinoa pilaf: substitute bulgur or quinoa for the rice.

Wild Rice, Barley and Mushroom Pilaf Casserole

For a vegetarian version, use vegetable stock instead of chicken stock. Barley is a traditional favourite for pilafs, and wild rice adds wonderful taste and texture. This pilaf can be also be used as a turkey stuffing. If your bird is large, you could serve it with traditional bread stuffing inside and pilaf in the neck cavity.

1/2 cup	wild rice	125 mL
2 tbsp	butter	30 mL
2 cups	coarsely chopped mushrooms	500 mL
3/4 cup	pearl barley, rinsed	175 mL
1/2 cup	each: chopped onion and celery	125 mL
1-1/2 cups	chicken stock	375 mL
1/4 cup	chopped parsley	50 mL
	Salt and pepper	

➜ Rinse wild rice thoroughly in sieve under cold running water. In saucepan, bring 3 cups (750 mL) water to boil; add wild rice and 1/2 tsp (2 mL) salt. Bring to boil, reduce heat and boil gently for 45 minutes or until rice is tender but still chewy. Drain and rinse in sieve under cold running water; set aside. Meanwhile, in large shallow saucepan, melt half of butter. Add mushrooms and sauté lightly; remove and set aside. Add remaining butter to pan; heat until melted. Add barley, onion and celery; cook, stirring, until vegetables are softened, about 5 minutes. Add stock and bring to boil. Reduce heat, cover and simmer for 35 minutes or until liquid is absorbed and barley is tender but still chewy (add a little more liquid if all has been absorbed before barley is cooked). Add parsley, wild rice and mushrooms; mix gently. Season to taste with salt and pepper. Transfer to covered casserole. (Can be prepared in advance to this point and refrigerated.) Bake in 375F (190C) oven for about 20 minutes (or microwave on High for about 5 minutes) until heated through, stirring once or twice. **Makes 6 to 8 servings.**

Paella

This adaptation of the classic Spanish dish is a great choice for informal dinner parties; it looks impressive and tastes terrific. You can adjust the ingredients and call it "sort-of paella" as I often do, using Italian sausage, increasing or decreasing the seafood and adding clams if available. Short-grain rice is traditional, but long-grain is fine, too (the paella will have a looser texture). If you don't have a paella pan, serve this in a very shallow large round serving bowl (you can often find good-looking, inexpensive ones at Italian and Portuguese food shops and hardware stores).

1 tbsp	olive oil	15 mL
3/4 lb	chorizo or hot Italian sausage	375 g
2 lb	chicken thighs	1 kg
1 tsp	saffron	5 mL
3 cups	hot chicken stock	750 mL
1	large onion, chopped	1
4	cloves garlic, minced	4
1	each: sweet red and green pepper, chopped	1
1	can (28 oz/796 mL) tomatoes	1
1 tsp	paprika	5 mL
1/2 tsp	each: dried thyme, oregano, salt, pepper	2 mL
2 cups	short-grain rice	500 mL
1 cup	frozen peas	250 mL
16	fresh mussels, scrubbed	16
3/4 lb	large shrimp, peeled and deveined	375 g
	Lemon wedges for garnish	

➜ In very large skillet or paella pan over medium-high heat, heat oil. Add sausage and brown on all sides; remove, cut into thick slices and set aside. In skillet, brown chicken in batches; remove and set aside with sausage. Stir saffron into hot stock; set aside. To skillet, add onion, garlic and peppers; cook over medium heat until softened, about 5 minutes. Add stock, tomatoes (crush as you add them), paprika, thyme, oregano, salt and pepper. Bring to boil. Stir in rice; reduce heat to medium-low. Add chicken and sausages, nestling them into the rice. Simmer uncovered, stirring occasionally, until rice is nearly tender and liquid nearly absorbed, about 20 minutes. Add peas, mussels and shrimp, nestling them into the rice. Cook for 10 minutes or until rice is tender, shrimp are pink and mussels are opened. Discard any unopened mussels. Serve garnished with lemon wedges. **Makes about 8 servings**.

Risotto

Making risotto properly requires a little patience but produces one of the world's ultimate comfort foods. Traditionally served as a first course, it also makes a good main course with a green salad. For the proper creamy texture, it's essential that you use Italian short-grain rice; arborio is the most readily available; carnaroli and vialone nano are even better if available. As variations on the theme, a wide variety of ingredients—mushrooms, seafood, prosciutto or pancetta, fresh greens, squash, zucchini or radicchio—are often added during cooking, or a tiny drizzle of truffle oil added at the end.

5 cups	(approx) chicken stock	1.25 L
2 tbsp	olive oil	30 mL
1 tbsp	butter	15 mL
1/2 cup	finely chopped onion	125 mL
1	clove garlic, minced	1
1-1/2 cups	arborio rice	375 mL
1/2 cup	white wine (optional)	125 mL
1/2 cup	freshly grated parmesan cheese	125 mL
	Salt and pepper	

➔ In saucepan, bring stock to simmer; keep hot over low heat. In large heavy saucepan over medium heat, heat olive oil and butter. Add onion and garlic; cook until softened but not browned. Add rice and cook, stirring constantly, for 2 minutes. Add white wine (if using); stir until almost absorbed. Add 1 cup (250 mL) of the stock; cook, stirring constantly with wooden spoon, until liquid is almost completely absorbed. Continue adding stock, 1/2 cup (125 mL) at a time, stirring almost constantly after each addition until liquid is absorbed before adding more, until rice is very creamy with a slight firmness at the centre, about 20 minutes. Stir in parmesan; add salt and pepper to taste. Serve immediately. **Makes 4 servings**.

Jamaican Rice and Peas

Every Caribbean island has its own version of rice and peas, using various kinds of dried peas and beans. The tiny red peas (sometimes called cow peas) that make this one authentically Jamaican are available in West Indian shops and some supermarkets; other dried red peas or beans could be substituted. This is delicious with curried chicken or fish.

1/2 cup	small dried red peas	125 mL
1-1/2 cups	water	375 mL
1/2 cup	coconut milk	125 mL
1 cup	long-grain rice	250 mL
1	small onion, chopped	1
1/4 tsp	dried thyme	1 mL
1/2 tsp	salt	2 mL
Pinch	pepper	Pinch

➔ In saucepan, boil peas in water until tender, about 1 hour. Drain and measure cooking liquid; add coconut milk plus enough water to make 2 cups (500 mL) of liquid. Return liquid and peas to saucepan. Add rice, onion, thyme, salt and pepper. Cover and simmer until liquid is absorbed and rice is tender, about 30 minutes. Add salt and pepper to taste if needed. **Makes about 4 servings**.

Beans Basics

Dried legumes—beans, peas and lentils (collectively known as pulses)—are not only the basics of countless delicious dishes but also tops in nutritional value (low in fat and high in protein, complex carbohydrate, fibre, B-vitamins, folic acid and several minerals). You'll find a great variety of dried beans, peas and lentils, including packaged mixtures for soups, in bulk food stores and most supermarkets. Many kinds of beans are available canned (and some frozen); they are convenient to use in place of cooked beans in most recipes. One 19-oz (540 mL) can of beans, drained, equals about 2 cups (500 mL) cooked beans. Or you can economize by cooking beans from scratch; keep a stock of them in the freezer for extra convenience. Dried beans keep almost indefinitely, stored in tightly covered containers in a dry, cool place (although older beans take longer to cook).

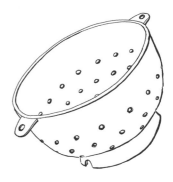

Soaking and Cooking Beans:

1 cup (250 mL) dried beans will yield 2 to 3 cups (500 to 750 mL) cooked beans. Dried beans and whole peas must be soaked before cooking; split peas and lentils do not require soaking. There are two soaking methods.

Quick-Soak: Rinse beans and place in large saucepan with 3 times their volume of water. Bring to boil and boil gently for 2 to 3 minutes. Remove from heat, cover and let stand for 1 hour.

Long-Soak: Rinse beans and place in large bowl with 3 times their volume of cold water; let soak for about 12 hours.

To cook: Drain and rinse soaked beans. Place in large saucepan with fresh water to cover beans by about 3 inches (8 cm). Do not add salt or acidic ingredients during cooking (prevents beans from softening). Bring to boil, reduce heat, cover and simmer until tender but slightly firm to the bite. Cooking times depend on freshness of beans (older take longer); cooking in hard water or at high altitudes also takes longer. *Navy beans (white pea beans), great northern, pinto, romano, kidney, fava, lima, adzuki and small red beans* take from 45 minutes to 1-1/4 hours; *chick peas* (garbanzos) about 1-1/2 hours; *soybeans* about 3 hours. Unsoaked *split peas and green or brown lentils* take 25 to 45 minutes, most red lentils 10 to 15 minutes. Soaked or cooked beans can be kept in refrigerator for up to 3 days or frozen.

Tofu is made from soybean curd and is extremely versatile, taking on the flavour of whatever it's cooked with. Choose firm or extra-firm tofu for stir-fries and grilling; soft and silken tofu for shakes, soups, dressings, spreads and desserts. Tempeh is made from fermented soybeans and has a chewy texture.

Grains Basics

Canada's Food Guide recommends 5 to 12 servings of grain products (breads, cereals, rice, pasta) per day as low-fat sources of fibre, carbohydrate and B-vitamins. Check out bulk food stores for a variety of interesting grains to use in breads, soups, salads and pilafs. Cooked grains make great alternatives to rice and potatoes; for extra flavour, they can be cooked in stock instead of water; add some chopped onion, celery, carrots or mushrooms if desired. Add salt and pepper to taste at end.

Basic Method for Cooking Grains:

In heavy saucepan, bring measured amount of water to boil, add about 1/4 tsp (1 mL) salt per cup (250 mL) of grain. Stir in grain; reduce heat, cover and simmer until tender; drain off any excess water. Most grains triple in bulk when cooked (e.g., 1 cup/250 mL raw will yield about 3 cups/750 mL cooked).

Barley: Husked, polished kernels called pearl or pot barley. Simmer 1 part barley with 3 parts water for about 45 minutes. (See Basic Method, above.) Used as side dish in soups, stuffings, pilafs and casseroles.

Bran (wheat or oat): Outer layer of kernels; very high in fibre; used in cereals and baked goods.

Bulgur: Wheat kernels that have been steamed, dried and crushed. Available coarse, medium and fine (use medium if recipe doesn't specify). Because it's partially cooked, bulgur is quick to prepare; stir 1 part bulgur into 1-1/2 parts boiling water and simmer for 15 minutes. (See Basic Method, above.) As an alternative to cooking, bulgur can be soaked in hot water for 30 minutes. Bulgur is commonly used for Tabbouleh Salad (page 56). To use in pilaf, see Basic Rice Pilaf (page 132).

Cornmeal: Fine and coarse grinds; used for baking, coatings, cooked cereal and polenta.

Cracked wheat: Whole wheat kernels, crushed but not precooked. Simmer 1 part cracked wheat with 2 parts water for 30 to 40 minutes. (See Basic Method, above.)

Grits: Means any coarsely ground grain, but commonly refers to hominy grits (see Hominy).

Groats: Refers to any crushed grain, most commonly buckwheat groats (see kasha).

Hominy: Dried white or yellow corn kernels treated with alkali to remove hulls. Used in traditional Native Canadian cooking, especially corn soup. Ground hominy grits are used in the American South to make a cooked dish similar to polenta.

Kasha: Roasted buckwheat groats. Cover kasha with boiling water and let stand for 10 to 15 minutes.

Millet: Small whole kernels; similar flavour to brown rice. Simmer 1 part millet with 2 parts water for about 40 minutes. (See Basic Method, above.)

Oats: Rolled oats used for porridge and in baking are available as quick-cooking oats (which cook in about 5 minutes) or large-flake oats (also called old-fashioned; they take about 15 minutes to cook). For cooked cereal, follow package directions. Large-flake and quick oats are interchangeable in most recipes. "Instant" oats, usually packaged with sugar and other flavourings, are precooked and cannot be substituted for regular oats. True "oatmeal" (sometimes labelled "Scotch," "Irish" or "steel-cut" oats) is a coarse meal that takes longer to cook than rolled oats.

Quinoa: Tiny bead-shaped grain native to ancient Peru; very high in protein; mild flavour. Rinse, then simmer 1 part quinoa with 2 parts water for about 15 minutes. (See Basic Method, page 136.) Use like rice in main dishes, soups, salads. To use in pilaf, see Basic Rice Pilaf (page 132).

Spelt: An ancient variety of large-kernel wheat. Cook as for wheat berries.

Wheat berries: Unprocessed whole wheat kernels. Soak overnight, then simmer 1 part wheat berries with 3 parts water for about 1 hour. (See Basic Method, page 136.)

Couscous: A staple of North African cooking, couscous looks like a grain but is a tiny pasta made from semolina. Packaged precooked couscous is widely available in supermarkets. Follow package directions. OR place couscous in saucepan or bowl and pour in boiling water (use 1-1/4 cups/300 mL water to 1 cup/250 mL couscous); cover and let stand for 10 minutes; fluff with fork. Couscous is quite bland but lends itself to all kinds of variations and additions. For extra flavour, prepare it with stock (chicken, meat or vegetable) instead of water.

For a pilaf-type side dish, sauté some chopped vegetables (onion, garlic, celery, sweet peppers) in a little oil before adding couscous and hot stock. For a North African variation, add chopped dried apricots, raisins, slivered almonds and a touch of cinnamon. Or season with cumin and hot pepper flakes, or with grated lemon or orange rind and a little dried thyme. For a salad, toss couscous with cooked chick peas and chopped grilled vegetables, or with chopped plum tomatoes, green onions, lots of chopped fresh mint, basil or parsley, and a light garlic or lemon vinaigrette.

Polenta

For traditional polenta, use an Italian-style coarse-grained cornmeal (or 2 parts coarse and 1 part fine cornmeal for creamier texture). Instant polenta (which cooks in about 5 minutes) is available, but most brands have less flavour and softer texture than the traditional. Precooked polenta sold in plastic-wrapped tubes is very bland. There's nothing like the real thing.

3 cups	water	750 mL
1 tsp	salt	5 mL
1 cup	cornmeal	250 mL

➡ In heavy-bottomed pot, bring water to gentle boil; add salt. Gradually add cornmeal in a fine, steady stream, whisking constantly with a wire whisk to prevent lumping. Reduce heat to low and cook, stirring often with a long-handled wooden spoon, for 20 to 30 minutes or until mixture is very thick and pulls away from sides of pan. Remove from heat. For extra flavour, stir in 1 tbsp (15 mL) of unsalted butter and 1/4 cup (50 mL) freshly grated parmesan. To serve polenta soft, spoon directly out of pot into serving dish. If you want it a bit firmer, pour onto platter or wooden board, let it firm up for a few minutes, then cut into thick slices. **Makes 4 servings.** Serve polenta with any stewed or braised meat or poultry or a chunky sauce. Many Italian recipes also use firm polenta for layered baked dishes.

🔥 **Grilled Polenta:** Pour hot polenta into a lightly oiled shallow pan and spread into a slab about 1/2 inch (1 cm) thick (use spatula dipped in hot water); chill until firm. Cut into squares or triangles, brush with olive oil and grill, broil or cook in skillet until lightly browned. Serve as main-course accompaniment. For appetizers, top small squares with roasted peppers, ratatouille or pesto; or sprinkle with asiago, gorgonzola or goat cheese and broil until melted

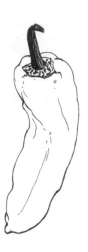

Mediterranean Spicy Rice and Beans ⸙

Lots of flavour, colour and texture make this a winner for family dinners or casual entertaining. It goes well with grilled Italian sausages but is also a satisfying vegetarian dish on its own.

1 tbsp	olive oil	15 mL
1 cup	each: chopped onions, celery, sweet red pepper	250 mL
2	cloves garlic, minced	2
1 tsp	dried basil	5 mL
1/2 tsp	each: dried rosemary, oregano, ground cumin	2 mL
1/2 tsp	salt (less if stock is salty)	2 mL
Pinch	hot pepper flakes	Pinch
	Freshly ground pepper	
1 cup	long-grain rice	250 mL
1-1/2 cups	chicken or vegetable stock	375 mL
1	can (19 oz/540 mL) red kidney beans, drained	1
1	can (28 oz/796 mL) tomatoes	1

➜ In large heavy saucepan over medium heat, heat oil. Add onions, celery, red pepper and garlic; cook, stirring, until onions are softened. Add basil, rosemary, oregano, cumin, salt, hot pepper flakes and a few grindings of pepper. Add rice, stock, beans and tomatoes (crushed). Bring to boil. Transfer to 10-cup (2.5 L) casserole. Bake, covered, in 350F (180C) oven for 45 to 60 minutes or until rice is tender; stir once halfway through baking. **Makes 6 servings.**

Maple Baked Beans ❧

A great choice for a wintry day when you're in the mood for real baked beans. This traditional version includes maple syrup for mellow flavour and makes a satisfying supper with brown bread and coleslaw. For a vegetarian version, omit the salt pork.

1 lb	white pea beans (2 cups/500 mL)	500 g
1/3 cup	each: maple syrup, molasses, ketchup	75 mL
1 tsp	each: salt, dry mustard	10 mL
1/4 tsp	pepper	1 mL
1	medium onion, chopped	1
4 oz	salt pork or bacon, in one piece	125 g

➜ Soak beans by long-soak or quick-soak method (see page 135). Drain beans and place in large saucepan. Cover with cold water; bring to boil, reduce heat, cover and simmer until just tender but still holding their shape, about 45 minutes. Drain and place beans in bean pot or casserole. Mix together maple syrup, molasses, ketchup, mustard, salt, pepper and onion; add to beans and stir gently to mix. Tuck salt pork into centre. Add enough water to just cover beans. Cover and bake in 300F (150C) oven for 4 hours or until beans are very tender; check occasionally and add a little more water as needed to keep beans moist; uncover for the last half hour; add salt to taste if needed. **Makes 6 to 8 servings.**

Bistro Lentils with Smoked Sausage

This recipe from food writer Johanna Burkhard makes an easy, earthy supper dish that tastes great on a late-fall evening. For a variation, you can start with fresh smoked sausage; brown it first, then add vegetables, lentils and stock (or half stock, half white wine); simmer until tender and add vinegar and seasonings at the end. For dishes like this, use small green lentils that hold their shape in cooking, such as Eston lentils grown on the Canadian prairies.

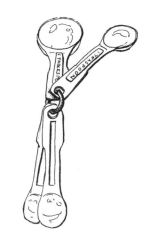

3-1/2 cups	chicken stock	875 mL
1-1/2 cups	lentils, rinsed	375 mL
1/2 tsp	dried thyme	2 mL
2 tbsp	olive oil	30 mL
1 cup	diced red onions	250 mL
3	cloves garlic, minced	3
2	carrots, diced	2
1 cup	diced fennel or celery	250 mL
1	sweet red pepper, diced	1
2 tbsp	balsamic vinegar	30 mL
1/2 lb	cooked smoked sausage, cut into chunks	250 g
	Freshly ground pepper	
1/4 cup	chopped parsley	50 mL

➜ In large saucepan, bring stock to boil over high heat. Add lentils and thyme; reduce heat, cover and boil gently for 30 to 40 minutes or until lentils are tender (some kinds take longer). Meanwhile, heat oil in nonstick skillet over medium heat. Add onions, garlic, carrots and fennel; cover and cook, stirring often, until softened. Add red pepper; cook for 2 minutes more or until vegetables are just tender. Stir in vinegar. Add vegetables and sausage to lentils in saucepan; season with pepper to taste. Cover and cook for 5 to 8 minutes or until sausage is heated through. (Add more stock or water if necessary to prevent lentils from sticking.) Stir in parsley. Serve warm or at room temperature. **Makes 6 servings**.

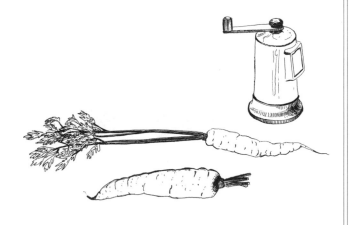

Marvellous Meatless Chili

This quick, hearty chili is a hit with everyone, vegetarian or not. It's flavourful, colourful, low-fat and high-fibre, and the bulgur adds a satisfying meaty texture. Serve with tortilla crisps (page 21) or crusty bread.

3 tbsp	vegetable oil	45 mL
2	large onions, chopped	2
2 tsp	each: chili powder, groundcumin, dried oregano	10 mL
1/4 tsp	hot pepper flakes or cayenne	1 mL
3	cloves garlic, minced	3
2	sweet green peppers, diced	2
1 tsp	minced jalapeño pepper (optional)	5 mL
1	can (28 oz/796 mL) tomatoes, undrained, chopped	1
2 tbsp	tomato paste	30 mL
1/2 cup	water	125 mL
1/2 cup	bulgur	125 mL
1	can (19 oz/540 mL) each: black beans and red kidney beans, drained and rinsed	1
1-1/2 cups	canned or frozen corn kernels	375 mL
	Salt and pepper	

Toppings (optional):

> shredded cheddar cheese,
> sour cream,
> chopped fresh coriander

→ In large heavy saucepan over medium heat, heat oil. Add onions, chili powder, cumin, oregano and hot pepper flakes; cook, stirring often, until onions are softened, about 10 minutes. Add garlic and green peppers; cook, stirring, for 1 minute. Add jalapeño (if using), tomatoes, tomato paste and water; bring to boil. Stir in bulgur, black beans, kidney beans and corn. Reduce heat, cover and simmer, stirring occasionally, for 15 minutes or until bulgur is tender. Add salt and pepper to taste. Serve with toppings if desired. **Makes 6 servings.**

Eggs & Cheese

Eggs by the dozen and a basketful of cheeses give star performances in streamlined classics flavoured for today

Eggs Basics

Poached eggs: Fill wide shallow saucepan with water about 2 inches (5 cm) deep. Bring to boil; reduce to simmer. Break 1 egg into a small cup. With a spoon, swirl the simmering water into a small whirlpool (this will help form egg into rounded shape); holding cup close to surface of water, slip egg into water. Repeat with remaining eggs. Poach in gently simmering water for 2 to 3 minutes (test by gently touching with finger; yolk should feel soft and slightly set). Remove with slotted spoon.

Eggs cooked in the shell: Two methods produce satisfactory results; try both and take your pick.

- *Method 1:* Bring saucepan of water to boil (use enough water to cover eggs by at least 1 inch/2.5 cm). With slotted spoon, slowly lower eggs into water. Bring water back to boil, immediately reduce heat to simmer and start timing. *For soft-cooked eggs,* simmer for 3 to 5 minutes, depending on how soft you like them. *For hard-cooked eggs,* simmer for 12 minutes. Drain and immediately run cold water over eggs in pan until they are cooled; this stops the cooking and prevents a grey ring from forming around the yolks (which is caused by overcooking).

- *Method 2:* Place eggs in single layer in saucepan. Add cold water to cover by at least 1 inch (2.5 cm). Cover pan; bring quickly to boil, then remove from heat. *For soft-cooked eggs,* let stand in hot water, covered, for 3 to 5 minutes. For *hard-cooked eggs,* let stand in hot water, covered, for 25 minutes; drain and immediately run cold water over eggs until cooled.

Eggs Safety: Thorough cooking of eggs is recommended for high-risk groups (the very young, the elderly, pregnant women and people whose immune systems are suppressed). Others may choose to eat raw or lightly cooked eggs. Whatever your choice, use proper handling methods: Purchase Canada Grade A eggs only. Buy from a reliable retailer where eggs are refrigerated properly. Buy only eggs with clean, uncracked shells. Take eggs home directly from store and refrigerate immediately. Keep eggs refrigerated until you are ready to use them. Use by "best before" date on carton. Serve food containing raw or lightly cooked egg immediately, or refrigerate and use within a day. If you do not wish to use raw egg whites in recipes calling for them, you can use refrigerated pasteurized egg whites sold in cartons at grocery stores.

Cooking Tips: Eggs separate better when cold, but beat to a higher volume when at room temperature. To bring cold eggs to room temperature, do not leave out on kitchen counter. Instead, put whole eggs in a bowl of warm water for a few minutes. To warm egg whites, place in bowl over warm water; stir occasionally.

To freeze raw eggs: Raw egg whites can be frozen as is, in airtight container. To freeze yolks or whole eggs, put them in bowl and mix gently; add 1/2 tsp (2 mL) salt OR 1 tbsp (15 mL) sugar for every 1 cup (250 mL) egg. Freeze in small quantities so only what is needed can be thawed. Thaw in refrigerator and use only in recipes where eggs are thoroughly cooked.

Cheese Choice

Cheese shops (and many supermarkets) offer a dazzling array for every taste and use. Sampling some new varieties is an enjoyable way to become familiar with the wide range of choices and to discover some new favourites. Enjoy the versatility of cheese for breakfast, lunch and snacks; in salads, main dishes, fondues and desserts; and with wine.

All cheeses are best kept refrigerated. Fresh (unripened) cheeses should be served cold. Serve all other cheeses at room temperature (remove from refrigerator 1 hour before serving). Cheese is made from the milk of cows, goats, sheep, even water buffalo. Cheeses are usually classified in categories from fresh to hard, depending on how they are made as well as the length and method of ripening.

Fresh: Unripened cheeses; soft and creamy with a slight tang. Include cottage cheese, cream cheese, mascarpone, neufchâtel, quark and ricotta.

Soft: Surface-ripened with "bloomy" rinds and smooth texture. Common examples are brie and camembert.

Semi-soft: A large group divided according to ripening process. Unripened semi-soft cheeses such as mozzarella and bocconcini have an elastic texture. Interior-ripened, which are generally mild, include havarti, monterey jack, muenster and Saint Paulin. Surface-ripened have a more pronounced, sometimes pungent, flavour; they include feta, limburger and oka.

Firm: Interior-ripened; range from mild to sharp, depending on how long and by which method they have ripened. Includes brick, caciocavallo, cheddar, cheshire, colby, danbo, emmenthal, farmer's, fontina, friulano, gloucester, gouda, jarlsberg, leicester, marble, port salut, provolone, raclette, samsoe, swiss and tilsit.

Hard: Cooked and pressed, with a pronounced flavour and dry graininess due to the long ripening process. Asiago, parmesan and romano are in this category; the true parmesan is Parmigiano-Reggiano.

Blue: Distinctive blue veining and piquant flavour; can be soft or firm. Examples are danish blue, gorgonzola, roquefort and stilton.

Goat's milk cheese (chèvre): Ranges from fresh (mild flavour) to soft (saltier, more pronounced) to semi-soft and hard (flavour becomes saltier and stronger with age).

Sausage and Mushroom Scramble

Spice up brunch with this lively Tex-Mex take on traditional eggs and sausages. Serve with corn-bread squares or muffins (page 168).

6	hot Italian or other spicy sausages	6
1/2 cup	chopped onion	125 mL
1	clove garlic, minced	1
1	each: small sweet red and green pepper, cut into short strips	1
1 tbsp	(or to taste) minced jalapeño pepper	15 mL
2 cups	sliced or quartered small mushrooms	500 mL
1/4 tsp	(or to taste) hot pepper flakes	1 mL
	Salt and pepper to taste	
2 tbsp	butter	30 mL
12	eggs	12
1/2 cup	milk	125 mL
1/2 cup	each: shredded monterey jack and cheddar cheese	125 mL

➡ In nonstick skillet over medium heat, brown sausages on all sides; cover pan, reduce heat and cook for about 15 minutes or until cooked through. Remove sausages and cut into small pieces; set aside. To skillet, add onion, garlic, peppers and mushrooms; cook until softened but not browned. Return sausages to skillet. Add hot pepper flakes, salt and pepper. Keep warm over low heat. In very large nonstick skillet, melt butter over medium-high heat. Beat eggs lightly with milk; pour into skillet. Cook, stirring, until nearly set but still very moist. Add sausage mixture and cheese; stir gently until eggs are set but still moist. Add salt and pepper if needed. Serve immediately. **Makes 6 to 8 servings**.

Easy Eggs Benedict

Uncork the champagne and indulge in this brunch classic. Doing it right demands a good hollandaise sauce. This quick sauce tastes like the classic even though the butter has been pared back somewhat, and it's a snap to prepare using the microwave and blender.

	Quick Hollandaise Sauce (recipe at right)	
4	eggs	4
2	English muffins, split in half	2
4	slices cooked ham, prosciutto or smoked salmon	4

➡ Have pan of water simmering and ready to poach the eggs. Then quickly make the hollandaise and cover the blender tightly so sauce stays warm. Poach the eggs (see page 142). While eggs are poaching, toast muffins. Place muffins on 4 plates. Top with ham and poached egg. Spoon sauce over each. **Makes 4 servings**.

Quick Hollandaise Sauce:

3	egg yolks	3
1 tbsp	lemon juice	15 mL
Pinch	each: salt and white pepper	Pinch
1/2 cup	butter (in glass measuring cup)	125 mL

➡ In blender, combine egg yolks, lemon juice, salt and pepper; blend about 5 seconds. Heat butter in microwave on High until bubbling hot, about 1-1/2 minutes. With blender running, add hot butter slowly in thin stream through the hole in the lid. The sauce will thicken as the butter is added (takes only about 30 seconds).

Vegetable Frittata

Italian frittatas, the easiest of all omelets because they require no folding, make satisfying midweek suppers as well as weekend breakfasts. Use any combination of vegetables you like; traditional versions often include browned diced potatoes or some leftover pasta.

1 tbsp	olive oil	15 mL
1/4 cup	chopped onion	50 mL
1-1/2 cups	vegetables such as chopped sweet red pepper, sliced zucchini, coarsely chopped cooked broccoli, sliced mushrooms, or mixture	375 mL
1	clove garlic, minced	1
1/2 tsp	salt	2 mL
	Freshly ground pepper to taste	
6	eggs	6
1 cup	shredded mozzarella cheese	250 mL
2 tbsp	each: chopped fresh parsley and basil	30 mL
2 tbsp	grated parmesan cheese	30 mL

➜ In 10-inch (25 cm) nonstick skillet over medium heat, heat oil. Add onion; cook until softened a little, about 1 minute. Add vegetables; cook, stirring, for 3 minutes or until just tender. Stir in garlic, salt and pepper. In bowl, whisk eggs; stir in mozzarella, parsley and basil. Pour into skillet; stir briefly to mix. Cook, lifting edges with spatula during the first minute or 2 to allow uncooked eggs to flow underneath, until edges are set, centre is still moist and bottom is golden brown, about 5 minutes. Sprinkle with parmesan. Wrap skillet handle in foil if it's not ovenproof. Place frittata under preheated broiler for 1 to 2 minutes or until just set. Slide onto serving plate and cut into wedges. **Makes 4 servings**.

Classic French Omelet

A simple, satisfying supper for one. It's also easy to fix, short-order-style, for house guests, or makes the perfect breakfast in bed for someone special.

2	eggs	2
2 tsp	water	10 mL
Pinch	each: salt and pepper	Pinch
1 tsp	butter	5 mL
	Fillings (see below)	

➜ Have the fillings ready before you start cooking the omelet. In small bowl, lightly whisk together eggs, water, salt and pepper. Heat 7- to 8-inch (18 to 20 cm) nonstick skillet or omelet pan over medium-high heat; add butter and heat until it foams up and subsides but before it starts to brown. Pour in egg mixture and stir for 10 seconds. Cook, shaking pan occasionally and pushing egg from edges to centre to allow uncooked portions to flow underneath, for 1 minute or until almost set but still very moist. Spoon filling across centre; cook for another few seconds until underside is light golden. Fold over one-third of omelet (away from handle and toward the centre), then tilt pan and roll omelet onto plate so it is folded in three. **Makes 1 serving**.

Fillings: (about 1/4 cup/50 mL per omelet) shredded cheese (any kind); sautéed mushrooms; chopped fresh tomatoes with basil; chopped grilled vegetables or ratatouille (reheated in microwave); chopped cooked spinach with some crumbled feta or chèvre; chopped roasted red peppers; shredded grilled chicken; diced prociutto or ham; cooked crab, shrimp, smoked salmon.

Souffléd Sweet Omelet

Sweet omelets, laced with liqueur and topped with berries, are rather a novelty and make an interesting brunch dish or dessert for a small group (especially if your guests like to gather in the kitchen, since the omelets must be cooked immediately before serving). One omelet also makes a sweet little indulgence to share after dîner à deux.

2	eggs, separated	2
1 tbsp	each: granulated sugar, fruit liqueur	15 mL
1 tbsp	unsalted butter	15 mL
	Sweetened berries or sliced fruit; icing sugar	

→ In bowl, beat egg whites until stiff but not dry. In separate bowl, beat yolks with sugar and liqueur; fold into whites. Preheat broiler. In heavy ovenproof 8-inch (20 cm) skillet, melt butter; pour in egg mixture and spread evenly. Cook over medium-low heat, without stirring, until omelet is puffy and bottom is lightly browned, about 2 minutes. Broil about 8 inches (20 cm) below heat until top is lightly browned, about 2 minutes. Quickly spoon some berries over middle of omelet. With spatula, gently fold omelet in half to cover berries. Slide out onto warm plate. Sift icing sugar over top and sprinkle with more berries. If desired, drizzle with more liqueur. Serve immediately. **Makes 1 serving**.

Quiche by Any Other Name

Having bid adieu to Lorraine and many other quiches that were so popular in the '70s and '80s, we've moved on to more fashionable savoury pies, usually called tarts. The fillings are a bit shallower and showier, the flavours more intense, but they are Lorraine's relatives nonetheless. Here are two examples that are delicious by any name.

Asparagus and Goat Cheese Tart: Using Basic Pastry (page 216), roll out and fit pastry into 9- to 10-inch (23 to 25 cm) flan pan (about 1 inch/2.5 cm deep) with removable bottom. Pre-bake for 10 minutes in 375F (190C) oven.

Filling: Trim 3/4 lb (375 g) asparagus, peel stalks. Cook in large skillet of boiling water until tender, about 5 minutes. Drain and rinse under cold water. Cut off tips and set aside; chop stalks. In bowl, beat 2 eggs with 1/2 cup (125 mL) light cream; stir in chopped asparagus; season with salt and pepper. Pour into pastry shell. Arrange asparagus tips on top. Crumble 2 oz (60 g) goat cheese over top. Bake in 375F (190C) oven for 20 minutes or until set. Let cool until just warm. **Makes 4 to 6 servings**.

Red Pepper, Broccoli and Mushroom Tart: Prepare pastry shell as for Asparagus and Goat Cheese Tart.

Filling: In large nonstick skillet over medium-high heat, heat 1 tbsp (15 mL) olive oil. Add 1 chopped small onion, 1 minced garlic clove and 3/4 cup (175 mL) each chopped sweet red pepper, tiny broccoli florets and sliced small mushrooms. Stir-fry until vegetables are tender-crisp; add salt and pepper to taste. Let cool. In bowl, beat 2 eggs with 1/2 cup (125 mL) light cream. Add vegetable mixture and 1/2 cup (125 mL) shredded provolone or friulano cheese. Pour into pastry shell. Bake same as for Asparagus and Goat Cheese Tart.

Cheese Soufflé

Soufflés are much easier than many people imagine; this is a good basic one that can be made with many kinds of cheeses. Try swiss instead of cheddar (or half of each plus a little parmesan), or add some chèvre (goat cheese) for a French accent.

	Grated parmesan cheese	
3 tbsp	butter	45 mL
3 tbsp	all-purpose flour	45 mL
1 cup	milk	250 mL
1/2 tsp	salt	2 mL
1/4 tsp	dry mustard	1 mL
Pinch	pepper	Pinch
4	eggs, at room temperature, separated	4
1 cup	shredded old cheddar cheese	250 mL

➡ Butter a 6-cup (1.5 L) soufflé dish and sprinkle lightly with parmesan. In heavy saucepan over medium heat, melt butter. Whisk in flour; cook, stirring, until bubbling. Gradually whisk in milk; bring to boil, whisking constantly, and cook until thick and smooth, about 2 minutes. Whisk in salt, mustard and pepper. Remove from heat and whisk in yolks, one at a time. Add cheese; stir until melted. Transfer mixture to large bowl. In another bowl, beat egg whites until stiff but not dry. Stir a spoonful of the whites into cheese mixture to lighten it, then gently fold in remaining whites. Pour into prepared soufflé dish; very gently smooth the top. Bake in a preheated 375F (190C) oven for 30 to 35 minutes or until well risen and golden brown. Serve immediately. **Makes 4 servings**.

Swiss Cheese Fondue

An après-ski favourite that never goes out of style, cheese fondue can be made with wine or beer or flavoured with liqueur such as kirsch. Experimenting with different kinds and combinations of cheeses is interesting, too. This good basic recipe will get you started. In heavy saucepan, combine 1-1/2 cups (375 mL) white wine, 1 tbsp (15 mL) lemon juice and 1 lightly crushed garlic clove. Heat over medium heat until bubbles form around edge. Remove garlic. Toss 4 cups (1 L) shredded swiss cheese with 1 tbsp (15 mL) cornstarch. Add to wine, a handful at a time, stirring until melted. Transfer to fondue pot. Serve with small chunks of crusty bread and fondue forks for dipping. **Serves 4** as a light meal.

Harvest Strata

Layered stratas are splendid make-aheads for entertaining at brunch and can be made with a great variety of ingredients. Similar dishes have become fashionably known as "savoury bread puddings." This easy, colourful version is one of food writer Rose Murray's favourites for weekend house guests.

6	thick slices white bread	6
	Butter	
2 cups	shredded old cheddar cheese (about 8 oz/250 g)	500 mL
1	sweet red pepper, diced	1
3	green onions, sliced	3
1	small zucchini, diced	1
4	eggs	4
2-1/2 cups	milk	625 mL
1 tsp	each: dry mustard, Worcestershire sauce	5 mL
1/2 tsp	each: salt, dried thyme	2 mL
2 tsp	dried basil	10 mL
	Freshly ground pepper	

➜ Butter bread on one side; cut into 1/2-inch (1 cm) cubes. Arrange in greased shallow 11- x 7-inch (2 L) baking dish. Sprinkle with cheese. Scatter red pepper, green onions and zucchini on top. In bowl, whisk together eggs, milk, mustard, Worcestershire sauce, salt and thyme; pour over vegetables. Sprinkle with basil and pepper to taste. Cover and refrigerate overnight. Bake, uncovered, in 350F (180C) oven for 1 hour or until golden. **Makes 6 servings**.

Make-Ahead French Toast

Ideal for a leisurely weekend brunch, this convenient version of French toast can be assembled ahead of time and refrigerated overnight, then cooked in a skillet or baked in the oven. The French call French toast pain perdu or "lost bread" because it's made with stale bread that would have been wasted. Be sure to use bread that is a day or two old; if it's too fresh, the toast will be soggy. For this recipe, you will need most of a 1-lb (500 g) loaf; egg bread has good flavour and texture, but you can use any good Italian or French bread or even croissants.

8	(approx) slices (1 inch/2.5 cm thick) slightly stale egg bread*	8
4	eggs	4
1 cup	milk	250 mL
2 tbsp	granulated sugar	30 mL
1 tsp	vanilla	5 mL
1/4 tsp	salt	1 mL

* Slices should be about 4 x 3 inches (10 x 8 cm); larger ones can be halved or trimmed to fit.

➜ Arrange bread slices in single layer in 13- x 9-inch (33 x 23 cm) glass or ceramic dish. In bowl, whisk together eggs, milk, sugar, vanilla and salt. Pour over bread; let stand for 5 minutes; turn slices over. Cover with plastic wrap; refrigerate for at least 1 hour or up to 12.

To cook on stovetop: Melt a little butter in skillet over medium heat; add bread, a few slices at a time, and cook, turning once, until golden brown on both sides.

To bake: Place slices on well-buttered baking sheet (preferably nonstick). Bake in 400F (200C) oven for 10 minutes; turn slices over and bake for about 7 minutes longer or until slightly puffy and golden. Serve immediately, with warmed maple syrup or other toppings (see page 180). **Makes 4 servings**.

Asparagus to Zucchini...

Vegetables

The good earth delivers. Take it from there.

At the Market

"Eat your vegetables," say the nutritionists. And taking that advice has never been so easy, interesting and delicious. Farmers' markets, specialty grocers and supermarket produce sections are overflowing with an awesome array of choices in every category. There are two main rules for satisfaction: Buy the freshest possible, and don't over-cook. Here's a look at familiar favourites and recent arrivals:

Greens: A profusion of interesting greenery is definitely upstaging bagged spinach. Fresh bunches of **leaf spinach**, **beet greens** and **Swiss chard** (both white- and red-stemmed varieties) abound. Wash thoroughly in cold water, then cook, with only the water clinging to the leaves, in a saucepan just until wilted. Robust, stronger-flavoured varieties include: **rapini** (also called broccoli rabe and broccoletti di rape), **kale**, **mustard greens**, **turnip greens**, **dandelion greens**, **collards**, **sorrel**. They're best braised or cooked briefly in boiling water. (See also Salad Greens, page 45.)

Brassicas: This family, also known as cruciferous vegetables, earns lots of attention for its cancer-preventing qualities, plus it's a powerhouse of nutrients. It includes **broccoli**, **broccoflower**, **cauliflower** (white, purple and green), **cabbage** (green, red and crinkly Savoy) and **brussels sprouts**. Mild-flavoured **Chinese cabbage** (also called **napa** and **sui choy**) is pleasant in salads, soups and stir-fries. **Bok choy** has a thick white stem, dark green leaves, slightly bitter taste and crunchy texture (excellent in stir-fries). Baby bok choy is delicious just steamed.

Stalks and Sprouts: **Celery** is an essential in soups, stocks, stir-fries, stuffings and salads, and good braised on its own. **Fennel**, sometimes incorrectly called anise, has a lovely licorice taste and crisp texture; the bulb can be sliced for grilling or salads, the feathery leaves used as garnish. **Artichokes** require patience in preparing and eating but are worth it (see page 161).

Fiddleheads: The curled-up fronds of a fern that grows wild in many parts of Canada, are a springtime treat (they're also available frozen). Sauté, steam or boil 4 to 5 minutes or until tender; toss with butter and a squeeze of lemon juice. **Asparagus** is another treasure worth waiting for locally in the spring. Cook it just tender-crisp in the microwave or in a large skillet of simmering water; it's also delicious grilled. All kinds of fresh **sprouts** and **shoots** are popping up at produce counters—unusual bean varieties, alfalfa, radish, even corn. Pea shoots or sprouts are the tender sweet leafy tips of young snow pea plants; look for them in Asian markets.

Fresh Peas and Beans: **Green peas** are always best fresh-picked from your own garden, a you-pick farm or farmers' markets. At grocery stores, you can usually find good-quality **snow peas** or **sugar snap peas** and fresh **green and yellow beans**. In Asian markets you'll see **yard-long beans**, and in some Italian markets fresh **fava** beans (broad beans) and **limas**. (See also Dried Peas and Beans, page 135.) In some markets, you'll also see **okra**, the small green pod vegetable used commonly in the cooking of the American South and the Caribbean.

Onions: This big family includes the familiar **yellow** and **white** cooking onions; slightly milder **red**; sweet **Spanish** and **Bermuda**; super-sweet **Vidalia**, **Walla Walla** and **Maui**; **pearl onions** (white, yellow and red); **green onions** (also called scallions); **chives**, **leeks**, **garlic** and **shallots**.

Eggplant: There are two main types. Most common is the large, shiny, purple-black variety used in Mediterranean and Middle Eastern cooking. The most common Asian eggplants are small and slender, thinner-skinned, and dark to light purple. Some recipes call for slicing and salting the large eggplant to remove any bitterness and to draw out excess moisture before cooking; Asian eggplants don't require this.

Tomatoes: Always best in season and locally grown; otherwise, high-quality Canadian greenhouse/hothouse tomatoes do just fine. Round slicing tomatoes are the familiar favourites; most are red, but orange and yellow are also available. Attractive clusters of tomatoes are sold still on the vine. **Beefsteak** are a jumbo variety (some weigh over 1 lb/500 g), very juicy and flavourful. **Plum** tomatoes (also called roma or Italian) have an elongated shape, meaty flesh, rich flavour and less juice than round tomatoes. They are the best tomatoes for sauces, grilling, roasting and oven-drying. **Mini-tomatoes** are very sweet and ideal for snacking or salads; varieties include red, orange and yellow cherry tomatoes and tiny yellow pear-shaped ones. Look for specialty growers' **heirloom varieties** of tomatoes at farmers' markets; the shapes, colours and tastes are amazing and worth a premium price. (See also Sun-dried Tomatoes, page 236.)

Roots and Tubers: Our familiar Canadian root vegetables—**potatoes, carrots, parsnips, rutabaga, beets**—remain stalwarts in traditional cooking as well as showing off in today's comfort-food creations. The yellow-fleshed **rutabaga** is still "turnip" to many Canadians, but true **turnips** (small, white with purple tops) are becoming more familiar; they are white-fleshed and pleasantly peppery, raw or cooked. **Kohlrabi** ("cabbage turnip" in German) looks like a light green turnip with long stems sprouting from it; it's mild and crisp, excellent as crudités or cooked. More southern climes send us **sweet potatoes** (rich orange flesh) and all kinds of **yams** (many sizes but mostly large and lumpy; bland white to yellow flesh). Yams are common in West Indian markets, as are **breadfruit** (a large tropical fruit that's like a starchy vegetable when cooked) and **plantain** (a relative of bananas but always cooked before eating). **Taro** (or **dasheen**) is another starchy root and tastes like potato; the leaves of these plants are called **callaloo** in the Caribbean. **Jicama** is a brown turnip-shaped tropical tuber with sweet, crisp white flesh that is popular for salads and crudités. **Jerusalem artichokes** are not artichokes but knobby little tubers, crisp and white inside, good raw or cooked. **Celeriac** (also called celery root) is another knobby brown bulb; its creamy, nutty flesh is excellent grated for salads or cooked like potato. Celeriac discolours when exposed to air, so should be dropped into acidulated water when peeled. Garden-fresh **radishes** (red and white) are not just for slicing as garnishes; they make delicious nibbles when dipped into sweet butter or salt. **Daikon** is a long white mild-flavoured Asian radish that's good grated, cooked or pickled.

Sweet Peppers: Also called bell peppers. Members of the capsicum family that includes hot chile peppers and the in-between kinds (banana peppers, Shepherd, cubanelle, peperoncini, cherry and Hungarian wax peppers), which can range from mild to quite hot. All sweet peppers are green at first, then ripen to red, becoming sweeter and fuller-flavoured as they mature. Orange, yellow, brown, purple and almost-white varieties are also available. Field and greenhouse production provides a colourful year-round supply. Though expensive in midwinter, just one sweet red pepper can be worth it for the bright boost of colour and flavour it adds to cold-weather cooking. (See also Roasted Peppers, page 236.)

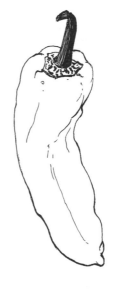

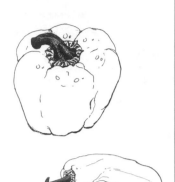

Chile Peppers: Small in size, big in flavour and ranging from medium-hot to searing. The heat comes from a compound called capsaicin, which is concentrated in the seeds and ribs (remove them for less heat). Be very careful when handling chiles; wear rubber gloves if you have sensitive skin; wash hands very thoroughly and don't rub your eyes after touching chiles. A great variety can be found in specialty shops and many supermarkets. The most widely available is **jalapeño** (short, tapered, green), which is considered medium-hot but can vary, so taste before using; it can be substituted for other chiles in recipes by adjusting the quantity. Jalapeños are also sold canned and bottled (chopped, sliced, pickled). The hottest of all chiles is the **habanero** (scrunchy rounded shape; green, orange, red). Also intensely hot are **Scotch bonnet** and **Jamaican hot** (small, bumpy lantern-shaped; red, orange, yellow, green; common in Jamaican cooking) and **Thai bird or bird's eye** peppers (tiny, slender, green or red). **Serrano** (tapered, usually green, medium-hot) is a staple of Mexican cooking; **poblano** is green, medium-sized and medium-hot. **Anaheim** is larger and milder.

Dried chiles are sold in small packages or in bunches; **ancho** chiles are dried poblanos; **pasillas** are long, wrinkled, black; chipotle is dried smoked jalapeño, also sold as **chipotle** en adobo (canned in a spicy tomato sauce). Crushed dried chiles are also called hot pepper flakes; bottled brands are usually labelled crushed red pepper.

Cayenne is finely ground dried chiles. Chili powder is a blend of spices including ground dried chiles.

Summer Squashes: (soft-skinned) Mild flavour and high moisture content. Range from teeny to huge, including **zucchini** (green and yellow varieties), **yellow crookneck** and **straightneck squash** and **scalloped pattypan**. **Chayote**, a pale green pear-sized variety, is called cho-cho in the Caribbean and choko in Australia. **Vegetable marrow** is larger, oval with yellow, green or striped skin and pale flesh.

Winter Squashes: (hard-skinned) Appear in a fascinating array of sizes and shapes, from gigantic hubbards to cute minis with endearing names like sweet dumpling, baked potato and jack-be-little. **Acorn** (or pepper): Deeply ridged and acorn-shaped; skin is green, orange-green or, less commonly, ivory. Pale orange tender flesh. Nutty flavour, slightly bland and enhanced by sweetening. **Buttercup:** Squat, round; dark green, bumpy skin with greyish spots and stripes. Flesh is deep orange, fine-textured and very sweet. **Kabocha** is similar to buttercup squash. **Butternut:** Long, straight neck with a larger round bottom that contains the seeds, light beige to tan smooth skin, yellow-orange fine-textured flesh, good flavour. **Hubbard:** Very large with a thick, tapered neck and lumpy skin, ranging from orange to green to blue-grey; flesh is yellow-orange, rather mealy and less sweet than other types. Midsize usually have better flavour than large ones. **Turban:** Look exotic with their striped turban tops, which makes them attractive for decorations; flavour can be bland.

Delicata, Sweet Dumpling and other small squashes: Wide variety of shapes and colours, often yellow or green with lighter streaks. Fine textured, yellowish flesh with sweet flavour. Smallest sizes are perfect for individual servings. **Spaghetti squash:** Oval with smooth yellow skin. Flesh is pale yellow and coarse; once cooked, it can be pulled into strands resembling spaghetti. It cooks easily in the microwave: Halve lengthwise and remove seeds; place cut side down in microwavable dish, add 1/4 cup (50 mL) water and cover with plastic wrap, leaving vent at one corner. Microwave on High for 6 to 10 minutes or until tender; let stand for 5 minutes. Loosen flesh from skin with fork; toss with a little butter, or serve with tomato sauce and grated parmesan.

To Cook Winter Squash: Baking is ideal and doesn't require peeling of the hard skin. Cut squash into halves, wedges or chunks and scoop out seeds and fibres. Halved small squashes can be stuffed if desired and baked cut side up. Unstuffed halves are best placed cut side down in greased baking dish; wedges or chunks can be covered loosely with foil. Bake in 400F (200C) oven until soft, about 45 minutes. For mashed squash, scoop the cooked flesh away from the skin; mash or purée in food processor until smooth. Squash, peeled or unpeeled, can also be microwaved until tender.

Mushrooms: Specialty mushrooms—exotic looking and wonderfully flavourful—have become familiar in supermarkets as well as specialty grocers. Most varieties are now cultivated in Canada (use them in recipes calling for "wild mushrooms").

Preparation Tips: Choose firm, dry fresh mushrooms; avoid shrivelled or damp. Store loose mushrooms in paper bag in refrigerator; commercially packaged mushrooms may be refrigerated as is (the porous plastic wrap allows air to circulate). Use within 4 days. Clean mushrooms just before using. If fairly clean, simply wipe with damp cloth, paper towel or soft brush. Otherwise, rinse quickly under cold running water, then wipe dry; do not soak. Most varieties of mushrooms are interchangeable in recipes. Cook briefly to retain tenderness. Add salt at end of cooking to prevent moisture loss. When sautéeing, don't overcrowd in pan or mushrooms will stew in their own juices. Sprinkle white mushrooms with lemon juice when raw or during cooking to retain colour.

Here's a guide to foraging in-store for fabulous fungi.

White Button: The most familiar and available; white to beige; size ranges from tiny to large enough to stuff. Mild flavour; use raw or cooked.

Cremini: Brown mushrooms similar to white button but more flavourful. Use in same ways as white.

Portobello: Tan to brown; very large with open caps; meaty texture; deep, earthy flavour. Portobellos are grown-up creminis. Cook sliced or whole; large caps are great for grilling. To remove stems, cut close to cap rather than breaking off.

Oyster: Cream to light grey; slightly ruffled fan-shaped caps; mild flavour. Brief cooking suits their delicate texture.

Shiitake: Fawn-coloured with open parasol-shaped caps; woodsy flavour, meaty texture. Remove tough stems before cooking.

Chanterelle: Trumpet-shaped with frilled edges; usually golden to orange; variety of sizes and flavours. Sauté whole to show off shape.

Enoki: White with tiny caps and long thin stems; delicate taste and texture. Cook very briefly; add to clear soups; use raw in salads or as garnish.

Porcini (cêpes): Usually imported and in dried form.

Dried Mushrooms: (usually porcini or shiitake) Though pricey, small quantities of dried mushrooms deliver a lot of flavour. To reconstitute, soak in warm water for 30 minutes (use strained soaking liquid to add flavour to sauces, soups and stews).

Basic Cooking Methods for Fresh Vegetables

Roasted Vegetables

Potatoes, carrots, parsnips, rutabaga and onions can all be roasted on their own or in any combination you like. Peel vegetables and cut into 1-1/2-inch (4 cm) chunks. Place in large bowl. Toss with just enough olive oil to coat lightly. Sprinkle lightly with salt and pepper (and a little dried rosemary or mixed Italian herbs and/or minced garlic if desired). Spread vegetables in single layer on rimmed shallow baking pan (preferably nonstick). Roast in 425F (220C) oven, stirring twice during cooking, until vegetables are tender and browned, about 45 minutes.

To Cook Beets

For all methods, first cut off beet tops, leaving about an inch of stem. After cooking, let cool slightly or run under cold water, then slip off skins.

Roasted Beets: Wrap beets individually in foil. Roast in 375F (190C) oven until tender when pierced with point of knife, about 1-1/2 hours for medium beets. Unwrap; let cool slightly (or run briefly under cold water) and slip off skins.

Boiled Beets: Cook beets in large saucepan of boiling water until tender, about 45 minutes.

Microwaved Beets: Pierce beets, place in microwavable dish and add water to 1/2 inch (1 cm) depth. Cover and microwave on High until tender, about 15 minutes.

Boiling: Nearly all vegetables can be cooked in boiling water (leave whole if small; otherwise slice or cut in chunks; cook just until tender). But most keep nutrients, colour, flavour and texture better if microwaved, steamed, grilled or roasted. There are some exceptions: potatoes for mashing (see page 157); artichokes (see page 161); green beans (see page 155). Boiling is also fine for corn on the cob, especially in large quantities. Don't add salt—it toughens the corn—and don't overcook; today's sweet tender corn needs only 2 or 3 minutes.

Steaming: A simple collapsible steamer rack that fits into a variety of pots is all you need. Add water to below the level of the rack, heat the water to boiling, add vegetables and cover tightly. Steaming just until tender-crisp retains nutrients and bright colour.

Microwaving: Most vegetables, from asparagus to zucchini, cook beautifully in the microwave, retaining their fresh flavour and colour. The basic method is simple: Place vegetables in shallow microwavable dish, add 2 to 4 tbsp (30 to 60 mL) water, cover with lid or vented plastic wrap, and microwave on High until just tender-crisp. The only trick is timing, which will vary depending on the quantity, size and density of the vegetables, and the power of your oven. Four servings of broccoli or carrots usually take 6 to 8 minutes, but start testing for doneness sooner. Remember to undercook slightly and allow 2 or 3 minutes of standing time afterwards, during which vegetables will continue to cook.

Grilling: Grilled vegetables have great flavour, and the grill marks add an appetizing appearance. Sliced eggplant, zucchini, peppers, fennel, onions, potatoes and mushrooms, asparagus spears—even radicchio—all grill beautifully. Grilling can be done on the barbecue, an indoor grill or ridged grill pan on stovetop. Have grill very hot; brush vegetables with oil and grill until nicely browned and just tender; most vegetables take 3 to 4 minutes on each side.

Roasting: Roasting caramelizes the natural sugars and adds a special depth of flavour to most vegetables. The word "roasted" has largely replaced "baked" (except for traditional "baked potatoes"), even for unpeeled whole vegetables such as sweet potatoes, squash and beets. Toss chunks of vegetables (especially potatoes, onions and root vegetables) with a little oil and roast uncovered in a shallow pan in a hot oven. Vegetables can also be roasted by placing them around meat or chicken in the roasting pan.

Braising: Means adding a little stock or other liquid to vegetables in saucepan, skillet or roasting pan, and cooking slowly, covered. The liquid softens and flavours the vegetables as it is absorbed and reduced. A good method for leeks, whole onions, carrots, fennel, brussels sprouts and sturdy greens.

Easy Combos and Dress-ups ☺

Seasonal Mixed Vegetable Stir-fry: See All-Purpose Super Stir-fry (page 118); omit meat.

Broccoli and Sweet Red Peppers: This pair is where peas and carrots used to be—everywhere. Broccoli (as a nutrient powerhouse) and red peppers (especially roasted) are culinary stars individually, but as a combo they're unbeatable for colour, flavour and nutrition. Try tossing them together in a stir-fry or salad with olive oil and garlic; crisp-cook or roast and marinate them for antipasto.

Green Beans with Almonds or Pine Nuts: Trim 1 lb (500 g) fresh green beans. Leave skinny beans whole; larger ones can be cut diagonally into pieces, or "frenched" (cut in half lengthwise). Plunge into a large pot of boiling lightly salted water; cook uncovered (for brightest colour) just until tender-crisp (remove a bean and taste for doneness; poking with a fork is deceptive). Drain well (if making ahead, refresh in cold water and drain again). In large skillet over medium heat, melt 2 tbsp (30 mL) butter; add 1/3 cup (75 mL) slivered almonds or pine nuts and stir until lightly browned. Add 1 minced garlic clove; cook for a few seconds (do not brown). Add beans and toss until hot. Season with salt and pepper to taste. **Makes 4 servings.** Sautéed mushrooms or chopped prosciutto (instead of the almonds or pine nuts) are also great additions to green beans (and peas).

French-Style Peas with Lettuce: Place 2 heads of Boston or Bibb lettuce (halved, and large outer leaves removed) in medium saucepan. (If desired, tuck in a few sprigs of fresh mint or thyme.) Add 3 cups (750 mL) fresh green peas, 2 tbsp (30 mL) butter and a pinch of sugar. Pour in 1/2 cup (125 mL) water. Bring to simmer over medium heat, reduce heat to low and cook for 10 to 15 minutes or until peas are tender. Drain well and serve hot. **Makes 4 servings.**

Broccoli or Cauliflower with Cheese Sauce: Top hot, drained vegetables with Microwave Cheese Sauce (page 128; makes enough for 4 to 6 servings). For an easy make-ahead **Broccoli-Cauliflower Gratin:** In casserole, combine 2 cups (500 mL) each well-drained cooked broccoli and cauliflower florets with the cheese sauce. Sprinkle top with buttered breadcrumbs (can be refrigerated, covered, for up to 8 hours). Bake in 350F (180C) oven for 30 minutes or until heated through.

Sautéed Broccoli or Rapini: This traditional Italian method also works well with other greens (chard, kale, mustard or collard). Cook 1 bunch broccoli or rapini briefly in boiling salted water until nearly tender; drain. In large skillet over medium heat, heat 2 tbsp (30 mL) olive oil. Add a sliced garlic clove and pinch of hot pepper flakes, then the broccoli or rapini. Cook, stirring, until tender, 3 to 4 minutes. Season with salt and pepper to taste. **Makes 4 servings.**

Brussels Sprouts with Pancetta: Toss steamed sprouts in skillet with crisp-fried chopped pancetta and red, yellow or orange sweet peppers.

Carrots, Celery and Fennel Parmigiana: Cut 2 carrots and 2 celery stalks into sticks or diagonal slices. Slice 1 fennel bulb lengthwise into eighths. Cook vegetables separately, in microwave or boiling water, until barely tender. Drain thoroughly. Combine vegetables in buttered baking dish. Add 1 tbsp (15 mL) soft butter and sprinkle lightly with salt and pepper; stir to mix. Sprinkle with 1/4 cup (50 mL) grated parmesan cheese. Bake in 375F (190C) oven until top is golden, about 25 minutes. **Makes 4 servings.**

Mixed Mushroom Sauté: Use 3 or 4 varieties of mushrooms (about 1 lb/500 g for 4 servings); cut large ones into pieces. In large skillet over medium-high heat, cook mushrooms in 2 tbsp (30 mL) each butter and oil, stirring often, until tender, about 4 minutes. Add salt and pepper to taste. For extra flavour, add a little minced garlic during cooking or add a splash of balsamic vinegar at the end.

Baked Potatoes with Toppings

A baked potato with a great-tasting topping makes a satisfying, nutritious supper. It's ready in minutes in the microwave; just add a salad.

Baked Potatoes: Use large baking potatoes; scrub well, then prick several times with a fork.

To Microwave: Place on paper towel; microwave on High until just tender, about 4 minutes for one potato, 7 minutes for two, 10 minutes for three; turn potatoes once during cooking. Let stand 5 minutes.

To Oven-Bake: In oven or toaster oven, bake at 400F (200C) for about 50 minutes or until tender.

Toppings: Make toppings while potatoes are baking in oven or during standing time after microwaving. Just before serving, cut a deep cross in top of each baked potato; squeeze lightly to open. Spoon topping over potato.

Italian Sausage, Peppers and Tomato Topping: Cut 1/2 sweet green pepper into strips; microwave in small covered dish on High for 1-1/2 minutes or until tender. Add 1/2 cup (125 mL) chunky tomato or thick pasta sauce and 1 sliced cooked Italian sausage; cover and microwave for 1 minute or until hot. Makes enough for 2 or 3 potatoes. As a variation, try *Spicy Mexican Topping*, using hot or mild salsa instead of pasta sauce.

Cheese, Ham and Broccoli Topping: In small covered dish, microwave 1 cup (250 mL) coarsely chopped broccoli on High for 1-1/2 minutes or until tender. Add 1/2 cup (125 mL) diced ham and 1 cup (250 mL) shredded cheddar cheese. Cover and microwave for 1 minute or until cheese is melted. **Makes enough for 2 or 3 potatoes.**

Light Scalloped Potatoes ♥

Satisfyingly creamy and flavourful, this low-fat version is a real winner. Use Yukon Gold potatoes for richest colour.

4 cups	thinly sliced peeled Yukon Gold potatoes (about 4 medium)	1 L
1 cup	chopped onions	250 mL
1/2 cup	chicken stock	125 mL
2 cups	1% or 2% milk	500 mL
2 tbsp	all-purpose flour	30 mL
Pinch	nutmeg	Pinch
	Salt and pepper to taste	
3/4 cup	shredded old cheddar cheese	175 mL
	Paprika	

→ In large saucepan of boiling salted water, cook potatoes for 5 minutes or until slightly tender; drain. Meanwhile, in large skillet over medium heat, cook onions in chicken stock for 4 minutes or until liquid has evaporated. In bowl, whisk together milk and flour; stir into onions. Bring to boil, stirring as it thickens; boil gently for 1 minute. Add nutmeg, salt and pepper. Combine sauce and potatoes, mixing gently but thoroughly. Pour into 8-cup (2 L) casserole. Cover with lid or foil and bake in 350F (180C) oven for 30 minutes or until potatoes are just tender. Uncover and sprinkle with cheese. Sprinkle lightly with paprika. Bake uncovered for 10 minutes or until cheese is melted and top is lightly browned. **Makes 6 servings.**

Perfect Mashed Potatoes

Back in style and better than ever, mashed potatoes are classic comfort food—plain and simple, or fashionably flavoured.

The Basics: Use all-purpose or baking potatoes, not new potatoes. For 4 servings, you will need about 1-1/2 lb (750 g). Peel and cut in large chunks. Place in large saucepan and cover with lightly salted water. Cover and bring to boil; reduce heat and boil gently for 15 minutes or until tender but not mushy. Drain well and place pot back over low heat for a minute or so to evaporate excess water. Meanwhile, in microwave or small saucepan, heat about 3/4 cup (175 mL) milk until hot (cold milk can be used, but hot gives creamier texture and doesn't cool the potatoes). Mash potatoes with potato masher until smooth and creamy, gradually beating in enough milk to give desired consistency. (Never mash potatoes in a food processor; they turn to glue.) Add salt and pepper to taste.

Garlic Mashed Potatoes: Boil potatoes with whole peeled garlic cloves (1 or 2 per potato); drain and mash potatoes and garlic together. OR squeeze the pulp from roasted garlic (page 236) into potatoes during mashing. OR add minced garlic to potatoes during mashing.

Herbed Mashed Potatoes: To hot mashed potatoes, add chopped fresh herbs to taste (chives, parsley, thyme, savory, oregano).

Cheesy Mashed Potatoes: To hot mashed potatoes, add grated parmesan, cheddar, swiss or other favourite cheese to taste. Add some chopped green onions if desired.

Buttermilk Mashed Potatoes: For a pleasant tangy flavour (and less fat), use buttermilk instead of milk in plain mashed potatoes or any of the variations above.

Smashed Potatoes: Can be made with peeled or unpeeled red potatoes. Mash coarsely with fork rather than potato masher, leaving potatoes a bit chunky. Add a drizzle of olive oil and some chopped green onions or herbs.

Oven-Baked French Fries

This method is much easier than deep-frying and produces crisp fries much lower in fat. For 4 servings, peel 4 large potatoes and cut into 1/2-inch (1 cm) thick sticks. Pat dry with paper towels. Place in large bowl; toss with 2 tbsp (30 mL) vegetable oil until coated. Spread in single layer on baking sheet (preferably nonstick). Bake in 450F (230C) oven for 30 minutes or until crisp and golden brown; turn them over halfway through baking. Sprinkle lightly with salt.

Variations: Cut peeled or unpeeled potatoes in slices or wedges rather than sticks.

Herbed: Sprinkle potatoes with 1 tbsp (15 mL) dried herbs along with the oil.

Parmesan: After turning potatoes over during baking, sprinkle lightly with grated parmesan cheese.

Mixed Mashes

Different combinations of mashed vegetables add delicious variety to your menus. Try mashing potatoes together with parsnips, rutabaga, squash, sweet potatoes or carrots (all can be cooked with the potatoes or separately). Or combine squash with rutabaga or sweet potatoes, or carrots with parsnips. For extra smoothness, purée the vegetables in a food processor. If combining with potatoes, mash the potatoes separately by hand, then add the purée.

Pommes Frites: These are real French fries—slender, tender, crisp and golden brown. A two-step frying method is the secret. For 4 servings, peel 4 to 6 baking potatoes and cut into long sticks about 1/4 inch (1 cm) in width. Rinse in cold water, then place in bowl of ice water. Pour vegetable oil to depth of about 3 inches (8 cm) in large, deep saucepan. Heat oil to 325F (160C). Drain potatoes and dry thoroughly. Drop them, a handful at a time, into hot oil; after first addition, turn up heat under pot to bring temperature back up quickly; after all potatoes have been added, turn heat back down to maintain 325F (160C). Fry potatoes, stirring occasionally, for 10 minutes or until just starting to brown. Remove and drain on paper towels. Heat the oil to 375F (190C). Return potatoes to oil and fry until crisp and golden brown, about 2 to 3 minutes. Drain on paper towels. Serve immediately.

Orange-Glazed Carrots or Sweet Potatoes

A shiny glaze brightens up the flavour and colour of orange vegetables; these are both good with roast pork, chicken or turkey.

4	medium carrots or 2 large sweet potatoes	4
1 tbsp	butter	15 mL
2 tbsp	packed brown sugar	30 mL
2 tbsp	orange juice concentrate	30 mL

→ Peel vegetables and cut into thick slices. Cook in saucepan of boiling salted water about 10 minutes until tender but still firm; drain. (Or place in covered dish with a little water and microwave on High for about 6 minutes.) In large skillet over medium-high heat, melt butter. Stir in brown sugar and orange juice concentrate until melted and smooth. Add drained vegetables; cook, stirring and spooning sauce over vegetables, until hot and glazed, about 2 minutes. **Makes about 4 servings**.

Tomato-Zucchini Sauté ☺

A tasty, colourful vegetable dish that takes only 5 minutes to make.

1 tbsp	each: butter, olive oil	15 mL
2	small zucchini, sliced	2
1 cup	cherry tomatoes	250 mL
1	clove garlic, minced	1
1 tbsp	chopped parsley	15 mL
1 tbsp	chopped fresh basil or rosemary (or 1 tsp/5 mL dried)	15 mL

Salt and pepper

→ In large skillet over medium heat, melt butter with oil. Add zucchini and cook, stirring, until nearly tender, about 3 minutes. Add tomatoes, garlic, parsley and basil. Cook, stirring gently, for about 2 minutes or just until tomatoes are softened and hot (if overcooked, they will collapse). Add salt and pepper to taste. **Makes about 3 servings**.

Braised Red Cabbage with Red Onion and Apples

This makes a flavourful sweet-and-sour accompaniment to pork, turkey, chicken or sausages.

2 tbsp	vegetable oil	30 mL
1-1/2 cups	chopped red onion	375 mL
8 cups	thinly sliced red cabbage	2 L
2	cloves garlic, minced	2
2	apples, peeled, cored, chopped	2
1 cup	chicken stock	250 mL
1/4 cup	red wine vinegar	50 mL
2 tbsp	brown sugar	30 mL
1	bay leaf	1

Salt and pepper

→ In large heavy saucepan over medium heat, heat oil. Add onion and cook for 5 minutes or until softened. Stir in cabbage, garlic and apples. Cook, stirring frequently, for 5 minutes or until cabbage begins to wilt. Stir in chicken stock, vinegar, sugar and bay leaf. Reduce heat, cover and simmer, stirring occasionally, for 45 minutes or until cabbage is soft and liquid has evaporated. Remove bay leaf. Season with salt and pepper to taste. **Makes 4 servings.**

Glazed Braised Shallots or Pearl Onions

Whole peeled shallots or pearl onions, braised and glazed with balsamic vinegar and red wine, make a great-looking, delectable side dish for roast poultry or meats. Pearl onions are now available in yellow, white and red; use an assortment if you can. To peel them easily, loosen the skins by dropping the onions into saucepan of boiling water for 1 minute, drain and rinse under cold water.

➜ Place shallots or onions in large deep skillet or shallow saucepan. Add water, wine, vinegar, sugar and salt. Bring to boil, reduce heat to simmer; cover and cook for 15 minutes or until nearly tender (large shallots will take a little longer). Uncover pan, raise heat to medium-high and cook until liquid has reduced to a syrupy glaze, about 5 minutes; stir occasionally to coat shallots or onions. Sprinkle with pepper to taste. **Makes about 6 servings**.

1-1/2 lb	whole shallots or pearl onions, peeled	750 g
1/4 cup	each: water, red wine, balsamic vinegar	50 mL
1 tbsp	granulated sugar	15 mL
Pinch	salt	Pinch

New Vegetable Hodgepodge

"July is hodgepodge time in Nova Scotia," says Halifax food writer Marie Nightingale, "and connoisseurs of this dish head for you-pick farms throughout the province for the freshest from the fields." Farmers dig up tiny new "hodgepodge potatoes" and fingerling carrots to accompany the first pickings of peas and beans. Hodgepodge is not only a traditional way to welcome the early harvest but also fits perfectly into today's focus on vegetable-appreciation.

➜ Choose a variety of tender young vegetables—tiny new potatoes, finger-length carrots, green and yellow beans, green peas or snow peas. For 6 to 8 servings, use about 2 cups (500 mL) of each plus 2 or 3 chopped green onions. Give vegetables a quick scrub under running water; if too large to leave whole, cut in half.

Place potatoes in large pot with about 1 inch (2.5 cm) of boiling water; cover and boil gently for 2 to 3 minutes. Add carrots, cook for another 1 to 2 minutes, then add beans. Leave cover off (so beans retain bright colour) and cook for 2 minutes more. Add peas and onions and cook gently until all vegetables are just tender. Cooking time will vary a bit, depending on the size of the vegetables; the trick is to start with those that take longest and work down so none overcook. Tiny beets and cauliflower and broccoli florets can be cooked separately and added to the pot. Nova Scotians traditionally add cream, butter, salt, pepper and a sprinkle of parsley at the end, but the vegetables are also delicious with just a little butter, a squeeze of lemon juice or chopped fresh herbs.

Skillet Ratatouille

Though a classic dish of Provence and made with vegetables favoured along the Mediterranean and in the Middle East, ratatouille is right at home in Canadian kitchens, especially in late summer. The skillet method is traditional; the roasted version a little deeper-flavoured and more convenient.

3 tbsp	extra-virgin olive oil	45 mL
2	onions, coarsely chopped	2
4	cloves garlic, minced	4
1	can (28 oz/796 mL) plum tomatoes, chopped	1
1	medium eggplant, cut into 3/4-inch (2 cm) chunks	1
3	small zucchini, cut into 3/4-inch (2 cm) chunks	3
1	each: sweet red and green pepper, cut into short strips	1
2 tbsp	each: chopped fresh basil and Italian parsley	30 mL
1/2 tsp	salt	2 mL
	Freshly ground pepper	

➜ In large shallow heavy saucepan over medium-high heat, heat oil. Add onions and garlic; cook until softened but not browned. Add tomatoes and their juice; cook for 5 minutes or until thickened. Add eggplant, zucchini and red and green peppers; cook for 15 to 20 minutes or until vegetables are tender. Stir in basil, parsley, salt and pepper to taste. Serve warm or at room temperature over pasta, polenta or on its own. **Makes 6 to 8 servings**.

Roasted Ratatouille: Instead of canned tomatoes, use 3 chopped fresh tomatoes. Instead of minced garlic, use 8 peeled whole garlic cloves. Toss all ingredients together in large shallow roasting pan. Roast in 400F (200C) oven, stirring occasionally, for 45 minutes or until tender. (Same mixture can be cooked, wrapped in individual foil packages, on barbecue.)

Tomatoes Provençal

Bright red tomatoes with a crisp topping taste delicious and look great (especially alongside a green vegetable or salad) as accompaniment to chicken, chops or fish.

4	medium tomatoes	4
	Salt and pepper	
1 cup	coarse fresh breadcrumbs	250 mL
1/4 cup	grated parmesan cheese	50 mL
2 tbsp	chopped parsley	30 mL
1/2 tsp	each: dried basil and oregano	2 mL
2	cloves garlic, minced	2
2 tbsp	each: melted butter, olive oil	30 mL

➜ Cut tomatoes in half crosswise; gently squeeze out seeds and juice. Place cut side up in small baking dish. Sprinkle lightly with salt and pepper. In small bowl, combine breadcrumbs, parmesan, parsley, basil, oregano and garlic; toss with butter and oil. Spoon crumb mixture generously on top of each tomato half. Bake in 350F (180C) oven for 20 minutes or until tomatoes are tender and topping is golden brown. **Makes 4 to 8 servings**. (Serve one tomato half per person if serving another vegetable, otherwise two halves each.)

Peppers Stuffed with Spicy Rice and Shrimp

Rice-stuffed peppers are long-time favourites but take on new flavour with extra spicing and shrimp. Chopped cooked spicy sausage can be used instead of shrimp. Use large peppers for a main dish, smaller ones for a side dish. For 3 to 4 servings, halve the recipe.

6	large (or 8 medium) sweet green or red peppers	6
2 tbsp	vegetable oil	30 mL
1-1/2 cups	chopped onions	375 mL
3	cloves garlic, minced	3
2/3 cup	each: chopped celery, sweet peppers	150 mL
1 tsp	each: paprika, dried basil	5 mL
1/2 tsp	each: salt, dried thyme	2 mL
1/4 tsp	cayenne	1 mL
1	can (28 oz/796 mL) tomatoes (chop; reserve juice)	1
3 cups	cooked long-grain rice	750 mL
3/4 lb	cooked small shrimp	375 g
	Chopped parsley	

➜ Cut tops off peppers; remove seeds and membranes. Trim bottoms so they stand straight. Bring large pot of water to boil; boil peppers gently for 2 minutes. Drain peppers cut side down on paper towels; set aside. In large saucepan or skillet, heat oil. Add onions, garlic, celery and diced peppers; cook over medium heat until softened. Stir in seasonings, tomatoes, rice and shrimp. Add enough of reserved tomato juice (about 1/2 cup/125 mL) to moisten filling. Taste and adjust seasoning. Spoon filling into peppers. Place in baking dish; cover tightly with foil. Bake in 350F (180C) oven for 15 to 20 minutes or until filling is hot. Sprinkle with parsley. **Makes 6 to 8 servings**.

Herbed Lemon-Garlic Butter

This recipe is one of my brother Garry's long-time favourites to serve as a dipping sauce for artichokes or lobster, and to use as a basting sauce for grilled or broiled fish, especially trout. Heat 1 cup (250 mL) clarified butter until melted. Add 2 tbsp (30 mL) fresh lemon juice and 1 tbsp (15 mL) each chopped fresh chives, parsley and garlic. Add dill, tarragon or thyme to taste (about 1 tbsp/15 mL chopped fresh or 1 tsp/5 mL dried).

Clarified Butter: In small heavy saucepan over low heat, heat butter until melted. Pour into glass measuring cup or bowl. Let stand a few minutes until solids have settled to bottom. Skim off foam that has risen to top. Carefully pour off the clear liquid (this is the clarified butter); discard solids left behind. Clarified butter can be used immediately or stored in a covered jar in the refrigerator for up to 2 weeks.

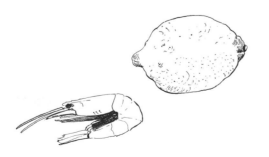

Artichokes

To prepare: Cut off stem flat with base and remove tough lower leaves. With scissors, snip tips off remaining leaves; rub cut surfaces with lemon juice. Place in large pot, stem side down (if you squeeze them in together they won't bob around); add boiling water to cover. Boil uncovered for 30 to 45 minutes or until leaves pull off easily and knife can be easily inserted into bottom. Remove from pot and drain well upside down.

To eat: Remove one leaf at a time, dipping fleshy end into melted butter, hollandaise or other sauce (see Herbed Lemon-Garlic Butter). Then scrape away the thistly "choke" in the centre and eat the deliciously meaty heart.

Rutabaga and Apple Bake

A layer of spiced apples mellows the robust flavour of rutabaga in this easy casserole.

1	large rutabaga, 2-1/2 lb (1.25 kg)	1
1 tbsp	butter	15 mL
	Salt and pepper	
2 cups	thinly sliced apples	500 mL
2 tbsp	packed brown sugar	30 mL
1/4 tsp	each: cinnamon, nutmeg	1 mL

Topping:

1/2 cup	dry breadcrumbs	125 mL
2 tbsp	packed brown sugar	30 mL
2 tbsp	butter, melted	30 mL

➜ Peel and cut rutabaga into chunks; cook in boiling salted water until tender. Mash with 1 tbsp (15 mL) butter; season with salt and pepper to taste. Layer half in greased 8-cup (2 L) baking dish. Toss apples with 2 tbsp (30 mL) sugar, cinnamon and nutmeg; arrange evenly on top. Cover with remaining rutabaga.

Topping: Combine breadcrumbs, sugar and butter; sprinkle on top. Bake in 350F (180C) oven for 50 to 60 minutes or until apples are fork-tender. **Makes 6 servings.**

Easy "Cabbage Roll" Casserole ✤

This layered dish offers the flavour of cabbage rolls without the fuss of making them. Serve with light sour cream or drained yogurt (page 239) seasoned with a little dill.

1-1/2 lb	ground beef	750 g
2	onions, chopped	2
2	cloves garlic, minced	2
1 tsp	salt	5 mL
1/4 tsp	pepper	1 mL
1	can (14 oz/398 mL) tomato sauce	1
1 cup	water	250 mL
1/2 cup	rice	125 mL
4 cups	shredded cabbage (shredded in food processor or with knife)	1 L

➜ In nonstick skillet, brown beef, stirring to break it up. Stir in onions, garlic, salt, pepper, tomato sauce and water; bring to boil. Stir in rice; cover and simmer for 10 minutes or until rice is partially cooked. Place half of shredded cabbage in greased 11- x 7-inch (28 x 18 cm) or 9-inch (23 cm) square baking dish. Cover with half of beef mixture. Repeat layers. Do not stir. Cover and bake in 350F (180C) oven for 1 hour or until rice is tender. **Makes about 6 servings.**

Rolling in Doughs...

Quickbreads, Yeast Breads

Marvellous muffins, perfect tea scones, foolproof focaccia—fast and fresh from your kitchen

Best Bran Muffins

Made with either wheat or oat bran, this recipe produces a dozen just-the-right-size, great-tasting, good-for-you muffins.

Just starting to explore the pleasures of baking? Or want a fast update on ingredients, methods and equipment? See Baking Tips, pages 240-41.

2	eggs	2
1 cup	milk	250 mL
1/2 cup	vegetable oil	125 mL
1/4 cup	molasses	50 mL
3/4 cup	packed brown sugar	175 mL
1-1/2 cups	natural wheat bran	375 mL
1-1/2 cups	all-purpose flour	375 mL
2 tsp	baking powder	10 mL
3/4 tsp	salt	4 mL
1/2 tsp	baking soda	2 mL
1 cup	raisins	250 mL

➡ In large bowl, beat together eggs, milk, oil, molasses and sugar until well blended. Stir in bran; let stand for 5 minutes. In small bowl, mix together flour, baking powder, salt and baking soda. Add to egg mixture, stirring just until combined. Stir in raisins (don't overmix). Spoon into greased or paper-lined muffin tins, filling to top. Bake in 400F (200C) oven for 20 to 22 minutes or until firm to touch. **Makes 12 muffins**.

Honey-Oat Bran Muffins: Use honey instead of molasses and oat bran instead of wheat bran.

Blueberry-Bran Muffins: use fresh (or frozen, unthawed) berries instead of raisins.

Carrot-Orange Muffins

Lightly spiced, fruity carrot muffins (often called by sunny names such as "morning glory" at bakeshops and coffee houses) are perennial favourites for breakfast-on-the-go.

2	eggs	2
1/4 cup	vegetable oil	50 mL
1/4 cup	buttermilk, sour milk, yogurt or orange juice	50 mL
1 tsp	vanilla	5 mL
1 tbsp	grated orange rind	15 mL
1 cup	each: grated carrot, apple	250 mL
1/2 cup	each: raisins, chopped pecans	125 mL
1-1/2 cups	all-purpose flour	375 mL
1/2 cup	packed brown sugar	125 mL
1/4 cup	wheat germ	50 mL
1 tsp	cinnamon	5 mL
1 tsp	baking soda	5 mL
1/2 tsp	salt	2 mL

➡ In large bowl, whisk together eggs, oil, buttermilk and vanilla. Stir in orange rind, carrot, apple, raisins and pecans. In medium bowl, mix together flour, sugar, wheat germ, cinnamon, baking soda and salt. Add to carrot mixture, stirring just until combined (don't overmix). Spoon into greased or paper-lined muffin tins, filling to top. Bake in 400F (200C) oven for 20 minutes or until firm to touch. **Makes 12 muffins**.

Blueberry, Cranberry or Apple Muffins

Choose your favourite fruit—all three make deliciously moist muffins. The optional sugar-and-spice topping is especially complementary to the apple variation.

2 cups	all-purpose flour	500 mL
1/2 cup	granulated sugar	125 mL
1 tbsp	baking powder	15 mL
1/2 tsp	salt	2 mL
1 cup	blueberries (fresh or frozen, unthawed) or coarsely chopped cranberries (tossed with 1 tbsp/15 mL sugar) or chopped peeled apples	250 mL
2	eggs, lightly beaten	2
1 cup	milk or yogurt	250 mL
1/4 cup	melted butter or vegetable oil	50 mL
1 tbsp	grated lemon rind	15 mL

Topping (optional):

1/4 cup	brown sugar	50 mL
1/4 tsp	each: nutmeg, cinnamon	1 mL

→ Mix together flour, granulated sugar, baking powder and salt. Stir in fruit. In separate bowl, combine eggs, milk, butter and lemon rind. Add to dry ingredients, stirring just until moistened. Spoon into greased or paper-lined muffin tins, filling almost to top. Add optional topping. Bake in 400F (200C) oven for 20 to 22 minutes or until tester comes out clean. **Makes about 12 muffins**.

Topping (if using): Combine brown sugar, nutmeg and cinnamon; sprinkle on muffins.

Beer and Cheddar Muffins

These savoury muffins taste great with a big bowl of chili. The recipe is from Calgary Herald *food editor Cinda Chavich.*

2 cups	all-purpose flour	500 mL
2 tbsp	granulated sugar	30 mL
1 tsp	baking powder	5 mL
1/2 tsp	each: dry mustard, salt	2 mL
1 cup	beer	250 mL
1/4 cup	vegetable oil	50 mL
1	egg	1
1-1/4 cups	shredded old cheddar cheese	300 mL

→ In large bowl, mix together flour, sugar, baking powder, mustard and salt. In separate bowl, whisk together beer, oil and egg; stir in cheese. Add to flour mixture; stir just until combined. Spoon into greased muffin tins. Bake in 400F (200 C) oven for 20 to 25 minutes or until golden brown and firm to touch. **Makes about 9 large muffins**.

Banana Bread

This is one of the easiest-ever recipes for popular banana bread. Use overripe bananas for best flavour and moistness.

2	eggs	2
3/4 cup	granulated sugar	175 mL
1/2 cup	vegetable oil	125 mL
1 cup	mashed overripe bananas (about 3 medium)	250 mL
1/2 cup	plain yogurt or sour cream (low-fat or regular)	125 mL
2 cups	all-purpose flour	500 mL
1 tsp	each: baking powder, baking soda	5 mL
1/2 tsp	salt	2 mL

➜ In large bowl, beat eggs; add sugar, oil, bananas and yogurt; beat with electric mixer or whisk until thoroughly blended. In small bowl, mix together flour, baking powder, baking soda and salt. Add to banana mixture; stir until combined. Pour into greased and floured 9- x 5-inch (23 x 13 cm) loaf pan. Bake in 350F (180C) oven (or 325F/160C for glass or dark nonstick pan) for 55 to 60 minutes or until tester comes out clean; don't overbake. Let cool in pan for 5 minutes, then turn out onto rack to cool completely.

Banana-Cherry or Banana-Cranberry Bread: Stir 1 cup (250 mL) coarsely chopped dried cherries or dried cranberries into flour mixture.

Spiced Banana Coconut Bread: Add 1/2 cup (125 mL) flaked or finely shredded unsweetened coconut and 1/2 tsp (2 mL) each cinnamon, nutmeg and allspice to flour mixture.

Banana Muffins: Spoon batter into paper-lined muffin tins, filling almost to top. Bake in 375F (190C) oven for 20 to 25 minutes or until tester comes out clean. Makes about 12.

Nuts and Seeds Bread

A pleasantly textured, flavourful loaf to slice and serve buttered or plain.

2 cups	all-purpose flour	500 mL
1 tsp	each: baking powder, baking soda	5 mL
1/2 tsp	salt	2 mL
3/4 cup	packed brown sugar	175 mL
1/2 cup	chopped nuts	125 mL
2 tbsp	each: wheat germ, sesame seeds, poppyseeds	30 mL
2	eggs, beaten	2
1 cup	buttermilk	250 mL
1/3 cup	vegetable oil	75 mL

➜ In large bowl, combine flour, baking powder, baking soda, salt and sugar; mix thoroughly. Add nuts, wheat germ, sesame seeds and poppyseeds. In separate bowl, whisk together eggs, buttermilk and oil. Add to dry ingredients, stirring just until blended. Turn into greased 9- x 5-inch (23 x 13 cm) loaf pan. Bake in 350F (180C) oven (or 325F/160C for glass or dark nonstick pan) for 1 hour or until tester comes out clean. Let cool in pan for 5 minutes, then turn out onto rack to cool completely.

Pancakes

With basic ingredients on hand, whipping up a batch from scratch is as easy as using a mix and rewards you with fresh homemade flavour. Serve with maple syrup or try some of the toppings on page 180.

1-1/2 cups	all-purpose flour	375 mL
1 tbsp	granulated sugar	15 mL
1 tbsp	baking powder	15 mL
1/2 tsp	salt	2 mL
1	egg	1
2 cups	milk	500 mL
2 tbsp	vegetable oil	30 mL

➔ In large bowl, mix together flour, sugar, baking powder and salt. In small bowl, whisk together egg, milk and oil. Add to dry ingredients, stirring until almost smooth (there will be a few small lumps). Heat large nonstick skillet over medium-high heat. Brush lightly with additional vegetable oil. Using 1/4 cup (50 mL) measure for easy pouring, pour batter onto pan, making 3 or 4 pancakes at a time. Cook until bubbles form on surface and underside is browned, about 2 minutes. Turn and cook until browned on second side, about 1 minute. Cook remaining batter same way, brushing pan with oil between each batch. Serve hot. **Makes about 14 pancakes**.

Buttermilk Pancakes: Reduce baking powder to 2 tsp (10 mL) and add 1/2 tsp (2 mL) baking soda. Substitute buttermilk for milk.

Wholewheat or Buckwheat Pancakes: Use 1 cup (250 mL) all-purpose and 1/2 cup (125 mL) wholewheat or buckwheat flour.

Blueberry, Cranberry or Peach Pancakes: After pouring batter into skillet, sprinkle each pancake with a few fresh or frozen blueberries, coarsely chopped cranberries (tossed with a little sugar) or chopped peaches. (This distributes the fruit more evenly than stirring it into the batter, and prevents blueberries from turning the pancakes blue.)

Crêpes

In blender, combine 4 eggs, 1 cup (250 mL) milk, 1/4 cup (50 ml) water, 2 tbsp (30 mL) melted butter, 1 cup (250 mL) all-purpose flour and 1/2 tsp (1 mL) salt. For sweet crêpes, add 1 tbsp (15 mL) granulated sugar. Blend until smooth. Cover and refrigerate for 1 hour.

Heat 7- to 8-inch (18 to 20 cm) crêpe pan (preferably nonstick) over medium-high heat; brush with unsalted butter. Using scant 1/4 cup (50 mL) for each crêpe, pour batter into pan, tilting to cover bottom thinly; pour excess batter back into remaining batter. Cook until lightly browned on underside; turn and cook other side until lightly browned. Repeat until batter is used up, stacking cooked crepes on plate. **Makes 12 to 16 crêpes**.

Crêpes can be wrapped around all sorts of sweet or savoury fillings. For dessert crêpes, fill with sliced fruit such as strawberries or peaches, or try the spiced apple or hot banana-rum toppings on page 180. Roll up and dust with icing sugar; add a dollop of whipped cream if desired. Crêpes are also delicious simply sprinkled with sugar and lemon juice, then folded in quarters.

For savoury crêpes, fill with cooked fresh asparagus, ratatatouille (page 160), shrimp or crabmeat. Roll up and place in shallow baking dish. Drizzle with butter and sprinkle with grated parmesan or other cheese; or top with cheese sauce (page 128) or béchamel (page 238) and sprinkle with parmesan; heat in 400F (200C) oven for 10 minutes or until heated through.

Cornbread

Corn kernels make this extra-corny, and two kinds of peppers add a zap of colour and a little heat. Sharp cheese can also be added for extra flavour and moistness. Cornbread makes a great accompaniment to salads, soups, chili, barbecued chicken or ribs.

1 cup	each: cornmeal, all-purpose flour	250 mL
1 tbsp	granulated sugar	15 mL
1 tbsp	baking powder	15 mL
1/2 tsp	baking soda	2 mL
1 tsp	salt	5 mL
1-1/4 cups	fresh, frozen or canned corn kernels	300 mL
1/3 cup	finely chopped sweet red pepper	75 mL
2 tbsp	minced jalapeño pepper	30 mL
1 cup	shredded old cheddar cheese (optional)	250 mL
2	eggs	2
1 cup	buttermilk or soured milk	250 mL
1/4 cup	vegetable oil	50 mL

→ In large bowl, combine cornmeal, flour, sugar, baking powder, baking soda and salt; mix thoroughly. Stir in corn, red pepper, jalapeño and cheese (if using). In small bowl, beat together eggs, buttermilk and oil. Add to corn mixture; stir just until combined. Spread batter in greased 8-inch (20 cm) square baking pan. Bake in 400F (200C) oven for 25 minutes or until golden brown and tester comes out clean. Serve warm or cooled, cut in squares.

Cornbread Muffins: Spoon batter into greased muffin tins, filling 3/4 full. Bake for 15 to 18 minutes. **Makes about 12 muffins**.

Popovers

A great alternative to Yorkshire pudding, popovers are easier, are much lower in fat and can be made ahead and reheated.

2	eggs, at room temperature	2
1 cup	milk, at room temperature	250 mL
1 tbsp	butter, melted	15 mL
1 cup	all-purpose flour	250 mL
1/2 tsp	salt	2 mL

→ Preheat oven to 450F (230C) and generously grease 12 muffin cups. In bowl, beat eggs very lightly; stir in milk and butter. Add flour and salt, mixing with a fork just until nearly smooth (there may be a few small lumps). Fill muffin cups 1/2 full. Bake for 15 minutes; reduce heat to 350F (180C) and bake 15 minutes longer or until well puffed and browned. With popovers still in pan, cut a small slit in each to vent steam; turn oven off and return pan to oven for 10 minutes. When done, popovers should be well browned and crisp outside, and nearly hollow inside. Remove from pan and serve hot. (Can be made ahead and reheated in pan in 350F/180C oven for about 5 minutes.) **Makes 12.**

Tea Biscuits

Fresh-baked biscuits—warm, tender and flaky— make the simplest meal seem special, and are delicious accompaniments to soups or salads. Basic tea biscuits are quick and easy to make after a little practice (a light touch is the secret). Then try Quick Cinnamon Rolls made with the same dough (see Sidebar).

2 cups	all-purpose flour	500 mL
1 tbsp	granulated sugar	15 mL
4 tsp	baking powder	20 mL
1 tsp	salt	5 mL
1/2 cup	shortening (or half butter, if desired)	125 mL
3/4 cup	milk	175 mL

➔ In large bowl, combine flour, sugar, baking powder and salt; cut in shortening until mixture looks like coarse crumbs. Add milk all at once, stirring quickly with a fork to make a soft, sticky dough. Turn out onto lightly floured surface. Gather into ball and knead very lightly about 10 times. Roll or pat out to 3/4-inch (2 cm) thickness and cut into 3-inch (8 cm) rounds; place on ungreased baking sheet. Bake in 425F (220C) oven for 10 to 12 minutes or until golden brown. **Makes 12 biscuits.**

Cheese Tea Biscuits: Omit sugar. Add 1/2 tsp (1 mL) dry mustard. After cutting in shortening, stir in 1 cup (250 mL) shredded cheddar cheese.

Herbed Tea Biscuits: Omit sugar. After cutting in shortening, stir in 1 tbsp (15 mL) chopped parsley or chives and/or 1/2 to 1 tsp (2 to 5 mL) crushed dried herbs such as sage, savory, rosemary, thyme, dillweed or mixed herbs.

Quick Cinnamon Rolls: (For Cinnamon Buns made with yeast, see page 171.) Prepare Tea Biscuit dough. Roll out to 10-inch (25 cm) square. Mix together 2/3 cup (150 mL) brown sugar, 1 tsp (5 mL) cinnamon, 1/4 cup (50 mL) melted butter and 1/3 cup (75 mL) raisins; spread evenly over dough. Roll up; pinch long edge to seal. Cut into 9 slices. Place slices, cut side down, evenly spaced in greased 8-inch (20 cm) cake pan. Bake in 425F (220C) oven for 15 to 20 minutes or until golden brown. Let stand in pan for about 3 minutes, then turn out onto rack. Serve warm. **Makes 9 rolls.**

Wholewheat Soda Bread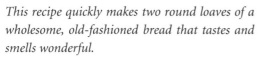

This recipe quickly makes two round loaves of a wholesome, old-fashioned bread that tastes and smells wonderful.

2 cups	each: all-purpose flour, wholewheat flour	500 mL
1/4 cup	granulated sugar	50 mL
2 tsp	each: baking soda, baking powder	10 mL
1-1/2 tsp	salt	7 mL
1/4 cup	butter	50 mL
1	egg	1
1-1/2 cups	buttermilk	375 mL

➔ In large bowl, mix together flours, sugar, baking soda, baking powder and salt. Cut in butter until it looks like fine crumbs. In small bowl, beat egg and add buttermilk. Add all at once to dry ingredients, stirring with fork to make a soft dough. Turn out onto lightly floured surface; knead gently about 10 times. Cut dough in half. Shape into two round loaves. Place on greased baking sheet. Flatten loaves slightly, and with a sharp knife cut a shallow X on top on each. Bake in 375F (190C) oven for 45 minutes or until tester inserted in centre comes out clean and loaves sound hollow when tapped on bottom. Let cool on racks.

Soda Bread Variations

Beer-Caraway Soda Bread: Add 1 tbsp (15 mL) caraway seeds to dry ingredients. Reduce buttermilk to 3/4 cup (175 mL) and add 3/4 cup (175 mL) beer.

Blueberry-Honey Soda Bread: Increase all-purpose flour to 3 cups (750 mL) and decrease wholewheat flour to 1 cup (250 mL). After cutting in butter, stir in 1 cup (250 mL) fresh or frozen (unthawed) blueberries. Add 1/4 cup (50 mL) liquid honey to wet ingredients.

Cream Tea Scones ✤

Delicious served with butter, jam and stiffly whipped cream (which substitutes nicely for English clotted cream).

2 cups	all-purpose flour	500 mL
2 tbsp	granulated sugar	30 mL
1 tbsp	baking powder	15 mL
1/2 tsp	salt	2 mL
1/2 cup	butter	125 mL
1	egg	1
2/3 cup	milk or light cream	150 mL

➜ In mixing bowl, combine flour, sugar, baking powder and salt. Cut in butter until mixture looks like coarse crumbs. In small bowl, beat egg lightly; remove 1 tbsp (15 mL) of beaten egg and reserve for topping. To remaining egg, add milk; add mixture all at once to dry ingredients, stirring with a fork to make a light, soft dough. Gather into a ball and turn out onto lightly floured surface. Knead lightly a few times until smooth. Roll or pat out to 3/4-inch (2 cm) thickness. Cut into 2-1/2-inch (7 cm) rounds. Place on ungreased baking sheet. Brush tops with reserved egg. Bake in 425F (220C) oven for 12 to 14 minutes or until golden brown. **Makes about 12 scones**.

Raisin or Currant Scones: Add 1/2 cup (125 mL) raisins or currants to dry ingredients after cutting in butter.

Ginger-Orange Scones: Add 1 tsp (5 mL) ground ginger, 1 tbsp (15 mL) grated orange rind and 1/4 cup (50 mL) chopped candied ginger to dry ingredients after cutting in butter.

Lemon-Cranberry Scones: Add 1 tbsp (15 mL) grated lemon rind and 1/2 cup (125 mL) dried cranberries to dry ingredients after cutting in butter. Sprinkle tops of scones with granulated sugar.

Savoury Scones with Onion, Red Pepper and Pancetta: In skillet, cook 1/4 cup (50 mL) chopped pancetta in a little olive oil (bacon may be substituted for pancetta; omit oil). Add 1/4 cup (50 mL) chopped onion and cook until softened. Add 1/4 cup (50 mL) chopped sweet red pepper and cook briefly. Set aside. Prepare Cream Tea Scone recipe, omitting sugar and egg and decreasing butter to 1/3 cup (75 mL). Add pancetta mixture and 1/2 tsp (2 mL) dried oregano to the dry ingredients.

Basic Sweet Dough

This rich yeast dough can be used for small rolls, cinnamon buns or festive breads in fancy shapes.

1 tsp	granulated sugar	5 mL
1/2 cup	warm water	125 mL
1	pkg active dry yeast	1
1/2 cup	milk	125 mL
1/4 cup	butter	50 mL
1/4 cup	granulated sugar	50 mL
1-1/2 tsp	salt	7 mL
2	eggs, beaten	2
4 cups	(approx) all-purpose flour	1 L

➔ In large mixing bowl, dissolve 1 tsp (5 mL) sugar in the warm water. Sprinkle in yeast; let stand 10 minutes or until frothy. Meanwhile, in microwave or small saucepan over low heat, heat together milk, butter, 1/4 cup (50 mL) sugar and salt, stirring to melt butter; let cool to lukewarm. Add cooled liquid and eggs to yeast mixture. Add 1-1/2 cups (375 mL) flour; beat with electric mixer for 2 minutes. Gradually stir in enough flour to make a soft, slightly sticky dough. On lightly floured surface, knead for 5 minutes or until smooth and springy. Place in large greased bowl, turning dough to grease all over. Cover and let rise in a warm place until doubled, about 1-1/4 hours. Punch down.

If using one half of dough for one of these variations, the other half can be refrigerated or frozen (see Refrigerator Dough in Sidebar).

Crescent Rolls: Divide Basic Sweet Dough in half. One half will make 12 rolls. Roll out dough to 16-inch (40 cm) circle. Cut into 12 wedges. Roll up from wide ends. Place rolls, with points underneath, on greased baking sheet. Curve ends into crescent shapes. Repeat with second half of dough if desired. Cover and let rise until doubled, about 40 minutes. Bake in 375F (190C) oven for 15 to 20 minutes or until golden brown. Let cool on rack.

Cinnamon Buns: Divide Basic Sweet Dough in half. One half will make 9 cinnamon buns. Roll out dough to rectangle about 12 x 9 inches (30 x 23 cm). Spread with 1/4 cup (50 mL) very soft butter. Sprinkle evenly with mixture of 1/2 cup (125 mL) brown sugar and 1 tsp (5 mL) cinnamon. Sprinkle with 1/3 cup (75 mL) raisins. Roll up from narrow end and pinch long edge to seal. With sharp knife, slice into 9 pieces. Place in greased 9-inch (23 cm) square baking pan. Repeat with second half of dough if desired. Cover and let rise in warm place until doubled, about 45 minutes. Bake in 375F (190C) oven for 25 to 30 minutes or until dark golden brown and buns sound hollow when tapped. **Sticky Buns or Chelsea Buns:** In microwave or saucepan, melt together 1/2 cup (125 mL) each butter and brown sugar; pour into 9-inch (23 cm) square baking pan. Sprinkle with 1/2 cup (125 mL) coarsely chopped pecans or walnuts. Place 9 Cinnamon Bun slices on top. Let rise and bake as for Cinnamon Buns. When baked, turn pan upside-down on rack and let stand to allow syrup to run into the buns. **Braided Festive Bread:** After punching down Basic Sweet Dough, knead in 1 cup (250 mL) chopped candied peel or dried fruit (mixture of dried cherries, dried cranberries and golden raisins). Divide dough into 3 equal parts. Roll each part into a rope about 16 inches (40 cm) long. Place ropes side by side; braid together loosely; press ends together to seal and tuck under. Place on greased baking sheet. Cover and let rise until doubled, about 45 minutes. Bake in 375F (190C) oven for 30 minutes or until golden brown and loaf sounds hollow when tapped. Remove to rack to cool. Dust with icing sugar or drizzle with icing (icing sugar mixed with a little milk and a drop of almond flavouring) and decorate with candied fruit if desired.

Refrigerator Dough: After placing kneaded dough in greased bowl, cover tightly with plastic wrap and refrigerate for up to 2 days. If not doubled in bulk, let rise at room temperature before punching down and shaping. The kneaded dough can also be frozen in a plastic bag; let thaw in refrigerator.

The dough can also be refrigerated **after shaping**. This is convenient if you want to serve fresh-baked bread for breakfast or brunch. After the dough has been shaped and placed on baking sheet or in pan, cover with plastic wrap, leaving room for expansion. Refrigerate for up to 24 hours. If it has not doubled in size while refrigerated, let it finish rising at room temperature, then bake.

Best Basic White Bread

Although surrounded by wonderful bakeshops and awesome bread machines, sometimes one simply feels a need to knead. And with some basic know-how and a little practice, you can happily venture into all sorts of healthy or fancy creations. Here are some satisfying loaves to get you started.

1 tsp	granulated sugar	5 mL
1-1/2 cups	warm water	375 mL
1	pkg active dry yeast	1
1/2 cup	milk	125 mL
2 tbsp	granulated sugar	30 mL
2 tbsp	butter	30 mL
2 tsp	salt	10 mL
5 cups	(approx) all-purpose flour	1.25 L

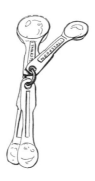

→ In large mixing bowl, dissolve 1 tsp (5 mL) sugar in the warm water. Sprinkle yeast into water; let stand 10 minutes or until frothy. Meanwhile, in microwave or small saucepan, heat milk with 2 tbsp (30 mL) sugar, butter and salt until warm; stir to melt butter; let cool to lukewarm. Add to yeast mixture. Stir in 3 cups (750 mL) flour; beat with electric mixer for 2 minutes. Gradually stir in enough of the remaining flour to make a soft dough. Knead on lightly floured surface for 10 minutes or until smooth and springy. Place in large greased bowl, turning dough to grease all over. Cover and let rise in warm place until doubled, about 1-1/2 hours. Punch down. Divide dough in half; shape each half into smooth ball. Roll out to 12- x 8-inch (30 x 20 cm) rectangle. Roll up from narrow end; pinch seam and ends to seal. Place in two greased 8-1/2- x 4-1/2-inch (22 x 12 cm) loaf pans. Cover and let rise until doubled, about 1 hour. Bake in 400F (200C) oven for 30 minutes or until loaves sound hollow when tapped on bottom. Remove from pans; let cool on racks. **Makes 2 loaves**.

Basic Brown Bread: (60% wholewheat) Use 3 cups (750 mL) wholewheat flour and 2 cups (500 mL) all-purpose flour.

Dinner Rolls: After punching down risen dough, divide it into 20 portions (the easiest way is to cut dough in half, shape into two logs and cut each into 10 pieces). Shape each piece into a smooth ball or oval, pinching dough together on the underside. Place about 2 inches (5 cm) apart on greased baking sheets. Cover and let rise until doubled, about 30 minutes. Bake in 400F (200C) oven for 15 to 20 minutes or until rolls sound hollow when tapped on bottom. **Makes 20**.

Dill-Ricotta Bread ❦

As food and travel writer for the Edmonton Journal, *Judy Schultz writes about bistros in Paris, bakers in Tuscany and chefs in Canton, but never forgets her Canadian Prairie roots. Her favourite recipes reflect the seasonal rhythms of Prairie life and food preparation, along with updated methods and ingredients. This traditional no-knead "casserole bread" gets an update using fresh dill instead of dried, ricotta instead of cottage cheese, and an extra-easy food processor method. It's delicious served warm from the oven (or toasted the next day).*

1/2 tsp	granulated sugar	2 mL
1/4 cup	warm water	50 mL
1	pkg active dry yeast	1
1 cup	ricotta or creamed cottage cheese	250 mL
1	egg	1
1	green onion, chopped	1
2 tsp	dry mustard or Dijon mustard	10 mL
2 tsp	mustard seeds	10 mL
1/3 cup	minced fresh dill (or 2 tbsp/30 mL dried)	75 mL
1 tbsp	granulated sugar	15 mL
1 tbsp	butter, melted	15 mL
1 tsp	salt	5 mL
1/4 tsp	baking soda	1 mL
2-1/2 cups	all-purpose flour	625 mL

➜ In small bowl, dissolve 1/2 tsp (2 mL) sugar in the warm water; sprinkle yeast into water. Let stand 10 minutes or until frothy. In microwave or saucepan, warm cheese to lukewarm. In food processor, combine cheese, egg, onion, dry mustard, mustard seeds, dill, 1 tbsp (15 mL) sugar, butter, salt and baking soda. Process until smooth. Add yeast and 1 cup (250 mL) of the flour; process for 30 seconds. Add half of remaining flour and process until flour is incorporated. Add remaining flour; process until dough forms a ball and cleans the sides of the bowl. Turn dough into well-greased and floured 6-cup (1.5 L) casserole or soufflé dish. Cover and let rise in warm place until doubled, about 45 minutes. Bake in 350F (180C) oven for 40 minutes or until lightly browned and bottom of loaf sounds hollow when tapped. Turn out onto rack to cool.

Oatmeal Bread ✦

Bread made with oats and molasses is a long-time favourite in the Maritimes, where it is called Porridge Bread or Rolled Oats Bread (to most Maritimers, "oatmeal" refers to a coarse-grained meal, not rolled oats); Halifax food writer Marie Nightingale calls it the most popular traditional bread still made in the region. Some old-time recipes called for leftover porridge, a lot more molasses and an all-day rising; this version is lighter but moist and flavourful. Try the mini-loaves for a dinner party, especially at harvest time; they look great placed individually on the bread-and-butter plate at each place setting.

1 cup	quick-cooking oats (not instant)	250 mL
1-1/4 cups	boiling water	300 mL
1/4 cup	molasses or honey	50 mL
1/4 cup	butter	50 mL
1-1/2 tsp	salt	7 mL
1 tsp	granulated sugar	5 mL
1/2 cup	warm water	125 mL
2	pkg active dry yeast	2
2	eggs, lightly beaten	2
5 cups	(approx) all-purpose flour	1.25 L

Topping (optional):

lightly beaten egg; rolled oats

→ In large bowl, combine oats, boiling water, molasses, butter and salt; let stand until luke-warm. Dissolve sugar in warm water; sprinkle yeast into water and let stand for 10 minutes or until frothy. To oat mixture, add dissolved yeast, eggs and 2 cups (500 mL) of the flour. Beat for 2 minutes with electric mixer or vigorously by hand. Gradually add enough of remaining flour to make a soft dough, mixing first with wooden spoon and then with hands. Knead on lightly floured surface for about 8 minutes until smooth and springy. Place in large greased bowl, turning dough to grease all over. Cover and let rise until doubled, about 1 hour. Punch down. Cut in half and shape into 2 loaves. Place in 2 greased 8-1/2- x 4-1/2-inch (22 x 12 cm) loaf pans. (Dough may also be shaped into 4 balls, placing 2 side by side in each pan.) Let rise until doubled, about 40 minutes. If desired, brush tops of loaves with lightly beaten egg and sprinkle with oats (large-flake or regular). Bake in 375F (190C) oven for 45 to 50 minutes or until loaves sound hollow when tapped on bottom. Remove from pans and let cool on racks. **Makes 2 loaves**.

Oatmeal Mini-Loaves or Buns: Cut dough into 16 equal pieces. Shape into small loaves and place in greased mini loaf pans (3/4 cup/175 mL capacity) OR shape into oval buns and place on greased baking sheets. Cover and let rise in warm place for 30 to 40 minutes or until doubled. Brush tops with lightly beaten egg and sprinkle with oats. Bake in 375F (190C) oven for 30 to 40 minutes or until loaves or buns sound hollow when tapped on bottom. **Makes 16**.

174

Focaccia

Fresh-baked focaccia—warm from the oven, crispy on the outside, soft and puffy inside—is wonderful with salads, soups or cut into small pieces for pre-dinner appetizers with drinks. Focaccia is easy to make at home from scratch (see below) or using the good pizza dough now readily available in supermarkets and bakeries. The dough is usually sold refrigerated in a plastic bag; if frozen, let it thaw in the bag in refrigerator.

1 lb	pizza dough (purchased or homemade)	500 g
1 tbsp	extra-virgin olive oil	15 mL
2 tsp	each: chopped fresh oregano and rosemary (or 1/2 tsp/2 mL each dried)	10 mL
1/2 tsp	coarse salt	2 mL

➡ If dough is refrigerated, bring to room temperature before using. Place dough on lightly oiled baking sheet. Press out into an oval or rectangle about 11 x 7 inches (28 x 18 cm). Cover loosely with plastic wrap and let stand in a warm place for 45 minutes or until slightly risen. With fingertips, press indentations into dough to give dimpled surface. Brush with olive oil. Sprinkle with herbs and salt. Bake in 400F (200C) oven for 20 to 25 minutes or until golden brown. Let cool slightly. Serve warm, cut into squares or wedges.

Foccacia Variations

Parmesan Focaccia: Omit salt. After the first 10 minutes of baking, sprinkle with 1/4 cup (50 mL) grated parmesan cheese.

Onion and Garlic Focaccia: Cook 1/2 cup (125 mL) chopped onion and 1 minced garlic clove in 1 tbsp (15 mL) olive oil until softened but not browned. Spread over dough before sprinkling with herbs.

Black Olive and Sun-dried Tomato Focaccia: Sprinkle dough with 1/2 cup (125 mL) each chopped pitted kalamata olives and sun-dried tomatoes (oil-packed) along with the herbs.

Sage and Red Onion Focaccia: Sauté 1 red onion (halved and sliced) in 1 tbsp (15 mL) olive oil until softened. Spread over dough. Sprinkle with 3 tbsp (45 mL) chopped fresh sage. Omit other herbs.

Pizza or Focaccia Dough

This is the equivalent of 1 lb (500 g) store-bought pizza dough. Makes enough for two 12-inch (30 cm) thin-crust pizzas OR one 14-inch (35 cm) thick-crust pizza OR six 7-inch (18 cm) pizzas OR one focaccia. For Pizza, see page 32.

2-1/2 to 3 cups	all-purpose flour	625 to 750 mL
1 pkg	quick-rising instant yeast	1 pkg
3/4 tsp	salt	4 mL
1 cup	hot water (125F/50C)	250 mL
2 tbsp	olive oil	30 mL

➡ In large bowl, mix 2 cups (500 mL) of the flour with yeast and salt. Stir in hot water and oil. Gradually stir in enough of remaining flour to make a soft dough. Knead on lightly floured surface until smooth and elastic, about 5 minutes. Shape dough into ball, cover and let rest on floured surface for 10 minutes before rolling or pressing out. Dough can be wrapped in plastic bag and refrigerated for up to 8 hours, or frozen for up to 1 month (thaw in refrigerator). Bring dough to room temperature before using.

Food Processor Method: Place 3 cups (750 mL) flour, yeast and salt in food processor bowl; process for 5 seconds to mix. Add oil. With machine running, slowly pour 1 to 1-1/4 cups (250 to 300 mL) hot water through feed tube just until ball forms; continue processing for 30 to 45 seconds to knead dough. With floured hands, shape into smooth ball; cover and let rest on floured surface for 10 minutes.

Herbed Garlic Bread

Vary this as you wish for buffets, barbecues or soup-and-salad lunches. Instead of wrapping the loaf in foil, toast the slices on the grill or under the broiler, or heat on a baking sheet in the oven (400F/200C for about 10 minutes). Use butter or olive oil as desired, vary the herbs to taste, add parmesan or not. For plain garlic bread, omit the herbs.

1	large loaf crusty bread Italian or French (about 16 x 4 inches/40 x 10 cm)	1
1/2 cup	butter, softened	125 mL
2	cloves garlic, minced	2
2 tbsp	minced chives or green onions	30 mL
2 tbsp	chopped parsley	30 mL
1/4 tsp	each: dried basil, oregano, crushed rosemary	1 mL
1/4 cup	grated parmesan cheese (optional)	50 mL

→ Cut bread into thick slices on the diagonal. Mix butter with remaining ingredients. Spread on one side of bread slices. Reassemble into loaf shape. Wrap in foil, leaving top slightly open. Place in 375F (190C) oven for 15 minutes or until heated through. **Serves 6 to 8**.

Roasted Garlic Bread: Replace minced garlic with the pulp squeezed from 1 head of roasted garlic (page 236).

Olive Oil Garlic Bread: Use olive oil instead of butter; omit chives and parsley. Brush on both sides of bread slices; grill or broil for a few minutes on each side until lightly browned.

Garlic Baguette: Cut baguette loaf in half lengthwise. Spread or brush with garlic mixture; broil until lightly browned OR wrap in foil and heat through. To serve, cut into 8 to 10 portions.

Breadsticks: Half of Pizza Dough (page 175) or 1/2 lb (250 g) store-bought pizza dough will make 12 breadsticks about 12 inches (30 cm) long. (Make shorter lengths if you prefer.) Roll out dough to large rectangle about 1/4 inch (5 mm) thick. Cut into strips about 1 inch (2.5 cm) wide. Gently twist each strip several times; place 1 inch (2.5 cm) apart on greased baking sheets. Beat 1 egg white with 1 tbsp (15 mL) water; brush over breadsticks. Sprinkle lightly with poppyseeds, sesame seeds, grated parmesan or dried herbs. Bake in 425F (220 C) oven for 10 to 15 minutes or until golden brown.

How Sweet It Is...

Desserts

A perfect pear, the finest chocolate,
the silkiest sabayon...you deserve it

Easy Fruit Desserts ☻

Fresh Fruit Sauces (Coulis)

Strained purées of uncooked fruit are often called by the French name, coulis. Usually used as decorative drizzles or spooned into pools on dessert plates, these bright-coloured, fresh-flavoured sauces are a breeze to make using either fresh or frozen unsweetened fruit.

Raspberry Coulis: In food processor, purée 2 cups (500 mL) fresh raspberries or 1 thawed package (10 oz/300 g) frozen unsweetened raspberries. Push purée through sieve to remove seeds. Stir in sugar to taste (about 3 tbsp/45 mL). **Makes about 1 cup** (250 mL). (*Note*: Puréeing the raspberries makes the sauce slightly cloudy; for brightest colour, omit puréeing and just push thawed berries through sieve.)

Other fruit coulis (such as mango, peach, apricot, strawberry, blueberry) can be made in the same way; simply purée chopped, fully ripe fresh fruit or thawed unsweetened fruit, adding a little water if needed, a squeeze of lemon juice, and sugar to taste.

Sabayon-Topped Fruit Gratinée: For each serving, place a layer of fresh blueberries or sliced peaches, nectarines, apples or pears in an individual gratin dish. Top with a layer of sabayon (see Zabaglione, page 187), letting fruit just poke through. Sprinkle with a teaspoon of sugar. Place under preheated broiler for a few minutes, until topping starts to brown slightly. Serve hot, sprinkled with a little fruit brandy or liqueur if desired.

Figs with Mascarpone: Blend creamy mascarpone cheese with a little maple syrup or liquid honey, then use teaspoonfuls of the mixture to top halves of fresh ripe figs. The colour contrast with purple-black Mission figs is particularly eye-catching.

Fruit Takes the Cake: Use slices of Lemon Poppyseed Pound Cake (page 201), All-Purpose White Cake (page 199) or Basic Sponge Cake (page 203) as the base for individual servings of sliced fruit and berry combinations—nectarines and blueberries; papaya and raspberries; mango and strawberries. Drizzle with one of the fruit coulis (see Sidebar), then top with whipped cream or crème fraîche.

Strawberries with Balsamic Reduction: Choose a good-quality balsamic vinegar (the classic dark one, or the newer white). For 4 servings, gently simmer 1/2 cup (125 mL) until reduced by half; it should be syrupy. Trail it by teaspoonfuls over sliced strawberries in individual serving bowls. Bring the pepper mill to the table and invite diners to use it for a new take on how good our favourite berry can taste.

Almost-Instant Berry Sauce over Melon Cubes: Purée fresh strawberries, raspberries or blueberries in blender or food processor; strain if desired. Drizzle over cubes of firm-fleshed melon such as honeydew or cantaloupe.

Peaches and Blueberries with Creamy Orange Sauce: Mix together 1/2 cup (125 mL) each plain yogurt and light sour cream and 1/4 cup (50 mL) each granulated sugar and thawed orange juice concentrate. Spoon over sliced peaches and blueberries (or other seasonal fruit) in stemmed glasses. **Makes 4 servings.**

Fruit Salad Bowl: Beautiful and delicious for brunch or a dessert. Use any combination of fruit in season. In summer, it's peaches, berries, nectarines, apricots and seedless grapes. At other times of year, check what's most attractive in the produce market: grapes work all year; so do oranges and their small cousins (mandarins, clementines); seasonal melons add sweetness and substance; kiwifruit slices add sparkle and nutritious elements; everyone loves bananas.

For 4 to 6 servings: In glass serving bowl, place 4 cups (1 L) mixed fruit (if using kiwi or bananas, add just before serving). Add 2 cups (500 mL) orange juice and 1/4 cup (50 mL) lime or lemon juice. If desired, stir in orange liqueur to taste. Add sugar to taste (preferably fruit sugar, which dissolves quickly). Cover and refrigerate for up to 1 day. Garnish with sprigs of mint. To serve, spoon fruit and its juice into stemmed glasses; use small spoons for the fruit and sip the juice.

For a version with a little more punch and sparkle, substitute sparkling white wine for the orange juice and liqueur; add wine just before serving.

Strawberry Dipping Dessert: One of the most delicious ways to eat strawberries is also one of the simplest. Just dip whole strawberries first into light sour cream or drained yogurt (page 239), then into brown sugar or maple sugar. For a buffet, set out pretty bowls of strawberries, cream and sugar; at a dinner table, provide each person with a plate of strawberries and small dishes of cream and sugar.

Chocolate-Dipped Strawberries or Dried Apricots: For 24 pieces of fruit, gently melt about 4 oz (125 g) high-quality semisweet dark or milk chocolate until smooth. Dip fruit partially into chocolate, then place on waxed or parchment paper until chocolate sets. Store in an airtight container in refrigerator. Can also be used for slices of pineapple, small clusters of seedless grapes, seeded orange slices, apple or pear slices (brush lightly with lemon juice first to prevent discolouring) and wedges of kiwifruit. Dried-fruit versions make fine holiday gifts.

Grilled Fruit: Summer or winter, any time your grill (or stovetop grill pan) is hot, cook dessert there, too. Cook fruit just until hot and marked by the grill, turning once or twice. Cooking times vary with the fruit's ripeness and the barbecue's heat, but as a rough guide, peach halves take 6 to 8 minutes, pineapple slices about 10 minutes. For grilled fruit kabobs, thread smaller pieces onto bamboo skewers that have first been soaked in water for 20 minutes, or use a hinged grilling basket. Try halves, thick slices or wedges of peaches, nectarines, apricots, plums, mango, pineapple, pears, apples, firm bananas—or a mixture.

Fruit and Cheese Dessert Plate: For each guest, arrange a dessert plate with pretty groupings of fruit: a few perfect strawberries, halved passionfruit, a fresh fig, a tiny bunch of grapes (frosty from the freezer), small slices of melon, mango or papaya. Garnish with fresh mint. Add small slices of goat cheese or wedges of brie or camembert, and 2 or 3 small cookies or sweet crackers.

Fruit Fools: A classic dessert that couldn't be easier to make. Simply fold any sweetened puréed fruit (apricot, peach, mango, raspberry, strawberry, blueberry or mixture of berries) into whipped cream; leave some streaks of fruit through the cream. (Rhubarb Fool is traditional; use stewed rhubarb made by simmering chopped rhubarb until soft with a little water and sugar to taste.) For 4 servings, use 1 cup (250 mL) fruit purée and 1 cup (250 mL) whipping cream (whipped and sweetened to taste). For a lower-fat version, reduce whipping cream to 1/2 cup (125 mL); whip cream and fold into 1 cup (250 mL) extra-thick or drained yogurt (plain or vanilla-flavoured; see page 239); sweeten to taste.

Fruit Parfaits: Use same yogurt cream mixture as for Fruit Fools (above); layer it with fruit purée and fresh berries or sliced fruit in parfait or stemmed glasses. Chill before serving.

Top It Off

Use these easy, delectable toppings on ice cream, crêpes or pancakes, or as dessert sauces over cake or fruit. Most will keep several days in refrigerator.

Speedy Fruit Sauce: In microwave or saucepan, heat together equal parts high-quality jam and a compatible fruit-flavoured liqueur. (Raspberry, apricot and red currant jam all work well.) Add some chopped preserved ginger if extra punch is desired. Serve warm or chilled, over sliced fresh fruit or berries.

≋ Microwave Chocolate Sauce: In 2-cup (500 mL) glass measure or bowl, combine 1/2 cup (125 mL) chocolate chips or 2 oz (60 g) chopped semisweet chocolate, 1/4 cup (50 mL) light cream, 2 tbsp (30 mL) corn syrup and 1 tbsp (15 mL) softened butter. Microwave on High for 1 minute; stir. Microwave 1 minute longer; stir until smooth. Stir in 1/2 tsp (2 mL) vanilla. Let cool 5 minutes. Serve warm or cool; store at room temperature, or refrigerate and reheat before serving. **Makes about 2/3 cup** (150 mL).

≋ Microwave Butterscotch Sauce: In 4-cup (1 L) glass measure or bowl, combine 1/2 cup (125 mL) brown sugar, 1/4 cup (50 mL) each softened butter and light cream and 2 tbsp (30 mL) corn syrup. Microwave on High for 1 minute; stir. Microwave 1 minute longer; stir until smooth. Stir in 1/2 tsp (2 mL) vanilla. Let cool 5 minutes. Serve warm or cool; store at room temperature, or refrigerate and reheat before serving. **Makes about 2/3 cup** (150 mL).

Hot Banana-Rum Topping: Peel and slice 2 firm bananas. In skillet over medium heat, melt 2 tbsp (30 mL) butter. Stir in 1/4 cup (50 mL) each brown sugar and rum (or orange juice) and a pinch each of cinnamon and nutmeg. Add bananas; cook, stirring gently, just until bananas are slightly softened, about 1 minute. Serve hot on vanilla ice cream. **Makes about 4 servings**.

Raspberry-Blueberry Topping: In small heavy saucepan, combine 1 cup (250 mL) fresh or frozen unsweetened blueberries, 1/3 cup (75 mL) granulated sugar and 1 tbsp (15 mL) cornstarch. Stir in 1/2 cup (125 mL) water. Bring to boil, stirring; boil gently, stirring, for about 1 minute until thickened. Gently stir in 1 cup (250 mL) fresh or frozen unsweetened raspberries and 2 tsp (10 mL) lemon juice. If using frozen raspberries, heat about 1 minute longer. Serve warm or cold. **Makes about 1-1/2 cups** (375 mL).

Spiced Apple Topping: In small heavy saucepan, combine 2 thinly sliced peeled apples, 2 tbsp (30 mL) each raisins and granulated sugar, pinch each of cinnamon and nutmeg, and 1/4 cup (50 mL) water. Cook over medium-high heat, stirring often, until apples are tender, about 5 minutes. Serve warm. **Makes about 1 cup** (250 mL).

Maple-Nut Topping: In small heavy saucepan, combine 1/2 cup (125 mL) pure maple syrup and 1/4 cup (50 mL) each corn syrup, water and granulated sugar. Bring to boil, stirring. Boil, uncovered, for 5 minutes. Add 1/2 cup (125 mL) coarsely chopped pecans or walnuts; boil 5 minutes longer, stirring occasionally. Let cool (sauce will thicken); stir to distribute nuts evenly through sauce. **Make about 1 cup** (250 mL).

Fruit Classics, Warm or Cold

Poached Pears in Red Wine: Peel 4 firm ripe pears, cut in half and remove cores with melon baller. (To prevent discolouring, place pears in bowl of water with a little lemon juice.) In large saucepan, combine one 750 mL bottle red wine, 1 cup (250 mL) water, 3/4 cup (175 mL) granulated sugar, the peel (in long strips, no white part) of 1/2 orange and 1/2 lemon, 1 cinnamon stick and 4 whole cloves. Bring to boil, stirring to dissolve sugar. Place pears in liquid and poach for 15 minutes or until just tender. Remove pears to serving dish. Boil wine syrup until reduced by half. Pour over pears. Serve warm or chilled. **Makes 4 servings.**

Winter Fruit Compote: Fresh-tasting and not too sweet, this dessert takes advantage of dried and canned fruits while waiting for summer fruit season. In casserole, combine 28-oz (796 mL) can of pear halves and 1 cup (250 mL) of their juice, 1 cup (250 mL) each dried apricots and large pitted prunes, 1/2 cup (125 mL) dried cherries or cranberries, 1/4 cup (50 mL) brown sugar and 1 tsp (5 mL) ground ginger. Cover and bake in 375F (190C) oven for 30 minutes or until apricots are soft. Serve warm or cold, with a dollop of vanilla yogurt or frozen yogurt. **Makes 6 servings.**

Easy Apple Strudel

Flaky layers of phyllo enclose a tasty apple filling in this streamlined version of traditional strudel. It can also be made with pears, plums or apricots. Enjoy with a good cup of coffee. (For working with phyllo, see Sidebar.)

3	apples, peeled and cored	3
1/4 cup	granulated sugar	50 mL
1/4 cup	chopped pecans, walnuts or almonds	50 mL
1/4 cup	raisins or dried cranberries	50 mL
1 tsp	grated lemon rind	5 mL
1/2 tsp	cinnamon	2 mL
2 tbsp	each: fine dry breadcrumbs, granulated sugar	30 mL
1/3 cup	(approx) butter, melted	75 mL
6	sheets phyllo pastry (16 x 12 inches/40 x 30 cm), thawed if frozen	6
	Icing sugar	

➡ Coarsely chop or thinly slice apples. In bowl, toss apples with 1/4 cup (50 mL) sugar, nuts, raisins, lemon rind and cinnamon; set aside. Combine breadcrumbs and 2 tbsp (30 mL) sugar; set aside. Place 1 sheet of phyllo on flat surface (keep remaining pastry covered with damp tea towel). Brush sheet of phyllo lightly with melted butter (about 2 tsp/10 mL); sprinkle with about 2 tsp (10 mL) breadcrumb mixture. Top with remaining sheets of phyllo one at a time, brushing each with butter and sprinkling with crumbs. Spoon apple mixture along one long edge of phyllo, leaving about 2 inches (5 cm) clear at edges. Starting at filled edge, carefully roll up strudel, folding in short edges. Place seam side down on buttered baking sheet. Brush with melted butter. Cut 5 diagonal slashes in top of strudel. Bake in 400F (200C) oven for 15 minutes; reduce heat to 350F (180C) and bake for 30 minutes longer or until golden brown. Let cool for 15 minutes on baking sheet. Serve warm or at room temperature. Before serving, dust top with sifted icing sugar. Slice with sharp serrated knife. **Makes 6 servings.**

Working with Phyllo

Frozen phyllo pastry is available in most supermarkets. One package contains about 18 sheets 16 x 12 inches (40 x 30 cm). Thaw package overnight in refrigerator. After removing required number of sheets, wrap unused portion airtight in plastic wrap; it can be stored in refrigerator for up to 2 weeks or refrozen immediately. Phyllo is easy to work with but dries out quickly; keep it covered with a damp tea towel as you work, removing sheets as you need them.

Phyllo Dessert Cups: These look great filled with ice cream or mousse and fresh fruit. For 6 dessert cups, you will need 4 sheets of phyllo. Stack 2 sheets; brush top lightly with melted butter. With sharp knife or pizza cutter, cut in half lengthwise, then in three crosswise, to make 6 squarish pieces. Place in 6 greased muffin cups (points of pastry should extend over top edges of cups). Repeat with 2 more stacked sheets of phyllo, making 6 more squares; place them crosswise over the first squares in muffin cups. Bake in 400F (200C) oven for 6 minutes or until golden. Let cool. (Can be stored in airtight container for up to 2 days.)

Apples Basics

Come fall, apples are the fruit of everyone's eye. Many Canadian communities mark autumn's harvest with festivals celebrating the apple's great diversity. Supermarkets and greengrocers offer a fair range of choices, but for a taste of less-common and heirloom varieties, seek out fall fairs, farmers' markets and roadside stands in orchard country. Not all apples are created for all purposes. Some are best eaten out of hand; others bake beautifully or make fine pies. Here's a guide to help you pick the right apple—and discover some new favourites.

For pies: Northern Spy is excellent for flavour and texture; Golden Delicious holds its shape well for open-face tarts. McIntosh is fine if you like a softer texture (or mix with firmer apples). Fairly tart apples make the best pies; adjust the amount of sugar in your recipe as required. Different varieties of apples can be combined to give the texture and sweet-tart balance you prefer (mix firm and soft; juicy and drier; tart and sweet).

For baked apples: Idared, Mutsu and Northern Spy hold their shape well.

For smooth sauces: Empire, Gravenstein, McIntosh and Royal Gala break down readily.

For cakes, baked puddings, chunky sauces: Cortland, Golden Delicious, Granny Smith, Idared, Mutsu, Northern Spy and Spartan (chopped or sliced) soften but hold their shape.

Popular Varieties:

Cortland: Red-orange striped skin; sweet-tart, crisp; white flesh resists browning when cut.

Empire: Dark red with stripes and tiny dots; cream flesh; sweet-tart, firm.

Golden Delicious: Yellow skin with five bumps on base; yellowish flesh; sweet, firm; keeps shape when cooked.

Granny Smith: Light green; tart, crisp, juicy; firm texture.

Gravenstein: Yellow or green, striped with red; tart, crisp, juicy.

Idared: Bright red with greenish-yellow patches; sweet-tart, very firm.

Jersey Mac: Red with yellow-green shoulder; tart, crisp; early eating apple.

Jonagold: Bright red over gold; sweet-tart, crisp, juicy.

Jonathan: Bright red, small; sweet-tart, crisp, juicy.

McIntosh: Deep red with green patch on side; sweet-tart, juicy; becomes soft when cooked.

Mutsu or Crispin: Green-yellow, medium-large; sweet-tart, firm, juicy.

Northern Spy: Bright red stripes; tart, firm; excellent for pies.

Paulared: Dark red; tart, very firm.

Red Delicious: Deep red, elongated shape with five bumps at base; sweet, crisp, juicy; excellent for eating and salads, not for cooking.

Royal Gala: Yellow skin with pink streaks; sweet, crisp, juicy.

Russet: Brown-yellow skin; firm cream to yellow flesh; sweet and aromatic; best eaten fresh.

Spartan: Dark red over faint stripes; sweet-tart, crisp, juicy

Fast and Easy Mousses ≈ ⊕

(Lemon, Lime, Orange, Raspberry, Cranberry, Cappuccino or Maple) This streamlined method produces delicious, creamy little mousses that are perfect make-aheads for a dinner party. The recipe gives you a choice of five fruit flavours as well as cappuccino and maple variations. Frozen concentrates conveniently provide intense flavour and the yogurt adds a slight tang.

1	envelope unflavoured gelatin	1
3/4 cup	granulated sugar	175 mL
3/4 cup	cold water	175 mL
3/4 cup	thawed frozen concentrate (raspberry or cranberry cocktail, orange juice, lemonade or limeade)	175 mL
3/4 cup	plain yogurt	175 mL
3/4 cup	whipping cream, whipped	175 mL

➜ In microwavable bowl, mix together gelatin and sugar. Stir in water. Microwave on High, stirring once or twice, for 1 minute or until gelatin and sugar are dissolved and mixture is clear. (Alternatively, heat in small saucepan over low heat until dissolved.) Stir in thawed concentrate. Chill, stirring occasionally, until slightly thickened (about 1 hour in refrigerator or 20 minutes in freezer). Whisk in yogurt until smooth. Fold in whipped cream. Spoon into stemmed glasses. Chill until firm, about 3 hours. Garnish each serving with a small dollop of whipped cream; for citrus mousses, top with shreds of zest; for raspberry or cranberry, top with mint sprigs or whole berries. **Makes 4 servings**.

Cappuccino Mousse: Instead of concentrate, use extra-strong coffee (can be made with instant espresso powder). Garnish with grated chocolate, chocolate curls, chocolate-coated coffee beans or a dusting of cocoa.

Maple Mousse: Reduce sugar to 1/4 cup (50 mL). Instead of concentrate, use maple syrup. Garnish with coarse maple sugar or chocolate curls.

♥ **Light and Easy Mousse:** Prepare Fast and Easy Mousse in any flavour, but instead of whipped cream, fold in 3 egg whites beaten until stiff but not dry. If you don't wish to use raw egg whites, use refrigerated pasteurized egg whites sold in small cartons.

A Trio of Flavours: For an attractive presentation, make 3 mousses of different flavours (such as lemon, raspberry and maple). Chill in separate bowls until firm. For each serving, place a large, oval-shaped spoonful of each flavour on dessert plate. Drizzle with Raspberry Coulis or other fruit purées (page 178) and/or Chocolate Drizzle (page 204). Garnish with small fresh edible flowers.

Lemon Snow on Raspberry Coulis: Prepare mousse using lemonade concentrate. Pour into small moulds rinsed in cold water. Chill until firm. Unmould onto individual dessert plates. Spoon Raspberry Coulis (page 178) around (not under) each. Garnish with mint and shreds of lemon zest.

Classic Chocolate Mousse

Rich, smooth, dark, delicious. For an even denser mousse, omit the egg whites and use an extra 1/2 cup (125 mL) whipping cream (stir the sugar into the egg yolk mixture). If you don't wish to use raw egg whites, use pasteurized refrigerated egg whites (available in cartons in most supermarkets).

8 oz	semisweet or bittersweet chocolate, chopped	250 g
1/4 cup	strong coffee	50 mL
1/4 cup	unsalted butter, cut into cubes	50 mL
3	eggs, separated	3
1 cup	whipping cream	250 mL
1/4 cup	granulated sugar	50 mL

➜ In heavy saucepan over low heat, melt chocolate in coffee. Whisk in butter until smooth. Whisk in egg yolks and continue to cook, stirring, for 2 minutes. Pour into large bowl and let cool to room temperature. Whip cream; set aside. Beat egg whites to soft peaks; gradually add sugar, beating to stiff peaks. Fold egg whites and whipped cream into chocolate mixture. Spoon into small dessert cups. Chill thoroughly, at least 2 hours. Garnish with whipped cream if desired. **Makes about 8 servings**.

Hot Apricot Soufflés 🕐 ♥

Individual soufflés make an impressive finale for a dinner party. These are surprisingly simple to prepare, rise like magic in the oven and are a popular fat-free alternative to traditional choco-late or liqueur-flavoured soufflés.

	Apricot purée (see below)	
3	egg whites, at room temperature	3
1/4 tsp	cream of tartar	1 mL
1/4 cup	granulated sugar	50 mL
	Icing sugar	

➜ Prepare apricot purée (see below). Butter four 8-oz (250 mL) or five 6-ounce (175 mL) soufflé dishes or ramekins; dust with granu-lated sugar, shaking out excess. Place dishes in a baking pan; set aside. With electric mixer, beat egg whites with cream of tartar to soft peaks; gradually add sugar, beating until mix-ture holds stiff peaks. Stir about one-quarter of the whites into the apricot purée to lighten it, then fold the mixture gently but thoroughly into remaining whites. Pour into prepared dishes, filling to top. (Can be prepared to this point and refrigerated for up to 2 hours.) Bake in 350F (180C) oven for 20 to 25 minutes or until well risen above the rim and golden brown on top. Dust with icing sugar. Serve immediately. Makes 4 or 5 servings.

Apricot purée: For best flavour and colour, use good-quality dried apricots that are soft and bright orange. In small saucepan, combine 4 ounces/125 g (3/4 cup/175 mL) chopped dried apricots, 1 cup (250 mL) water and 1/4 cup (50 mL) granulated sugar. Bring to boil, reduce heat, cover and simmer for 20 minutes. Do not drain. Add 1 tbsp (15 mL) lemon juice. Purée until very smooth in blender or food processor; let cool. (Can be made several days ahead and refrigerated.)

Fresh Fruit Trifle ♥

Always a crowd-pleaser, layered trifle shows off best in a straight-sided glass bowl.

4 cups	(approx) cake pieces*	1 L
1/4 cup	sweet sherry or fruit juice	50 mL
1/2 cup	raspberry jam or 1 cup (250 mL) Raspberry Coulis (page 178)	125 mL
3 cups	fruit (berries, sliced peaches, mango, kiwi)	750 mL
3 cups	Quick Custard Sauce (see Sidebar)	750 mL
1 cup	whipping cream	250 mL

* Use Basic Sponge Cake (page 203) or buy a packaged frozen pound cake; cut into small slices or fingers about 1/2 inch (1 cm) thick.

➜ Line bottom of 8-cup (2 L) glass serving bowl with half of the cake pieces. Drizzle with half of the sherry. Dot with half of the jam (or drizzle with Raspberry Coulis). Cover with half of the fruit and spread with half of the custard. Repeat layers, reserving some fruit for garnish. Cover and refrigerate for at least 4 hours or up to 8 hours. Before serving, whip cream and spread or pipe on top. Garnish with reserved fruit. **Makes 8 servings**.

Crème Brûlée

With divinely rich, smooth custard under a crackly burnt-sugar topping, crème brûlée remains one of the most popular desserts on restaurant menus. It's not difficult to make at home if you have a really hot broiler, or even better, a small blowtorch like chefs use for melting the sugar. For a variation, place a few fresh raspberries, strawberries, blueberries, peach slices or pieces of candied ginger in the ramekins before pouring in the custard.

1-1/2 cups	whipping cream	375 mL
4	egg yolks	4
1/4 cup	granulated sugar	50 mL
1 tsp	vanilla	5 mL
1/4 cup	granulated sugar	50 mL

➜ Heat cream almost to boiling. In bowl, whisk together egg yolks, 1/4 cup (50 mL) sugar and vanilla until blended. Gradually whisk in hot cream. Pour into four 3/4-cup (175 mL) ramekins. Place in shallow baking pan. Pour hot water into pan to come halfway up sides of ramekins. Bake in 350F (180C) oven for 35 to 40 minutes or until custard is set. Remove from water; let cool, then refrigerate until well chilled, at least 2 hours. Before serving, sprinkle top of each custard evenly with remaining sugar. Place under preheated broiler (or use blowtorch) until sugar melts and turns dark golden brown. Chill for at least 10 minutes or up to 3 hours (any longer and the sugar may soften). **Makes 4 servings**.

≋ Quick Custard Sauce: You can make custard sauce from tinned custard powder or even buy canned sauce. However, if you want the flavour of home-made but don't want to fuss with double boilers, you can make a fast, foolproof custard sauce very satisfactorily in the microwave. This recipe is also lower in fat than the traditional, using milk instead of cream and fewer eggs.

In 4-cup (1 L) glass measure or microwavable bowl, mix together 1/4 cup (50 mL) granulated sugar and 2 tbsp (30 mL) cornstarch; whisk in 1-1/2 cups (375 mL) milk until smooth. Microwave on High for 4 to 5 minutes, whisking twice during cooking, or until sauce comes to full boil and thickens. In small bowl, whisk 2 eggs; whisk in a little of the hot sauce, then whisk mixture back into sauce. Microwave on Medium for 30 seconds. Stir in 1 tsp (5 mL) vanilla. If too thick, whisk in more milk. **Makes about 2 cups (500 mL)**.

Serve warm as **pouring sauce** for desserts (sauce may also be chilled; it will thicken, but you can whisk in a little milk to thin it if desired). For a **soft custard for trifle**, chill the sauce thoroughly before using (cover surface with plastic wrap to prevent skin forming).

Baked Custards ❦

Perfect baked custard is a simple pleasure—smooth, soft-firm, scented with nutmeg. Various proportions of whole eggs, yolks, milk and cream can be used, but this straightforward version using whole eggs and milk turns out just right every time. You could use light cream for a richer custard, but whole milk works fine (don't substitute low-fat milk or the custard will be watery). If you have leftover egg yolks to use up, you can use 4 yolks in place of 2 of the eggs in this recipe.

2 cups	homogenized milk	500 mL
3	eggs	3
1/3 cup	granulated sugar	75 mL
Pinch	salt	Pinch
1 tsp	vanilla	5 mL
	Nutmeg	

→ Heat milk in microwave or saucepan just until hot (don't boil; if skin forms, strain through sieve). In bowl, whisk together eggs, sugar and salt just until combined. Slowly add hot milk, stirring with whisk (for smooth texture, don't whisk until frothy). Stir in vanilla. Place six 3/4-cup (175 mL) custard cups or ramekins in large baking pan. Pour custard mixture into cups. Sprinkle lightly with nutmeg. Pour hot water into pan to come halfway up sides of cups. Bake in 350F (180C) oven for 40 minutes or just until knife inserted in custard comes out clean. Remove cups from water. Serve warm or chilled. **Makes 6 servings**.

Crème Caramel

Rich but still light, simple but never bland, crème caramel (often with flavours of orange, coffee, cinnamon or liqueur) concludes any dinner in style. This French bistro classic has popular counterparts in many countries: in Spain, Portugal and Mexico, it's "flan," perfect after a spicy dinner. Crème caramel is a little firmer than plain baked custard so it will unmould easily. Caramelizing the sugar is not difficult; just watch it closely and remove from heat as soon as it turns dark golden brown.

Caramel: In heavy saucepan or skillet, combine 1 cup (250 mL) granulated sugar and 1/4 cup (50 mL) water. Heat over medium-high heat, stirring often, until sugar has dissolved; continue to cook, without stirring, until mixture turns dark golden brown. Remove from heat and immediately divide among six 3/4-cup (175 mL) ramekins or custard cups, swirling to coat bottom of each with caramel (it will harden quickly). (For easy cleanup of the saucepan, add hot water and bring to boil to dissolve caramel residue.)

Custard: Prepare recipe for Baked Custards but instead of 3 eggs, use 4 eggs plus 2 egg yolks. Instead of milk, use 1 cup (250 mL) each milk and whipping cream. Pour into caramel-lined cups and bake as for Baked Custards. Remove cups from water; let cool, then refrigerate until cold, about 3 hours. To unmould, run knife around edge of each custard and invert onto serving plate; caramel will run down sides of custard. (If any caramel sticks to cups, microwave for a few seconds until melted; pour over custard.) **Makes 6 servings.**

Zabaglione

Whether it's called zabaglione (Italian) or sabayon (French), this classic dessert is delectably luxurious though light and frothy. It has to be prepared just before serving but takes only a few minutes (and the "ching-ching-ching" sound of whisking coming from the kitchen will add to your guests' anticipation while waiting for dessert). Marsala is the traditional flavouring, but anything from champagne to orange juice can be substituted.

4	egg yolks	4
1/4 cup	granulated sugar	50 mL
1/2 cup	dry Marsala wine	125 mL

➡ In metal bowl, whisk egg yolks with sugar until pale and creamy. Set bowl over saucepan of simmering water; add Marsala and whisk until mixture is tripled in volume and holds soft peaks. Pour into stemmed glasses and serve immediately. **Makes 4 servings.** Zabaglione can also be served chilled.

Zabaglione semifreddo: Freeze zabaglione in individual soufflé dishes or small loaf pan.

Tiramisù

Following a long debut on fashionable menus of the '80s, tiramisù has settled in as a familiar favourite in Canada as in Italy. Many versions of this recipe are made with uncooked eggs; here, whipping cream is used instead, but you could replace it with 3 stiffly beaten egg whites (you can use refrigerated pasteurized egg whites sold in small cartons). The Italian crisp ladyfinger biscuits called "savoiardi" are the ones to use if you can find them; otherwise, soft ladyfingers are fine, but let them dry out before using. If you don't wish to use liqueur, increase espresso to 1 cup (250 mL).

12 oz	mascarpone cheese (1-1/2 cups/375 mL)	375 g
2 tbsp	granulated sugar	30 mL
4 tbsp	coffee liqueur	60 mL
3/4 cup	whipping cream, whipped	175 mL
3/4 cup	cold espresso coffee (can be made with instant espresso powder)	175 mL
20	(approx) crisp ladyfingers (enough for two layers; trim to fit if necessary)	20
1 tbsp	cocoa	15 mL

➡ In bowl, beat together mascarpone, sugar and half of the liqueur until soft and light. Fold in whipped cream. In shallow dish, combine espresso and remaining liqueur. Dip ladyfingers one at a time into espresso mixture just to moisten (do not soak); arrange in single layer in 8-inch (20 cm) square glass or ceramic dish. Spread with half of the mascarpone mixture. Dip remaining ladyfingers and arrange in dish to make a second layer. Spread with remaining mascarpone mixture. Dust top with sifted cocoa. Cover with plastic wrap and refrigerate for at least 4 hours. Cut in squares. **Makes 6 to 8 servings.**

Pavlova

A traditional favourite in Australia and New Zealand, this light-as-air dessert is said to be named after the ballerina Anna Pavlova. Sliced strawberries and kiwifruit are classic toppings; passionfruit pulp can be drizzled over or folded into the cream; fresh raspberries, peaches or mango are also delicious. A good pavlova starts with a type of meringue shell that's crispy on the outside with a soft, marshmallow-like centre.

4	egg whites, at room temperature	4
1 cup	granulated sugar	250 mL
1 tbsp	cornstarch	15 mL
2 tsp	white vinegar	10 mL
1 tsp	vanilla	5 mL
1 cup	whipping cream	250 mL
1 tbsp	icing sugar	15 mL
3 cups	(approx) fresh fruit	750 mL

→ Line baking sheet with parchment paper; trace 9-inch (23 cm) circle on paper. With electric mixer, beat egg whites to soft peaks. Very gradually beat in sugar, beating until sugar is thoroughly dissolved and mixture holds stiff, shiny peaks. Beat in cornstarch, vinegar and vanilla. Spread onto traced circle on baking sheet, mounding sides up and making a very shallow depression in centre. Bake in 250F (120C) oven for 1-1/2 hours or until outside is crisp, dry and very lightly coloured. Turn oven off and leave pavlova shell inside until completely cooled. (Shell can be stored in airtight container for up to 2 days.) Place shell on serving plate. Whip cream with icing sugar to soft peaks. Fill pavlova shell with whipped cream and decorate with fruit. **Makes 8 servings**.

Tulip Dessert Cups

For an impressive dessert, fill these tulip-shaped crisp cookie cups with ice cream, sorbet or mousse; place on a pool of raspberry coulis on dessert plate, drizzle with melted chocolate and decorate with fresh berries. The cookies can also be shaped into classic tuiles (resembling curved roof tiles) by draping them while warm over a rolling pin.

2	egg whites	2
1/2 cup	granulated sugar	125 mL
1/3 cup	all-purpose flour	75 mL
1/4 cup	butter, melted	50 mL
2 tsp	water	10 mL
1 tsp	vanilla	5 mL

→ In bowl, beat egg whites, sugar, flour, butter, water and vanilla just until blended. Using 3 tbsp (45 mL) per cookie, drop onto parchment-lined baking sheets about 7 inches (18 cm) apart. Spread each into very thin 6-inch (15 cm) circle. Bake in 400F (200C) oven for 6 to 8 minutes or until just lightly browned at edges. Remove from oven and immediately remove cookies with a large metal spatula, one at a time, and place over lightly greased inverted glass (about 1-1/2 inches/4 cm in diameter). Working quickly, shape warm tuile with fingers to create a fluted cup. Let cool completely on the glass. Repeat with remaining cookies. (If too firm to mould, reheat in oven for 15 to 30 seconds or until softened.) **Makes 6 tulips**. (Can be stored in airtight container for up to 2 days.)

Meringue Shells: Fill a large shell or individual "nests" with whipped cream, custard, lemon curd or ice cream, topped with fruit if desired.

With electric mixer, beat 3 egg whites (at room temperature) with 1/4 tsp (1 mL) cream of tartar to soft peaks. Gradually beat in 3/4 cup (175 mL) granulated sugar, beating until mixture holds stiff peaks.

For **individual meringue shells**, spoon into 8 to 12 mounds on parchment-lined baking sheet. Use back of spoon to form hollow nests.

For **large meringue shell**, spread into a 9-inch (23 cm) round. Build up the sides, leaving a shallow depression in centre. Bake in 275F (140C) oven for 1 hour for individual shells, 1-1/2 hours for large shell, or until crisp, dry and very faintly coloured. Turn off oven and leave meringues in oven until completely cooled.

For **tiny meringue kisses**, use same mixture. If desired, fold in 1/2 cup (125 mL) chopped toasted almonds or hazelnuts. Pipe with a star tube, or drop by small spoonfuls, onto parchment-lined baking sheets. Bake for 30 minutes or until very faintly coloured.

Linzertorte ✤

This recipe from Toronto Star *food editor Marion Kane is a great example of the treasured traditional recipes that are passed down from one generation to another.*

Marion adapted this one from her mother's collection of favourite European-style cakes and tortes. Austrian in origin, it's a shallow, rich, nut-crusted tart that's superb with a good cup of tea or coffee.

1-1/4 cups	whole unblanched almonds	300 mL
3/4 cup	butter, softened	175 mL
1/2 cup	granulated sugar	125 mL
2	egg yolks (reserve 1 white)	2
1 tsp	finely grated lemon rind	5 mL
1 tbsp	lemon juice	15 mL
1 cup	all-purpose flour	250 mL
1 tbsp	cocoa	15 mL
1/2 tsp	cinnamon	2 mL
Pinch	ground cloves	Pinch
1 cup	(approx) good-quality raspberry jam	250 mL
	Icing sugar	

➜ In food processor, pulse almonds with on/off motion just until ground. In large bowl, using electric mixer, cream butter and sugar until fluffy. Add egg yolks, lemon rind and juice. Beat until smooth. In separate bowl, mix together flour, cocoa, cinnamon, cloves and almonds. Stir into butter mixture to form a soft dough. Gather dough into ball, wrap well in plastic wrap and refrigerate for at least 1 hour or overnight. (If chilled overnight, let soften at room temperature 30 minutes before continuing.)

With floured hands, evenly pat two-thirds of dough into bottom and about 1-1/4 inches (3 cm) up sides of 9-inch (23 cm) springform pan or fluted flan pan with removable bottom. Carefully spread jam over dough. On floured surface, roll remaining dough into oval 1/4 inch (5 mm) thick. Cut into strips 3/4 inch (2 cm) wide and arrange in lattice on top of jam, pressing edges into edge of torte. (The dough is delicate, so don't bother trying to weave it; just do it crisscross-style. If strips break, simply press them back together.) Lightly beat reserved egg white. Brush strips and edges of torte with egg white. Bake in 350F (180C) oven for 45 minutes or until pastry is well browned and jam is bubbling. Let cool completely in pan on rack. Remove sides of pan. Dust torte with sifted icing sugar. Cut in wedges and serve with vanilla ice cream or crème fraîche. **Makes 10 servings**.

Cheesecake

This classic cheesecake gets top marks for taste and texture. For a small cheesecase, halve the recipe and bake in 7-inch (19 cm) springform pan. Top it off with any fruit sauce, sweetened sliced fruit or berries.

Crust:

1-1/2 cups	graham wafer crumbs	375 mL
2 tbsp	granulated sugar	30 mL
1/4 cup	butter, melted	50 mL

Filling:

1-1/2 lb	regular cream cheese (3 250-g packages), softened	750 g
1 cup	granulated sugar	250 mL
4	eggs, separated	4
1/2 cup	sour cream	125 mL
1 tbsp	all-purpose flour	15 mL
1 tsp	vanilla	5 mL

Crust: Mix together crumbs, sugar and butter; press into bottom of 10-inch (25 cm) springform pan. Bake in 325F (160C) oven for 10 minutes. Let cool.

Filling: In large bowl, with electric mixer, beat cheese with sugar just until smooth. Beat in egg yolks, one at a time, until smooth. Blend in sour cream, flour and vanilla. Beat egg whites until stiff but not dry; fold into cheese mixture. Pour over cooled crust. Bake in 325F (160C) oven for 1 hour or until centre is just set. Turn oven off, prop door open a few inches and let cheesecake cool in oven for 1 hour. Remove from oven and run knife around inside edge of pan. Let cool completely (at least 2 hours) before removing sides of pan. Chill thoroughly before serving. Keeps well for 4 days refrigerated. **Makes about 12 servings.**

Fruit Crisp

Use apples, peaches, pears, apricots, plums, pitted cherries or a mixture of fruit for this ever-popular baked dessert. Add some raisins, dried cranberries, dried cherries or chopped candied ginger if you like. The fruit doesn't usually require sugar, but if it's too tart, sweeten with sugar or a drizzle of honey. The topping can be varied by adding chopped hazelnuts, sliced almonds or sesame seeds; or replace the oats with granola.

4 cups	fruit, peeled and sliced as necessary	1 L
1 tbsp	lemon juice	15 mL
1/2 cup	quick-cooking oats (not instant)	125 mL
1/4 cup	all-purpose flour	50 mL
1/2 cup	packed brown sugar	125 mL
1/4 tsp	cinnamon	1 mL
1/4 cup	butter	50 mL

➜ Toss fruit with lemon juice and place in 8-cup (2 L) baking dish. In bowl, mix together oats, flour, sugar and cinnamon. Cut in butter until crumbly. Sprinkle over fruit. Bake in 350F (180C) oven for 40 minutes or until topping is golden brown and fruit is tender. **Makes 4 servings.**

Strawberry-Rhubarb Cobbler

Good Filling — Don't serve too hot, it will be runny.

Food writer Johanna Burkhard uses this recipe for each fruit as it comes into season near her Niagara Peninsula home (frozen fruit can be used in the winter). Heating the fruit before adding the topping prevents the biscuit mixture from becoming soggy on the underside.

4 cups	chopped fresh rhubarb	1 L
2 cups	sliced strawberries	500 mL
3/4 cup	granulated sugar	175 mL
2 tbsp	cornstarch	30 mL
1 tsp	grated orange rind	5 mL

Biscuit Topping:

1 cup	all-purpose flour	250 mL
1/4 cup	granulated sugar	50 mL
1-1/2 tsp	baking powder	7 mL
1/4 tsp	salt	1 mL
1/4 cup	cold butter, cut into bits	50 mL
1/2 cup	milk	125 mL
1 tsp	vanilla	5 mL
	Additional granulated sugar	

➜ Place rhubarb and strawberries in 9-inch (2.5 L) round or square baking dish. In a small bowl, combine 3/4 cup (175 mL) sugar, cornstarch and orange rind; sprinkle over fruit and toss gently. Bake in 400F (200C) oven for 20 to 25 minutes (or 30 minutes if using frozen fruit) or until hot and bubbles appear around edges.

Topping: In mixing bowl, combine flour, 1/4 cup (50 mL) sugar, baking powder and salt. Cut in butter until mixture resembles coarse crumbs. In separate bowl, combine milk and vanilla; add to dry ingredients all at once and stir quickly to make a soft and sticky dough. Using large spoon, drop 8 separate spoonfuls of dough onto hot fruit; sprinkle with about 2 tsp (10 mL) sugar. Bake in 400F (200C) oven for 25 to 30 minutes longer, or until top is golden and fruit is bubbly. Serve warm, topped with vanilla ice cream. **Makes 8 servings**.

Blueberry-Peach Cobbler: Use 2 cups (500 mL) fresh or frozen blueberries and 4 cups (1 L) sliced peaches. Reduce sugar to 2/3 cup (150 mL).

Baked Lemon Pudding

Also called Lemon Sponge Pudding or Lemon Pudding Cake, this delicious dessert comes out of the oven with a fluffy cake-like topping over a creamy lemon sauce.

3/4 cup	granulated sugar	175 mL
3 tbsp	butter, melted	45 mL
3 tbsp	all-purpose flour	45 mL
1/4 tsp	salt	1 mL
3	eggs, separated	3
1 cup	milk	250 mL
1 tsp	grated lemon rind	5 mL
1/3 cup	lemon juice	75 mL

➜ In bowl, combine sugar, butter, flour, salt, egg yolks, milk, lemon rind and lemon juice. In separate bowl, beat egg whites until stiff; fold into batter. Pour into 8-cup (2 L) baking dish. Place in larger pan and add hot water to come halfway up sides of dish. Bake in 350F (180C) oven for 30 to 40 minutes or until set and lightly browned. **Makes 6 servings**.

Caramel-Apple Pudding ❦

Self-saucing puddings have come a long way since their humble beginnings as plain-and-simple "hasty puddings" in the 1930s. Today's versions are as easy to make as ever but taste even better. These two variations will please last-minute guests as well as the family.

1 cup	all-purpose flour	250 mL
1/3 cup	packed brown sugar	75 mL
2 tsp	baking powder	10 mL
1/4 tsp	salt	1 mL
3/4 cup	raisins	175 mL
1/2 cup	milk	125 mL
2 tbsp	butter, melted	30 mL
3/4 cup	thinly sliced peeled apples	175 mL

Sauce:

1 cup	packed brown sugar	250 mL
1 tbsp	all-purpose flour	15 mL
1 tbsp	butter, softened	15 mL
1-3/4 cups	boiling water	425 mL
2 tsp	vanilla	10 mL

➜ Mix together flour, sugar, baking powder, salt, raisins, milk and butter; spread in buttered 8-cup (2 L) baking dish. Arrange apple slices on top of batter.

Sauce: In bowl, mix together sugar and flour; blend in butter, boiling water and vanilla. Gently pour over batter. Bake in 350F (180C) oven for 35 to 40 minutes or until tester inserted in cake comes out clean. (Pudding will have formed a cake-like top with lots of sauce underneath.) **Makes 6 servings**.

Steamed Cranberry Pudding

Studded with cranberries (fresh, frozen or dried), this festive pudding is a great alternative to traditional plum pudding at Christmas. The recipe is a Prairie favourite from Judy Schultz, food and travel writer with the Edmonton Journal.

1/2 cup	butter, softened	125 mL
3/4 cup	granulated sugar	175 mL
2	eggs	2
1/2 cup	orange juice	125 mL
1 tsp	grated orange rind	5 mL
2-1/3 cups	all-purpose flour	575 mL
1 tbsp	baking powder	15 mL
1/2 tsp	salt	2 mL
1/2 cup	milk	125 mL
1-1/2 cups	cranberries (fresh, frozen or dried)	375 mL
	Custard sauce (page 185)	

➜ Cream together butter and sugar. Beat in eggs, orange juice and orange rind. In separate bowl, mix together flour, baking powder and salt; stir into creamed mixture alternately with milk. Fold in cranberries. Spoon into buttered and floured 8-cup (2 L) pudding mould or bowl (batter is thick; pack it well). Cover with lid or double thickness of buttered foil secured with string. Place on rack in large pot; add boiling water to halfway up side of mould. Cover and steam for about 2 hours (water should bubble gently; add more if necessary to maintain level); when done, tester inserted in centre of pudding should come out clean. Remove from water and let stand for 15 minutes before unmoulding. Serve with warm custard sauce (flavoured with orange liqueur if desired). **Makes 8 servings**.

Chocolate Fudge Pudding: (variation of Caramel-Apple Pudding) To the dry ingredients for the batter, add 2 tbsp (30 mL) cocoa. To dry ingredients for sauce, add 3 tbsp (45 mL) cocoa.

Baked Apples: For each serving, use 1 large apple. Remove core with apple corer or small knife. Peel the top one-third of each apple. Place apples in baking dish just large enough to hold them. Fill each core hole almost to top with raisins, then a spoonful of brown sugar, pinch of cinnamon and dot of butter. Pour apple juice or maple syrup, about 1/4 inch (5 mm) deep, around apples. Bake in 350F (180C) oven for 45 minutes or until tender; baste with juice once or twice during baking. Serve warm, with ice cream, whipped cream or custard sauce.

Creamy Rice Pudding

The stovetop method produces a delectably creamy pudding and is very easy, requiring only an occasional stir. The small proportion of rice to milk is correct, so don't be concerned. Be sure to use short-grain rice and do not rinse it—that's the secret to the creamy consistency. Also be sure to use whole milk even if you usually buy 1% or 2%; the recipe conveniently uses 1 litre of homogenized.

1/2 cup	short-grain rice (arborio or Italian-style)	125 mL
4 cups	homogenized milk	1 L
1/3 cup	granulated sugar	75 mL
1/4 tsp	salt	1 mL
1/3 cup	raisins	75 mL
1 tsp	vanilla	5 mL
	Cinnamon	

→ In large heavy saucepan, combine rice, milk, sugar and salt. Bring just to boil, stirring often. Reduce heat to very low, add raisins, cover and simmer very gently, stirring occasionally, for 50 minutes or until rice is very tender and pudding is very creamy and thickened somewhat (it will look a little soupy while hot, but thickens a lot more as it cools, and is just right when served slightly warm or chilled). Stir in vanilla. Remove from heat and let stand, uncovered, until just warm, stirring occasionally. (Pudding may also be served chilled.) Transfer to dessert dishes and sprinkle with cinnamon. **Makes 6 servings**.

Microwave Lemon Curd 〰

Old-fashioned lemon curd is back in vogue, turning up in stylish restaurant desserts and fancy bakeshop goodies. Here's today's way of making it fast, easy and more delectable than ever. Microwaving avoids the problems of the old methods (fussing with double boilers, sticking or lumping, and wondering if it's thick enough). This version is fast, foolproof, extra-lemony in flavour and lower in sugar and butter than old-time recipes. Use lemon curd as a delicious filling for tarts or meringue shells, for spreading on toast or scones, or as a cake filling.

3	eggs	3
3/4 cup	granulated sugar	175 mL
1 tbsp	grated lemon rind	15 mL
1/2 cup	lemon juice	125 mL
2 tbsp	butter, softened	30 mL

→ In microwavable bowl, whisk together eggs and sugar. Whisk in lemon rind, lemon juice and butter. Microwave on High for 2 minutes; whisk until smooth; microwave on High for 2 to 3 minutes longer until it boils and thickens slightly; whisk again until smooth. Let cool, then refrigerate (it will thicken much more as it chills). May be stored in covered jar in refrigerator for up to 1 week. **Makes 1-1/2 cups** (375 mL), enough for 24 2-inch (5 cm) tarts.

Baked Rice Pudding: In 4-cup (1 L) baking dish, combine 1 cup (250 mL) cooked rice, 1/3 cup (75 mL) granulated sugar, 2 beaten eggs, pinch of salt, 1/2 tsp (2 mL) vanilla and 2 cups (500 mL) hot milk. Stir in 1/3 cup (75 mL) raisins if desired. Place dish in larger pan of hot water. Bake in 325F (160C) oven for 30 minutes; stir. Sprinkle lightly with nutmeg. Bake for 30 minutes longer or until softly set. **Makes 4 servings**.

Extra-Easy Rice Pudding: In saucepan, combine 1 cup (250 mL) cooked rice, 1 cup (250 mL) milk, 2 tbsp (30 mL) granulated sugar, 1/4 cup (50 mL) raisins and 1 tsp (5 mL) vanilla. Cook over medium heat until very hot but not boiling, stirring occasionally. In small bowl, beat 1 egg; stir in a little of the hot pudding, then return it to saucepan, stirring quickly to mix. Remove from heat, cover and let stand until just warm, stirring occasionally (pudding thickens as it cools). Sprinkle each serving lightly with cinnamon. **Makes 2 servings**.

Bread Pudding Variations

Raisin-Bread Pudding with Apples: Omit raisins. Use raisin bread and add 2 chopped peeled apples.

Bread and Butter Pudding: Instead of bread cubes, use 4 large slices bread. Remove crusts, spread slices with butter and cut in strips or squares. Place half in bottom of baking dish; sprinkle with raisins; pour in half of custard mixture; repeat layers.

Berry Bread Pudding: Make Bread and Butter Pudding, increasing sugar to 2/3 cup (150 mL) and omitting raisins; sprinkle 1/2 cup (125 mL) raspberries or blueberries over each layer of bread.

Bread Pudding ✦

Originally designed to use up stale bread during hard times, bread puddings have now been reinvented in all kinds of flavours from banana-orange to chocolate-rum. Use slightly dry, firm-textured white bread or egg bread for this recipe, which makes a soft pudding with slightly crusty sides. For a more custardy pudding, place baking dish in larger pan filled with hot water to come halfway up sides.

3	eggs	3
1/3 cup	granulated sugar	75 mL
1 tbsp	butter, melted	15 mL
1 tsp	vanilla	5 mL
1/4 tsp	each: nutmeg, salt	1 mL
2 cups	hot milk	500 mL
3 cups	cubed bread	750 mL
1/3 cup	raisins	75 mL
	Icing sugar	

➜ In large bowl, beat eggs with sugar until foamy. Add butter, vanilla, nutmeg and salt. Stir in hot milk. Add bread and raisins; mix well. Turn into buttered 6-cup (1.5 L) baking dish. Bake in 350F (180C) oven for 50 to 60 minutes or until set. Let stand for about an hour before serving. Dust top with icing sugar. **Makes 4 to 6 servings.**

Cream Puffs ✦

Lighter-than-air crispy puffs filled with whipped cream are a retro treat now back in favour. This dough is called chou paste and is used for many French pastries such as éclairs and profiteroles. With the addition of cheese, they become cheese puffs or gougères (see page 14). They can be made mini-size for savoury fillings.

1 cup	water	250 mL
1/2 cup	butter	125 mL
1 cup	all-purpose flour	250 mL
1/4 tsp	salt	1 mL
4	eggs	4
	Whipped cream; icing sugar	

➜ In small heavy saucepan, combine water and butter; bring to full boil. Reduce heat; add flour and salt all at once, and beat with wooden spoon until mixture forms a smooth ball that leaves side of pan. Remove from heat. With electric mixer, beat in eggs one at a time, beating well after each addition; continue beating until smooth and shiny. Chill for a few minutes until fairly firm. Drop by 8 large or 12 medium spoonfuls onto lightly greased baking sheet, mounding each in centre. Bake in 425F (220C) oven for 15 minutes; reduce heat to 350F (180C) and bake for 20 to 30 minutes longer or until puffed and golden. Remove from oven and cut a small slit with point of knife in each puff. Cool thoroughly. Slice tops off each puff; remove any moist dough inside (puffs should be almost hollow). Just before serving, fill with whipped cream and dust tops with icing sugar. **Makes 8 large or 12 medium puffs.**

Chocolate Truffles

Very easy to make, and much less expensive than store-bought, melt-in-the-mouth truffles are a special treat for any occasion and make great gifts. For an alcohol-free flavouring, use orange or raspberry juice concentrate or extra-strong coffee instead of liqueur.

6 oz	semisweet chocolate, coarsely chopped	175 g
6 tbsp	whipping cream	90 mL
2 tbsp	rum or liqueur (such as orange, coffee, raspberry, hazelnut)	30 mL
	Coating: cocoa, icing sugar, finely chopped nuts or melted semisweet chocolate	

➜ Place chocolate and cream in bowl. Place over saucepan of simmering water; melt slowly, stirring often. Remove from heat; beat well with whisk. Blend in rum or liqueur. Chill until firm. Shape into small balls. Roll in cocoa, icing sugar or nuts, or dip into melted chocolate. Store in refrigerator. **Makes about 30.**

Marbled Cranberry-Chocolate Bark

Jewel-like dried cranberries dot these holiday treats or gifts. This easy candy is a good project for little kids to help with or for bigger kids to do on their own.

6 oz	semisweet or bittersweet chocolate	175 g
6 oz	white chocolate	175 g
1 cup	dried cranberries	250 mL
1 cup	toasted whole unblanched almonds (optional) (see page 237)	250 g

➜ In bowls set over saucepan of simmering water, melt dark and white chocolate separately (see page 240). Stir half of the cranberries and almonds (if using) into dark chocolate; stir remainder into white chocolate. Drop spoonfuls of chocolate, alternating dark and white, onto baking sheet lined with parchment or waxed paper. With point of knife, swirl dark and white chocolate together to create a marbled effect. Gently tap baking sheet to smooth surface of chocolate. Chill until firm. When cool, break into pieces.

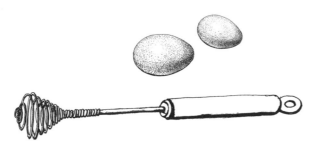

Chocolate and Cocoa

Chocolate and cocoa both come from cocoa beans. After harvesting, the beans are processed, leaving the chocolate liquor from which chocolate and cocoa are produced. The liquor contains cocoa butter, the natural fat that gives chocolate its melting quality.

Unsweetened chocolate is made from pure chocolate liquor with no sugar added and is used only for baking and desserts, not for eating on its own. *Bittersweet and semisweet* chocolate can be used interchangeably; bittersweet has slightly lower sugar content and slightly stronger chocolate flavour. Both are used in desserts and baking but are sweet enough to eat on their own. *Sweet chocolate* is slightly sweeter and has a milder chocolate flavour than semisweet.

Milk chocolate has milk added and has lighter colour and flavour; it can be eaten on its own as well as used in recipes.

Chocolate chips are specially formulated to soften yet hold their shape during baking. Do not use in place of pure chocolate unless indicated in recipe.

White chocolate contains cocoa butter but not chocolate liquor, so is not actually chocolate. In recipes, be sure to use pure white chocolate, not artificial, which does not melt evenly.

Cocoa is a dry, unsweetened powder made from chocolate liquor that has had most of the cocoa butter removed. Cocoa is therefore lower in fat than chocolate. Do not confuse it with sweetened instant chocolate drink mix.

Strawberry Shortcake ❧

Traditional shortcake, made with a rich biscuit dough and slathered with fresh fruit and whipped cream, is dessert perfection, especially when the cake is still warm from the oven. Strawberries, raspberries, blueberries, sliced peaches or a mixture of fruit all make wonderful shortcakes.

➜ To make the shortcake, prepare the dough for Cream Tea Scones (page 170). Roll out and cut into 8 individual shortcakes OR pat into one 8-inch (20 cm) round on a baking sheet and, with a knife, score the top in 8 wedges. Sprinkle with granulated sugar. Bake in 400F (200C) oven for 15 minutes for individual cakes, 20 to 25 minutes for large cake, or until golden brown and baked through. Meanwhile, lightly sprinkle sugar over about 3 cups (750 mL) sliced strawberries; let stand until juicy. Whip 1 cup (250 mL) whipping cream. Split shortcake (preferably warm) and fill with strawberries and whipped cream. To serve large shortcake, cut in wedges. **Makes 8 servings.**

Frozen Raspberry-Mango Cake ♥

This take on ice cream cake is virtually fat-free and very easy to prepare. Fruit ices contain no fat but are still smooth and flavourful; mango and raspberry make a tantalizing combo, but you can use any favourite flavours of fruit ice, gelato, sorbet, sherbet, low-fat ice cream or frozen yogurt. Low-fat pound cake can be found in the freezer section of most supermarkets.

1	pkg (320 g) frozen low-fat pound cake	1
1/3 cup	raspberry jam	75 mL
2 cups	each: mango and raspberry ice	500 mL
	Toppings (optional): sliced mango, whole raspberries, Raspberry Coulis (page 178)	

➜ Cut cake into slices about 5/8 inch (1.5 cm) thick (you will use about 3/4 of the cake). Line bottom of 8-inch (20 cm) springform pan with cake (trim pieces to fit, leaving no spaces). Spread cake with jam. Let mango ice soften slightly at room temperature; transfer to bowl and stir just until soft enough to spread but not melted. Spread evenly over jam; place in freezer for 10 minutes. Meanwhile, soften and stir raspberry ice same as for mango ice; spread over mango layer. Cover with plastic wrap and freeze for 3 hours or until firm. (May be removed from pan and stored in airtight freezer bag for up to 1 month.) To serve, remove sides of pan; cut frozen cake into wedges. If desired, top with mango slices and raspberries; drizzle with Raspberry Coulis. **Makes 8 servings.**

Ice Cream Cakes for kids' parties: Prepare same as Frozen Raspberry-Mango Cake, above, but omit pound cake and jam. Choose any combination of ice creams or sherbets to make 2 or 3 layers of different colours. Decorate top with piped whipped cream if desired; sprinkle with crushed cookies, candies or nuts, or drizzle with butterscotch or chocolate sauce.

For a Hallowe'en party, **Spider Ice Cream Cake** is easy, spooky and fun. For the layers, use chocolate ice cream topped with orange sherbet. For a spiderweb topping: Use storebought chocolate sundae syrup (not melted chocolate, which hardens too quickly to draw a web). Spoon about 1/4 cup (50 mL) syrup into small plastic bag with one tiny corner snipped off. Pipe chocolate circles in bull's eye pattern on top of frozen orange layer. Use toothpick to pull lines through circles from centre to outside edge. Decorate with a few chocolate, licorice or plastic spiders.

Summertime Kid-Pleasers

Ice Cream Sandwiches: Spread thick layer of slightly softened ice cream between flat round cookies or thin rice crispy squares; freeze in zip-top plastic bags.

Frozen Banana Pops: Peel mini-bananas, or larger ones cut in pieces, and insert wooden stick in end of each. Freeze in plastic bags. Eat plain or rolled in chocolate or caramel sauce and chopped nuts or coconut. Kids also love frozen bunches of grapes.

Peach Pops: In food processor, purée 4 peeled, pitted peaches with 2 tsp (10 mL) lemon juice and 1/4 cup (50 mL) granulated sugar. Freeze in popsicle moulds or ice cube trays; insert sticks when mixture is half frozen.

Berry Pops: Purée 1-1/2 cups (375 mL) strawberries, blueberries or raspberries; strain. Add 1/2 cup (125 mL) fruit juice concentrate, 1 cup (250 mL) water, and sugar or honey to taste. Freeze as for Peach Pops.

Fruit Yogurt Pops: Combine 1 jar (about 200 mL) apricot (or other fruit) junior baby food with 1/2 cup (125 mL) orange juice, 2 cups (500 mL) plain yogurt, and honey to taste. Freeze as for Peach Pops.

196

Let Us Eat...

Cakes

Fast-and-easy favourites to please your
sweetie, celebrate a birthday, delight a child,
wow the bridge club

Fast and Easy Snacking Cake

Just starting to explore the pleasures of baking? Or want a fast update on ingredients, methods and equipment? See Baking Tips, page 240-41.

Use overripe bananas (great flavour!) or leftover canned pumpkin or applesauce to make a moist, flavourful cake that can be whipped up in 10 minutes. Use as a snacking cake or quick dessert or for lunchboxes. Frost with a simple buttercream (page 204) or just dust with icing sugar.

2	eggs	2
1/3 cup	vegetable oil	75 mL
1/2 cup	each: granulated sugar, packed brown sugar	125 mL
1 cup	mashed overripe bananas (about 3)	250 mL
1-1/2 cups	all-purpose flour	375 mL
1 tsp	baking powder	5 mL
1/2 tsp	each: baking soda, salt	2 mL

➔ In large bowl, combine eggs, oil and granulated and brown sugars; with electric mixer, beat until smooth and creamy, about 1 minute. Add bananas and beat until blended in, about 30 seconds. In separate bowl, mix together flour, baking powder, baking soda and salt; stir in at low speed until blended, about 30 seconds. Pour into greased and floured 8- to 9-inch (20 to 23 cm) square cake pan. Bake in 350F (180C) oven for 40 to 45 minutes or until tester comes out clean.

Pumpkin or Applesauce Cake: Instead of bananas, use 1 cup (250 mL) canned pumpkin purée or 3/4 cup (175 mL) smooth applesauce. To the flour mixture, add 1 tsp (5 mL) cinnamon and 1/4 tsp (1 mL) each nutmeg, allspice and ground cloves.

Pumpkin-Gingerbread: Instead of bananas, use 1 cup (250 mL) canned pumpkin purée. Instead of brown sugar, use 1/2 cup (125 mL) molasses. To flour mixture, add 2 tsp (10 mL) ground ginger and 1/4 tsp (1 mL) each cinnamon, nutmeg, allspice and ground cloves. Serve warm, with whipped cream. **Makes 6 to 8 servings**.

Chocolate Snacking Cake

This version is extra-moist and chocolaty but low-fat, and a fun recipe for little kids to help make.

1-1/2 cups	all-purpose flour	375 mL
1 cup	granulated sugar	250 mL
3 tbsp	cocoa	45 mL
1 tsp	each: baking powder, baking soda	5 mL
1/2 tsp	salt	2 mL
1/3 cup	vegetable oil	75 mL
1 tbsp	white vinegar	15 mL
1 tsp	vanilla	5 mL
1 cup	warm water	250 mL
1/2 cup	chopped walnuts (optional)	125 mL

➔ In mixing bowl, combine dry ingredients (except nuts); mix thoroughly. Add liquid ingredients; stir with whisk until blended. Add nuts (if using). Pour into lightly greased 8-inch (20 cm) square cake pan. Bake in 350F (180C) oven for 30 minutes or until tester comes out clean.

Instant Chocolate Icing: Sprinkle baked cake, while still hot, with about 1 cup (250 mL) chocolate chips OR top with a single layer of peppermint patties (round chocolate-coated patties with mint cream filling); spread when softened.

Fruit Streusel Coffeecake

Warm from the oven, this is one of the ultimate accompaniments to a good cup of coffee. This easy-mix cake is good with a variety of fruit toppings; for a plainer coffeecake, omit the fruit.

1-1/2 cups	all-purpose flour	375 mL
1 tsp	baking powder	5 mL
1/2 tsp	baking soda	2 mL
1/4 tsp	salt	1 mL
3/4 cup	granulated sugar	175 mL
1/3 cup	very soft butter	75 mL
1	egg	1
3/4 cup	buttermilk	175 mL
1 tsp	vanilla	5 mL
2 to 3	thinly sliced apples, peaches or plums, or 1 cup (250 mL) fresh blueberries	2 to 3

Streusel:

1/3 cup	packed brown sugar	75 mL
1/4 cup	all-purpose flour	50 mL
1/2 tsp	cinnamon	2 mL
2 tbsp	butter	30 mL

➤ In mixing bowl, combine flour, baking powder, baking soda, salt and sugar; stir thoroughly to mix. Add butter, egg, buttermilk and vanilla. With electric mixer, beat at low speed until moistened, then at medium speed for 1 minute, scraping sides of bowl often (batter is thick). Spread batter evenly in greased and floured 9-inch (23 cm) square or round cake pan. Top evenly with fruit.

Streusel: In small bowl, mix together brown sugar, flour and cinnamon. Cut in butter until crumbly. Sprinkle over fruit. Bake in 350F (180C) oven for 35 to 40 minutes or until cake tester comes out clean. Let cool on rack until just warm.

Upside-Down Cake: Use same batter as for Streusel Coffeecake. In bottom of the pan, spread 1/4 cup (50 mL) melted butter and 3/4 cup (175 mL) brown sugar. Over this, arrange 1-1/2 cups (375 mL) sliced apples, plums, peaches, mangoes, papaya, or blueberries. Carefully spread cake batter over fruit. When baked, let cool for a few minutes, then loosen edges of cake with a knife and carefully invert pan onto serving plate.

All-Purpose White Cake: The batter for the Fruit Streusel Coffeecake can also be used to make a moist and buttery small white cake in just one bowl. Once you get used to measuring a few ingredients, the method is as easy as a mix. Bake in an 8-inch square pan. Use the cake as a dessert with fruit or fruit sauce, or top squares of it with whipped cream and sweetened sliced strawberries. For an easy frosting, Broiled Topping (page 204) tastes great on this cake. For a big, fast birthday cake, place two square cakes side by side on a tray to make a rectangular cake; frost and decorate as desired.

Carrot Cake

Every bit as good as the traditional versions, this recipe uses much less oil. For speedy grating of carrots, use the shredding disc on your food processor.

4	eggs	4
1 cup	each: granulated sugar, packed brown sugar	250 mL
1/2 cup	vegetable oil	125 mL
1/2 cup	carrot purée (see Sidebar)	125 mL
2 cups	all-purpose flour	500 mL
2 tsp	baking powder	10 mL
1 tsp	each: baking soda, salt	5 mL
1-1/2 tsp	cinnamon	7 mL
1/2 tsp	each: nutmeg, allspice	2 mL
3 cups	lightly packed grated raw carrots	750 mL
1/2 cup	each: raisins, finely chopped nuts (optional)	125 mL

→ Grease and flour baking pan. This recipe adapts to many pan sizes: Use one 10-inch (25 cm) tube or bundt pan OR 13- x 9-inch (33 x 23 cm) rectangular pan OR two 9-inch (23 cm) layer pans OR three 8-inch (20 cm) layer pans.

In large bowl, with electric mixer, beat eggs until frothy. Add granulated and brown sugars gradually, beating until light. Beat in oil and carrot purée. In separate bowl, mix together flour, baking powder, baking soda, salt, cinnamon, nutmeg and allspice; stir in. Stir in grated carrots and raisins and nuts (if using). Pour into prepared pan(s). Bake in 350F (180C) oven for 1 to 1-1/4 hours for tube or bundt pan, 40 to 50 minutes for rectangular pan, 35 to 40 minutes for layers or squares, or until tester comes out clean. Let cool for 5 to 10 minutes in pan before turning out onto rack. When cool, dust with icing sugar or frost with Cream Cheese Frosting (page 204).

Carrot Purée

In many updated recipes, fruit or vegetable purées are being used as fat replacements; in this cake, carrot purée also adds great colour and flavour. For the purée, a jar of baby-food strained carrots is perfect; or you can purée cooked carrots in a food processor. Applesauce or puréed squash could be used instead.

Chocolate Layer Cake

Many people who don't do much baking still like to make a home-baked birthday cake. Here's a dark, moist, very chocolaty cake that's fast and virtually foolproof. Microwave Lemon Curd (page 193) makes a great filling; for frosting, use Easy Glossy Chocolate Frosting or Chocolate Buttercream (page 204).

2 cups	sifted cake-and-pastry flour	500 mL
1-1/2 cups	granulated sugar	375 mL
3/4 cup	sifted cocoa	175 mL
1-1/2 tsp	baking powder	7 mL
1/2 tsp	each: baking soda, salt	2 mL
1/2 cup	very soft butter	125 mL
2	eggs	2
1-1/2 cups	buttermilk	375 mL
1 tsp	vanilla	5 mL
1/2 cup	hot water	125 mL

→ Lightly grease two 8-inch (20 cm) round layer cake pans; line bottoms with parchment or waxed paper. Into large mixing bowl, sift together flour, sugar, cocoa, baking powder, baking soda and salt. Add butter, eggs, buttermilk and vanilla. With electric mixer, beat at low speed for 1 minute, scraping bowl often. Then beat at medium speed for 2 minutes, scraping bowl occasionally. Add hot water and mix just until combined. Pour batter into prepared pans. Bake in 350F (180C) oven for 30 to 35 minutes or until tester comes out clean. Let cool in pans for 10 minutes. Turn out onto racks and let cool completely.

Pan Variations: Use 9-inch (23 cm) layer pans (cake will be shallower). Use rectangular cake pan (13- x 9-inch/33 x 23 cm); bake for 40 to 45 minutes.

Lemon-Poppyseed Pound Cake

Much easier than traditional pound cake (which has more eggs and no baking powder and requires a great deal of beating), this recipe produces a moist, fine-textured, easy-to-slice cake. The basic recipe make one loaf cake that adapts well to flavour variations. **For a bundt or tube pan, double the recipe and bake for 1 hour or until tester comes out clean.**

1/2 cup	butter, softened	125 mL
3/4 cup	granulated sugar	175 mL
2	eggs	2
1 tsp	vanilla	5 mL
1-1/2 cups	all-purpose flour	375 mL
1 tsp	baking powder	5 mL
1/4 tsp	salt	1 mL
1/2 cup	milk	125 mL
2 tbsp	each: grated lemon rind, poppyseeds	30 mL

➜ With electric mixer, cream together butter and sugar until light and fluffy. Add eggs one at a time, beating well after each addition; then beat for 1 more minute at high speed. Beat in vanilla. In small bowl, mix together flour, baking powder and salt; stir into creamed mixture alternately with milk. Stir in lemon rind and poppyseeds. Turn batter into greased and floured 8-1/2- x 4-1/2-inch (22 x 12 cm) loaf pan. Bake in 325F (160C) oven for 50 to 60 minutes or until tester comes out clean. Let cool for 10 minutes in pan, then turn out onto rack and let cool completely.

Fruited Pound Cake: Omit poppyseeds and lemon rind. Stir in 1 to 1-1/2 cups (250 to 375 mL) dried fruit (cranberries, cherries, raisins, currants or mixture) or chopped candied fruit (peel, pineapple, ginger, cherries or Christmas cake mixture).

Seed Cake: Stir in 1 tbsp (15 mL) caraway seeds.

Glazed Lemon Loaf: Make Lemon-Poppyseed Pound Cake, omitting the poppyseeds. Let baked cake cool for 10 minutes in pan. Meanwhile, in microwave or small saucepan, heat together 1/4 cup (50 mL) each lemon juice and granulated sugar until sugar is dissolved. Prick surface of cake all over with fork. Slowly pour warm glaze over warm cake, letting it soak in. Let cool completely in pan, then turn out.

Angel Food Cake ♥

Very popular once again because of its very low fat content, angel food cake is as easy to make from scratch as from a mix and much better tasting.

1 cup	sifted cake-and-pastry flour	250 mL
1/2 tsp	salt	2 mL
1-1/2 cups	granulated sugar	375 mL
1-1/2 cups	egg whites (12 to 14), at room temperature	375 mL
1 tsp	cream of tartar	5 mL
1 tsp	vanilla	5 mL
1/2 tsp	almond extract	2 mL

➜ Sift together flour, salt and 3/4 cup (175 mL) of the sugar; set aside. In large bowl, with electric mixer, beat egg whites with cream of tartar to soft peaks. Very gradually add remaining 3/4 cup (175 mL) sugar, beating constantly until mixture holds stiff, glossy peaks. Beat in vanilla and almond extract. Sift flour mixture, one-quarter at a time, over egg whites; fold in each addition gently but thoroughly. Turn batter into 10-inch (25 cm) tube pan (capacity 16 cups/4 L). Run knife through batter to eliminate any air pockets; gently smooth the surface. Bake in 350F (180C) oven for 40 to 45 minutes or until cake springs back when touched. Turn pan upside down (if it doesn't have feet, hang it over a bottle or inverted funnel); let cake cool completely. When cool, loosen cake by running knife around inside edges and tube; remove cake from pan (if using loose-bottomed pan, run knife between cake and base to remove).

Chocolate Angel Cake: Reduce flour to 3/4 cup (175 mL) and add 1/4 cup (50 mL) sifted cocoa; sift with other dry ingredients.

Hold the yolks: if you'd rather not have a dozen leftover egg yolks to use up, you can purchase small cartons of pasteurized refrigerated egg whites in most supermarkets; a 250 mL carton is equivalent to 8 egg whites.

Fast-and-Fancy Dessert Cakes

Why settle for a storebought cake of mediocre quality, or spend a small fortune on a fancy layered torte from a bakeshop? With one basic cake recipe (Basic Sponge Cake and variations, page 203), you can create good-looking, great-tasting dessert cakes in all kinds of flavours and shapes, dressed up with easy fillings, frostings and decorations for every occasion. All make about 8 servings each.

(Basic Sponge Cake and variations, page 203)

Jelly Roll or **Lemon Roll:** Bake Basic or Lemon Sponge Cake in jelly roll pan; roll up and let cool as directed. Unroll cake and spread with about 1-1/2 cups (375 mL) raspberry jam or jelly or Lemon Curd (page 193). Roll up again and dust with icing sugar. Cut into slices.

Chocolate Cream Roll: Bake Chocolate Sponge Cake in jelly roll pan; roll up and let cool as directed. Unroll cake and spread with Whipped Cream Filling (see Sidebar). Roll up again and dust with icing sugar. Cut into slices.

Yule Log: A holiday tradition, called Bûche de Noel in French Canada, yule logs are often intricately decorated, but here's a simplified version: Bake Basic, Chocolate or Hazelnut Sponge Cake in jelly roll pan; roll up and let cool as directed. Unroll cake and drizzle with rum or coffee liqueur; spread with Whipped Cream Filling (see Sidebar). Roll up and spread outside of log with Mocha Buttercream (page 204; double the recipe). Run a fork along length to simulate bark. Decorate with candied fruit and fresh holly.

Layered Chocolate Cream Cake: Bake Chocolate Sponge Cake in jelly roll pan; don't roll up. Cut cooled cake into 3 equal rectangles. Assemble into a rectangular 3-layer cake, filled and frosted with Whipped Cream Filling (see Sidebar). If desired, decorate with Glossy Chocolate Frosting (page 204) piped through a decorating tube. Chill cake thoroughly before serving; cut into slices.

Chocolate Mousse Cake: Bake Chocolate Sponge Cake in springform pan. With long serrated knife, split cooled cake into 3 horizontal layers. Fill and frost with Chocolate Mousse (page 184; chill mousse to spreading consistency); or fill with Chocolate Mousse and frost with whipped cream or Chocolate Whipped Cream (see Sidebar). Decorate with grated chocolate, chocolate curls, Chocolate Drizzle (page 204) or Glossy Chocolate Frosting (page 204) piped through a decorating tube.

Hazelnut Torte: Bake Hazelnut Sponge Cake in springform pan. With long serrated knife, split springform cake into 3 horizontal layers. Assemble into layered torte, filling between layers with Whipped Cream Filling (see Sidebar) or Buttercream Frosting (page 204; use desired flavour). Frost outside of torte with whipped cream. Decorate top with whole hazelnuts and dust with cocoa through a small sieve. OR Gently press chopped hazelnuts into cream on sides of torte and decorate top with whipped cream piped through a decorating tube.

Fresh Fruit Cream Torte: Bake Basic or Lemon Sponge Cake in springform pan. With long serrated knife, split cake into 3 horizontal layers. Assemble into layered torte, filling between layers with Whipped Cream Filling (see Sidebar) and a scattering of fresh fruit (raspberries, blueberries, blackberries, sliced strawberries, peaches, mango, etc). Spread top of cake with whipped cream and garnish with more fruit.

Whipped Cream Filling or Frosting: Whip 1 cup (250 mL) whipping cream to soft peaks; gradually add 1/4 cup (50 mL) icing sugar and beat just until thick enough to spread (be careful not to over-beat). For flavouring, add a few drops of vanilla, or about 2 tbsp (30 mL) liqueur (such as hazelnut or amaretto). Makes enough to fill rolled cake, or to fill or frost a layered torte; double the recipe if you want both filling and frosting.

Chocolate Whipped Cream: increase icing sugar to 1/2 cup (125 mL) and mix it with 2 tbsp (30 mL) cocoa.

Mocha Whipped Cream: dissolve 1 tbsp (15 mL) instant coffee in 2 tsp (10 mL) hot water; let cool and add to Chocolate Whipped Cream along with cocoa mixture. Refrigerate cakes after filling or frosting with whipped cream.

Basic Sponge Cake

This versatile recipe produces a good basic sponge cake (vanilla, lemon, chocolate or hazelnut) that can be used for all the Fast-and-Fancy Dessert Cakes on page 202. Bake it in a springform pan for layered round tortes, or in a sheet pan for rolled cakes or rectangular layers. You can also use the basic cake for Trifle (page 185) or to serve like strawberry shortcake (topped with whipped cream and strawberries or mixed fresh fruit).

The recipe includes a tiny bit of baking powder to make it more foolproof than traditional sponge cakes; it's also much simpler than classic genoise cakes that require careful folding in of dry ingredients and melted butter.

1 cup	sifted cake-and-pastry flour	250 mL
1/4 tsp	each: baking powder, salt	1 mL
4	eggs, at room temperature	4
3/4 cup	granulated sugar	175 mL
1/4 tsp	cream of tartar	1 mL
2 tbsp	water	30 mL
1 tsp	vanilla	5 mL

➜ Preheat oven to 325F (160C). Prepare baking pan: Use a 15- x 10-inch (30 x 20 cm) jelly roll pan (line with parchment or greased waxed paper) OR a 9- to 10-inch (23 to 25 cm) springform pan (line the bottom with a circle of paper).

In small bowl, sift together flour, baking powder and salt; set aside. Place egg whites in large bowl and yolks in medium bowl (use fairly deep bowls for efficient beating of eggs). With electric mixer at high speed, beat egg whites with cream of tartar until they hold soft peaks; gradually beat in 1/4 cup (50 mL) of the sugar, beating until whites hold stiff peaks; set aside. Using same beaters (don't bother washing them), immediately beat egg yolks with 1/2 cup (125 mL) sugar until thick and pale in colour, about 2 minutes at high speed. Beat in water and vanilla. Add flour mixture and stir in, with mixer at very low speed, just until combined. Stir about one-quarter of beaten whites to yolk mixture to lighten it, then add yolk mixture to whites and fold together gently but thoroughly. Pour batter into prepared pan and spread evenly.

Springform pan: Bake for 45 minutes or until cake springs back when touched lightly. Invert cake onto wire rack and let cool completely in pan. To remove, run knife around edge of cake to loosen it, then remove sides of pan.

Jelly roll pan: Bake for 20 minutes or until cake springs back when touched lightly. Invert cake onto a tea towel sprinkled with icing sugar. Remove pan; peel paper off cake. If using for a rolled cake, gently roll the warm cake up in the towel. Place on wire rack and let cool completely. If using cake for rectangular layers, don't roll up in towel; just let stand until cool.

Lemon Sponge Cake: Use lemon juice instead of water, and 1 tbsp (15 mL) grated lemon rind instead of vanilla.

Chocolate Sponge Cake: Instead of 1 cup (250 mL) flour, use 1/2 cup (125 mL) each flour and sifted cocoa.

Hazelnut Sponge Cake: Instead of 1 cup (250 mL) flour, use 1/2 cup (125 mL) each flour and finely ground hazelnuts (available at bulk food stores).

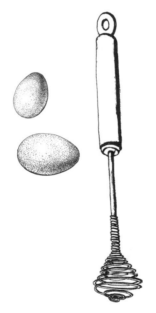

Frostings

Vanilla Buttercream Frosting: This traditional simple icing makes a satisfying finish for any cake and lends itself to many flavour variations. The recipe makes enough for the top of a small square or round cake; to frost top and sides, double the recipe. For a large rectangular cake, triple it; for a layer cake, quadruple it.

In bowl, combine 2 tbsp (30 mL) softened butter, 1 cup (250 mL) icing sugar, 1 tbsp (15 mL) cream or milk and 1/2 tsp (2 mL) vanilla. Beat until smooth, preferably with electric mixer. If too thin, add a little more icing sugar; if too thick, add a little more cream or milk.

Chocolate Buttercream: Add 1 oz (30 g) melted unsweetened chocolate.

Coffee Buttercream: Instead of cream, use cold espresso or strong coffee.

Mocha Buttercream: Make Chocolate Buttercream, using cold strong coffee instead of cream.

Orange or Lemon Buttercream: Add 1 tbsp (15 mL) grated orange or lemon rind.

Almond or Hazelnut Buttercream: Use almond or hazelnut extract instead of vanilla.

Easy Glossy Chocolate Frosting: This is soft, shiny, not too sweet and extra-easy to make. In small bowl in microwave or small heavy saucepan over low heat, melt 1 cup (250 mL) chocolate chips or 3 oz (90 g) semisweet chocolate. Add 1/2 cup (125 mL) sour cream; stir until smooth. Add 1 cup (250 mL) icing sugar; beat until smooth. If necessary, chill for a few minutes. Makes enough for top and sides of small square or round cake; for top only, halve recipe; for rectangular cake, double recipe; for layer cake, triple recipe.

Broiled Topping: Let cake cool in pan for about 5 minutes after baking. Meanwhile, in small heavy saucepan, combine 1/4 cup (50 mL) butter, 1/2 cup (125 mL) brown sugar, 2 tbsp (30 mL) milk and 3/4 cup (175 mL) flaked or shredded (preferably unsweetened) coconut. Bring to boil, stirring; boil gently for 1 minute. Spread over warm cake. Place under broiler until bubbly and golden brown (this takes only a couple of minutes; watch closely). Makes enough for 8- to 9-inch (20 to 23 cm) square or round cake.

Fast Fluffy Frosting: A streamlined version of old-fashioned "seafoam" or boiled icing, this snowy-white frosting is fat-free, foolproof and not too sweet. In microwave or small saucepan, bring 1 cup (250 mL) corn syrup to a full boil. Meanwhile, with electric mixer, beat 2 egg whites (at room temperature) with 1/4 tsp (1 mL) cream of tartar until mixture holds soft peaks. Beating constantly at high speed on mixer, gradually add hot syrup in a thin stream; continue beating until frosting holds stiff, shiny peaks. Beat in 1 tsp (5 mL) vanilla or 1/2 tsp (2 mL) almond extract. Makes enough to generously frost large layer cake or angel food cake. (Recipe may be halved for smaller cake.) For a special-occasion cake, swirl the frosting into peaks and sprinkle lightly with chopped nuts, grated chocolate, candied flowers or a few fresh edible petals, or drizzle with melted chocolate. This frosting doesn't keep well; use cake same day it's frosted.

Cream Cheese Frosting: The classic topping for carrot cake (page 200). With electric mixer, cream together 8 oz (250 g) softened cream cheese, 1/4 cup (50 mL) softened butter and 2 tsp (10 mL) vanilla. Gradually beat in enough icing sugar (about 3 cups/750 mL) to give smooth, spreadable consistency. Makes enough to frost rectangular, tube or layer cake. For small cakes (such as 8-inch/20 cm square), halve the recipe.

Chocolate Drizzle: (for drizzling over white icing on cakes or for decorating cookies or squares) Melt 1 oz (30 g) semisweet chocolate with 1/4 tsp (1 mL) vegetable oil. Drizzle from tip of small spoon (or from small, heavy plastic bag with a tiny corner snipped off). Makes enough for decorative drizzle on one cake, small pan of squares or about a dozen biscotti; double as necessary.

Chocolate Glaze (Ganache): This gives a smooth, shiny finish. In saucepan, heat 1 cup (250 mL) whipping cream until hot but not boiling. Remove from heat and add 8 oz (250 g) chopped semisweet chocolate; stir until melted and smooth. Let cool to lukewarm. Pour over top of cake, letting it run down sides; spread sides with knife or metal spatula if necessary. Makes enough for one 8-inch (20 cm) cake.

Hurray for Hermits! Bravo, Biscotti!

Cookies, Bars & Squares

A treasure trove of favourites for every occasion

Just starting to explore the pleasures of baking? Or want a fast update on ingredients, methods and equipment? See Baking Tips, page 240.

Oatmeal Raisin Cookies

Crisp, chewy oatmeal cookies—great for dessert, snacks and brownbag lunches.

3/4 cup	butter or shortening, softened	175 mL
1 cup	packed brown sugar	250 mL
1	egg	1
1 tsp	vanilla	5 mL
1 cup	all-purpose flour	250 mL
1/2 tsp	each: baking soda, salt	2 mL
1-1/2 cups	quick-cooking oats (not instant)	375 mL
3/4 cup	raisins	175 mL

➜ In large bowl, cream together butter and sugar. Beat in egg and vanilla. In separate bowl, mix together flour, baking soda, salt and oats; stir into creamed mixture. Stir in raisins. Drop by spoonfuls 2 inches (5 cm) apart on greased baking sheets. Flatten to 1/2 inch (1 cm) with fork. Bake in 375F (190C) oven for 10 to 12 minutes or until golden brown (don't over-bake). Let cool on sheets for 5 minutes, then remove to racks to cool. **Makes about 24.**

Chocolate Chip Oatmeal Cookies: Omit raisins if desired. Add 1 cup (250 mL) chocolate chips or chopped semisweet chocolate.

Double Ginger Crackle Cookies ✤

A favourite coast-to-coast in Canada, this time-tested recipe needed no updating except for an extra hit of chopped ginger (leave it out if you want the traditional version). The cookies flatten slightly as they bake, ending up crackled on top, crisp on the outside and slightly soft in the centre.

3/4 cup	shortening, softened	175 mL
1 cup	granulated sugar	250 mL
1	egg	1
1/4 cup	molasses	50 mL
2 cups	all-purpose flour	500 mL
2 tsp	baking soda	10 mL
1/4 tsp	salt	1 mL
1 tbsp	ground ginger	15 mL
1 tsp	each: cinnamon, ground cloves	5 mL
1/2 cup	finely chopped candied ginger	125 mL
	Granulated sugar for coating	

➜ In large bowl, cream together shortening and sugar. Beat in egg and molasses. In separate bowl, mix together flour, baking soda, salt and ground spices; blend into creamed mixture. Stir in candied ginger. Shape into balls 1 inch (2.5 cm) in diameter. Roll in sugar. Place 2 inches (5 cm) apart on greased baking sheets. Bake in 350F (180C) oven for 8 to 10 minutes or until golden brown. Don't overbake; cookies should be slightly soft when removed from oven. Let cool on baking sheets for a few minutes, then remove to racks to cool completely. **Makes about 40.**

Chocolate Chip Cookies

Rich in taste and texture, crispy at the edges, soft and chewy in the middle—for most chocolate chip cookie lovers, this is perfection. (If you prefer a slightly firmer cookie, increase flour to 2-1/4 cups/550 mL and do not chill dough.)

1/2 cup	each: butter and shortening, softened	125 mL
3/4 cup	packed brown sugar	175 mL
1/2 cup	granulated sugar	125 mL
2	eggs	2
2 tsp	vanilla	10 mL
2 cups	all-purpose flour	500 mL
1 tsp	baking soda	5 mL
1/2 tsp	salt	2 mL
1-1/2 cups	chocolate chips	375 mL
1 cup	chopped walnuts or pecans	250 mL

➜ In large bowl, cream together butter, shortening, brown sugar and granulated sugar until well blended. Beat in eggs and vanilla. In small bowl, mix together flour, baking soda and salt; stir into creamed mixture. Stir in chocolate chips and nuts. Chill dough for 20 minutes or until firm (this prevents cookies from spreading too much during baking). Drop by heaping spoonfuls (about 1-1/2 tbsp/20 mL dough for each cookie) onto lightly greased baking sheets, spacing cookies 2 inches (5 cm) apart. Slightly flatten each cookie to an even thickness of about 1/2 inch (1 cm). Place oven rack slightly above centre of oven. Bake one sheet of cookies at a time in 350F (180C) oven for 9 to 11 minutes or until cookies are golden brown but still slightly soft in centre. Don't overbake. Let cool on baking sheet for 5 minutes, then remove to rack to cool completely. **Makes about 4 dozen.**

Chocolate Chunk Cookies: Use chopped semisweet or bittersweet chocolate instead of chips. For easy chopping, chocolate should be at warm room temperature; with sharp knife, cut into 1/2-inch (1 cm) chunks.

Reverse Chocolate Chip Cookies: (dark chocolate cookies dotted with white chocolate): Add 1/2 cup (125 mL) cocoa along with the flour. Use white chocolate chips or chunks instead of dark chocolate.

Hermits

Soft, spicy cookies chock-full of fruit and nuts, hermits are perennial best-sellers at bakeshops— but even better homemade.

1/2 cup	each: butter and shortening, softened	125 mL
1 cup	packed brown sugar	250 mL
1/2 cup	granulated sugar	125 mL
2	eggs	2
1 tsp	vanilla	5 mL
2-1/2 cups	all-purpose flour	625 mL
1 tsp	baking powder	5 mL
1/2 tsp	baking soda	2 mL
1 tsp	cinnamon	5 mL
1/2 tsp	each: nutmeg, allspice, ground cloves, salt	2 mL
1-1/2 cups	raisins	375 mL
1/2 cup	each: chopped dates and nuts	125 mL

➜ In large bowl, cream together butter and shortening; gradually add sugars, creaming until light. Beat in eggs and vanilla. In separate bowl, mix together flour, baking powder, baking soda, spices and salt; stir into creamed mixture. Stir in raisins, dates and nuts. Drop by spoonfuls onto greased baking sheets. Bake in 350F (180C) oven for 8 to 10 minutes or until lightly browned. Let cool on baking sheets for a few minutes, then remove to racks to cool completely. **Makes about 4 dozen.**

Peanut Butter Cookies

Hide the cookie jar if you don't want these to disappear immediately. They are everything peanut butter cookies should be: pleasantly crunchy, peanutty-flavoured, and crisscrossed with fork marks for the traditional look.

1/2 cup	butter, softened	125 mL
1 cup	packed brown sugar	250 mL
3/4 cup	smooth peanut butter	175 mL
1	egg	1
1 tsp	vanilla	5 mL
1-1/2 cups	all-purpose flour	375 mL
1-1/2 tsp	baking powder	7 mL
1/4 tsp	baking soda	1 mL
Pinch	salt	Pinch
	Halved peanuts (optional)	

➜ In large bowl, cream together butter and sugar. Add peanut butter, creaming thoroughly. Beat in egg and vanilla. In separate bowl, mix together flour, baking powder, baking soda and salt. Blend into creamed mixture. Shape into balls 1-1/4 inches (3 cm) in diameter; place on lightly greased baking sheets. Flatten slightly with floured fork (in one direction or crisscross). If desired, top each cookie with a peanut half. Bake in 350F (180C) oven for 10 to 12 minutes or until lightly browned. Let cool on baking sheets for a few minutes, then remove to racks to cool completely. **Makes about 40.**

Almond Crescents ✿

Almost everyone with a Canadian Christmas recipe collection has a recipe for cookies like these. They might be called Vanillekipferl, Mexican Wedding Cakes, Russian Tea Cakes or Melting Moments, depending on whose grandma or which 1950s cookbook the recipe came from. Here's our family's favourite version. You can use store-bought ground almonds, but for ultimate taste and texture, grind whole almonds in a food processor. Hazelnuts may be substituted for almonds. The cookies can be formed into small balls instead of crescents.

1 cup	butter, softened	250 mL
1/2 cup	icing sugar	125 mL
2 tsp	vanilla	10 mL
1-3/4 cups	all-purpose flour	425 mL
1 cup	coarsely ground or very finely chopped blanched almonds	250 mL
	Icing sugar for dusting	

➜ Cream butter; gradually add icing sugar, creaming until light. Beat in vanilla. Gradually stir in flour and almonds, mixing only until blended. Shape into small crescents, using about 1 tbsp (15 mL) dough per crescent. Place on ungreased baking sheets. Bake in 350F (180C) oven for 25 to 30 minutes or until very lightly browned. Remove to racks to cool. When cool, roll in icing sugar to coat lightly. **Makes about 60.**

Classic Shortbread ✦

This is the basic, old-fashioned Scottish-style shortbread. It's quick and easy to make and keeps well in tightly covered tins. The dough may be rolled out and cut into small rounds or bars, or pressed into wooden shortbread moulds. Extra-fine sugar is labelled superfine, fruit or berry sugar; you can make your own by processing regular granulated sugar in a food processor for a few seconds. Rice flour gives traditional texture but can be replaced with all-purpose flour. Icing sugar or brown sugar may be substituted for granulated sugar.

1 cup	butter, at cool room temperature	250 mL
1/2 cup	extra-fine granulated sugar	125 mL
1-3/4 cups	all-purpose flour	425 mL
1/4 cup	rice flour	50 mL

→ Cream butter well. Blend in sugar, creaming thoroughly. In separate bowl, combine flours; using wooden spoon, gradually blend into creamed mixture. Press into ball and knead lightly on floured board until smooth. Pat dough into ungreased 9-inch (23 cm) square metal cake pan, or into a large round, about 1/2 inch (1 cm) thick, on baking sheet, or into metal pie plate. Prick all over with fork. Bake in 275F (140C) oven for 45 minutes or until set and faintly browned. When almost cool, cut into pieces and remove from pan; let cool thoroughly on rack. **Makes about 30 pieces.**

Food Processor Shortbread: Omit rice flour and increase all-purpose flour to 2 cups (500 mL). In food processor, combine flour and sugar; process for a few seconds to mix. Cut very cold butter into 8 cubes; add to flour mixture. Pulse on and off for about 30 seconds or until mixture forms fine crumbs; stir through crumbs with fork to make sure no large lumps of butter remain. Process for a few seconds longer just until mixture starts to clump together to form a ball; don't over-process. Turn mixture into ungreased 9-inch (23 cm) square metal cake pan. Press out evenly. Prick with fork and bake as for Classic Shortbread.

Whipped Shortbread: With electric mixer, beat 1 cup (250 mL) softened butter with 1/2 cup (125 mL) icing sugar. Sift together 1-1/2 cups (375 mL) all-purpose flour and 1/2 cup (125 mL) cornstarch; stir gradually into butter mixture. Shape into balls about 1-1/4 inches (3 cm) in diameter. Place on ungreased baking sheet. Bake in 300F (150C) oven for 20 to 25 minutes or until firm to touch and faintly browned at edges. **Makes about 32.**

Chocolate Chunk Shortbread Cookies: Prepare Whipped Shortbread (above). Before shaping into balls, stir in 4 oz (125 g) semi-sweet chocolate chopped in small chunks (or 1 cup/250 mL chocolate chips). **Makes about 40.**

Variations: Instead of chocolate, add chopped candied ginger or cherries, dried cranberries or cherries, or pecan pieces.

Oats and Nuts Shortbread: Cream 1 cup (250 mL) softened butter with 1/2 cup (125 mL) brown sugar and 1/4 cup (50 mL) granulated sugar. Gradually stir in 1-1/2 cups (375 mL) all-purpose flour, 3/4 cup (175 mL) quick-cooking oats (not instant) and 1/4 cup (50 mL) finely chopped pecans or walnuts. On lightly floured surface, roll out to 1/4-inch (5 mm) thickness. Cut into 2-inch (5 cm) rounds, diamonds, triangles or fingers. Place on lightly greased baking sheets. Prick each cookie several times with fork. Bake in 325F (160C) oven for 16 to 18 minutes or until lightly browned. **Makes about 4 dozen.**

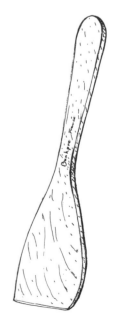

Take-Your-Pick Cookies

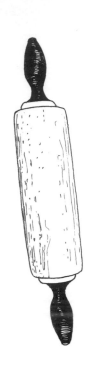

A life-saver at Christmas or any time of year when you want one kind or a whole variety of cookies in short order. This basic dough adapts to all kinds of shaping and flavouring variations; it's fast to mix, easy to handle, and you don't even have to grease the pans. The dough can be wrapped and refrigerated for a few days, or frozen before or after shaping. The baked cookies all freeze well, too.

This makes enough for about 4 dozen small cookies. Each variation uses one-half of the dough and makes about 2 dozen. (Basic Dough recipe can be doubled if desired.)

Basic Dough

1 cup	butter, soffened	250 mL
1-1/2 cups	sifted icing sugar	375 mL
1	egg	1
2 tsp	vanilla	10 mL
3 cups	all-purpose flour	750 mL
1/2 tsp	baking soda	2 mL
1/2 tsp	salt	2 mL

➡ In large bowl, cream together butter and icing sugar. Beat in egg and vanilla. In separate bowl, mix together flour, baking soda and salt. Stir gradually into creamed mixture. Divide dough in half. Shape cookies as desired (see variations, below).

To Bake: Place cookies on ungreased baking sheets. Bake in 350F (180C) oven for 8 to 12 minutes (depending on thickness of cookies) until firm to touch and very lightly browned. Let cool slightly on baking sheets, then remove to wire racks to cool completely.

Slice-and-Bake Cookies: Keep a few rolls of these in the freezer and be ready for last-minute bake sales, kids' parties or empty cookie jars. For each roll, use one-half of the prepared basic dough and blend in your choice of flavour additions: For **Cranberry-Orange,** add 1/4 cup (50 mL) finely chopped dried cranberries and 2 tsp (10 mL) grated orange rind. For **Fruit-and-Nut,** add 1/4 cup (50 mL) each finely chopped nuts and chopped raisins or mixed candied fruit. For **Lemon Poppyseed,** add 2 tsp (10 mL) each poppyseeds and grated lemon rind.

To shape dough, form it into a log about 2 inches (5 cm) in diameter; wrap tightly with plastic wrap and chill in refrigerator or freezer until firm. When ready to bake, cut into 1/4-inch (5 mm) slices. See To Bake, left.

Cut-Out Cookies: Roll dough to a little less than 1/4-inch (5 mm) thickness; cut out with cookie cutters in shapes to suit the occasion. Decorate after baking: Pipe or spread cookies with decorator icing (can be purchased in small tubes from cake-decorating shops and most supermarkets). Before icing hardens, decorate with chocolate sprinkles, tiny candies, raisins or candied fruit. OR spread or drizzle cookies with chocolate icing (melted chocolate chips are easiest) and sprinkle with chopped nuts.

Shaped Cookies: For **Crescents or Snowballs,** shape small pieces of dough into crescents or 1-inch (2.5 cm) balls; after baking, roll in icing sugar. For **Hazelnut or Cherry Centres,** wrap small pieces of dough around hazelnuts or candied cherries to form smooth balls; after baking, roll in icing sugar. For **Nutty Chocolate Logs,** shape dough into small logs about 2 inches (5 cm) long and 1/2 inch (1 cm) in diameter; after baking and cooling, dip ends of logs into melted chocolate, then into finely chopped nuts. For **Ginger Sparkles,** blend 1/3 cup (75 mL) finely chopped candied ginger into one half of prepared basic dough; shape into 1-1/4-inch (3 cm) balls and roll in granulated sugar before baking.

Nutty Biscotti

Recipes for biscotti abound, some producing crisp, crunchy cookies, others extra-firm for dunking in cappuccino; some are tiny, some giant. This recipe is a happy medium, firm enough for coffee-dunking but not tooth-breaking. Using melted butter makes the cookies close-textured and easier to slice; you can also use half butter and half vegetable oil, or even olive oil when the flavour is desirable, such as in the lemon-almond variation.

2	eggs	2
2/3 cup	granulated sugar	150 mL
1/3 cup	butter, melted and cooled	75 mL
1-1/2 tsp	vanilla	7 mL
1/2 tsp	almond extract	2 mL
2 cups	all-purpose flour	500 mL
2 tsp	baking powder	10 mL
1/2 tsp	salt	2 mL
1/2 cup	coarsely chopped hazelnuts or almonds	125 mL

➡ In large bowl, beat eggs; gradually beat in sugar, butter, vanilla and almond extract. In small bowl, mix together flour, baking powder and salt; stir in to make soft, sticky dough. Stir in nuts. Turn dough out onto lightly floured surface and knead into smooth ball. Divide in half; shape each piece into log 6 inches (15 cm) long. Place logs 4 inches (10 cm) apart on lightly greased baking sheet. Flatten each log to 4 inches (10 cm) wide with slightly rounded edges. Bake in 325F (160C) oven for 30 minutes or until pale golden and not quite firm to the touch. Let cool on baking sheets for 3 minutes. Transfer logs to cutting board; with sharp knife, cut on slight diagonal into 1/2-inch (1 cm) thick slices. Arrange slices upright (with both cut sides exposed) about 1 inch (2.5 cm) apart on baking sheet. Reduce oven temperature to 300F (150C). Bake slices for 25 minutes or until firm and dry. Let cool. Store in airtight container. **Makes about 20**.

Biscotti Variations

Orange or Ginger-Nut: Stir in 1/4 cup (50 mL) chopped candied orange peel or candied ginger and 1 tbsp (15 mL) grated orange rind along with nuts.

Chocolate-Nut: Replace 1/2 cup (125 mL) of the flour with sifted cocoa.

Lemon-Almond: Add 1 tbsp (15 mL) grated lemon rind; use unblanched almonds.

Cranberry-Pistachio: Omit hazelnuts or almonds. Add 1/4 cup (50 mL) each chopped dried cranberries and shelled pistachios.

Anise: Add 1 tbsp (15 mL) anise seed along with nuts. Substitute anise extract for almond.

Crisp Lemon Wafers

Crisp, light and lemony, these are pleasantly summery cookies to enjoy with iced tea. For a variation, substitute lime for lemon.

1/2 cup	butter, softened	125 mL
1 cup	granulated sugar	250 mL
1	egg	1
1 tbsp	grated lemon rind	15 mL
2 tbsp	lemon juice	30 mL
1-3/4 cups	all-purpose flour	425 mL
1/2 tsp	each: salt, baking soda, ground ginger	2 mL
Topping:		
	granulated sugar, grated lemon rind	

➡ Cream together butter and sugar; beat in egg, lemon rind and lemon juice. In separate bowl, combine flour, salt, baking soda and ginger; gradually blend into creamed mixture. Cover and refrigerate until firm. Shape dough into cylinder 1-3/4 inches (4 cm) in diameter. Wrap in plastic and chill until very firm (or freeze). With sharp knife, cut dough into very thin slices (1/8 inch/3 mm or less); place on greased baking sheets 2 inches (5 cm) apart.

Topping: Sprinkle cookies lightly with sugar and grated rind. Bake in 375F (190C) oven for 6 to 8 minutes. Let cool for 2 minutes on baking sheets; remove to wire racks to cool completely. **Makes about 5 dozen**.

Fudgy Brownies

Rich, moist and chewy—just what brownie-lovers love best.

2 oz	unsweetened chocolate, melted	60 g
1/2 cup	butter, melted	125 mL
1 cup	granulated sugar	250 mL
2	eggs	2
1 tsp	vanilla	5 mL
1/2 cup	all-purpose flour	125 mL
1/2 cup	chopped walnuts	125 mL

➡ In bowl, combine chocolate, butter, sugar, eggs and vanilla; beat well. Gently stir in flour only until no streaks remain. Stir in nuts. Spread in greased 8-inch (20 cm) square cake pan. Bake in 350F (180C) oven for 20 to 25 minutes until barely firm to the touch; don't overbake. Let cool; cut in squares. Frost if desired.

Date Squares ♣

Called Matrimonial Cake in some parts of Canada, date-filled oatmeal squares have been around forever but remain popular all across the country. Today's fillings are not as sweet (this one adds tangy orange marmalade to the dates and omits the usual sugar entirely), but otherwise these squares are right out of grandma's cookbook. Mincemeat can replace the date filling.

Filling:

3 cups	chopped dates	750 mL
1 cup	orange juice	250 mL
1/4 cup	orange marmalade	50 mL
1 tbsp	lemon juice	15 mL

Base and Topping:

1-1/2 cups	quick-cooking oats (not instant)	375 mL
1-1/2 cups	all-purpose flour	375 mL
1 cup	packed brown sugar	250 mL
1 tsp	baking soda	5 mL
1/4 tsp	salt	1 mL
3/4 cup	butter, melted	175 mL

➡ *Filling:* In heavy saucepan, combine all ingredients. Cook, stirring, over medium heat until thickened and fairly smooth, about 10 minutes. Let cool.

Base and Topping: In bowl, mix together dry ingredients. Add butter, mixing thoroughly to make crumbly mixture. Press half of mixture into 9-inch (23 cm) square OR 11- x 7-inch (28 x 18 cm) cake pan. Spread filling evenly over base. Sprinkle with remaining crumb mixture; press down lightly. Bake in 350F (180C) oven for 30 to 35 minutes or until lightly browned. Let cool. Cut into squares.

Raisin Squares: Replace date filling with raisin filling.

Raisin Filling:

2 cups	raisins	500 mL
1 cup	brown sugar	250 mL
1/4 cup	cornstarch	50 mL
1-1/2 cups	water	375 mL
2 tbsp	lemon juice	30 mL
2 tsp	grated lemon rind	10 mL

➡ In heavy saucepan, mix together raisins, sugar and cornstarch. Stir in water, lemon juice and rind. Cook, stirring, until mixture comes to boil and thickens. Let cool.

Lemon Squares   ❧

Of the hundreds of recipes for traditional squares, this tangy, not-too-sweet kind remains a top favourite.

Base:

1/2 cup	butter, softened	125 mL
1/4 cup	granulated sugar	50 mL
1 cup	all-purpose flour	250 mL

Topping:

2	eggs	2
1 cup	granulated sugar	250 mL
2 tbsp	all-purpose flour	30 mL
1/2 tsp	baking powder	2 mL
1/4 tsp	salt	1 mL
	Grated rind of 1 lemon	
3 tbsp	lemon juice	45 mL
	Icing sugar for dusting	

➜ *Base:* Cream butter with sugar; blend in flour until crumbly. Press into bottom of 8-inch (20 cm) square cake pan. Bake in 350F (180C) oven for 15 minutes or until very lightly browned.

Topping: In bowl, beat eggs. Beat in sugar. Stir in flour, baking powder, salt, lemon rind and juice. Pour over base. Bake in 350F (180C) oven for 25 minutes or until just set. Let cool. Dust with icing sugar. Cut into small squares.

Energy Bars

Easy, chewy, tasty and good for you! Keep these handy when you need a little boost.

1-1/2 cups	quick-cooking oats (not instant)	375 mL
1/2 cup	each: all-purpose flour, brown sugar	125 mL
1/2 cup	each: chopped dried apples and dried cranberries or raisins	125 mL
1/4 cup	slivered almonds	50 mL
2 tbsp	each: toasted wheat germ, sesame seeds	30 mL
1 tsp	cinnamon	5 mL
1	egg	1
1/4 cup	each: vegetable oil, corn syrup	50 mL

➜ In large bowl, combine oats, flour, sugar, dried apples and cranberries, almonds, wheat germ, sesame seeds and cinnamon. In small bowl, beat egg with oil and corn syrup. Add to oats mixture and mix until well combined. Press firmly into 9-inch (23 cm) square baking pan. Bake in 350F (180C) oven for 20 minutes or until lightly browned. Let cool on rack. Cut into 1- x 3-inch (2.5 x 8 cm) bars. Store in tightly covered container. **Makes 27 bars**.

❧ **Butter Tart Squares:** (for the taste of butter tarts without the trouble of making them). *Base:* Same as Lemon Squares. *Topping:* In bowl, beat 2 eggs. Beat in 1 cup (250 mL) brown sugar. Stir in 2 tbsp (30 mL) melted butter, 2 tbsp (30 mL) all-purpose flour, 1/2 tsp (2 mL) baking powder, 1 tsp (5 mL) vanilla and 1 cup (250 mL) raisins. Pour over base. Bake in 350F (180C) oven for 30 minutes or until set. Let cool and cut into small squares.

Nanaimo Bars ✤

Nanaimo Bars have been made in Canadian homes for decades and their great appeal has inspired scads of variations. You'll see them in coffee houses and bakeshops, flavoured with mint, espresso or orange, and layers maybe in reverse colours. Here's the classic, irresistible as ever.

Bottom Layer:

1/2 cup	butter	125 mL
1/3 cup	cocoa	75 mL
1/4 cup	granulated sugar	50 mL
1	egg, beaten	1
1-1/2 cups	graham wafer crumbs	375 mL
1 cup	flaked coconut (preferably unsweetened)	250 mL
1/2 cup	finely chopped walnuts	125 mL

Middle Layer:

1/4 cup	butter	50 mL
3 tbsp	milk	45 mL
2 tbsp	custard powder	30 mL
2 cups	sifted icing sugar	500 mL

Top Layer:

4 oz	semisweet chocolate	125 g
2 tbsp	butter	30 mL

➤ *Bottom Layer:* In small heavy saucepan over low heat, melt butter with cocoa and sugar. Add egg and cook, stirring, until slightly thickened, about 2 minutes. Stir in crumbs, coconut and nuts. Press into 9-inch (23 cm) square cake pan. Chill for about 5 minutes.

Middle Layer: Beat together butter, milk, custard powder and icing sugar until very smooth. Spread over bottom layer. Chill until firm.

Top Layer: In small heavy saucepan over low heat, melt chocolate with butter, stirring until smooth. Cool slightly and pour over middle layer; jiggle pan to smooth out the chocolate evenly. Chill until chocolate is set but not quite firm. Mark into bars or squares with knife (this prevents cracking of chocolate if cut when cold). Chill until firm. Cut into bars or squares.

Peanut Butter Cereal Squares 😀

Make these crunchy unbaked squares in just a few minutes. They're almost like candy but do have the redeeming qualities of such wholesome ingredients as cereal, peanut butter and nuts. As a variation, shape the mixture into small balls and roll in sesame seeds or coconut.

1-1/2 cups	each: cornflakes, crisp rice cereal	375 mL
1/2 cup	chopped peanuts	125 mL
3/4 cup	corn syrup	175 mL
1/4 cup	packed brown sugar	50 mL
1/2 cup	peanut butter	125 mL

Topping:

1 cup	chocolate chips	250 mL
1/2 cup	peanut butter	125 mL

➤ In large bowl, combine cereals and peanuts. In small saucepan, heat corn syrup with sugar just until bubbling, stirring to dissolve sugar. Remove from heat and add peanut butter; stir until smooth. Pour over cereal and mix well. With greased hands, press firmly into buttered 8-inch (20 cm) square pan.

Topping: In small saucepan over low heat, melt chocolate chips with peanut butter, stirring until smooth. Spread over mixture in pan. Chill until firm. Cut into small squares.

Pies & Pastries

Dazzle 'em with deep-dish peach pie,
a free-form galette or the ultimate butter tart

Basic Pastry

There's no great mystique to making pastry. You don't have to settle for a store-bought frozen pie crust or, at the other extreme, fuss with a classic pâte brisée. You also don't need a lot of fancy equipment, although a few simple tools do make pastry-making a breeze, even for novice cooks: a pastry blender for cutting in the fat, a good rolling pin, and a pastry cloth and rolling pin cover to eliminate sticking. Glass pie plates brown the crust evenly and allow you to see when the underside is done. Measuring accurately saves time and guesswork. Cake-and-pastry flour is easiest to work with; if using all-purpose flour, be sure not to overhandle the pastry. This recipe uses a combination of shortening and butter; shortening makes tender, flaky pastry that's easy to handle, and butter adds flavour and colour. The shortening can be at room temperature; the butter must be very cold. If you are novice baker, use 3/4 cup (175 mL) shortening and no butter; this makes very easy-to-handle pastry.

Just starting to explore the pleasures of baking? Or want a fast update on ingredients, methods and equipment? See Baking Tips, page 240.

Lattice-Top Pie: Prepare same as double-crust pie but instead of top crust, make lattice topping: Cut pastry into strips about 1/2 inch (1 cm) wide. Arrange strips about 1 inch (2.5 cm) apart on top of filling, weaving lengthwise and crosswise strips. Trim ends evenly; fold overhang under pastry on rim; press together gently and flute.

2-1/4 cups	cake-and-pastry flour or 2 cups (500 mL) all-purpose flour	550 mL
1/2 tsp	salt	2 mL
1/2 cup	shortening	125 mL
1/4 cup	cold butter, cut in small cubes	50 mL
4 to 6 tbsp	cold water	60 to 90 mL

➡ In large bowl, mix together flour and salt. With pastry blender, cut in shortening and butter until mixture looks like fine crumbs with a few larger pieces. Add water, 1 tbsp (15 mL) at a time, stirring quickly with fork, adding just enough water to hold dough together. Press into a ball; divide in half. Makes enough for 1 double-crust or 2 single-crust 9-inch (23 cm) pies, or about 24 3-inch (8 cm) or 36 2-inch (5 cm) tart shells.

Single-Crust Pie: On lightly floured surface or pastry cloth, roll out dough to a round about 1/8 inch (3 mm) thick. Roll pastry loosely around rolling pin, then unroll it into pie plate; ease it into place without stretching dough. Trim edges, leaving about 1/2 inch (1 cm) overhang; turn under the overhang to make a double thickness; flute the edge. (If using fluted flan pan, press pastry gently against sides.) Fill and bake as directed in recipe.

To bake unfilled pie shell: Prick pastry all over with fork (for regular pie plate or tart shells, this is enough to prevent puffing up during baking; for flan, line pricked pastry shell with parchment or foil and fill with pie weights or dried beans). Bake in 400F (200C) oven until golden brown, 15 to 20 minutes for regular pie plate, 10 to 15 minutes for tart shells. For flan, bake for 10 minutes, then remove foil and weights; bake for 10 minutes longer or until golden brown.

Double-Crust Pie: Roll out dough as for single crust; fit into pie plate and trim edges even with rim. Add filling. Roll out top crust and place over filling. Trim edge of top crust, leaving 1/2-inch (1 cm) overhang. Tuck overhang under edge of bottom crust. Press together and flute edge. Cut several slashes as steam vents in top crust. Glaze and bake as directed in recipe.

Double-Crust Fresh Fruit Pies

Prepare Basic Pastry and follow instructions for Double-Crust Pie. For filling, combine prepared fruit and sugar (see amounts in chart). Stir in *1/4 cup (50 mL)* **all-purpose flour** *(unless otherwise noted)* and *1 tbsp (15 mL)* **lemon juice.** *Spoon filling into pie shell; dot with 1 tbsp (15 mL)* **butter if desired.** *Cover with plain or lattice-top crust.* **Glaze:** *With fork, beat together 1* **egg yolk** *and 2 tsp (10 mL)* **water.** *Brush over top crust. Sprinkle lightly with granulated sugar. Bake in 425F (220C) oven for 15 minutes; reduce heat to 350F (180C) and bake for 35 to 45 minutes longer or until fruit is tender and crust is golden brown.*

	Prepared Fruit	Sugar
Apple	5 cups (1.25 L) sliced	1/2 cup (125 mL); reduce flour to 1 tbsp (15 mL); add 1/2 tsp (2 mL) cinnamon
Apple-Cranberry	3 cups (750 mL) sliced apples; 2 cups (500 mL) cranberries	1 cup (250 mL); reduce flour to 1 tbsp (15 mL)
Blueberry	5 cups (1.25 L)	3/4 cup (175 mL)
Peach	5 cups (1.25 L) sliced	3/4 cup (175 mL)
Peach-Blueberry	4 cups (1 L) sliced peaches; 1 cup (250 mL) blueberries	3/4 cup (175 mL)
Pear	5 cups (1.25 L) sliced	3/4 cup (175 mL)
Plum	5 cups (1.25 L) sliced	1 cup (250 mL)
Raspberry	4 cups (1 L)	1 cup (250 mL)
Rhubarb	4 cups (1 L) in 3/4-inch (2 cm) pieces	1-1/4 cups (300 mL)
Sour cherry	4 cups (1 L)	1 cup (250 mL)
Strawberry-Rhubarb	3 cups (750 mL) strawberries; 2 cups (500 mL) chopped rhubarb	1 cup (250 mL)

Sweet Pastry

Quickly made in a food processor, this is the classic pastry for glazed fruit tarts.

1-1/2 cups	all-purpose flour	375 mL
1/4 cup	icing sugar	50 mL
1/2 cup	very cold butter, cut into cubes	125 mL
1	egg, lightly beaten	1

➜ In food processor, combine flour, icing sugar and butter. Process until mixture looks like fine crumbs. Add egg and process very briefly, just until mixture starts to clump together. Gather into a ball; flatten to a disk on parchment or waxed paper; wrap and chill for 30 minutes. Roll out, fit into pan(s) and bake. (See instructions for Single-Crust Pie, page 216.) Makes enough for one 9- to 10-inch (23 to 25 cm) flan or eight 4-inch (10 cm) tarts.

Fruit Pie Variations

Frozen Fruit Pies: If using frozen fruit instead of fresh, thaw just enough to separate if necessary. Proceed as with fresh fruit, but use cornstarch instead of flour (cornstarch has double the thickening power to compensate for the extra juice in frozen fruit; it also produces a clearer juicy filling). Increase baking time by about 20 minutes.

Fruit Crumble Pie: Instead of top crust, use Crumble Topping (especially suitable for apple, peach and pear). Mix together 1/2 cup (125 mL) all-purpose flour, 1/4 cup (50 mL) brown sugar and 1/4 tsp (1 mL) cinnamon. Cut in 1/4 cup (50 mL) cold butter until mixture looks like coarse crumbs. Sprinkle evenly over fruit filling. Bake as for double-crust pie, reducing baking time by a few minutes if filling has thickened, underside is baked and topping is golden brown.

Deep-Dish Fruit Pie: Omit bottom crust. Place fruit mixture in 8-inch square (20 cm) baking dish. Roll out pastry to a 10-inch (25 cm) square. Place pastry on top of fruit; fold edges under. Cut several slashes in top and brush with glaze (1 egg yolk beaten with 2 tsp/10 mL water). Bake as for double-crust pie, reducing baking time by about 10 minutes or until fruit is tender and pastry is golden brown.

Bumbleberry Pie

Now included among the most-popular Canadian fruit pies, bumbleberry is made with various combinations of berries along with apples and sometimes rhubarb or other fruit. This version has beautiful colour and delightful flavour; the filling is delectably soft and juicy; serve slightly warm or completely cooled. If blackberries are unavailable, use extra blueberries.

If you are using frozen berries, add 1 tsp (5 mL) cornstarch per cup (250 mL) of frozen berries, along with the flour.

2 cups	thinly sliced peeled apples	500 mL
1 cup	each: fresh raspberries, blueberries, blackberries, sliced strawberries	250 mL
1 tbsp	lemon juice	15 mL
3/4 cup	granulated sugar	175 mL
6 tbsp	all-purpose flour	90 mL
1/4 tsp	cinnamon	1 mL
	Pastry for double-crust 9-inch (23 cm) pie	

Glaze:

	1 egg yolk, 2 tsp (10 mL) water, granulated sugar

→ In large bowl, combine apples and berries. Sprinkle with lemon juice. In separate bowl, mix together sugar, flour and cinnamon. Add to fruit; stir gently to mix. Roll out half of pastry and fit into pie plate. Fill with fruit mixture. Roll out remaining pastry for top crust (plain or lattice). Place over fruit. Seal edges well and flute; cut several slits in top crust if not lattice.

Glaze: With fork, beat together egg yolk and water; brush over top crust; sprinkle with sugar. Bake in 425F (220C) oven for 15 minutes; reduce heat to 350F (180C) and bake for 35 to 40 minutes longer or until golden brown. Let cool on rack.

Rhubarb Custard Pie ❧

A delectable, old-fashioned treat with a tart-sweet, slightly creamy filling, this always sells out at farmers' markets—but is even better fresh from your own oven.

3 cups	rhubarb (3/4-inch/2 cm pieces)	750 mL
2	eggs	2
2 tbsp	butter, melted	30 mL
1 cup	granulated sugar	250 mL
3 tbsp	all-purpose flour	45 mL
	Pastry for double-crust 9-inch (23 cm) pie	

→ Place rhubarb in large bowl. In small bowl, whisk together eggs and butter. Mix together sugar and flour; stir into egg mixture until smooth. Add to rhubarb and stir to mix well. Spoon into pastry-lined pie plate. Top with pastry, preferably lattice crust. Bake in 425F (220C) oven for 10 minutes; reduce heat to 350F (180C) and bake for 30 to 40 minutes longer or until filling is softly set. Let cool on rack. Serve at room temperature.

Saskatoon Pie

In saucepan, simmer 4 cups (1 L) saskatoon berries in 1/4 cup (50 mL) water for 10 minutes. Add 2 tbsp (30 mL) lemon juice. Stir in 3/4 cup (175 mL) granulated sugar mixed with 3 tbsp (45 mL) flour. Fill and bake as for Double-Crust Pies (page 216).

Glazed Fruit Tarts

Always irresistible, these individual tarts can be made with any seasonal berries or fruit. The French patisserie look is easy to achieve using shallow fluted tartlet pans; you can also use this recipe for one large tart (use 9-inch/23 cm fluted flan pan with removable bottom). The creamy filling of ricotta and light cream cheese is much easier and lower-fat than traditional pastry cream; if ricotta is unavailable, you could use all cream cheese.

8 to 12	baked shallow tartlet shells (3- to 4-inch/8 to 10 cm) (use Sweet Pastry, page 217)	8 to 12
3 cups	(approx) fresh strawberries, raspberries, blueberries, blackberries or sliced peaches (or mixture)	750 mL
1/2 to 3/4 cup	red currant jelly	125 to 175 mL

1/2 cup	each: light cream cheese, ricotta	125 mL
1/2 cup	icing sugar	125 mL
1 tbsp	orange juice concentrate or orange liqueur	15 mL

➜ With electric mixer, beat together cream cheese, ricotta, icing sugar and orange juice concentrate until smooth. Spread in bottom of pastry shells. Arrange berries on top. In microwave or saucepan, heat jelly just until melted; let cool slightly. Spoon over berries to glaze. **Makes 8 to 12 tarts.**

Fruit Galette

The French term galette applies to a variety of rather flat cakes and tarts but is most commonly used for free-form pies like this. Much easier to make than a traditional pie, it doesn't even require a pie plate—just wrap the pastry around the filling.

	Pastry for double-crust 9-inch (23 cm) pie	
4 cups	peeled sliced peaches, apples, pears or plums	1 L
1/2 cup	granulated sugar	125 mL
2 tbsp	all-purpose flour	30 mL
1/2 tsp	cinnamon (for apples only)	2 mL
1 tbsp	butter	15 mL
1	egg white, lightly beaten	1
1 tbsp	granulated sugar for sprinkling	15 mL

➜ Roll pastry into a 14-inch (35 cm) round; roll it up on the rolling pin and transfer to baking sheet. In large bowl, gently toss fruit with sugar and flour (and cinnamon if using). Place fruit mixture in centre of pastry, mounding it up and leaving 2 inches (5 cm) of pastry uncovered around the edges. Dot fruit with butter. Fold pastry up over fruit to create a border, pleating loosely, leaving fruit exposed in centre. Brush pastry with egg white and sprinkle with sugar. Bake in 425F (220C) oven for 15 minutes. Reduce heat to 375F (190C) and bake for 30 to 40 minutes longer or until fruit is tender and pastry is lightly browned. Serve slightly warm. **Makes 6 servings.**

Pumpkin Pie   ✤

A classic harvest-time pie with hard-to-beat flavour. Evaporated milk, commonly used in traditional recipes and now available in low-fat versions, is a popular option to cream. Be sure to use pure pumpkin purée, not the kind labelled "pumpkin pie filling," which contains added ingredients. Recipe may be doubled for 2 pies, using 28-oz (796 mL) can pumpkin.

2	eggs	2
1	can (14 oz/398 mL) pumpkin purée	1
3/4 cup	packed brown sugar	175 mL
1 tsp	cinnamon	5 mL
1/2 tsp	each: ground ginger, allspice, nutmeg, salt	2 mL
1 cup	light cream or evaporated milk	250 mL
	Unbaked 9-inch (23 cm) pie shell	
	Whipped cream	
	Chopped candied ginger (optional)	

➔ In large bowl, whisk eggs well. Add pumpkin purée, sugar, spices, salt and cream; stir with whisk until well mixed. Pour into pie shell. Place pie on rack below centre of oven. Bake at 425F (220C) for 15 minutes; reduce heat to 350F (180C) and bake for 30 to 35 minutes or just until knife inserted in centre comes out clean. Let cool completely. Top with whipped cream; garnish with a sprinkle of ginger if desired.

Butter Tarts   ✤

An all-Canadian classic, butter tarts have been a favourite forever and remain a special treat (though not as often!). This filling is the popular runny kind but not overly sweet.

1/4 cup	raisins or pecan halves	50 mL
12	unbaked 3-inch (8 cm) tart shells	12
1/4 cup	butter, softened	50 mL
1/2 cup	packed brown sugar	125 mL
1/4 cup	corn syrup or maple syrup	50 mL
1	egg	1
1 tsp	white vinegar	5 mL
1 tsp	vanilla	5 mL
Pinch	salt	Pinch

➔ Sprinkle raisins evenly in tart shells. Cream together butter and brown sugar; beat in corn syrup, egg, vinegar, vanilla and salt. Pour into shells, filling each 3/4 full. Bake in 375F (190C) oven for 15 minutes or until golden brown. Let cool in pans for a few minutes, then remove to rack and let cool completely. **Makes 12 tarts**.

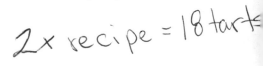

2x recipe = 18 tarts

Satisfying Sipping...

Beverages

Tall cool ones (short hot ones, too)

Tea Time

Whether it's good old orange pekoe, Earl Grey or English Breakfast, exotics like Darjeeling or Lapsang, or fragrant herbal brews, tea is hot, hot, hot—fast becoming the beverage of choice for more and more people each year and giving coffee some real competition for breakfast, restorative breaks, afternoon refreshment or evening indulgence.

To Make a Proper Cuppa: For 2 cups of tea (6 oz/175 mL each), use 1 tea bag (2-cup size) or 1 rounded teaspoonful of loose tea, and 1-1/2 cups (375 mL) water. For more servings, increase quantities, using same proportions. In kettle, bring fresh cold water to full, rolling boil. Warm teapot with a little boiling water; swish around and pour out. Place tea bags or loose tea in warmed pot; pour in boiling water. Let steep for 3 to 5 minutes for tea bags or 5 minutes for loose tea. Discard tea bags or strain loose tea as you pour into cups.

Iced Tea: Make double-strength hot tea (double the number of tea bags or amount of loose tea). After steeping, remove bags or strain; let cool. Pour over ice in tall glasses, add sugar and lemon, and garnish with fresh mint if desired. Iced tea can be made with any type of tea—try a herbal tea for a really refreshing summertime drink.

Minted Iced Tea: For each 2 to 3 servings, add 1/4 cup (50 mL) chopped fresh mint leaves to the brewing tea.

Chai

Spicy, milky tea, steeped in the traditions of India, makes a lovely finale to an exotic Indian meal and is gaining popularity in Canada as a satisfying beverage any time of day. There is no definitive recipe for chai; make it as spicy or mild as you wish. This version has a good balance of flavours; you could add one small star anise if you like. For the tea itself, orange pekoe is fine, Darjeeling more authentic.

2 cups	boiling water	500 mL
2	2-cup tea bags (preferably Darjeeling)	2
2	3-inch (8 cm) pieces cinnamon stick	2
1	slice fresh ginger, 1/2 inch (1 cm) thick	1
8	whole black peppercorns	8
4	whole cloves	4
1 tsp	cardamom seeds	5 mL
1 cup	milk	250 mL
	Sugar to taste	

➔ In saucepan, pour boiling water over tea and spices; add milk and stir. Bring just to boil; reduce heat to low and simmer very gently for about 5 minutes. Strain and serve. Add sugar to taste. **Makes 3 cups** (750 mL), 3 to 4 servings.

Coffee

Coffee houses are brimming over with all kinds of coffee from all corners of the world. The best approach is to buy small quantities and experiment to find the types, roasts, grinds and proportions you prefer.

How to Make: Experts recommend using 1-1/2 to 2 tbsp (20 to 30 mL) of ground coffee per 6 oz (175 mL) water, no matter what brewing method you use. If you find the coffee too strong or weak, you are probably using the wrong grind for your method. Use coarse grind for plunger/press-type pots, medium grind for a flat-bottom basket filter, fine grind for cone-shaped filters, and extra-fine for manual-drip cone filters and espresso machines. The roast (light to dark) greatly affects the flavour of the coffee. For maximum flavour, grind your own beans in a coffee grinder as you need them; store beans and ground coffee in an airtight container. Keep all your brewing equipment sparkling clean. Make your coffee with fresh cold water. Don't let brewed coffee sit on the warmer for more than a few minutes; transfer to an insulated carafe if necessary. New gadgets for coffee include milk frothers, which look like plunger-type glass coffee pots and make ordinary coffee look like cappuccino (and, as a bonus, low-fat milk foams better than full-fat milk); several brands are available in kitchen shops.

Quick Latte: Mix together equal parts very strong coffee or espresso and hot milk that has been frothed with frother or whisk.

Iced Coffee: Make double-strength coffee; let cool to room temperature, then cover and refrigerate. Sweeten as desired, and pour over ice in tall glasses. For a variation, add a scoop of vanilla, coffee or chocolate ice cream or frozen yogurt.

Mochaccino

Perfect for fireside sipping, après-ski or après-dinner, this extra-chocolaty cappuccino is low-fat and easy to make (you don't need a cappuccino machine). Using cocoa rather than high-fat chocolate or high-sugar chocolate syrup gives very good flavour at low calorie count and cost. For the liqueur-laced option, choose any favourite flavour (crème de cacao, amaretto, hazelnut, coffee, orange or cinnamon are all good); instead of liqueurs, you can use the no-alcohol flavoured syrups available at specialty coffee shops. A low-fat foamed milk topping is easy to make with a milk frother; if you do have a cappuccino machine, use it for the espresso and milk.

1/4 cup	each: unsweetened cocoa, granulated sugar	50 mL
1/4 cup	boiling water	50 mL
2 cups	hot espresso or very strong dark-roast coffee	500 mL
2 cups	hot milk	500 mL
3/4 cup	liqueur or flavoured syrup to taste (optional)	175 mL
3/4 cup	low-fat milk, foamed (or whipping cream, whipped)	175 mL
	Grated chocolate, sifted cocoa or cinnamon	

→ In small bowl, mix together cocoa and sugar; add boiling water, stirring with a whisk until smooth (may be made ahead and stored in covered jar).

For 6 servings: In large pitcher, combine coffee and milk (if not steaming hot, heat in microwave or saucepan). Stir in cocoa mixture. If desired, add liqueur or flavoured syrup to taste. Pour into six 1-cup (250 mL) mugs. Top each with foamed milk or whipped cream. Sprinkle with chocolate, cocoa or cinnamon.

For single serving: In mug, combine 1/3 cup (75 mL) each coffee and milk, 1 tbsp (15 mL) cocoa mixture and about 2 tbsp (30 mL) liqueur or flavoured syrup if desired.

Hot Chocolate: For each serving, in saucepan over medium heat or in microwave, heat 1 cup (250 mL) milk with 1 oz (30 g) chopped semisweet chocolate until steaming, stirring occasionally to melt chocolate. Add a few drops of vanilla and a little sugar to taste if desired. Pour into mugs. Top with foamed milk or whipped cream, or whisk until frothy before pouring into mugs.

Hot Cocoa: For each serving, in mug, mix together 1 tbsp (15 mL) each dry unsweetened cocoa and granulated sugar. Stir in a little cold milk to make a smooth paste. Fill mug with hot milk, stirring to blend. OR fill mug with cold milk; heat in microwave until steaming.

Fruit Smoothies

Fruit smoothies are upscale milkshakes and can be made with virtually any fruit and fruit juice. To ensure a really cold smoothie, be sure to use some frozen ingredients, such as frozen fruit, juice concentrate, frozen yogurt, ice cream, sherbet or crushed ice.

Frozen Fruit Smoothie: Frozen fruit makes this thick and cold. (For convenience, freeze chopped fruit in small plastic bags.) In blender, combine 1/2 cup (125 mL) each frozen coarsely chopped bananas, peaches and strawberries with 2 cups (500 mL) milk, 1/4 cup (50 mL) orange juice concentrate and 2 tbsp (30 mL) honey. Blend until smooth. **Makes 4 cups** (1 L), about 4 servings. For variations, replace half of the milk with yogurt, frozen yogurt, low-fat ice cream or sherbet.

Tropical Fruit Smoothie: Make same as Frozen Fruit Smoothie, but instead of frozen fruit, use diced fresh pineapple, papaya and mango, and add 1/2 cup (125 mL) crushed ice. Instead of milk, use chilled canned unsweetened coconut milk.

Bumbleberry Smoothie: Teamed with a low-fat muffin, this flavourful shake makes a quick, healthy breakfast. In blender, combine 3/4 cup (175 mL) each fresh or frozen raspberries, blueberries and strawberries with 1 cup (250 mL) chilled apple juice, 3/4 cup (175 mL) vanilla-flavoured yogurt and 1/2 cup (125 mL) crushed ice. Blend until smooth, adding sugar to taste if needed. **Makes 4 cups** (1 L), 2 to 4 servings.

Real Lemonade

This convenient concentrate is a delicious old-fashioned refresher that conjures up lazy summer afternoons on a shady verandah. Citric acid (available at drugstores) adds a little extra zip. For limeade, replace lemons with limes.

3/4 cup	lemon juice	175 mL
2 tbsp	grated lemon rind	30 mL
3 cups	granulated sugar (preferably superfine or fruit sugar)	750 mL
2 tbsp	citric acid (optional)	30 mL
2 cups	boiling water	500 mL

➜ In heatproof glass jar with lid, combine all ingredients; stir until sugar is dissolved. Cover and refrigerate. For each serving, mix 2 to 4 tbsp (30 to 60 mL) concentrate with 3/4 cup (175 mL) cold water, or to taste. **Makes 4 cups** (1 L) **concentrate**. Will keep for`about 2 weeks in refrigerator.

Mulled Wine

A warm and welcoming libation for guests on a cold winter's day.

1	bottle (750 mL) red wine	1
1/2 cup	orange juice	125 mL
1/2 cup	granulated sugar	125 mL
1/2	each: orange and lemon, sliced	1/2
3	whole cloves	3
3	3-inch (8 cm) pieces cinnamon stick	3
1	2-inch (5 cm) piece unpeeled fresh ginger	1

➜ In large saucepan over low heat, combine all ingredients. Simmer gently for 30 minutes or until hot and fragrant. Strain before serving. **Makes about 6 servings** (5 oz/150 mL each).

Mulled Cider

This timeless favourite wafts delicious aromas through the house. The spices can be tied in a cheesecloth bag for easy removal. Ciders vary in sweetness, so taste during mulling: if too tart, stir in more brown sugar; if too sweet, add a few squeezes of lemon juice.

8 cups	apple cider (fresh or hard)	2 L
2 tbsp	brown sugar	30 mL
1	each: thinly sliced lemon and orange	1
8	each: whole cloves, whole allspice	8
8	cardamom seeds (optional)	8
6	3-inch (8 cm) pieces cinnamon stick	6

➜ In large saucepan, combine all ingredients. Simmer for 20 minutes or until hot and fragrant. Strain before serving. **Makes about 10 servings** (6 oz/175 mL each).

Spiked Spiced Cider: Just before serving, stir in 1 cup (250 mL) dark rum, calvados or brandy and a little more sugar to taste.

Sangria

A big pitcher of fruit-flavoured wine makes a favourite summer refresher. These are the proportions for a classic Spanish sangria; if desired, add some orange liqueur, cream sherry, sliced peaches, apple wedges or strawberries.

1	each: sliced lemon, lime and orange	1
1/4 cup	(or to taste) fruit sugar	50 mL
1/2 cup	brandy	125 mL
1	bottle (750 mL) red wine	1
1-1/2 cups	(or to taste) sparkling mineral water	375 mL

➜ In large pitcher, combine lemon, lime and orange slices, sugar, brandy and wine. Chill for about 2 hours. Just before serving, add sparkling water and lots of ice cubes. **Makes about 6 servings** (6 oz/175 mL each).

White Wine Sangria: Use white wine instead of red. If desired, replace brandy with orange liqueur.

Rosé Sangria: Use rosé wine instead of red.

Brunch Bubblies

Kir: Pour a splash of cassis (black currant liqueur) into a champagne flute and fill with chilled sparkling white wine. For Kir Royale, use champagne instead of sparkling wine.

Mimosa: In stemmed glass, combine equal parts chilled fresh-squeezed orange juice and sparkling white wine. For Minted Mimosa, add a few slivered leaves of fresh mint and garnish with a mint sprig.

Kids' Party Punch 👦

The purple colour and citrus-grape flavour make this a popular punch, especially if it has frozen seedless grapes instead of ice cubes. For a Hallowe'en party, gummy-worm ice cubes are a big hit.

1	can (12 oz/341 mL) lemonade concentrate	1
1	can (12 oz/341 mL) orange juice concentrate	1
4 cups	purple grape juice	1 L
6 cups	soda water or sparkling water	1.5 L

➡ Combine all ingredients in punch bowl or large pitcher. **Makes about 20 servings** (5 oz/150 mL each).

To freeze grapes: Wash seedless red or green grapes, pat dry and freeze in single layer on baking sheet; transfer to plastic freezer bag.

Four-Fruit Punch

An out-of-the-ordinary combination of juices makes a flavourful, alcohol-free alternative that's great for festive or casual gatherings any time of the year.

1	bottle (40 oz/1.14 L) cranberry cocktail	1
3 cups	each: white grape juice, pineapple juice	750 mL
1/2 cup	lemon juice	125 mL
3 cups	soda water or sparkling water	750 mL
	Slices of lemon, lime, kiwifruit	

➡ Combine all ingredients except soda and fruit. Chill thoroughly. Pour over ice in punch bowl and add soda and fruit slices. **Makes about 20 servings** (6 oz/175 mL each).

Raspberry Champagne Punch

Celebrate in style with this sparkling pink punch. Any moderately priced champagne-style bubbly wine will do nicely as the base. For ice cubes that won't dilute the flavour or colour, freeze raspberry juice (made from concentrate plus water) in ice cube trays; if desired, add a whole raspberry to each cube when half frozen. Or make a raspberry ice ring in a ring mould.

1	can (12 oz/341 mL) raspberry juice concentrate	1
1 cup	orange liqueur	250 mL
1	bottle (750 mL) sparkling mineral water	1
1	bottle (750 mL) sparkling white wine	1

➡ In punch bowl, combine raspberry concentrate and liqueur. Just before serving, add ice cubes and pour in sparkling water and wine. **Makes about 14 servings** (5 oz/150 mL each).

Bottle the Harvest...

Preserves &
Unpreserves

Small-batch jams, herbed jellies,
super salsas and spicy chutneys

Sweet Sensations: A Jam Session in Six Easy Steps

To Sterilize Jars: Wash jars in dishwasher or hot soapy water and rinse. Boil jars in boiling-water canner or large pot of water for 10 minutes. Keep jars hot until filling. Other equipment (such as funnel and ladle) should also be sterilized (5 minutes in boiling water).

To Fill, Seal and Process Jars: Using a sterilized wide-mouthed canning funnel or glass measuring cup, ladle or pour hot jam into hot sterilized jars, leaving 1/4-inch (5 mm) space from the top of the jar (1/2 inch/1 cm for freezer jam). Wipe jar rim with clean damp cloth to remove any stickiness. Cover with new snap lids that have been boiled for 5 minutes to soften sealing compound. Screw on jar rings just until they feel tight to your fingertips. To process, place on rack in boiling-water canner (jars must be covered with at least 1 inch/2.5 cm water). Boil for 5 minutes (10 minutes for chutneys and relishes). Remove jars and place on towel to cool. Store jars in cool, dark place. If any jars have not sealed properly, refrigerate and use within 3 weeks. A jar is properly sealed when the lid has curved downward and remains so when pressed (you usually hear a "snap" during cooling).

Note: Melted paraffin wax is no longer considered a safe method for sealing jars.

This simple method makes delicious jams without commercial pectin. (For recipes using pectin, see the package leaflet or contact manufacturer.) These small-batch jams can be stored in the refrigerator for several weeks or conveniently frozen for up to a year. For pantry storage, process in boiling-water bath.

Refer to chart below for amounts of prepared fruit and sugar. Each yields about 4 cups (1L).

1. **Prepare fruit**. Choose firm ripe fruit, free of bruises. Wash just before using and drain well. Remove stems and pits; crush soft fruit with potato masher; chop firmer fruit in food processor. Place fruit in a large heavy-bottomed stainless steel saucepan or Dutch oven (at least 4-quart/4 L capacity; must be large enough to allow a full rolling boil).

2. **Add sugar and 1/4 cup (50 mL) lemon juice**. Stir over low heat until sugar is dissolved. Increase heat and bring to full rolling boil, stirring frequently. Boil hard, uncovered, for minimum time shown on chart.

3. **Test for jam stage**. While jam is cooking, place two saucers in freezer to chill. When ready to test for jam stage, remove pot from heat, spoon some of the jam onto one of the cold saucers and return to freezer for 2 minutes or until cold. Jam is ready when it is softly set and forms a mass that moves slowly when plate is tilted. If not thick enough, return pot to heat and continue boiling, testing on cold saucer at 2-minute intervals until jam stage is reached. Remove from heat and skim off any foam.

4. **Let stand for 5 minutes**, stirring occasionally to prevent floating fruit.

5. **Fill hot sterilized jars; seal** (see Sidebar). Let stand at room temperature for 24 hours.

6. **Store** in refrigerator for up to 3 weeks, or freeze for up to 1 year. Otherwise, **process filled jars in boiling-water bath** (see Sidebar).

	Prepared Fruit	**Sugar**	**Boiling Time**
Apricot	5 cups (1.25 L) chopped	3 cups (750 mL)	10–15 min.
Blueberry	5 cups (1.25 L) lightly crushed	3 cups (750 mL)	15–20 min.
Peach	5 cups (1.25 L) crushed	3 cups (750 mL)	15–20 min.
Raspberry	4 cups (1 L) lightly crushed	4 cups (1 L)	10–15 min.
Strawberry	4 cups (1 L) lightly crushed	4 cups (1 L)	15–20 min.

Bumbleberry Jam

1 cup	crushed strawberries	250 mL
1 cup	each: raspberries, blueberries, blackberries, chopped rhubarb	250 mL
5 cups	granulated sugar	1.25 L
1	pouch (85 mL) liquid pectin	1

➡ In Dutch oven or large heavy-bottomed pot, mix fruits together thoroughly. Bring to boil over high heat, stirring constantly. Reduce heat and simmer for 10 minutes or until rhubarb is soft. Stir in sugar. Bring to full rolling boil; boil for 2 minutes. Remove from heat and stir in pectin. Stir for 5 minutes (to prevent floating fruit). Skim off any foam. Fill and seal jars (see page 228). Store in refrigerator for up to 3 weeks, or process in boiling-water bath (see page 228). **Makes about 5 cups** (1.25 L).

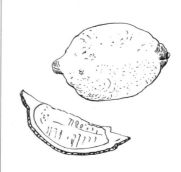

Raspberry Sugar Plum Jam

2 cups	finely chopped yellow plums (red plums can be substituted)	500 mL
2 cups	raspberries	500 mL
5 cups	granulated sugar	1.25 L
1/4 cup	lemon juice	50 mL
1	pouch (85 mL) liquid pectin	1

➡ In Dutch oven or large heavy-bottomed pot, combine plums, raspberries, sugar and lemon juice; mix thoroughly. Bring to boil over high heat, stirring constantly; boil hard for 1 minute. Remove from heat and immediately stir in pectin. Skim off any foam. Fill and seal jars (see page 228). Store in refrigerator for up to 3 weeks, or process in boiling-water bath (see page 228). **Makes about 6 cups** (1.5 L).

Ginger Pear Jam

A combination of fresh and candied ginger adds sparkle to the mellow flavour of pears.

4 cups	finely chopped peeled, cored pears (about 2 lb/1 kg or 5 large pears)	1 L
4 cups	granulated sugar	1 L
2 tbsp	grated fresh ginger root	30 mL
1/4 cup	lime juice	50 mL
1/2 cup	diced candied ginger	125 mL

➡ In large Dutch oven or large heavy-bottomed pot, mix together pears, sugar, ginger root, and lime juice. Bring to boil, stirring often. Boil for 12 to 15 minutes, stirring often; test for jam stage (see page 228). Stir in candied ginger. Fill and seal jars (see page 228). Store in refrigerator up to 3 weeks, or process in boiling water bath (see page 228). **Makes about 4 cups** (1L).

Rhubarb Chutney

This excellent, inexpensive chutney rivals the most costly store-bought. The recipe, from food writer Rose Murray, has been scaled down to make a small batch that can be stored in the fridge. It's spicy-hot, great as a condiment for meats or with cream cheese on crackers.

1 cup	packed brown sugar	250 mL
3/4 cup	cider vinegar	175 mL
1-1/2 tsp	ground ginger	7 mL
1/2 tsp	each: salt, allspice, cinnamon	2 mL
1/4 tsp	each: ground cloves, cayenne, pepper	1 mL
3 cups	rhubarb cut in 1-inch (2.5 cm) pieces	750 L

1	jalapeño or other chile pepper, minced	1
1 tbsp	each: minced fresh ginger and garlic	15 mL
1/2 cup	chopped onion	125 mL
1/2 cup	golden raisins	125 mL

→ In heavy saucepan, combine sugar, vinegar, ground ginger, salt, allspice, cinnamon, cloves, cayenne and pepper. Bring to boil, stirring to dissolve sugar. Add rhubarb, jalapeño, fresh ginger, garlic, onion and raisins. Return to boil, reduce heat and simmer, uncovered and stirring often, for about 1 hour or until thick. **Makes about 2 cups** (500 mL).

Chili Sauce   ❧

Homemade spicy-sweet chili sauce is a distinctly Canadian condiment. It's unlike anything sold in stores (though some bottled salsas come close) and remains a favourite for using up late-summer produce (and for making the kitchen smell wonderful). Here's an easy small-batch recipe that can be doubled if you have a prolific garden. If you want the sauce hotter, add 1 small chile pepper, seeded and minced.

4 cups	peeled chopped tomatoes	1 L
1	onion, chopped	1
1	sweet red or green pepper, chopped	1
2	stalks celery, chopped	2
1	apple or pear, peeled and chopped	1
1 cup	white vinegar	250 mL
1/3 cup	granulated sugar	75 mL
1/2 tsp	each: cinnamon, ground ginger, salt	2 mL
1/4 tsp	each: allspice, pepper, hot pepper flakes	1 mL

→ In large heavy stainless steel saucepan, combine all ingredients. Bring to boil, reduce heat and boil gently, uncovered, until thick, about 1-1/2 hours, stirring occasionally. Fill sterilized canning jars, leaving 1/2-inch (1.5 cm) headspace. Seal and process in boiling-water bath for 15 minutes (see page 228). **Makes about 4 cups** (1 L).

Quick-Pickled Vegetables: A one-day marinating in the refrigerator produces tasty pickled vegetable sticks to enjoy with snacks, sandwiches or grilled meats. Start with about 3 cups (750 mL) vegetables cut into sticks 1/2 inch (1 cm) thick. Use one kind or a mixture (sweet peppers, carrots, cucumber, zucchini, cauliflower). If using carrots, blanch in boiling water for 1 minute, drain and refresh in cold water. Place vegetables in large glass bowl. In saucepan, combine 1 cup (250 mL) each white wine vinegar and water, 1/4 cup (50 mL) granulated sugar, 1/2 tsp (2 mL) each dried oregano and salt, and 2 slivered garlic cloves. Bring to boil, stirring to dissolve sugar. Let cool. Pour over vegetables. Cover and chill for 24 hours (or up to 1 week for carrots, 2 or 3 days for others).

Red and Green Pepper Jelly

This attractive jelly, speckled with red and green, is popular for gift-giving. Serve with meats or add a small dollop to cream cheese on crackers for appetizers.

1 cup	each: finely chopped red and green sweet peppers	250 mL
1 to 2	jalapeño peppers, minced (optional)	1 to 2
6-1/2 cups	granulated sugar	1.625 L
1-1/2 cups	cider vinegar	375 mL
1/2 tsp	hot pepper sauce	2 mL
2	pouches (85 mL each) liquid pectin	2

➡ In Dutch oven or large heavy-bottomed pot, mix together peppers, sugar, vinegar and hot pepper sauce. Bring to full rolling boil over high heat. Remove from heat and let stand for 20 minutes. Return to heat and return to full rolling boil; boil for 2 minutes. Remove from heat and stir in pectin; continue stirring for 5 minutes to prevent floating peppers. Skim off any foam. Fill and seal jars (see page 228). Store in refrigerator for up to 3 weeks, or process in boiling-water bath (see page 228). **Makes about 5 cups** (1.25 L).

Rosemary Apple Cider Jelly

Serve this savoury jelly with roast chicken, lamb or pork; or use as glaze, brushing over meats or poultry during last 10 minutes of roasting or grilling.

2 cups	apple cider	500 mL
2 tbsp	cider vinegar	30 mL
1/4 cup	chopped fresh rosemary	50 mL
3-1/2 cups	granulated sugar	875 mL
1	pouch (85 mL) liquid pectin	1

➡ In large saucepan, combine apple cider, vinegar and rosemary; bring to boil over high heat. Reduce heat and simmer for 20 minutes. Pour through strainer into 2-cup (500 mL) measure; discard rosemary. Measure steeped cider, adding additional cider or water to equal 2 cups (500 mL). Pour steeped cider into Dutch oven or large heavy-bottomed pot. Add sugar and bring to full rolling boil over high heat, stirring frequently. Stir in liquid pectin; bring back to rolling boil for 30 seconds. Remove from heat; skim off foam. Fill and seal jars (see page 228). Store in refrigerator for up to 3 weeks, or process in boiling-water bath (see page 228). **Makes about 4 cups** (1 L).

Herbed Wine Jelly: Instead of apple cider, use 1-1/2 cups (375 mL) white wine, 1/2 cup (125 mL) apple cider or juice or water, and 2 tbsp (30 mL) white or cider vinegar. Add 2 tbsp (30 mL) chopped fresh herbs: rosemary, thyme, sage, savory or tarragon.

Herbed Vinegars: Use dill, chervil, chives or chive blossoms, purple basil, savory or tarragon. Place about 1 cup (250 mL) herb flowers/leaves in a clean wide-mouth canning jar. Heat 2 cups (500 mL) white wine vinegar until very hot but not boiling; pour over herbs in jar. Cover with plastic lid, or place plastic wrap over top before adding metal lid. Store in cool dark place for at least 48 hours; shake jar occasionally. Strain out herbs and discard. Pour into clean glass bottle, adding sprigs of fresh herbs if desired. Seal; label with name and date. Store in cool, dark place for up to 1 year. Use in salad dressings and marinades.

Cranberry Sauces and Relishes

See **Apples** page 182.

For **Preserved Lemons**, see page 99.

Basic Cranberry Sauce: In saucepan, combine 12-oz (340 g) package (about 3 cups/750 mL) fresh or frozen cranberries and 1 cup (250 mL) each water and granulated sugar. Bring to boil, reduce heat and boil gently, stirring often, for 10 minutes or until skins pop. Let cool (sauce will thicken as it cools). Store in covered container in refrigerator for up to 2 weeks. **Makes about 2 cups** (500 mL).

Microwave Cranberry Sauce: In 8-cup (2 L) glass measure or large microwavable bowl, combine 3 cups (750 mL) cranberries, 1 cup (250 mL) granulated sugar and 1/2 cup water or cranberry juice. Microwave uncovered on High for 7 to 10 minutes, stirring twice during cooking, until cranberries pop and soften. Stir well, crushing berries. Let cool.

Baked Cranberry Sauce: Baking retains the shape of the berries for an attractive sauce. Spread 3 cups (750 mL) cranberries in shallow layer in glass baking dish. Add 3/4 cup (175 mL) sugar and 1/2 cup (125 mL) water. Cover with foil and bake in 350F (180C) oven for 30 minutes, stirring occasionally, or until berries are tender.

Cranberry-Orange or Cranberry-Port Sauce: Make Basic Cranberry Sauce, using 1/2 cup (125 mL) each water and orange juice or port. Add 1 tbsp (15 mL) grated orange or lemon rind. For **Gingered Cranberry Sauce**, add 1/4 cup (50 mL) chopped candied ginger or 1 tbsp (15 mL) grated fresh ginger.

Cranberry-Orange Relish: In food processor, combine 2 cups (500 mL) fresh cranberries, 1 unpeeled orange (quartered and seeded) and 1/2 cup (125 mL) granulated sugar. Process until chopped. Add more sugar to taste if needed. Refrigerate for 2 days before serving. **Makes about 2 cups** (500 mL).

Applesauce

Experiment with different kinds of apples (alone or in combination) to discover how deliciously varied the flavour of homemade applesauce can be. Also take advantage of seasonal specials on apples in bulk, and prepare a large batch of applesauce; it freezes well packed in airtight containers.

Basic Applesauce: Peel, core and slice or coarsely chop 6 apples. Place in heavy saucepan; add 2 tbsp (30 mL) granulated sugar and 1 tbsp (15 mL) lemon juice. Depending on juiciness of apples, add 1/4 to 1/2 cup (50 to 125 mL) water or apple juice. Cover and cook over medium-low heat, stirring occasionally, until soft, about 15 minutes. Taste and add more sugar if needed. Sauce may be left chunky, mashed lightly or puréed until smooth in food processor. **Makes about 2 cups** (500 mL).

Alternatively: Cook in covered dish in Microwave for about 5 minutes on High. OR Bake in covered dish (omit the water) in 350F (180C) oven for 30 minutes or until soft.

Pink Applesauce: Use unpeeled thin-skinned red apples.

Spicy Applesauce: After cooking, stir in a large pinch (or to taste) each of cinnamon, nutmeg and allspice.

Gingered Applesauce: Before cooking, add 1/4 cup (50 mL) chopped candied ginger.

Cranberry Applesauce: Before cooking, add 1 cup (250 mL) cranberries. Increase water to 3/4 cup (175 mL) and sugar to 1/4 cup (50 mL). After cooking, pass through food mill to remove seeds, or purée and strain through coarse sieve.

Fresh Tomato Salsa

This is a typical salsa mexicana. Make it mild, medium or hot by adjusting the amount of minced jalapeños.

1 lb	plum tomatoes	500 g
1/2 cup	finely chopped red onion	125 mL
2	cloves garlic, minced	2
1 tbsp	(or to taste) minced jalapeño pepper	15 mL
1/4 cup	(or to taste) chopped fresh coriander	50 mL
1 to 2 tbsp	(to taste) lime juice or red wine vinegar	15 to 30 mL
	Salt to taste	

➡ Cut tomatoes in half lengthwise; squeeze out seeds. Chop tomatoes (you should have about 2 cups/500 mL). In bowl, combine all ingredients, stirring well. Let stand for about 30 minutes to develop flavour. Best eaten fresh but can be refrigerated for a few days. **Makes about 2-1/2 cups** (625 mL).

Variations: Stir in 1/2 cup (125 mL) (or to taste) cooked or canned black beans, corn kernels, chopped cucumber, avocado or black olives.

Mango Salsa

All kinds of fruit salsas can be made as variations of this one. Just replace one or both of the mangoes with peaches, pineapple, papaya, kiwifruit, melon or apricots.

2	mangoes, peeled and chopped	2
1	sweet red pepper, chopped	1
2	green onions or 1 small red onion, chopped	2
1	small jalapeño or other chile pepper, seeded and minced	1
2 tbsp	chopped fresh coriander, parsley or mint	30 mL
2 tbsp	lime or lemon juice	30 mL
1 tbsp	olive oil	15 mL
	Salt and pepper to taste	

➡ Combine all ingredients, stirring gently to mix well. Can be stored in refrigerator for up to 2 days. **Makes about 3 cups** (750 mL).

Black Bean Mango Salsa: Replace 1 mango with 1 cup (250 mL) drained canned black beans.

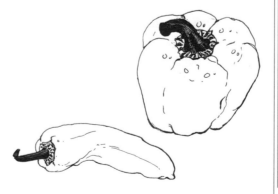

Salsas

The bottled salsa sold in supermarkets has apparently overtaken ketchup as the North American condiment of choice. These chunky cooked tomato sauces are convenient and flavourful additions to our tables, but not the same as the traditional salsas of Mexico and other countries. "Salsa" simply means sauce in Spanish and Italian. In Mexico, salsas are either uncooked or briefly "fried." The most popular is salsa mexicana (also called salsa cruda or pico de gallo), served with everything from tacos and tortilla crisps to chicken, fish, meat and egg dishes. Another favourite, salsa verde, is made with cooked green tomatillos. Uncooked salsas are easy-to-make, low-fat condiments that use all kinds of ingredients from tomato to mango and black beans.

Pesto

The aroma of fresh basil charms us all year, but when the crop is at its late-summer peak, the urge to make vats of pesto is inescapable. Give in. It freezes well.

2 cups	packed basil leaves	500 mL
2	cloves garlic	2
1/4 cup	pine nuts	50 mL
1/2 cup	olive oil	125 mL
1/2 cup	freshly grated parmesan (preferably Reggiano) or mixture of parmesan and romano	125 mL
	Salt and pepper to taste	

➜ In food processor or blender, combine basil, garlic and pine nuts; process until chopped. With machine running, gradually add oil, processing until smooth.

Stir in parmesan, salt and pepper. Transfer to small bowl; to prevent pesto from discolouring, press plastic wrap directly onto surface or cover with a thin film of oil. May be stored in refrigerator for up to 5 days. **Makes about 1-1/4 cups** (300 mL).

Pesto with Sun-dried Tomatoes: Add 6 oil-packed sun-dried tomatoes to processor along with basil; replace half of the olive oil with oil drained from the tomatoes.

Basil/Parsley Pesto: Substitute Italian parsley for half of the basil.

Coriander, Arugula or Mint Pesto: Substitute fresh coriander, arugula or mint (or half mint, half parsley) for basil.

Nut Pesto: Instead of pine nuts, use 1/2 cup (125 mL) pistachios, cashews, pecans, blanched almonds or sunflower seeds. To enhance their flavour, toast lightly in oven or skillet; let cool before adding to pesto.

Lower-Fat Pesto: Omit pine nuts. Replace half of the oil with chicken stock or with 2 tbsp (30 mL) each orange and lemon juice.

To Freeze Pesto: Prepare pesto, omitting parmesan. Place pesto in freezer containers (cover surface of pesto with thin film of oil) or in plastic freezer bags, or in ice cube trays (when frozen, remove cubes to freezer bag). Freeze for up to 6 months. Thaw in refrigerator (not microwave). After thawing, stir in parmesan.

Tip: To perk up colour after thawing, stir in 2 tbsp (30 mL) chopped parsley.

Uses for Pesto:

- Pasta Sauce: Dilute pesto with a little of the pasta cooking water, or mix pesto with cream. See Pesto Pasta (page 124).

- Spoon pesto onto baked potatoes or stir into mashed potatoes.

- Stir into sour cream, yogurt, mayonnaise or cream cheese for dips, spreads or dressings for potato or pasta salads.

- Stir a spoonful into marinades for chicken or lamb, or into vinaigrettes for salads.

- Add a dollop to omelets, frittatas or risottos.

- Spread pesto over pizza crust before adding toppings, or dot spoonfuls on top.

- Spread pesto on grilled bread for bruschetta or crostini.

References

Miscellaneous Basics

The following are called for in various recipes throughout.

Roasted Garlic: Slice about 1/2 inch (1 cm) off top of each head of garlic to expose tops of cloves. Remove outer layers of papery skin from heads. Place, cut side up, in small baking dish; drizzle with a little olive oil; cover dish tightly with foil. (Alternatively, wrap garlic completely in foil instead of placing in baking dish.) Bake in 350F (180C) oven for 45 minutes or until very soft. Squeeze out the softened garlic. For recipes using roasted garlic, see index.

Roasted Peppers: Roasting peppers brings out their full, sweet flavour and adds a hint of smokiness.

Sweet red peppers are the most common kind roasted (and are available in jars at the supermarket); yellow and orange are also good, as are banana peppers and large chiles.

To roast, place whole peppers over medium-high heat on the grill or under the broiler. Cook, turning occasionally, until blistered and charred all over, about 15 minutes. (Alternatively, for broiling, peppers can be halved lengthwise, flattened slightly and broiled on skin side without turning.) Place roasted peppers in bowl, cover and let stand for 15 minutes. Peel off skin; cut peppers in quarters lengthwise and remove seeds. Roasted red peppers are delicious on bruschetta, crostini, burgers and pizza; in sandwiches, salads, dressings, spreads and dips (see index for recipes).

To serve roasted peppers as antipasto: Drizzle with extra-virgin olive oil and sprinkle with salt and pepper. OR marinate in a simple vinaigrette of olive oil and red wine vinegar, with a little garlic if desired. Serve at room temperature.

Roasted Tomatoes: Roasting gives tomatoes a very sweet, concentrated flavour. Cut plum tomatoes into halves or quarters lengthwise. Place, cut side up, in single layer on oiled or parchment-lined baking sheet. Push sliver or thin slice of garlic into flesh of each tomato piece. Brush or drizzle lightly with olive oil and sprinkle with salt and pepper. Roast in 350F (180C) oven for 1-1/2 hours or until slightly shrivelled. Serve warm or at room temperature as an appetizer with mild goat cheese and crusty bread, or in a grilled focaccia sandwich with thinly sliced asiago or parmesan, or as a side dish with grilled meats or fish.

For **Roasted Tomato Pasta Sauce**, coarsely chop roasted tomatoes (for chunky sauce) or purée in food processor; add a little olive oil if needed to thin the sauce and chopped fresh basil to taste.

"Sun-dried" Tomatoes: Oven-drying is an easy and economical way to dry your own tomatoes. Cut plum tomatoes in half lengthwise and remove seeds and core. Place, cut side up, on rack on baking sheet and sprinkle lightly with salt. Bake in 175 to 200F (80 to 100C) oven for 7 to 8 hours or until leathery (they should feel dry but still pliable). Let cool; if some are still moist, return to oven until dry. Pack into clean jars or small plastic freezer bags and store in refrigerator for up to 3 months (can also be frozen). To rehydrate, place in boiling water for 1 to 2 minutes, or cover with hot water and let stand for 20 minutes or until softened; drain well. If desired, dried tomatoes can be covered with olive oil in a jar; store in refrigerator and use within 1 week (longer storage is not recommended for unprocessed product).

Caramelized Onions: These have a deliciously sweet, mellow flavour and rich golden brown colour. In large skillet over medium heat, heat 2 tbsp (30 mL) olive oil. Add 4 thinly sliced medium onions; cook, stirring occasionally, until golden brown, about 10 minutes. Add 2 tbsp (15 mL) each granulated sugar and red wine vinegar or balsamic vinegar. Sprinkle lightly with salt and pepper. Cook, stirring often, until onions are very tender and rich golden brown, about 10 minutes. **Makes about 1 cup** (250 mL). Serve warm or at room temperature on crostini or bruschetta, in sandwiches or burgers, with grilled steak or as a pizza topping (see index for recipes).

Roasted Chestnuts: With a sharp knife, cut a slit or cross through the shell on flat side of each chestnut. Place chestnuts in heavy skillet with a few drops of vegetable oil. Cook over medium heat, shaking pan frequently to prevent scorching, for a few minutes until shells and inner brown skins are loosened and can be easily removed. Peel while warm. Chestnuts can also be roasted in a long-handled chestnut pan over an open fire, or in baking pan in 425F (220C) oven for 20 minutes.

236

Toasted Nuts: Spread nuts on baking sheet and bake in 350F (180C) oven, shaking occasionally, for 5 to 10 minutes or until fragrant and lightly toasted. Or toast in dry skillet over medium heat for 2 to 3 minutes, tossing nuts occasionally. For hazelnuts, transfer to tea towel and rub off skins.

Croutons: Use day-old Italian or French bread, cut into 1/2-inch (1 cm) cubes. In large bowl, toss with olive oil (about 2 tsp/10 mL per cup/250 mL cubes). For flavoured croutons, add a sprinkle of dried herbs, garlic powder, grated parmesan, hot spices or chili powder. Spread on baking sheet. Bake in 375F (190C) oven until crisp and golden, about 5 minutes.

Breadcrumbs: (can be stored in freezer up to 3 months) *Coarse breadcrumbs* (also called soft or fresh breadcrumbs): Use slightly dry bread or rolls (about 2 days old). Process briefly in food processor or crumble by hand into coarse crumbs. About 3 slices of bread or 1 large roll makes 1 cup (250 mL) crumbs. *Fine dry breadcrumbs:* If you're pressed for time, use storebought, but homemade taste better. Use very dry bread slices (or dry in 350F/180C oven for a few minutes until crisp); break into chunks and process to fine crumbs in food processor.

Stock Up on Flavour

Good stock is a must for great-tasting soups, stews, sauces and many other dishes.

Making your own is not difficult and you can freeze it in convenient amounts for later use. If you are short of freezer space, you can make concentrated stock by boiling it down until reduced, then freezing in small containers or ice cube trays (when frozen, remove cubes to freezer bags); dilute with water before using. Any large pot will do for making stock, but a large stock pot with a separate perforated liner makes straining very easy.

Good fresh and frozen stocks are available in specialty shops, delis, butcher shops and fish markets. Canned stock (usually called broth or bouillon) is handy but expensive. In a pinch, bouillon cubes and powders will do, especially if you need just a small quantity of stock in a recipe; many are very salty, so be sure to reduce the salt in the recipe. Cubes and canned stock are available in low-salt and low-fat versions.

Chicken Stock: Get into the habit of keeping a bag in the freezer for necks, backs, wings and trimmings that can be used for stock. In large stock pot, place 4 lb (2 kg) chicken pieces (including any you've saved in freezer). Add 2 onions, 2 carrots, 2 celery stalks and 1 leek (optional), all cut in chunks; a small handful fresh parsley, 1 bay leaf, 1/2 tsp (2 mL) dried thyme, 8 peppercorns and enough cold water to cover by an inch. Bring to boil and skim off foam. Reduce heat and gently simmer uncovered for 1-1/2 hours. Strain. Refrigerate for about 8 hours; remove fat from surface. Store in refrigerator for up to 2 days or freeze. **Makes about 8 cups** (2 L). Turkey Stock can be made the same way.

Beef Stock: In shallow roasting pan, place 4 lb (2 kg) meaty beef bones such as shank. Add 2 onions, 2 carrots and 2 celery stalks (all cut in chunks). Roast in 425F (220C) oven for 1 hour or until browned, stirring occasionally. Transfer bones and vegetables to large stock pot. Pour 2 cups (500 mL) water into roasting pan, stir to scrape up brown bits and add to stock pot. Add small handful fresh parsley, 2 peeled garlic cloves,1/2 tsp (2 mL) dried thyme, 10 peppercorns, 1 bay leaf, 1 chopped tomato and enough water to cover by an inch. Bring to boil, skim off any foam, reduce heat and gently simmer, loosely covered, for about 2 hours. Strain. Refrigerate for about 8 hours; remove fat from surface. Store in refrigerator for up to 2 days or freeze. **Makes about 8 cups** (2 L).

Vegetable Stock: In stock pot, combine 2 onions, 1 leek, 2 carrots, 2 celery stalks and 2 tomatoes (all coarsely chopped). If desired, add 1/4 lb (125 g) chopped mushrooms or stems. Add small handful fresh parsley, 2 peeled garlic cloves, 1 bay leaf, 1/2 tsp (2 mL) dried thyme, 6 peppercorns and 8 cups (2 L) cold water. Bring to boil, reduce heat, cover loosely and simmer for 1 hour. Strain. Store in refrigerator for up to 2 days or freeze. **Makes about 8 cups** (2 L).

Fish Stock: In stock pot, combine 1-1/2 lb (750 g) fish bones, heads and tails (from lean, white-fleshed fish), a coarsely chopped onion, leek, carrot and celery stalk; 2 stalks parsley, 1 small bay leaf, pinch dried thyme, 4 peppercorns, 1/2 cup (125 mL) dry white wine and enough cold water to cover by an inch. Bring to boil, skim off any foam, reduce heat and gently simmer for 30 minutes. Strain. Store in refrigeraor for up to 2 days or freeze. **Makes about 6 cups** (1.5 L).

Barbecue Sauces

[handwritten: Easy basic BBQ Sauce ←]

All-Purpose Barbecue Sauce

Here's an excellent sauce for all seasons and reasons. Use it as a marinade, as a basting sauce during grilling, or in oven-baked or skillet dishes. (See Speedy Skillet Chops and Chicken, page 107; Barbecued Spareribs, page 85.)

1 tbsp	vegetable oil	15 mL
1/2 cup	finely chopped onion	125 mL
3	cloves garlic, minced	3
1 tsp	chili powder	5 mL
1/2 tsp	ground cumin	2 mL
1/4 tsp	dried ~~thyme~~ *mustard powder*	1 mL
1 cup	ketchup	250 mL
1/4 cup	each: cider vinegar, soy sauce *less vinegar*	50 mL
2 tbsp	brown sugar	30 mL
1 tbsp	Worcestershire sauce	15 mL
Dash	hot pepper sauce (to taste)	Dash

→ In heavy saucepan over medium heat, heat oil. Add onion and cook until softened. Add garlic, chili powder, cumin and thyme; cook, stirring, for 1 minute. Stir in remaining ingredients. Bring to boil, reduce heat, cover and simmer for 20 minutes. Let cool. (Sauce can be stored in covered jar in refrigerator for up to 2 weeks.) **Makes about 2 cups** (500 mL).

Easy Spicy Barbecue Sauce: Mix together 1 cup (250 mL) each ketchup and bottled hot salsa, 1/3 cup (75 mL) brown sugar, 1/4 cup (50 mL) cider vinegar, 2 tbsp (30 mL) Worcestershire sauce. Pureé in blender until smooth.

Chinese Barbecue Sauce: Mix together 3/4 cup (175 mL) each hoisin sauce and ketchup, 2 tbsp (30 mL) each soy sauce, honey and rice vinegar, 3 minced garlic cloves, 1 tbsp (15 mL) minced fresh ginger.

Maple Barbecue Sauce: Mix together 3/4 cup (175 mL) each maple syrup and ketchup, 1/4 cup (50 mL) brown sugar, 2 tbsp (30 mL) each cider vinegar and Worcestershire sauce, 1 tsp (5 mL) each dry mustard and salt.

Béchamel Sauce

Called béchamel in French and besciamella in Italian, this is the classic "white sauce" that was a familiar basic in Canadian kitchens for decades. Although it's rarely used now as a sauce on its own (as in once-common creamed vegetables or fish), it still serves as the basis of many other sauces (such as cheese sauce, see page 128).

Made with stock or other liquid instead of milk, it becomes a gravy for meat or poultry (see page 74). Béchamel sauce can also be flavoured with onions, chopped parsley or other herbs. Besciamella is used in many pasta dishes such as lasagne.

A classic béchamel or besciamella is a white sauce of medium thickness. For 1 cup (250 mL) sauce, use 2 tablespoons (30 mL) each butter and flour and 1 cup (250 mL) milk. (Use the same proportions if making larger or smaller amounts of sauce.)

In a heavy saucepan over medium heat, melt the butter. Whisk in the flour (this is called a roux); let it bubble gently for 1 to 2 minutes without browning. Gradually whisk in the milk. Cook, stirring constantly, until sauce comes to a boil and thickens; reduce heat to low and let simmer for about 3 minutes, stirring occasionally. Season to taste with salt, pepper and a pinch or two of nutmeg.

Dairy Products

The abbreviation "M.F." on dairy product labels refers to milk fat content.

Milk: Homogenized (whole) milk has about 3.25% M.F.; skim has less than 0.5%; 2% and 1% milk are in between. New milk products such as calcium-fortified and ultra-filtered are increasingly available. UHT (ultra-high temperature) milk in cartons lasts for several months without refrigeration.

Cream: Categorized by its milk fat content. The names vary somewhat across Canada, and you will also see different terms in recipes from other countries:

Whipping cream: About 35% M.F. Sometimes called heavy cream. Double cream (about 40% M.F.) has limited availability in Canada. Whipping cream is used whipped and unwhipped in recipes; it is also used in sauces that require reduction by boiling (lighter creams may separate or curdle).

Table cream: Usually 15 to 18% M.F. Also known as coffee cream. Can be used in recipes calling for light cream. Light cream is called single cream in British cookbooks.

Half-and-half: About 10% M.F. Also known as cereal cream or blend; can be used in recipes calling for light cream. 7% cream is available in some stores.

Crème fraîche: A smooth, thick cultured cream; common in Europe; increasing availability in Canada. You can make a satisfactory substitute by combining equal quantities of sour cream and whipped cream. Crème fraîche can also be made by adding a little buttermilk or sour cream to whipping cream and allowing it to stand at room temperature until thickened, but this method does not work well with ultra-pasteurized whipping cream.

Sour cream: About 14% M.F. Also available in light (low-fat) and no-fat versions. In most recipes, plain yogurt can be substituted. In baking, low-fat sour cream and yogurt can be substituted for higher-fat kinds; do not substitute no-fat versions.

Yogurt: Available in plain and flavoured varieties. Wide range of calorie and fat content (read labels), including low-fat and no-fat. Extra-thick yogurt is available in some stores. To make your own, see Drained Yogurt, below.

Drained Yogurt: Also called "thickened yogurt" or yogurt cheese," drained yogurt is thick, tangy, creamy and very versatile. It makes an excellent low-fat substitute for sour cream, cream cheese, whipped cream or mayonnaise in spreads, dips, dressings and sauces. Use it on its own as a baked potato topping, or sweetened slightly for a dessert topping.

It can be made with any plain yogurt (regular or low-fat, without thickeners such as starches, carageenan or agar; read the label). Special yogurt strainers can be purchased, and are convenient but not necessary. All you really need is a strainer placed over a bowl. Line strainer with cheesecloth, paper towel or coffee filter; place yogurt in strainer, cover with plastic wrap, and place in refrigerator until drained to desired thickness (the liquid will drain into the bowl). After 3 to 5 hours, the yogurt will have reduced to about three-quarters of its original volume and have the thickness of sour cream; after 8 to 12 hours it will be reduced by half, and as thick as soft cream cheese; left even longer (up to 48 hours), it will get even thicker.

Note: For recipes in this book that call for drained yogurt, use yogurt that has been drained to half its original volume (e.g. Start with 2 cups yogurt to make 1 cup drained yogurt).

Buttermilk: About 1% M.F. made from low-fat milk and bacterial culture. (At one time, it was the milk left over from churning butter.)

Evaporated milk: Canned milk available in whole or low-fat versions; made by evaporating milk to half its volume.

Condensed milk: Evaporated milk reduced even further and sweetened, available in whole or low-fat versions.

Baking Tips

- Read recipe through before beginning.

- Prepare pans and preheat oven before starting the recipe. Check your oven's accuracy occasionally with a reliable oven thermometer; if the oven dial is off a few degrees, you can adjust it each time it's used; if it's off more than 25F, it should be fixed.

- Measure accurately (see page 249). Improvisation is great in most cooking, but baking recipes are carefully balanced, so reliable results demand accurate measurements.

- If recipe calls for a measured amount of a sifted ingredient (e.g., 1 cup sifted cake-and-pastry flour), sift before measuring.

- If recipe calls for softened butter, use butter at warm room temperature; if room is cold, beat butter until softened, or warm it very gently in microwave.

- Check for doneness at the earliest time specified in the recipe. Check cakes and quickbreads with a cake tester or toothpick; it should come out clean, with no crumbs clinging to it. When done, cakes will start to pull away slightly from the edges of the pan and will spring back when lightly touched on top; yeast breads will sound hollow when tapped on the bottom.

- An electric mixer makes baking projects much easier. A hand-held model is satisfactory for most uses; if you do a lot of baking, a countertop model is much more efficient.

- If you don't do much baking, shop at bulk food stores for small quantities of ingredients such as specialty flours and spices.

- Baking pans: Good-quality shiny metal baking pans are best; they bake evenly and don't rust. If using glass baking dishes, reduce oven temperature by 25F.

  For nonstick pans, follow manufacturer's directions on labels; most say to reduce oven temperature or cooking time. If directions are unavailable, reduce oven temperature by 25F because nonstick surfaces, especially dark ones, tend to bake faster; this adjustment of temperature is especially important with large cakes because the edges will overbake before the centre is done. For some recipes, nonstick pans require a light greasing; follow manufacturer's directions and your own experience.

- Greasing pans: Shortening is best for greasing pans (butter and margarine tend to burn); oil is satisfactory for light greasing. Aerosol cooking spray is convenient (be sure to use a light touch); non-aerosol pumps, available in kitchenware shops, can be filled with your choice of oil and used for spraying the surface of baked goods as well as for greasing pans. If a recipe calls for a greased and floured pan, brush it with shortening or spray lightly with cooking spray, then sprinkle with flour, tilting pan and tapping to distribute flour thinly and evenly; tap out any excess. For most muffins, paper liners can replace greasing.

- Parchment paper is a great help in the kitchen. Line baking pans with it and nothing will stick—no greasing necessary. It can also be wiped off and re-used. Parchment in boxed rolls is available in bulk food stores, specialty shops and some supermarkets.

- Cookie-baking tips: Baking sheets without sides provide better heat circulation, more even browning and easier removal of cookies than rimmed baking sheets. Position oven racks in centre of oven or just above (so cookies don't brown too quickly on underside) and bake one sheet at a time. Underbake cookies very slightly, as they will continue to bake on the hot baking pan after removal from oven; let cool slightly, then remove cookies to wire racks to cool completely.

- To beat egg whites: Egg whites should be at room temperature (see Egg Safety: Cooking Tips, page 142). Use glass or metal, not plastic, bowl. Be sure bowl and beaters are clean; any trace of fat or yolk in the whites will inhibit proper beating.

  "Soft peaks" means the beaten whites will hold soft, droopy peaks when the beater is lifted. "Stiff peaks" means the whites will hold firm, shiny peaks that keep their shape; be sure to beat whites only until stiff but not dry. Many recipes call for the addition of a little cream of tartar to the whites, which helps to stabilize the foam.

- To melt chocolate: Chop chocolate into pieces. Melt slowly in bowl set over saucepan of hot, not boiling, water (the water should not touch bottom of bowl). OR Microwave at Medium until almost melted; remove from oven and stir until completely melted.

- To grate citrus rind (lemon, lime, orange): Use a hand-held metal grater; grate only the coloured part of the peel, avoiding the bitter white part. Rind is called zest in some cookbooks; in this book, zest refers to long shreds rather than grated rind; use a zester (a tool with small holes at one end) to make the shreds, or thinly peel off the coloured part of the rind and cut into fine shreds with sharp knife.

Know Your Flours

All-purpose flour: Canadian all-purpose flour is high-quality hard-wheat flour blended with a little soft-wheat flour. It is suitable for all baking, including bread. Unbleached all-purpose flour can be used interchangeably with regular all-purpose. Specialty bread flours and bread-machine flours, with higher gluten content, are also available. **Cake-and-pastry flour** is made from soft wheat and gives baked goods a tender, fine texture. It is not suitable for yeast breads. **Whole wheat flour** contains the whole kernel of wheat, including the bran and germ, and has a higher nutritional content than white flour. Store it in the refrigerator or freezer to prevent racidity. In most recipes, whole wheat can be substituted for up to half of the all-purpose flour called for. **Self-raising flour** is all-purpose flour with baking powder and salt added. **Stone-ground flour** is whole wheat flour ground between large flat stones; in only a few mills in Canada. **Other specialty flours** include rye, barley, buckwheat, cracked wheat, triticale (a cross between wheat and rye), soy, potato and rice. They are usually used in small quantities along with all-purpose flour.

• U.S. and European flours are different from Canadian. American all-purpose flour is a blend of hard and soft wheat flours, but varies by brand and region; it generally has a higher percentage of soft wheat than Canadian all-purpose. Most European flours are lower in protein than ours, and their "plain" flours are closer to our cake-and-pastry flour than to all-purpose flour.

The Scoop on Sugars

Granulated (white) sugar: Highly refined cane or beet sugar; the most common for everyday use; most brands are finely granulated.

Super fine sugar: Very finely granulated sugar; also called instant dissolving, powdered fruit sugar or berry sugar (you can make your own by whirling regular granulated sugar in a food processor). Called castor or caster sugar in Britain and Australia. **Decorating or coarse white sugar:** Large crystals used for decorating baked goods; can be found in cake-decorating shops and bulk food stores. **Icing sugar:** Finely powdered white sugar with a little cornstarch added; called confectioners' or powdered sugar in the U.S.A. **Brown sugar:** White sugar combined with molasses which gives it a soft texture. Light brown sugar is labelled golden or yellow by some manufacturers. Dark brown sugar (sometimes labelled old-fashioned) contains more molasses and is stronger-flavored. Light and dark are interchangeable in most recipes. **Raw sugar:** Sugar crystals left after processing of sugar cane syrup; "raw" sugars sold in North America have been purified. Available in fine to coarse dry crystals; similar to brown sugar in color and flavor. **Demerara** has medium golden crystals made from partly refined sugar plus a little molasses; **turbinado** is further refined and a little lighter in colour. A fine-textured form called "golden crystallized sugar" is packaged by some manufacturers. **Maple sugar:** Made by evaporating maple syrup; limited availability across Canada; for a small quantity in a recipe you can crumble maple sugar candy (often moulded in maple leaf shapes) sold in specialty shops.

Fats for Baking

Butter is used where a buttery flavour is desired; use salted or unsalted butter as directed in recipe; light or whipped butter is not suitable for baking. **Margarine** is made from vegetable oils plus flavorings and other ingredients. Hard margarine can be substituted for butter in recipes. Soft margarine has been formulated to remain spreadable when cold; in baking, it should be used only in recipes developed specifically for it. Light or whipped margarines are not suitable for baking. **Shortening** is made from hydrogenated vegetable oils and is virtually flavourless. Shortening can be stored at room temperature. It produces a tender "short" texture in pastry, and blends readily with other ingredients in doughs and batters; it can be substituted for butter where flavour is not important. **Lard** is made from animal fat and is used where old-fashioned flavour is desired, such as in some traditional pastry recipes. **Vegetable oils** are used in many baked goods and can also be substituted for melted fats; use mild-flavoured vegetable oils rather than olive oil unless specified in recipe.

Terms and Techniques

Like all sciences and art forms, cooking has its own terms for specific ways of doing things. If an unfamiliar term appears in a recipe, turn here for guidance.

Al dente: Means tender but still firm to the bite (literally "to the tooth" in Italian), referring to the doneness of pasta and sometimes to vegetables.

Bain-marie (water bath)**:** Larger pan of water in which a smaller pan or baking dish, usually containing egg-based mixtures, is placed to cook.

Bake: To cook, uncovered or covered, in oven. See also Roast.

Bake blind: To partially or completely bake a crust before filling. Pastry is lined with foil or parchment and filled with dried beans or pie weights to prevent it from puffing up.

Baste: To spoon or brush liquid (pan drippings or sauce) over food as it cooks, to keep it moist and/or add flavour.

Batter: An uncooked mixture—usually flour, liquid and other ingredients—thin enough to pour or spoon.

Beat: To mix vigorously until smooth or to introduce air, using electric mixer, egg beater, wire whisk, fork or spoon.

Blanch: To cook very briefly in boiling water. Used to remove skin from fruit, to enhance colour or to reduce bitterness or saltiness. After blanching, food is usually plunged into cold water to halt cooking. Vegetables are usually blanched before freezing.

Blend: See Mix.

Boil: To heat liquid until bubbles rise and break on surface; recipes may call for gentle or full rolling boil.

Braise: To brown at high heat, then add a small amount of liquid, cover and slowly simmer. Used for less-tender cuts of meat, sometimes for vegetables.

Bread: To coat with breadcrumbs, usually before frying or baking.

Broil: To cook under direct heat, usually the oven's upper element. See also Grill.

Brown: To cook quickly, usually at high heat, to deepen surface colour and intensify flavour; can be done in pan on stovetop, under broiler, on grill or in oven. See also Sear.

Butterfly: To halve horizontally, without cutting all the way through, so the two halves can be opened like butterfly wings. Done with meat or fish to be stuffed and rolled.

Caramelize: To brown food during cooking. Also means to cook sugar slowly until it melts and turns a deep golden brown.

Chiffonade: To cut (usually leafy greens or herbs) into fine strips.

Chop: To cut into small pieces (fine, medium or coarse) with knife or food processor. See also Mince.

Clarify butter: See page 161.

Cream: To beat fat such as butter or shortening, often with sugar, until thoroughly blended and light in texture.

Crush: To break into fine pieces.

Cube: To cut into cubes larger than 1/2 inch (1 cm). See also Dice.

Cut in: To work fat into flour until fat is in tiny pieces and mixture resembles coarse crumbs.

Dash: Less than 1/4 tsp (1 mL) of an ingredient. See also Pinch.

Deep-fry: To cook by submerging in hot fat.

Deglaze: To pour liquid (wine, stock, water) into pan after frying or roasting, then stir to loosen and incorporate the browned bits from the bottom.

Devein: To remove the black intestinal vein that runs along the outside curve of a shrimp or prawn.

Dice: To cut evenly into cubes, usually 1/2 inch (1 cm) or smaller. See also Cube.

Dredge: To dip pieces of food into coating such as flour, cornmeal, crumbs or icing sugar.

Emulsify: To mix insoluble ingredients so they hold together in suspension, such as oil incorporated into mayonnaise.

Fluff: To toss with a fork in order to separate grains.

Flute: To create a decorative edge on a pie crust.

Fold: To combine beaten egg whites or whipped cream with another mixture without losing any volume, by turning over gently with rubber spatula.

Fry: See Deep-fry, Pan-fry.

Glaze: To coat a surface with a thin layer (such as chocolate, icing, egg wash or syrupy mixture) to provide a shine.

Grate: To cut solids into small particles by rubbing against a grater.

Grease: To coat baking pan lightly with fat to prevent sticking. To grease and flour a pan: Brush with fat, then sprinkle with flour; tap pan to distribute flour evenly; shake out any excess.

Grill: To cook over a gas, electric or charcoal heat source (barbecue or indoor grill); can be simulated under broiler or on a ridged grill pan on stovetop.

Infuse: To flavour a liquid with herbs, spices or other seasonings, usually by simmering.

Julienne: To cut into match-like strips.

Knead: To work dough to make it smooth and springy, by hand, food processor or electric mixer with dough hook. Place ball of dough on floured surface; with fingertips, lift dough toward you, folding in half; press down with the heels of your hands. Turn dough and repeat according to recipe.

Macerate: Similar to marinating, but usually refers to fruit mixture and a sweet liquid or alcohol.

Marinate: To cover or coat food with a marinade (seasoned liquid or paste) and set aside to develop flavour or tenderize.

Mince: To chop into very fine pieces.

Mix (or Blend): To combine ingredients until evenly distributed, producing a mixture that is uniform in texture and colour.

Pan-fry: To cook in small amount of fat in skillet.

Parboil: To partially cook foods in boiling water.

Pinch: Less than 1/4 tsp (1 mL) of a dry ingredient. See also Dash.

Poach: To cook food gently in liquid that is simmering but not boiling.

Pot roast: Same as braise, but with larger cut of meat.

Pound: To flatten and/or tenderize meat or poultry, using a mallet or other heavy implement.

Reduce: To boil liquid rapidly to decrease volume and intensify flavours, especially in sauces.

Refresh: To place foods (usually vegetables) in cold water or ice bath immediately after boiling or poaching to halt cooking, set colour and crisp texture.

Roast: To cook in uncovered pan without added liquid, usually in oven. Refers commonly to meats, but also to vegetables and other foods. See also Bake.

Sauté: Originally meant to cook small pieces of food quickly, at high heat, in a small amount of fat, usually until just browned; now synonymous with pan-frying, in which food is cooked through.

Scald: To heat milk or cream just until tiny bubbles form around inside edge of pan.

Score: To cut shallow lines on meats to tenderize and/or allow marinade to penetrate surface, or on surface of dough to decorate.

Sear: To cook meat with intense heat to seal in juices, impart colour and add flavour. Usually done quickly in skillet or oven. See also Brown.

Shred: See Grate.

Simmer: To cook at just below boiling; liquid should be moving but not bubbling hard.

Skim: To remove fat or other material from surface of soup, stock, stew or sauce.

Sliver: To cut food into very thin strips.

Steam: To cook in a rack, over water, in a covered vessel.

Stew: To simmer less-tender cuts of meat, fruit or vegetables in liquid for a long time.

Stir: To mix thoroughly with a spoon, without beating.

Stir-fry: To cook bite-size pieces of food quickly in a small amount of oil over high heat, keeping the food in motion.

Strain: To remove solid matter from liquids by passing through a sieve, colander or cheesecloth.

Sweat: To draw out a food's juices by cooking, usually covered, over low heat, without browning. Vegetables such as onions are sweated to soften and develop flavour.

Toast: To heat briefly in oven, under broiler or in skillet, until lightly browned.

Toss: A word with two related meanings. A salad is tossed by gently lifting and turning the ingredients. Foods being cooked in a skillet are tossed by a rapid, slightly jerky, circular movement of the pan itself.

Truss: To secure wings and legs of a bird close to its body to give attractive appearance and hold in stuffing.

Whip: To beat rapidly to incorporate air, using wire whisk, electric mixer or hand-held egg beater.

Whisk: To mix briskly with a wire whisk.

Zest: The outer rind/peel of citrus fruit, without the white pith.

Global Pantry

Dramatic changes have taken place in Canadian grocery stores in recent years, and with them has come a new world of flavours. Many products that once seemed exotic—Dijon mustard, real parmesan, pesto, fresh chile peppers—have become so familiar they're now considered staples. The culinary traditions from which they came get nodding recognition, yet these ingredients have been adopted as our own. Italian foods, in particular, are firmly entrenched in our culinary vocabulary. But among the new items on the shelves are some that remain a bit mysterious while on their path to wide inclusion. This list explores the basics in that category, most of them products of our new awareness of things Asian and Latin American. Soon they may also be commonplace, supplanted by exciting new tastes from other corners of the globe.

The new basics (or soon-to-be-basics) in the produce department (fruits and vegetables), herbs and spices, grains and legumes, and oils and vinegars have descriptions elsewhere. Consult the index for specific items by name.

Black bean sauce: Fermented black beans combined with garlic and other seasonings; pungent and salty. Used as flavouring in Chinese cooking. Chinese black beans are also sold dry, unseasoned. Not to be confused with the larger dried or canned black beans used in western cooking.

Bonito flakes: Dried, salted, fermented fish flakes used in Japanese cooking.

Capers: Pickled buds of the caper bush; used extensively in Mediterranean cuisine. Sold bottled in brine. Traditional accompaniment to smoked salmon.

Chile oil: Flavoured oil made intensely hot by infusion with chile peppers.

Chile paste (Asian): Ground chile peppers, often mixed with garlic, beans and spices; brands vary in intensity.

Chili powder: A blend of dried chile peppers and other spices such as ginger, cumin, cayenne, oregano and mustard.

Chinese dried mushrooms: Add flavour and aroma to many dishes. Dried black mushrooms are common; other varieties include cloud ear, wood ear and shiitake. Usually rehydrated before using.

Coconut milk: Flavourful creamy liquid made from grated coconut mixed with water then strained; common in Southeast Asian and West Indian cooking. Available canned, in both regular and light versions. In some Thai brands, you'll find a thick layer of coconut "cream" on top of the milk; stir before using, unless recipe uses cream and milk separately. Be sure to buy unsweetened coconut milk, not the sweetened kind used for mixed drinks such as piña colada.

Curry paste: See Sidebar, page 117.

Curry powder: A blend of ground spices used to flavour Indian-style curried dishes. In traditional Indian cooking, spice mixtures called masalas are more often used.

Filé powder: Dried leaves of the sassafras plant. Used in gumbos and other Creole cooking for flavouring and thickening.

Fish sauce: Thin, salty, brown liquid, called nam pla in Thailand, nuoc nam in Vietnam, patis in the Philippines. Made from fermented fish, often anchovies, with spices and sugar; a key seasoning in Southeast Asia.

Galangal: Similar in appearance to fresh ginger root; slightly milder flavour; popular in Southeast Asian cooking.

Garam masala: See page 248.

Ghee: Clarified butter used in the cooking of India.

Harissa: Fiery paste of chiles and other spices used in North Africa.

Hoisin sauce: Thick, sweet, rich sauce made from soybean paste, garlic, vinegar, sugar and spices; common in Asian cooking, particularly Chinese.

Hot pepper sauce: Various commercial mixtures of hot chile peppers, vinegar and seasonings. Add flavour as well as heat; range from mild to fiery. Tabasco is one well-known brand.

Kaffir lime: Leaves of this Southeast Asian tree add intense citrus aroma and flavour to Asian dishes. Fresh leaves are more flavourful than dried.

Lemongrass: Long, thin leaves of this herb give an essential sour-lemon flavour to many Thai dishes. Usually sold dried, occasionally fresh.

Mirin: See Rice wine.

Miso: Fermented paste made from soybeans, used in Japanese cooking. Ranges in colour from white to yellow to reddish-brown (darkest is saltiest).

Nam pla: See Fish sauce.

Nori: Nutrient-rich paper-thin seaweed sheets used in Japanese cooking as a flavouring, a garnish and to wrap sushi.

Nuoc nam: See Fish sauce.

Oyster sauce: Thick, brown, richly flavoured sauce made from fresh oysters that are boiled, then seasoned with soy sauce, salt and spices; used widely in Chinese cooking.

Patis: See Fish sauce.

Peanut sauce: Purée of peanuts with various flavourings such as vinegar, hoisin sauce, chile peppers and ginger.

Plum sauce: Puréed plums, chili powder, vinegar, sugar and spices; a staple of Chinese cooking.

Rice vinegar: A staple in Chinese and Japanese cooking; milder than North American vinegars. Available unseasoned and seasoned (usually with sugar and salt).

Rice wine: Comes in dark and light varieties. Chinese rice wine is similar to dry sherry. Japanese versions include sake and the sweeter mirin.

Sambal: Spicy condiment common in South Asian cuisines. Usually based on chiles, ground into a paste and flavoured with salt and sugar. (Also called sambal ulek or sambal oelek.)

Sesame oil: Intensely flavoured aromatic oil made from sesame seeds; use sparingly. Look for the brown type, made from toasted seeds, not the bland, pale variety.

Soy sauce: Staple of Japanese, Chinese and other Asian cuisines; comes in wide range of flavours and intensities (specialty markets may offer 60 or more kinds). Light soy sauces are lighter in colour, consistency and flavour, and are preferred for most cooking. (Don't confuse them with sodium-reduced sauces, also labelled "light.") Dark soy sauce is thicker and strong-flavoured; use only when recipe calls specifically for it.

Tabasco sauce: See Hot pepper sauce.

Tahini: Sesame seed paste widely used in the Middle East.

Tamari: Dark, mellow sauce similar to soy but thicker.

Teriyaki sauce: Japanese condiment containing lime juice, ginger, garlic and soy sauce, usually thickened with cornstarch.

Truffle oil: Olive oil infused with the earthy flavour of truffles. Sold in small bottles at high prices. Drizzle into soups (especially mushroom) and risotto.

Wasabi: Japanese horseradish, usually sold as a green paste or powder.

Herbs and Spices

Herbs generally grow in temperate climates. Fresh or dried, they're the leaves and seeds of small plants and bushes. Some herbs have numerous varieties (sizes, colours, flavours). Herb flowers (such as chives) are also used as garnishes and in salads.

Spices generally come from tropical plants (seeds, berries, bark, roots). Store dried herbs and spices in tightly sealed glass or glazed ceramic containers, away from heat and light. Most should be replaced within 6 months to 1 year. Whole spices retain their flavour longer than ground. Check flavour of dried herbs by rubbing between fingers, then smell. If there's little scent, discard and restock.

Store fresh herbs in refrigerator in plastic bags (OR give ends of stems a fresh cut, then stand the bunch upright like flowers in a glass of water and cover loosely with plastic bag). Wash herbs with cold water just before using.

Herbs

Anise seed: Strong licorice flavour. Use crushed in cookies and cakes; add whole seeds to soups, stews, applesauce, vegetables (beets, carrots, cabbage).

Basil: Sold fresh and dried; hints of cloves and sage. Wide variety of leaf sizes, flavours and colours (such as purple); large-leaf sweet basil is most common. Essential for classic pesto, wonderful in tomato dishes, egg dishes, hearty soups and with fresh green vegetables.

Bay leaf: Sold whole; woodsy, robust flavour with a slight cinnamon-clove tinge. Super in meat and bean stews, stocks, marinades and pickles. Toss in water when boiling potatoes, carrots or pasta.

Bouquet garni: A small bundle of fresh herbs (usually parsley, thyme and bayleaf, sometimes with celery leaves added), tied together or wrapped in cheesecloth bag for easy removal after being used to flavour soups and stews.

Caraway seed: Taste is nutty, licorice, refreshing. Great in baking (rye bread, cakes, cookies), egg dishes, picnic salads (potato, coleslaw) and with robust vegetables (cabbage, carrots, spinach, beets, turnip, squash).

Celery seed: The seeds of wild celery; strong flavour. Use sparingly in soups, salads, meat dishes and pickling.

Chervil: Sold fresh; mild anise flavour. Complements egg dishes, fish, new potatoes, fresh peas and beans, baby carrots, asparagus, tomatoes.

Chives: Fresh is best; mild onion/garlic taste. Chop and toss into green and potato salads, omelets, devilled eggs, quiche, cheese spreads, dips, cream sauces and soups.

Cilantro: See Coriander, fresh.

Coriander, fresh: Also known as cilantro and Chinese parsley. Used extensively in Asian and Latin American cuisine. Flavour has hints of citrus and sage. Use in salsas, stir-fries and salads, and with seafood, fish and poultry. Fresh coriander root is also used in Southeast Asian cooking.

Coriander seed: Sold whole and ground; aromatic with hints of citrus and sage. Complements fish, chicken, meatloaf, stews (beef, lamb), beans and lentils, curry sauces, apple pie and sauce, bread puddings and rice puddings.

Dill: Sold fresh and dried (usually labelled dillweed); delicate, aromatic, like mild caraway. Excellent with seafood (salmon in particular), chicken, eggs, many vegetables (beets, carrots, cabbage, cauliflower, green beans, potatoes), salad dressings, soups. Dill seed is used in pickling and breads.

Fennel seed: Slight anise taste. Use in fish dishes, soups, salads and dressings.

Fines herbes: See page 248.

Herbes de Provence: See page 248.

Lavender: Strongly aromatic flowers and leaves; use fresh or dried as flavouring in custard sauces, cakes, cookies and desserts; a common component in herbes de Provence.

Lemon balm: Fresh, lemon-scented leaves; slightly bitter flavour. Excellent in teas and other beverages, salad dressings, and with poultry and fish.

Marjoram: Sold fresh and dried; aromatic, sweet, with resinous undertones. Complements roast meats, poultry, mushrooms and vegetables—especially corn, carrots, eggplant, green beans and cauliflower.

Mint: Sold fresh and dried. Aromatic, sweet, cooling. Traditional with lamb and in grain dishes such as tabbouleh; complements roast chicken, fish, tomatoes, green peas, fruit salads, iced tea, yogurt sauce and chilled soups.

Oregano: Sold fresh and dried. Strong, aromatic, pleasantly bitter. Use in tomato dishes, robust soups, vegetable dishes (broccoli, beans, peppers, carrots, peas, mushrooms, eggplant, squash) and with lamb, beef, pork, fish and chicken.

Parsley: Fresh is best. Flat-leaf Italian parsley has more flavour than common curly variety; both blend with other herbs. (Don't confuse Italian parsley with fresh coriander.) Peppery, refreshing. Use in soups, salads, tomato sauce and stews, and on eggs, boiled potatoes and other vegetables.

Rosemary: Sold fresh and dried. Pungent, sweet, pine-like. Complements lamb, veal, pork, poultry, mushrooms, eggplant, peppers, fruits, tomato sauces.

Sage: Sold fresh and dried; strong, musky, slightly bitter. A classic in poultry stuffing. Also complements pork, cheeses, onions, tomatoes, eggplant, green vegetables. Delicious in savoury biscuits.

Savory: Sold fresh and dried; pungent aroma and flavour with echoes of sage and thyme. Summer savory is slightly milder than winter savory and is best for cooking. Use with ground meats, poultry, lamb, soups and hearty vegetables.

Tarragon: Sold fresh and dried; fresh is best, but try to taste before buying (French tarragon has fine flavour; Russian tarragon is bland). Strongly aromatic with anise aspects. Essential for béarnaise sauce; great in mayonnaise, vinaigrettes and tomato soups, and in chicken, veal, fish and egg dishes.

Thyme: Sold fresh and dried; warm, aromatic, slightly clove-like. Complements meat, poultry, fish, soups (vegetable, pea, tomato, onion) and many hearty vegetables. Use chopped in biscuits and breads.

Spices

Allspice: Sold whole or ground; combines flavours of cloves, cinnamon and nutmeg. Use with squash and sweet potato, in barbecue and chili sauces, and in baked goods.

Cardamom: Sold whole or ground; pungently sweet. Use in Scandinavian baking (cookies, cakes), fruit salads and pies, rice pudding. Accents sweet potato and squash dishes.

Cayenne: Ground hot red chile pepper.

Chili powder: See page 244.

Cinnamon: Sold in sticks and ground; sweet, with slight heat. Use in apple dishes, dried fruit compotes, breads and buns, spice cakes and cookies, pies, rice pudding, chocolate drinks and desserts, mulled wine.

Cloves: Sold whole and ground; penetrating flavour both sweet and pungent. Use to stud baked ham, and onions and oranges for flavouring soups and stews. A common spice in chili sauce, gingerbread, spice cakes and cookies, plum pudding and fruit pies.

Cumin: Sold ground and as whole seeds; strong earthy taste. Seeds are best when toasted in a dry skillet before grinding or using whole. Embellishes chili con carne, tamales, stews, barbecue sauce, curries, fish, lamb, poultry, lentils, dried beans, chutneys.

Curry powder: See page 244.

Ginger: Sold fresh (ginger root), ground, candied and preserved in syrup; hot and spicy-sweet. A kitchen trojan for baking (cakes, cookies, gingerbread), desserts (particularly with pears and melon), meat and poultry dishes, vegetables (carrots, sweet potato), chutneys.

Mace: The covering of whole nutmegs. Usually sold ground. Delicate nutmeg-like flavour. Use in breads, soups, punches, fruit salads and desserts, and many kinds of baking. Also good with robust vegetables.

Mustard seed: Whole seeds are used in pickling and in meat dishes. Powdered dry mustard is finely ground mustard seeds; use as seasoning in meat and cheese dishes, salad dressings and sauces; can also be mixed with water to make hot mustard used as a condiment.

Nutmeg: Sold ground or grated; very spicy, sweet. Complements many vegetables (squash, spinach, cauliflower, onions), cream soups, seafood, baked goods, eggnog, fruit dishes, puddings and whipped cream.

Paprika: Sold ground; flavours range from mild to pungent and hot; colours range from bright orange to dark red. Hungarian paprika is usually considered the best for flavour. Use with poultry, veal, eggs and potatoes, and in goulash, soups, salad dressings. Paprika's red colour makes it popular as a garnish.

Saffron: Sold as threads. Dried stigma of the saffron crocus; hand-picking makes it very expensive. Adds distinctive mellow flavour and intense yellow colour to paella, risotto, couscous, bouillabaisse, yeast breads and cakes.

Star anise: Star-shaped pod sold whole or ground; licorice flavour; component of five-spice powder. Used in many Asian cuisines; complements meat and poultry.

Turmeric: Sold ground; musky, earthy aroma; slightly bitter taste; bright yellow colour. Use in chicken, fish, rice and egg dishes; curries, pickles and relishes.

Make your own mixtures

Recipes for spice and herb mixtures vary widely; these are typical combinations that will substitute satisfactorily when you can't find ready-made mixtures. For others, see Substitutions, page 255.

Cajun spice seasoning: Mix 2 tbsp (30 mL) chili powder, 1 tsp (5 mL) each onion powder and garlic powder, 1/2 tsp (2 mL) each ground cumin, cayenne, pepper and salt.

Fines herbes: Mix equal amounts of finely chopped fresh or dried chervil, chives, parsley and tarragon.

Five-spice powder: Mix equal parts ground cinnamon, cloves, star anise, fennel seed and peppercorns (szechuan, if possible).

Garam masala: Mixtures vary widely. Here's one: 1 tsp (5 mL) each black peppercorns, coriander seed, cardamom seed, cumin seed and whole cloves, 1/2 tsp (2 mL) anise seed and 1 cinnamon stick broken in pieces. Roast whole spices in skillet until fragrant (about 2 minutes); let cool. Grind in a spice grinder or with mortar and pestle.

Herbes de Provence: Mix equal amounts of dried basil, thyme, sage, savory, marjoram, rosemary, crushed bay leaves and lavender.

Measuring

Metric and imperial measures are both used in Canadian kitchens. Most Canadian recipes include both systems (in this book, imperial is on the left of the ingredient lists, metric on the right). When using a recipe, stick to one system or the other, not a combination, because the amounts are not exact equivalents.

Liquid measures: For measuring liquids, use standard glass measuring cups with graduated markings (imperial is on one side, metric on the other). When measuring, check the amount at eye level. Glass measuring cups are available in several sizes (1 cup/250 mL, 2 cups/500 mL, 4 cups/1 L, 8 cups/2 L).

L is the abbreviation for litre, mL for millilitre; 1 L equals 1000 mL.

1 cup equals 8 fluid ounces; 1 imperial pint equals 2-1/2 cups (20 fluid oz); 1 imperial quart equals 5 cups (40 fluid oz).

Dry measures are sold in sets of cups and spoons in graduated sizes. To measure a dry ingredient such as flour, spoon it into the measure and level off the top with the straight edge of a knife; don't tap or pack. (The exception is brown sugar, which should be packed enough to hold the cup shape when turned out.) **Measuring spoons** are used for small amounts of both dry and liquid ingredients.

Standard Imperial and Metric measures: The standard sizes for imperial dry measures and spoons are 1 cup, 1/2 cup, 1/3 cup, 1/4 cup; 1 tbsp, 1 tsp, 1/2 tsp, 1/4 tsp.

Canadian metric measures are also volume measures; they are similar to sets of imperial cups and spoons but are not exact equivalents. When the Canadian metric system was introduced in the 1970s, standard measures were established as follows: a set of three dry measures (250 mL, 125 mL, 50 mL) and a set of five small measures (25 mL, 15 mL, 5 mL, 2 mL, 1 mL). To measure 75 mL, use 50 mL plus 25 mL. These are the standard sets to use if you have them.

However, most sets of measuring cups and spoons now available in Canadian stores are marked with dual measures (imperial and metric), such as: 1 cup/250 mL (sometimes 240 mL); 1/2 cup/125 mL (sometimes 120 mL); 1/3 cup/80 mL (sometimes 75 mL); 1/4 cup/60 mL (sometimes 50 mL). Measuring spoons are usually marked as: 1 tbsp/15 mL, 1 tsp/5 mL, 1/2 tsp/2 mL and 1/4 tsp/1 mL; a 25 mL metric measure is rarely included. These sets are not manufactured in Canada and are not standard measures; the metric and imperial amounts are not exact equivalents (one or the other has been rounded off for conversion; sometimes the metric amount is accurate when measured, sometimes the imperial). Fortunately, the differences are small and don't matter in most recipes.

In Canadian recipes, almost all metric measuring is by volume (mL); the only weights you will see in a metric recipe (grams or kilograms) are for ingredients purchased by weight such as meats, cheese and produce. Different measuring systems are used in cookbooks from other countries, especially England and Australia. Most of these books include international conversion tables (not always accurate, and rarely including Canadian metric); others are published in North American editions, with recipes converted to U.S. measures (which are the same as our imperial measures, except for pints, quarts and gallons; 1 U.S. quart equals 4 cups/32 fluid ounces). In Europe, all measurements are metric; dry ingredients are usually weighed on a scale and liquids are measured by volume. British recipes use both imperial and metric measures; dry ingredients may be weighed in ounces or grams; liquids may be measured in fluid ounces or millilitres. Australian measures are all metric; all ingredients are measured by volume in cups (1 cup equals 250 mL); sometimes dry ingredients are given in weighed grams as well.

Equivalents: Baking Pans

(For other Baking Tips, see page 240.)

Baking pan sizes are no longer standardized as they once were. Many new pans (metal and glass) are slightly different in size from older ones of similar shape; they also vary from one manufacturer to another. Many are imported and some are labelled with a jumble of imperial and metric measurements old ones inherited from grandma or discovered at a garage sale. Many pans have no sizes marked on them, or are labelled in imperial when your recipe is metric, or in U.S. pints or quarts (different from imperial), or in linear measures when you (some accurate, some not). Most of us have also accumulated a variety of pans of odd sizes and shapes—interesting ones picked up on travels, unusual ones from import shops, nice need to know volume (or vice versa).

Don't hesitate to use different pans; just be sure they are very similar in dimensions and volume to the pan specified in the recipe. Don't use pans that are smaller in volume than called for (you risk overflow!); slightly larger is usually okay, although the baked product will be shallower. You can usually substitute pans of different shapes (such as round instead of square) if it has the same volume, but don't substitute a pan that is much deeper or shallower or longer or shorter than called for, even if the volume is the same.

When in doubt, check the following chart for equivalents. Measurements are based on the inside measure, across the top. To determine volume, measure the amount of water (or rice or sugar if pan has loose base) needed to fill the pan. To save time in the future, write the size on the bottom of your pan with a waterproof marker.

Note that these are average measurements and approximate equivalents; your pans may vary slightly. Pan sizes also vary somewhat depending on the slope of the sides.

	Dimensions		Volume	
	Imperial (inches)	Metric (centimetres)	Imperial (cups)	Metric (litres)
Round cake pans (layer pans)	8 x 1-1/2	20 x 4	5	1.2
	9 x 1-1/2	23 x 4	6	1.5
Deep round pan	8 x 2-1/2	20 x 6	8	2
Square cake pans	8 x 8 x 2	20 x 20 x 5	8	2
	9 x 9 x 2	23 x 23 x 5	10	2.5
Rectangular pans	11 x 7 x 1-1/2	28 x 18 x 4	8	2
	12 x 8 x 1-3/4	30 x 20 x 4.5	12	3
	13 x 9 x 2	33 x 23 x 5	14	3.5
Loaf pans	8-1/2 x 4-1/2 x 2-1/2	22 x 12 x 6	6	1.5
	9 x 5 x 2-1/2	23 x 13 x 6	8	2
Pie plates	9 x 1-1/4	23 x 4	4	1
	10 x 1-1/2	25 x 4.5	6	1.5
Tube pan	10 x 4	25 x 10	16	4
Bundt pan	10 x 3-3/4	25 x 9.5	12	3
Muffin/tart tins	3 x 1-1/4	8 x 3.5	1/2	125 mL
	2 x 3/4	5 x 2	1/4	60 mL
Springform pans	8 x 2-1/2	20 x 6	8	2
	9 x 2-1/2	23 x 6	10	2.5
	10 x 2-1/2	25 x 6	12	3
Jelly roll pan (rimmed baking sheet)	15 x 10 x 3/4	38 x 25 x 2	8	2
Soufflé dishes	7 x 3-1/2	18 x 8	6	1.5
	8 x 3-3/4	20 x 9.5	10	2.5
Flan/quiche pans	9 x 1-1/4	23 x 3	4	1
	10 x 1-3/4	25 x 4.5	6	1.5

Equivalents (Weight/Volume)

What do you do when a recipe calls for 3 cups of sliced mushrooms and you want to know how many to buy? Or 3 kg of potatoes and you have no scale? Or 1 cup of dried cranberries *and the bulk food store sells by metric weight? Here's a guide to approximate imperial/metric weight/volume equivalents.*

All Quantities Are Approximate
Note: 500 g is a little more than 1 lb.

Vegetables	Weight (as purchased; untrimmed)	Number	Volume (trimmed)
Asparagus	1 lb (500 g)	16–20 med. spears	3 cups (750 mL) pieces (1 in/2.5 cm)
Avocado	1/2 lb (250 g)	1 small	
Bean sprouts	3 oz (100 g)	–	2 cups (500 mL)
Beans, green or yellow	1 lb (500 g)	–	4 cups (1 L) pieces (1 in/2.5 cm)
Beets	1 lb (500 g)	3–4 medium	2 cups (500 mL) diced peeled
Broccoli	1-1/2 lb (750 g)	1 medium bunch	4 cups (1 L) florets
Cabbage	2 lb (1 kg)	1 medium	8 cups (2 L) shredded
Carrots	1 lb (500 g)	5 medium	3 cups (750 mL) diced or grated
Cauliflower	2 lb (1 kg)	1 medium	8 cups (2 L) florets
Celery	–	3 stalks	1 cup (250 mL) chopped
Corn	–	2 ears	1 cup (250 mL) kernels
Corn, whole kernel	–	12-oz (341 mL) can	1-1/3 cups (325 mL) drained
Cucumber	3/4 lb (375 g)	1 medium	2-1/2 cups (625 mL) diced
Eggplant	1-1/2 lb (750 g)	1 medium	5 cups (1.25 L) cubed
Garlic	–	1 medium clove	1 tsp (5 mL) minced
Green onions	–	2 medium	1/2 cup (125 mL) chopped
Leeks	1 lb (500 g)	2 medium	2 cups (500 mL) chopped (white and light green parts)
Legumes (beans, lentils, etc.)	–	19-oz (540 mL) can	2 cups (500 mL) drained
Mushrooms	1 lb (500 g)	–	6 cups (1.5 L) sliced
Onions	1 lb (500 g)	3–4 medium	2-1/2 cups (625 mL) chopped
		1 medium	3/4 cup (175 mL) chopped

All Quantities Are Approximate

Note: 500 g is a little more than 1 lb.

Vegetables	Weight (as purchased; untrimmed)	Number	Volume (trimmed)
Parsnips	1 lb (500 g)	6–8 medium	3 cups (750 mL) sliced
Peas, in pod	1 lb (500 g)	–	1-1/4 cups (300 mL) shelled
Potatoes	1 lb (500 g)	3 medium	3 cups (750 mL) sliced or cubed; 2-1/2 cups (625 mL) diced; 2 cups (500 mL) cooked mashed
Peppers, jalapeño	–	1 medium	1 tbsp (15 mL) minced
Peppers, sweet	1 lb (500 g)	3 medium	2 cups (500 mL) chopped
Rutabaga	2 lb (1 kg)	1 medium	6 cups (1.5 L) cubed; 5 cups (1.25 L) diced; 3 cups (750 mL) cooked mashed
Shallots	–	1 medium	1 tbsp (15 mL) minced
Snow peas	1 lb (500 g)	–	4 cups (1 L)
Spinach, fresh	10-oz (284 g) pkg	–	12 cups (3 L) untrimmed and lightly packed; 1-1/4 cups (300 mL) cooked
Spinach, frozen	300 g pkg	–	1-1/4 cups (300 mL) thawed and drained
Squash, winter	1 lb (500 g)	–	1-1/4 cups (300 mL) cooked mashed
Sweet potato	1 lb (500 g)	2 medium	2 cups (500 mL) cooked mashed
Tomatoes	1 lb (500 g)	3 medium	2 cups (500 mL) chopped
Tomatoes, canned	–	28-oz (796 mL) can	2-1/2 cups (625 mL) drained
Turnip, white	1 lb (500 g)	3 medium	3 cups (750 mL) cubed
Zucchini	1 lb (500 g)	3 (6-in/15 cm)	3 cups (750 mL) coarsely grated

All Quantities Are Approximate
Note: 500 g is a little more than 1 lb.

Fruits	Weight (as purchased; untrimmed)	Number	Volume (trimmed)
Apples	1 lb (500 g)	3 medium	3 cups (750 mL) sliced
Apricots	1 lb (500 g)	8–10 medium	2 cups (500 mL) chopped
Apricots, dried	1 lb (500 g)	–	3 cups (750 mL)
Bananas	1 lb (500 g)	3 medium	1 cup (250 mL) mashed
Berries	1-pint container	–	About 2 cups (500 mL)
Cherries	1 lb (500 g)		About 2-1/2 cups (625 mL) pitted
Cherries, dried	1/2 lb (250 g)	–	2 cups (500 mL)
Cranberries	1 lb (500 g)	–	4 cups (1 L)
	12-oz (350 g) pkg		3 cups (750 mL)
Cranberries, dried	1/2 lb (250 g)	–	2 cups (500 mL)
Kiwifruit	1 lb (500 g)	5–6 medium	3 cups (750 mL) sliced
Lemons	–	1 medium	3–4 tbsp (45–60 mL) juice; 2–3 tsp (10–15 mL) grated rind
Limes	–	1 medium	2 tbsp (30 mL) juice; 1 tsp (5 mL) grated rind
Mango	1 lb (500 g)	1 medium	1-1/2 cups (375 mL) diced
Melon, such as cantaloupe	1-1/2 lb (750 g)	1 medium	3 cups (750 mL) cubed
Oranges	1 lb (500 g)	2–3 medium	1 cup (250 mL) juice; 3 tbsp (45 mL) grated rind
Peaches	1 lb (500 g)	3–4 medium	2 cups (500 mL) sliced
Pears	1 lb (500 g)	3–4 medium	2 cups (500 mL) sliced
Pineapple	2-1/2 lb (1.25 kg)	1 medium	3 cups (750 mL) cubed
Plums	1 lb (500 g)	8 medium	3 cups (750 mL) sliced
Raspberries	1 lb (500 g)	–	4 cups (1 L) whole; 2 cups (500 mL) crushed
Rhubarb	1 lb (500 g)	6 stalks	3 cups (750 mL) pieces (1 in/2.5 cm)
Strawberries	1 lb (500 g)	–	4 cups (1 L) whole; 3 cups (750 mL) sliced; 2 cups (500 mL) crushed

All Quantities Are Approximate
Note: 500 g is a little more than 1 lb.

Baking Supplies	Weight	Volume
Candied fruit	1/2 lb (250 g)	1-1/12 cups (375 mL)
Chocolate chips	300 g pkg	1-3/4 cups (425 mL)
Dates	1 lb (500 g)	3 cups (750 mL) chopped
Nuts, chopped or ground	100 g pkg	About 1 cup (250 mL)
Raisins	1 lb (500 g)	3 cups (750 mL)
Shortening	1-lb (454 g) pkg	2-1/3 cups (575 mL)
Sugar, brown	1 lb (500 g)	2-1/2 cups (625 mL)
Sugar, granulated	1 lb (500 g)	2 cups (500 mL)
Sugar, icing	1 lb (500 g)	4 cups (1 L) sifted
Yeast	1 envelope active dry	Scant 1 tbsp (15 mL)

Dairy	Weight	Volume
Butter	1-lb (454 g) pkg	2 cups (500 mL)
Cheese (cheddar, swiss, mozzarella)	1/2 lb (250 g)	2 cups (500 mL) shredded
Cheese, parmesan	1/4 lb (125 g)	1 cup (250 mL) grated
Whipping cream	1 cup (250 mL)	About 2 cups (500 mL) whipped

Substitutions in a Pinch

(But only in a pinch!) It's always best to read through the recipe and be prepared ahead of time. But occasionally we all run out of an ingredient in the middle of a recipe, and emergency substitutions are useful if you can't make a quick trip to the store.

Sometimes a minor substitution makes little difference to the final product; avoid substitutions where the flavour or texture will be substantially altered.

If you don't have...		Substitute...
Allspice	1 tsp (5 mL)	1/2 tsp (2 mL) cinnamon plus pinch ground cloves
Anchovies	2 fillets, minced	1 tsp (5 mL) anchovy paste
Arrowroot: see Thickeners, page 256		
Baking powder	1 tsp (5 mL)	1/4 tsp (1 mL) baking soda plus 1/2 tsp (2 mL) cream of tartar
Balsamic vinegar	1 tbsp (15 mL)	1 tbsp (15 mL) red wine vinegar plus pinch granulated sugar
Butter, salted	1 cup (250 mL)	1 cup (250 mL) unsalted butter plus 1/2 tsp (2 mL) salt
Buttermilk	1 cup (250 mL)	1 tbsp (15 mL) vinegar or lemon juice plus enough milk to make 1 cup (250 mL); let stand 5 minutes
Chocolate, unsweetened	1 oz (30 g)	3 tbsp (45 mL) cocoa plus 1 tbsp (15 mL) butter
Cornstarch, potato starch: see Thickeners, page 256		
Egg	1 whole	2 egg whites (for lower fat)
	2 yolks	1 whole egg
Flour, cake-and-pastry	1 cup (250 mL)	1 cup (250 mL) less 2 tbsp (30 mL) all-purpose flour
Flour, self-raising	1 cup (250 mL)	1 cup (250 mL) all-purpose flour plus 1-1/2 tsp (7 mL) baking powder and 1/4 tsp (1 mL) salt
Herbs, fresh	1 tbsp (15 mL) chopped	1 tsp (15 mL) dried
Hot pepper substitutions: see page 256		
Italian seasoning		Equal parts dried basil, oregano, thyme, marjoram, sage, rosemary
Lemongrass	1 stalk	1 tsp (5 mL) grated lemon or lime rind
Poultry seasoning	1 tsp (5 mL)	3/4 tsp (4 mL) dried sage plus 1/4 tsp (1 mL) dried thyme

If you don't have...		Substitute...
Pumpkin pie spice	1 tsp (5 mL)	1/2 tsp (2 mL) cinnamon, 1/4 tsp (1 mL) ground ginger, pinch each nutmeg and ground cloves
Rice vinegar		White wine vinegar plus pinch granulated sugar
Rice wine		Dry sherry or vermouth
Sour cream	1 cup (250 mL)	1 cup (250 mL) yogurt
Sugar (superfine/fruit)		Granulated sugar processed in food processor until very fine
Tapioca: see Thickeners, below		
Yeast	1 tbsp (15 mL) or 1 cake	1 envelope active dry yeast

Thickeners: 2 tbsp (30 mL) all-purpose flour equals 1 tbsp (15 mL) cornstarch, potato starch or arrowroot OR 1-1/2 tbsp (22 mL) quick-cooking tapioca.

Hot pepper substitutions: The following are interchangeable in approximately equal amounts: hot pepper flakes, crushed dried chiles, cayenne, hot pepper sauce, chile paste. To replace 1 minced small fresh chile pepper, use 1/4 to 1/2 tsp (1 to 2 mL) of any of the above.

For Spice and Herb mixtures: see page 248.
For unfamiliar ingredients: see Global Pantry, page 244.

Safety First

Most food-borne illness can be prevented by proper handling and storage of food. Follow these rules to keep bacteria at bay:

- Keep everything in the kitchen very clean.
- Wash hands thoroughly with soap and water before handling food.
- Keep cold foods cold and hot foods hot—bacteria multiply quickly at room temperture; the danger zone is between 40F (4C) and 140F (60C).
- Never leave raw poultry, meat, fish, eggs or dairy products at room temperature.
- Keep your refrigerator temperature at or below 40F (4C) and freezer at 0F (−18C).
- Purchase frozen and refrigerated foods at the end of your shopping trip; store promptly at home.
- Thaw foods in refrigerator or microwave, not at room temperature; if thawed in microwave, finish cooking immediately.
- Refrigerate or freeze leftovers within 2 hours of cooking.
- Unsafe foods do not necessarily look or smell spoiled. If in doubt, throw it out.

Refrigerator Storage

Check best-before dates on perishable foods such as dairy products and vacuum-packed meats. The dates indicate how long foods will retain their freshness and be safe to eat if properly refrigerated, but don't apply once the package is opened. After opening, use within time indicated in list below. Some unopened dairy products can be used a few days after the best-before date but won't taste as fresh; use them for cooking or baking. Other foods such as fresh meats are labelled with a packaging date; if you can't use them within time indicated below, freeze immediately.

- Ground meats and sausage, raw: 2 days
- Poultry, raw: 1 to 2 days; cooked: 3 to 4 days
- Meat, raw or cooked: 3 to 4 days
- Fish and shellfish: 1 to 2 days
- Deli and vacuum-packed meats (opened): 3 to 5 days
- Poultry or meat casseroles, stews, soups: 2 to 3 days
- Firm cheese: several months
- Processed cheese (opened): 3 to 4 weeks
- Salad dressings and mayonnaise (opened): 2 months
  When in doubt, throw it out.

Freezing

For freezer storage, wrap foods airtight in heavy plastic freezer wrap or foil, or pack in freezer bags or airtight containers. Thaw in refrigerator or microwave, not at room temperature. Never refreeze raw foods that have thawed (including raw meat labelled "previously frozen" when puchased); they can be cooked and then refrozen.

Poultry and Meat

- Careful handling is especially important with raw chicken, turkey and all ground meats.
- After preparing raw poultry and ground meats, wash hands, knives, utensils and work surfaces thoroughly with hot soapy water. Sanitize cutting boards and countertops with chlorine bleach solution.
- Keep raw poultry and meat refrigerated and wrapped separately from other foods.
- Never return cooked food to a plate or bowl that held raw poultry or meat (such as when barbecuing).
- Marinate poultry and meat in refrigerator, if marinating time is longer than 30 minutes. If reusing marinade as a basting sauce, boil for 1 minute first.
- Cook poultry and ground meat thoroughly (no pink colour remains; juices run clear).
- For safety tips for thawing and stuffing turkey, see page 92.

Eggs: See page 142.

Flavoured oils

Homemade flavoured oils containing garlic or herbs must be refrigerated and used within 1 week, or they carry a risk of botulism. If accidentally left at room temperature, discard. If you make your own flavoured oils for drizzling on bread or vegetables, prepare them fresh and use promptly. If making for gifts, caution recipients to refrigerate and use within a week.

The Wine and Food Match-Maker

Wine puts the smile in good food. Pairing wine and food is fun, and you can be fearless because it's hard to mess up. The traditional rule of white wine with white meats and fish, red wine with red meats is a fine starting point, but it's a rule to break whenever you feel like it. For example, you can confidently serve reds with grilled or roasted pork, turkey, chicken, even salmon. Think of robust, oaky-smoky barrel-aged white wines as reds.

Fruit, acidity, tannins and sweetness all affect how wines work with a dish. Above all, the secret is balance: match light-bodied wines with light dishes, full-bodied wine with hearty fare. "Body" is determined by the level of alcohol (you'll find it on the label): 8–10% in a light-bodied wine; 10–12% medium; 12–16% full-bodied.

When cooking with wine, use a wine you enjoy drinking; its flavour will echo in the food. Avoid a riot of food flavours with a "serious" wine; a simple dish is the best foil.

Serving Tips

- If you're serving several wines, pour light-bodied before heavy, dry before sweet, white before red, young before old.

- Portions: For a reception or dinner, reckon about half a bottle per guest (a 26-oz/750 mL bottle equals about 6 glasses). For a wine-tasting, a 2-oz (60 mL) serving is sufficient.

- Stemware: Use narrow, tulip-shaped glasses filled no more than one-third to one-half full, and big enough to safely swirl, sniff the bouquet and sip the wine. All-purpose glasses are fine. White wine glasses are smaller to keep the wine chilled; red wine glasses are bigger to capture reds' more complex scents.

- Temperature: Serve white wines chilled and reds cool, not dulled by summer heat or a warm room. Using an ice bucket is fine, even for elegant reds and especially for light-bodied, fruity Beaujolais, Gamay or Merlot (5 to 10 minutes in ice water). Sparkling wine should be well chilled (8C/47F, or 15 minutes in an ice bucket).

- Wrap a napkin around the bottle as you lift it from an ice bucket.

- Pour from your guest's right without lifting the glass, twisting the bottle slightly as you finish to prevent drips.

Storing

You don't need a fancy cellar unless you buy ageable, collectible wines. Keep wine in a cool, dark place, away from vibrations or smelly things like paint; a cool closet that is not too dry or humid is fine. Store the bottles on their sides so corks stay moist and airtight. For longer storage, ideal humidity is 70–90%; ideal temperature is 13C (55F); otherwise just try to avoid dramatic fluctuations.

At the Wine Store

For light- and medium-bodied white and red wines, choose from cool regions like northern France and northern Italy, Germany, Ontario, British Columbia, Oregon, New York and New Zealand. These are great food wines, with zippy acidity to refresh the taste buds and brighten food flavours.

For full-bodied, oaky and fruity whites and reds, think Australia, Argentina, Chile, British Columbia, Ontario, California, Washington, Portugal, Spain, Greece, southern France, Italy, North Africa and South Africa.

Regional wines, naturally, go well with regional dishes; for example, Burgundy with coq au vin or boeuf bourguignon, Alsatian Riesling with ham or onion tart, Rioja with paella, Amarone with osso bucco, Okanagan Pinot Blanc with salmon, Niagara late-harvest Riesling with peaches.

VQA (Vintners' Quality Alliance): The Canadian appellation system that regulates standards of production, quality and origin, the consumer's assurance of top-quality Canadian wines.

Sugar code: These numbers indicate a wine's residual sugar (in grams per litre) and sweetness. O: very dry; 1–2: dry; 3–6: medium; 7 and over: sweet

Basic Wine Styles

Look for these names on the labels:

Light lively white: Bordeaux, Chablis, British Columbia and Ontario Riesling, Ontario Chardonnay, Italian Pinot Grigio, Mâcon, Mosel Trocken, Muscadet, Sauvignon Blanc, Soave, Vinho Verde

Medium-bodied fruity white: Chardonnay (Burgundy), Chenin Blanc, Fumé Blanc, Orvieto, Pinot Blanc, Pinot Gris, Riesling (dry, off-dry), Sancerre, Sémillon, Verdicchio

Full-bodied oaky white: Australia, California and British Columbia Chardonnay; estate-bottled Burgundy such as Meursault; Graves, Rhône, Rioja

Light lively red: Barbera, Bardolino, Beaujolais, young Bordeaux, Cabernet Franc, Chianti, Gamay, Merlot, Pinot Noir, Valpolicella

Medium-bodied fruity red: Beaujolais from named villages; older Bordeaux; Burgundy; Chianti Classico; Chile and South Africa Cabernet, Pinot Noir or Merlot; Douro (Portugal); Rioja; and blends such as Cabernet-Merlot

Full-bodied red: Amarone, Barbaresco, Barolo, chateau-bottled Bordeaux, California Cabernet, Dão (Portugal), Hermitage, Malbec, Petite Syrah, Rhône, Shiraz, Syrah, Zinfandel; and blends such as Cabernet-Shiraz from Australia

Naturally sweet: Barsac, Chenin Blanc, Icewine; late-harvest Gewürztraminer, Riesling, Sauvignon Blanc and Vidal; Sau-ternes, Tokay, Vin Santo

Dry fortified (sherries): Fino (light, bone-dry); Amontillado (darker, more pungent); Oloroso (nuttier, richer)

Sweet fortified: Cream Sherry, Madeira, Marsala, Muscat, Port

Rosé: dry to sweet; still or sparkling

Sparkling: Champagne (bone dry to sweet); good-value alternatives from Australia, Canada, France's Loire Valley, Germany, Italy (Prosecco and Asti Spumante), Spain, United States

Food and Wine Matches

Appetizers: dry sherry, sparking or light lively wine

Pâtés, foie gras: naturally sweet or sweet fortified

Oysters, mussels, clams: light lively white

Crab, lobster, scallops, shrimp: medium-bodied fruity white

Fish, white: light lively white or medium-bodied fruity white

Fish, oily (such as salmon): medium-bodied fruity white or light lively red

Smoked fish or meats: full-bodied oaky white or medium-bodied fruity red

Grilled or roasted lamb, pork, sausages, burgers, ribs: medium-bodied fruity red

Beef, venison: full-bodied red

Veal: full-bodied oaky white or light lively red

Chicken: light lively white or red

Turkey: light lively red or full-bodied oaky white

Goose, duck: light lively red

Ham: light lively white or red

Cold cuts, charcuterie, pizza: light lively red

Tomato-flavoured dishes: full-bodied red

Herb-flavoured dishes: light lively white

Citrus-flavoured dishes: light lively white

Hot and spicy dishes: off-dry Riesling, Gewürztraminer, sparkling wine, or beer from a local microbrewery

Chinese, Thai dishes: medium-bodied fruity white or Chinese beer

Teriyaki-flavoured dishes: full-bodied red

Curry-flavoured dishes: Start with a glass of wine before dinner, then switch to cold beer or mineral water.

Salads with vinegar: Drink mineral water instead of wine (vinegar makes wine taste sour) or make the salad dressing with sherry or fruit juice.

Desserts: naturally sweet or sweet fortified

Fruit desserts: naturally sweet or sparkling

Chocolate: sweet fortified or fruit liqueurs

Cheeses, mild: light lively red or medium-bodied fruity white

Cheeses, strong: full-bodied red or sweet fortified

Nuts: sweet fortified

Healthy Eating

Eating well requires a little planning—but don't most good things?

Healthy eating means making good choices, putting the focus on the foods you need every day, not on what you can't have. Good food is one of the great pleasures of life, and a healthy relationship with food—eating in moderation, choosing a wide variety of foods, including treats without overdoing it—means enjoyment, not guilt. Maintain a healthy body weight by being active and eating well.

Canada's Food Guide to Healthy Eating tells you the kinds of foods to choose and how much you need every day to get essential nutrients. Copies are available from your community or provincial health department.

Choose a variety of foods from each of the four food groups. The Food Guide gives a range of servings; young children can have the lowest number; male teenagers get the highest number; most other people can choose somewhere in between.

Here are the recommended number of servings for each of the food groups, followed by examples of one serving within each.

Grain Products: 5 to 12 servings each day (1 slice bread; 1/2 bagel or roll; 1/2 cup/125 mL pasta or rice). Choose whole-grain and enriched products often.

Vegetables and Fruit: 5 to 10 servings each day (1/2 cup/125 mL raw or cooked vegetables or fruit; 1/2 cup/125 mL juice; 1 cup/250 mL salad). Choose dark green and orange vegetables and orange fruits often.

Milk Products: Children, 2 to 3 servings each day; youths, 3 to 4 servings; adults, 2 to 4 servings (1 cup/250 mL milk; 1-1/2 oz/50 g cheese; 3/4 cup/175 mL yogurt). Choose lower-fat milk products often.

Meat and Alternatives: 2 to 3 servings each day (1-1/2 to 3 oz/50 to 100 g meat, poultry or fish; 1 to 2 eggs; 1/2 to 1 cup/125 to 250 mL beans; 2 tbsp/30 mL peanut butter). Choose leaner meats, poultry and fish, and use more dried peas, beans and lentils.

Tips for Trimming the Fat

- Use nonstick pans so you can use little or no fat.

- Grill or broil food instead of frying it.

- Remove fat from meat either before or after cooking.

- Watch portion sizes. Serve larger portions of nutritious low-fat foods and smaller portions of high-fat foods.

- Keep healthy snacks handy; avoid high-fat snacks.

- Use herbs and spices to increase flavour when you cut down on fat.

- When using high-fat foods, choose full-flavoured ones (such as extra-virgin olive oil instead of vegetable oil in salad; old cheddar cheese instead of mild) so you don't need to add as much.

- Choose low-fat versions of milk, cheese, sour cream, yogurt and mayonnaise.

- If you have favourite recipes that are high in fat, use a lower-fat version of the ingredients (such as sour cream). Change the cooking method (from frying to broiling, for example).

- If one dish on the menu is high in fat, eat a small portion and choose low-fat accompaniments.

- Remember to look at your whole day's fat intake, rather than the fat content of individual foods or meals. If you had a heavy lunch, make supper light. If you've really overdone it, don't despair. Reduce your intake for the next few days and step up your exercise.

- For reliable sources of nutrition information or advice on special diets, consult your public health department nutritionists, hospital dietitians or registered professional dietitians in private practice. For restricted diets (such as diabetics and allergies), contact the national or regional associations.

Menus

Spring Flings

Eastern Mediterranean Easter Dinner

- Hummus with pita (page 16)
- Avgolemono (page 38)
- Roast Leg of Lamb with rosemary and garlic (page 88)
- Rice Pilaf (page 132)
- Roasted Ratatouille (page 160)
- Spinach Salad with toasted pinenuts (page 237) and yogurt dressing (page 47)
- Minted Fruit Salad Bowl (page 178)
- Braided Festive Bread (page 171) or traditional Easter bread (purchased)

A Spring Brunch For Moms' Day

- Minted Mimosas (page 225)
- Asparagus Vinaigrette (page 50)
- Easy Eggs Benedict with smoked salmon (page 144)
- Pavlova with fresh fruit (page 188)

A Wedding Rehearsal Buffet

- White Wine Sangria (page 225) or Raspberry Champagne Punch (page 226)
- Smoked Salmon Torta (page 24)
- Avocado and Shrimp (page 26)
- Flower Salad (page 45)
- Maple-Mustard Glazed Ham (page 86)
- Light Scalloped Potatoes (page 156)
- Glazed Fruit Tart (page 219)

Tea For The Book Club

- Selection of teas (page 222)
- Tortilla Roll-ups with smoked salmon (page 20)
- Mini-pitas filled with cheese pâté and sliced cucumbers (page 20)
- Cream Tea Scones with fresh strawberries (page 170)
- Chocolate Chunk Shortbread Cookies (page 209)
- Lemon-Poppyseed Pound Cake (page 201)

Bistro Supper

- Moules à la Marinière (page 69)
- Poulet Rôti (Roast Chicken with Lemon, Rosemary and Garlic) (page 94)
- Pommes Frites (page 157)
- French-Style Peas with Lettuce (page 155)
- Mesclun Salad (page 49) with Balsamic Vinaigrette (page 46)
- Crème Brulée (page 185)

A Taste of Southeast Asia

- Spring Rolls with Dipping Sauce (page 23)
- Satays with Peanut Sauce (page 23)
- Pad Thai (page 129)
- Mango sorbet and almond cookies (purchased)

Happy Birthday (indoors or out)

- Layered Taco Dip (page 17)
- Chicken and Beef Fajitas (page 30)
- Chocolate Layer Cake (page 200)
- Real Lemonade (page 224)

The Good Old Summertime

Wave-the-Maple-Leaf Picnic

- Assorted dips and spreads (page 15)
- Grilled Flank Steak (page 54) and
    Oven-Fried Chicken (page 100)
- Fresh Tomato Salsa (page 233)
- Traditional Potato Salad (page 58)
- Strawberry Dipping Dessert (page 179)
- Nanaimo Bars, Lemon Squares,
    Butter Tart Squares (pages 213-214)

Neighbourhood Pool Party

- Bruschetta (page 13)
- Grilled Burgers (choice of meats or
    vegetarian), (pages 111-112)
- Mediterranean Pasta Salad (page 57)
- Mixed Bean Salad (page 55)
- Ice Cream with choice of Toppings (page 180)

A Caribbean Jump-Up

- Sangria (page 225) and Four-
    Fruit Punch (page 226)
- Caribbean Curry Chicken (page 102) or
    Jerk Chicken (page 101)
- Jamaican Rice and Peas (page 134)
- Creamy Cole Slaw (page 51)
- Sliced tomatoes and cucumbers (purchased)
- Tropical Fruit Salad Bowl (page 178)
- Spiced Banana Coconut Bread (page 166)

Seashore Supper

- Herb-Marinated Goat Cheese Salad (page 24)
- Canadian Cioppino (page 70)
- Black Olive and Sun-dried Tomato
    Focaccia (page 175)
- Blueberry-Peach Cobbler (page 191)

Summer Soup & Salad Suppers

- Cool Cucumber Soup (page 42) and
    Salade Niçoise (page 50)
- Gazpacho (page 42) and
    Chunky Chicken Salad (page 53)
- Mango Melon Soup (page 42) and
    Grilled Seafood Salad (page 54)

Dad's Day Off

- Easy Caesar Salad (page 47)
- Grilled rib-eye steaks (page 73) with
    Herb Butter (page 18)
- Grilled skewered new potatoes and
    onions (page 108)
- Cornbread (page 168)
- Rhubarb Custard Pie (page 218)

No-Labour Labour Day Barbecue

- Chicken Brochettes with Herbed Citrus
    Marinade (page 109)
- Marinated Vegetable Salad (page 57)
- Make-Ahead Cole Slaw (page 51)
- Herbed Garlic Bread (page 176)
- Grilled Peaches with ice cream (page 179)

Fall Feasting

Home From the Farmers' Market

- Autumn Salad with Honey-
    Broiled Apples (page 52)
- Roast Loin of Pork with Cider (page 84)
- Braised Red Cabbage with
    Red Onions and Apples (page 158)
- Baked Winter Squash (page 153)
- Plum Galette (page 219)

Traditional Thanksgiving Dinner

- Roasted Vegetable Soup (page 35)
- Roast Turkey (page 92) with
    Cranberry-Apricot Stuffing (page 93)
- Wild Rice, Barley and Mushroom Pilaf
    Casserole (page 132)
- Broccoli and Sweet Red Pepper Salad (page 155)
- Pumpkin Pie (page 220) with
    candied ginger and whipped cream

Kids' Hallowe'en Party

- Party Punch with
    gummyworm ice cubes (page 226)
- Nachos (page 21)
- Chicken Fingers with
    three Dipping sauces (page 22)
- Raw Vegetables with Herbed Dip (page 15)
- Spider Ice Cream Cake (page 196)

Grey Cup Grazing

- Crudités with two Creamy Dips (page 15)
- Hot Salsa Dip (page 18)
- Glazed Chicken Wings (page 22)
- Beef & Pork Chili with Ancho Sauce (page 80)
- Butterscotch Brownies and
    Fudgy Brownies (page 212)

Come for Coffee

- Fruit Streusel Coffeecake (page 199)
- Lemon-Cranberry Scones (page 170)
- Carrot-Orange Muffins (page 164)
- Chocolate-Nut Biscotti (page 211)
- Iced Coffee, Quick Latte, Moccachino (page 223)

Buon Appetito

- Antipasto Platter (page 12)
- Crusty Italian bread (purchased)
- Pesto Pasta (page 124) or Risotto (page 134)
    (first course portions)
- Veal Scaloppine (Piccata, Marsala or
    Mushroom) (page 87)
- Salad of arugula, radicchio and
    leaf lettuce (page 49)
- Zabaglione (page 187) and Lemon-
    Almond Biscotti (page 211)

Vegetarian Fall Fare

- Harvest Soup (page 35)
- Mediterranean Spicy Rice and Beans (page 138)
- Dill-Ricotta Bread (page 173)
- Caramel Apple Pudding (page 192)

Winter Warm-ups

Off the Slopes, Into the Soup

- Mulled Cider (page 225)

- A selection of hearty soups and breads
    (all make-ahead):
    Splendid Seafood Chowder (page 39)
    Country Kitchen Pea Soup (page 40)
    Minestrone with Sausage (page 34)
    Beer-Caraway Soda Bread (page 169)
    Oatmeal Bread (page 174)
    Crusty baguette or Italian bread (purchased)

- Winter Fruit Compote (page 181)

- Mochaccino (page 223) and
    Nutty Biscotti (page 211)

Un-Turkey Christmas Dinner

- Cranberry Consommé (page 38)

- Prime Rib au Jus (page 72)

- Brussels sprouts with pancetta (page 155)

- Roasted Vegetables (page 154)

- Glazed Braised Shallots or Pearl Onions (page 159)

- Steamed Cranberry Pudding with
    Custard Sauce (page 192)

Pub Party

- Seafood Bar
    steamed mussels (page 69)
    oysters on the half shell (page 62)
    smoked salmon torta (page 24)

- Deep-Dish Steak Pies (page 78)

- Make-Ahead Slaw (page 51)

- Quick-Pickled Vegetables (page 230)

- Fresh Fruit Trifle (page 185)

On a Cold Winter's Night

- Creamy Cauliflower Soup (page 35)

- Braised Lamb Shanks (page 89)

- Garlic Mashed Potatoes (page 157)

- Sautéed Rapini (page 155)

- Baked Fruit Crisp (page 190)

An Indian Curry Dinner

- Lamb or Vegetarian Curry (page 116) with
    Raita, poppadums and
    other accompaniments (page 102)

- Basmati Rice (page 131)

- Chai (page 222)

Memories of Mexico

- Guacamole with corn chips (page 17)

- Quesadillas (page 21)

- Tortilla Soup (page 41)

- Orange Crème Caramel (page 186)

A Valentine for Two

- Oysters on the Half Shell (page 62)

- Sautéed Steak with Red Wine Shallot
    Sauce (page 76)

- Mixed Mushroom Sauté (page 155)

- Salad of reds and greens with
    Herbed Vinaigrette (page 47)

- Hot Apricot Soufflés (page 184)

- Chocolate Truffles (page 195)

Easy Entertaining

Fuss-free dinner parties, casual or classy

Impromptu 1

- Prosciutto-Asparagus Bundles (page 25)
- Herbed Garlic Baguette (page 176)
- Quick Mixed Grill (lamb chops, red peppers, zucchini), (page 90)
- Peaches and Blueberries with Creamy Orange Sauce (page 178)

Impromptu 2

- Scallop Soup (page 38)
- Grilled Chicken Breasts (page 106) with Minted Marinade (page 110)
- Quinoa Pilaf (page 132)
- Cherry Tomato Salad (page 42)
- Figs with Mascarpone (page 178) or Fruit and Cheese Dessert Plate (page 179)

Make-ahead 1

- Country Kitchen Pea Soup, reheated (page 40)
- Herb-Roasted Chicken Breasts with Garlic, Potatoes and Carrots (page 96)
- Mixed Slaw with Apples and Lentils (page 51)
- Oatmeal Mini-Loaves (page 174)
- Fresh Fruit Trifle (page 185)

Make-ahead 2

- Pork and Beef Chili with Ancho Sauce (page 80)
- Creamy Coleslaw (page 51)
- Cornbread (page168)
- Cheesecake (page 190) with Raspberry-Blueberry Topping (page 180)

Easy Impressive

- Baked Brie Wedges on Mesclun (page 25)
- Roast Cornish Hens with Orange-Almond Rice Stuffing (page 96)
- Broccoli-Cauliflower Gratin (page 155)
- Orange-Glazed Carrots (page 158)
- Lemon Snow on Raspberry Coulis (page 183)
- Chocolate Angel Food Cake (page 201)

Easy Elegant

- Wild Mushroom Soup (page 36)
- Chicken Breasts with Prosciutto and Fontina (page 100)
- Risotto (page 134) or Rice Pilaf (page 132)
- Broccoli and Roasted Red Pepper Salad (page 48)
- A Trio of Flavours (Fast and Easy Mousses, page 183) or Tulip Dessert Cups (page 188)

Really Cool

- Cool Cucumber Soup (page 42)
- Salade Nicoise (page 50)
- Roasted Garlic Bread (page 176)
- Frozen Raspberry-Mango Cake (page 196)

Winter Fireside

- Mulled Wine or Cider (page 225)
- Mussels with Tomatoes and Basil (page 69)
- Swiss Cheese Fondue (page 147)
- Peach or Pear Crumble Pie (page 217)
- Mochaccino (page 223)

Summer Rustic

- Cedar-Planked Salmon (page 68)
- Wild Rice, Barley and
     Mushroom Pilaf Casserole (page 132)
- Mixed Cabbage Slaw (page 51)
- Bumbleberry Pie (page 218)

Classic Comforts

- Minestrone (page 34)
- Osso Bucco (page 89) or Italian Pot Roast (page 75)
- Polenta (page 138) or Garlic Mashed Potatoes (page 157)
- Carrots, Celery and Fennel Parmigiana (page 155)
- Tiramisù (page 187)

All Wrapped Up

- Mini-pitas with choice of fillings (page 20)
- Fish en Papillote (page 66)
- Peppers Stuffed with
     Spicy Rice (omit shrimp; page 161)
- Tomatoes Provençal (page 160)
- Herbed Garlic Bread (page 176)
- Chocolate or Hazelnut Roulade (page 202)

On the Patio

- Mango-Melon Soup (page 42)
- Sesame-Crusted Salmon on Greens (page 65)
- Fresh Berry Fool (page 179) with
     Crisp Lemon Wafers (page 211)

Indoors or Out

- Focaccia (page 175)
- Grilled or Broiled Butterflied Leg of Lamb (page 90)
- Bistro Potato Salad (page 58)
- Marinated Vegetable Salad (page 57)
- Fresh Fruit Cream Torte (page 202)

Indulgent

- Artichokes with Herbed Lemon-Dill Butter (page 161)
- Fettucine with Shiitake Mushrooms (page 126)
- Watercress salad with crumbled blue cheese,
     slivers of pear and balsamic dressing (page 49)
- Sabayon-Topped Fruit Gratinée (page 178) or
     Strawberries with Balsamic Reduction (page 178)
- Chocolate Truffles (page 195)

Company Chicken

- Avocado and Shrimp (page 26)
- Maple-Hoisin or Lemon-Garlic Chicken (page 98)
- Rice or Bulgur Pilaf (page 132)
- Stir-fried snow peas, pearl onions and
     mushrooms (page 118; omit meat)
- Hazelnut or Chocolate Roulade (page 202)

Taste of Spain

- Tapas (page 12)
- Paella (page 133)
- Mixed green salad with Citrusy Vinaigrette (page 46)
- Pears poached in red wine (page 181)

East Meets West

- Hot and Sour Soup (page 40)
- Steamed Sea Bass with Ginger (page 67)
- White Rice (page 130)
- Stir-fried broccoli & red peppers (page 118; omit meat)
- Chinese Cabbage Slaw (page 51)
- Fruit Takes the Cake (page 178)

Rush-Hour Suppers

Ready in about half an hour

For other side-dish salads, see Quick Tosses and Winning
Combinations, see pages 48-9

For Easy Fruit Desserts, see pages 178-9

Serve with green salad:

- Sauce-and-Toss Fast Pasta (pages 124-5)
- Baked Potatoes with Toppings
- Easy Macaroni and Cheese (page 128)
- Ravioli or Tortellini Casserole (page 126)
- Beef Noodle Skillet Dinner (page 82)
- Pasta e Fagioli (page 127)

Serve with crusty bread, biscuits or cornbread (from freezer):

- Super Stir-Fry (page 118)
- Quick Chili (page 80)
- Marvellous Meatless Chili (page 140)
- Vegetable Fritatta (page 145)
- Classic French Omelet (page 145)
- Sausage and Mushroom Scramble (page 144)

Serve with rice or noodles and green salad or microwaved broccoli:

- Speedy Skillet Chops
  or Chicken (3 variations; page 107)
- Fast Fish (3 variations; page 64)
- Grilled Fish (page 64)
- Herbed Rainbow Trout (page 67)
- Steamed Sea Bass with Black Bean Sauce (page 67)
- Glazed Chicken Wings (page 22)

Serve with make-ahead salads:

(Cole Slaw, page 51; Marinated Vegetable Salad, page 57;
Marinated Bean Salad, page 55)

- Oven-Fried Fish and Chips (page 66)
- Oven-Fried Chicken Fingers (page 100)
- Beef-Noodle Skillet Dinner (page 82)
- Easy Oven Stew, reheated (page 77)

Two-skillet suppers:

- Speedy Schnitzel (page 115) with
  Skillet Ratatouille (page 160)
- Pan-fried Fish Fillets (page 65) with
  Tomato-Zucchini Sauté (page 158)
- Pan-fried Pork Chops (page 85) with
  Orange-Glazed Carrots or Sweet Potatoes (page 158)

All-in-one suppers:

- Fajitas (page 30)
- Turkey or Chicken Burgers with toppings (page 112)
- Veggie Burgers with toppings (page 113)
- Pizza (storebought crust; choice of toppings; page 32)
- Turkey Parmigiana Panini (page 28)
- Pita or Tortilla Wraps (fillings pages 28-9)
- Six Easy Melts (page 29)
- Pad Thai (page 129)

Main-course salads; serve with crusty bread:

- Italian-Style Next-Day Salad (page 48)
- Cannellini and Tuna Salad (page 48)
- Salade Niçoise (page 50)
- Greek Salad (page 55)
- Grilled Chicken, Steak or Mushroom Salad (page 54)
- Warm Mushroom Spinach Salad (page 49)
- Mediterranean Pasta Salad (page 57)

Index

Tilapia, about, 63
Tiramisù, 187
Toast, defined, 243
Toast cups, 21
Tofu:
    about, 135
    hot-and-sour soup, 40
Tomato(es):
    about, 151
    and bocconcini with basil, 25
    bread salad, 56
    cherry tomato salad, 48
    how to crush or chopped canned, 122
    -pepper, spicy, with skillet chops
        or chicken, 107
    Provençal, 160
    roasted, 236
    salsa, 233
    -zucchini sauté, 158
Toppings:
    for baked potatoes, 156
    banana-rum, 180
    biscuit, 103
    broiled, for cakes, 204
    for canapés, 20
    chocolate sauce, 180
    cornmeal, 81
    for fish, 64
    fruit sauce, 180
    garlic potato for shepherd's pie, 79
    hot banana-rum, 180
    maple-nut, 180
    pastry, 103
    pizza, 32
    puff pastry, 103
    raspberry-blueberry, 180
    spiced apple, 180
    sweet, 180
Torta, smoked salmon, 24
Torte:
    fruit cream, 202
    hazelnut, 202
Tortellini casserole, 126
Tortillas:
    bowls, 80

chips, nachos, 21
crisps, 21
quesadillas, 21
roll-ups, 20
soup, 41
wrappers, 28-29
Toss, defined, 243
Tourtière, 86
Trifle, fresh fruit, 185
Tropical fruit smoothies, 224
Trout, about, 61
Truffle oil, about, 245
Truffles, chocolate, 195
Truss, defined, 243
Tubers, about, 151
Tulip dessert cups, 188
Tuna:
    about, 63
    and cannellini salad, 48
    melt, 29
    salade Niçoise, 50
    salad sandwiches, 30
Turban squash, about, 152
Turbot, about, 62
Turkey:
    breast, roasted, 93
    burgers, 112
    cutlets, grilled, 115
    drumsticks, 93
    fajitas, 30
    loaf, 115
    Parmigiana panini, 28
    pot pie, 103
    roasting methods, 92
    roasting pans, 92
    roasting times, 92
    salad sandwiches, 30
    -salsa melt, 29
    schnitzel, 115
    soup, 34
    stuffing, 93
    thawing frozen, 92
    thighs, roasted, 93
    wings, 93
Turmeric, about, 248

Turnip greens, about, 150
Turnips, about, 151
Tzatziki, 109

U
Upside-down cake, 199

V
Vanilla buttercream frosting, 204
Veal:
    chops, grilled, 106
    marsala, 87
    with mushrooms, 87
    osso bucco, 89
    piccata, 87
    scaloppine, 87
    schnitzel, 115
Vegetable marrow, about, 152
Vegetable oils, 44
Vegetables, 150-62
    basic cooking methods, 154
        boiling, 154
        braising, 154
        grilling, 154
        microwaving, 154
        roasting, 154
        steaming, 154
    crudités, 16, 17
    curry, 116
    frittata, 145
    grilled,
        melts, 29
        salad, 57
    hodgepodge of new, 159
    marinated, salad, 57
    mashes, mixed, 157
    pickled, 230
    roasted, 154
        soup, 35
    smoothies, 35
    stacked sandwich, 31
    stock, 237
Vegetarian burgers, 113